CONTEMPORARY JEWISH ETHICS

Sanhedrin Jewish Studies

GENERAL EDITOR:
David M.L. Olivestone

CONTEMPORARY

JEWISH
ETHICS

EDITED BY

Menachem Marc Kellner

Sanhedrin Press

NEW YORK

A teacher's discussion guide for *Contemporary Jewish Ethics* is available on request from the publisher.

For Jolene,
Proverbs 31:10–31

COPYRIGHT © 1978 by MENACHEM MARC KELLNER

Second Printing, 1979

SANHEDRIN PRESS,
a division of Hebrew Publishing Company
80 Fifth Avenue
New York, N.Y. 10011

Typographic design by Stanley Drate

Set by Burmar Technical Corporation

Library of Congress Cataloging in Publication Data

Main entry under title:

Contemporary Jewish ethics.

(Sanhedrin Jewish studies)
Bibliography: p.
1. Ethics, Jewish—Addresses, essays,
lectures.   2. Judaism—Addresses, essays,
lectures.   I. Kellner, Menachem Marc, 1946–
BJ1279.C66   296.3'85   78-5480
ISBN 0-88482-921-9
ISBN 0-88482-920-0 pbk.

PRINTED IN THE UNITED STATES OF AMERICA

Contents

ISSUES

BUSINESS ETHICS

SEXUAL ETHICS

THE HOLOCAUST

Preface

This volume grew out of my experience in the teaching of religious ethics and Jewish ethics in the Departments of Religious Studies at the University of Virginia and the College of William and Mary. I have long felt the need for a collection of representative writings on contemporary questions in Jewish ethics organized for teaching within the contexts of religious ethics and Jewish studies. I have sought, therefore, to include materials which describe the nature and scope of Jewish ethics as well as materials which exemplify the varying approaches of the Jewish tradition to contemporary moral problems. Thus, the essays in the first part of the book answer questions *about* Jewish ethics while the essays in the second part discuss a variety of issues from within the framework of Jewish ethics. The essays by Fackenheim, Samuelson, Jacobs and Leiman all address one of the central problems of religious ethics today: the question of whether or not there can be religious ethics at all in the face of the Kantian demand for moral autonomy. The essay by Lichtenstein addresses the question of whether or not there can be religious ethics at all in the face of the allegedly all-pervasive character of *halakhah*. Jewish ethicists have tended, when appealing to general halakhic/ethical norms or principles, to rely on two basic ideas: *imitatio dei,* and love of neighbor. Discussions of these two ideas are presented in the essays by Shapiro, Buber, Reines and Jacobs, in an attempt to analyze some of the basic principles of Jewish ethics. The essays in the second part of the book all address contemporary normative moral issues from a Jewish perspective; they are attempts to provide ethical and religious guidance from the perspective of Judaism on particular moral problems. I have tried, wherever possible, to include materials which are not only intrinsically valuable and interesting, but which also illuminate varying approaches to Jewish ethics and the problems it confronts.

In the introduction I have sought to locate the field of Jewish ethics within the general field of religious studies and to describe it in terms of its historical development. The notes to the introduction are primarily bibliographical; they direct the reader to sources available in English and to the major secondary studies. The chapter by David Feldman on *halakhah* is included to orient the reader in the literature of Jewish law, which plays so large a role in almost all discussions of Jewish ethics.

Both the publisher and I acknowledge with gratitude the permissions received from publishers and individual authors to reprint their material in this volume. In order to retain the editorial integrity of each individual chapter, no attempt has been made to make either the transliterations or the bibliographical citations within them uniform. However, obvious typographical errors have been corrected and footnotes have been renumbered where necessary in order to avoid confusion. Occasionally, the footnotes in one particular chapter refer to another essay which is also included in this book. This information is conveyed by an added note in square brackets which begins [See Kellner. . .].

It gives me great pleasure to acknowledge the assistance I have received in editing this book. Steven Schwarzschild, my friend and teacher, has been unfailingly helpful to me in every stage of its development. For this, and for much else, I am deeply indebted to him. Jim Childress, David Little, Hans Tiefel, and especially Gilbert Meilaender have made valuable suggestions and have saved me from many errors. They have contributed substantially to whatever usefulness this book might have. I am also grateful to my sister, Mrs. Tyra Lieberman, and to my brother, Rabbi Yisroel Kellner, for commenting on the introduction. David M. L. Olivestone, editor-in-chief of Hebrew Publishing Company, has carefully shepherded this book (and its author) through the various stages of its development. His contributions to the book, in terms of both organization and content, cannot be overstated. For this, and for his friendship, I am grateful.

M.M.K.

University of Virginia
June, 1977

GENERAL INTRODUCTION: THE STRUCTURE OF JEWISH ETHICS

The Structure of
Jewish Ethics

MENACHEM MARC KELLNER

The word *ethics* may be used and understood in many different ways. It is important, therefore, to define what ethics is in general before an attempt can be made to describe Jewish ethics in particular. Questions of ethics are, broadly speaking, questions of value. The province of ethics within the commonwealth of evaluative issues is determined by the particular values it seeks to understand, define and elucidate. These are generally accepted to be good and evil, right and wrong. Ethics, that is, deals with (1) the ends which truly fulfill human personality, (2) the character of moral agents, and (3) the nature of moral obligation.

Generally speaking, statements of or about ethics are divided into three groups: descriptive, normative and meta-ethical. *Descriptive ethics* simply describes actual moral behavior (i.e., behavior which may appropriately be described as good or evil, right or wrong) and actual moral reasoning. It does not attempt to prescribe or to judge such behavior.[1] *Normative ethics* purports to evaluate moral behavior

---

1. I am using the terms "ethics" and "morals" interchangeably here even though there are some differences in usage between them. The term "ethics" seems to have more of a practical, actional connotation than does "morals" (we say "medical ethics", for example, not "medical morals").

or to establish moral principles. It seeks to determine the *norm* or *norms* of moral behavior. *Meta-ethics* takes the judgments of normative ethics as its subject. Thus it seeks, not to make moral judgments, but to analyze their nature. Judgments of meta-ethics describe and analyze words (such as "good" or "bad") and judgments (such as "murder is wrong" or "one ought always seek to maximize the greatest good for the greatest number").

Traditionally, philosophers concerned with ethics sought to give general moral guidance. Such philosophers were not usually concerned with the details of moral behavior so much as with its basic principles and their justification. Since World War II, however, and until very recently, moral philosophers have increasingly given up the task of normative ethics in favor of pursuing the more purely philosophical questions of meta-ethics. The field of normative ethics was largely left to religious thinkers (often called "ethicists") who had always been active in it.[2]

The field of religious ethics is rather more difficult to define and describe than is that of philosophical ethics. Broadly speaking, it may be construed as the study of the ethical teachings of the various religious traditions.[3] In this sense it is purely descriptive. In the United States, however, in most academic contexts, "religious ethics" really means "Christian ethics," and it is most definitely normative (or sometimes meta-ethical) as opposed to descriptive. To characterize Christian ethics thus construed, we may say that it is primarily concerned with translating the general moral/religious teachings of the Christian faith into general principles of moral conduct and into specific moral injunctions. It is further characterized by the fact that almost all systems of Christian ethics seem to presuppose some single over-arching norm (often *agape*, or love). There is frequently disagreement over what the norm is or how to interpret it, but there is usually agreement that some such norm exists.

---

2. Good, brief descriptions of philosophical ethics may be found in William K. Frankena, *Ethics*, 2nd ed. (Englewood Cliffs, N.J., 1973), pp. 1-11, and in P. H. Nowell-Smith, *Ethics* (London, 1954), pp. 11-35. In the last few years, it should be noted, philosophers have once again been devoting attention to normative ethics. The appearance of John Rawls' *A Theory of Justice* and of such journals as *Social Theory and Practice* and *Philosophy and Public Affairs* are indicative of this renewed interest.

3. For a fuller, and very important discussion of the nature of religious ethics, see David Little and Sumner B. Twiss, "Basic Terms in the Study of Religious Ethics," in Outka and Reeder (eds.), *Religion and Morality* (New York, 1973), pp. 35-77. On the general question of the relationship between religion and morality, see the essays in the Outka and Reeder volume and the essays by Fackenheim, Samuelson, Jacobs, and Leiman in this book.

The situation in Christian ethics is conditioned by the fact that Christianity and its basic texts are fundamentally concerned with questions of faith. Thus, while no one could deny that the Christian religion is concerned with moral behavior, its specific teachings with respect to such behavior must be derived from the basic teachings of faith and are often a matter of dispute.[4]

Jewish ethical teaching, on the other hand, is conditioned by the fact that Judaism is a religion which emphasizes human behavior over general claims of theology and faith—a religion of pots and pans in the eyes of those who derogate its concern with actions.[5] Jewish tradition contains minutely detailed teachings regulating that behavior. The problem facing the Jewish ethicist, therefore, is not so much to derive moral obligations from general theological teachings but rather to justify his own undertaking in the face of the fact that the all-embracing character of Jewish law (halakhah) would seem to leave no room for supra-legal Jewish ethics as such.[6] To characterize

---

4. James Gustafson has devoted much attention to the delineation of the scope and content of Christian ethics. In particular, one ought to consult his *Christ and the Moral Life* (New York, 1968), chaps. 1 and 7; "What is the Contemporary Problematic of Ethics in Christianity?" *CCAR Journal* (January, 1968), pp. 14-26; and "Theology and Ethics," in his *Christian Ethics and the Community* (Philadelphia, 1971), pp. 83-100. Further relevant readings include Bernard Häring, "Essential Concepts of Moral Theology," in Gustafson and Laney (eds.), *On Being Responsible* (New York, 1968), pp. 86-108; Clyde A. Holbrook, "The Problem of Authority in Christian Ethics," *Journal of the American Academy of Religion* 37 (1969), pp. 26-48; Roger Mehl, *Catholic Ethics and Protestant Ethics* (Philadelphia, 1971), pp. 15-42; and Paul Ramsey, *Basic Christian Ethics* (New York, 1950), chaps. 3-6.

5. Among the comparative studies of Jewish and Christian ethics which may be consulted with profit are: Elie Benamozegh, *Jewish and Christian Ethics* (San Francisco, 1873); I. M. Blank, "Is There a Common Judeo–Christian Ethical Tradition?" in D.J. Silver (ed.), *Judaism and Ethics* (New York, 1970), pp. 95-108; Aḥad Ha'am (Asher Ginzberg) in Leon Simon (ed.), *Philosophia Judaica: Ahad Ha'am* (London, 1946), pp. 127-137; Joseph Klausner, "Jewish and Christian Ethics," *Judaism* 2 (1953), pp. 16-30; Kaufman Kohler, "Synagogue and Church in Their Mutual Relations, Particularly in Reference to the Ethical Teachings," in *Judaism at the World Parliament of Religions* (Cincinnati, 1894), pp. 114-126; and H. F. Rall and Samuel S. Cohon, *Christianity and Judaism Compare Notes* (New York, 1927). Two chapters of Benamozegh's work were separately translated into English by William Wolf and published in *Judaism* 13 (1964), pp. 220-227 and 346-350.

6. General studies of Jewish ethics as a whole include two works by Jacob Bernard Agus, *The Vision and the Way: An Interpretation of Jewish Ethics* (New York, 1960), and "Jewish Ethics," in his *Dialogue and Tradition* (New York, 1971), pp. 442-449. Other works include Simon Bernfeld (ed.), *The Foundations of Jewish Ethics* (New York, 1929 and 1968); Mordecai M. Kaplan, "A Philosophy of Jewish Ethics," in Louis Finkelstein (ed.), *The Jews: Their Role in Civilization* (New York, 1949 and 1971), pp. 32-64; Moritz Lazarus, *The Ethics of Judaism* (Philadelphia, 1900); and Mordecai Waxman, *Judaism: Religion and Ethics* (New York, 1958).

Jewish ethics simply, we may say that it attempts to show what Judaism, either in the guise of *halakhah,* or in some other form, teaches about moral issues.[7]

We may conveniently divide the literature of what has been called Jewish ethics into four main periods: Biblical, Talmudic, Medieval, and Modern. Strictly speaking, the Bible and Talmud do not fall under our view here: they are the sources of Jewish ethics but do not in any systematic sense devote themselves to that subject. Permeated as they are with moral concern, they contain almost no texts specifically given over to ethics.[8] Furthermore, in an important sense all Jewish ethics which takes *halakhah* seriously is Talmudic, not only because the Talmud is the source of *halakhah,* but because any attempt to determine a halakhic position on virtually any issue must begin with an analysis of the relevant Talmudic data. It is thus doubly difficult to talk of Talmudic ethics as such.[9]

The situation changes radically in the medieval period with the rise of a distinct Jewish ethical literature seeking systematically to ex-

---

7. For the definition of *halakhah* and other technical and Hebrew terms used throughout this book, consult the glossary.

8. The one notable exception to this generalization is the mishnaic tractate *Avot* ("Fathers"), a compilation of rabbinic moral maxims and homilies, and its related literature. Of the many translations of this text two are of particular importance: R. Travers Herford's *Ethics of the Talmud* (New York, 1962) presents a critical edition of the text, an accurate translation, and valuable historical notes. His introduction is particularly helpful: among other things, he explains how a work like *Avot* came to be included in the Mishnah. In his *Living Talmud* (New York, 1957), Judah Goldin presents the reader with a brilliant and elegant translation of the text coupled with a representative sampling of medieval Jewish commentaries on it. This makes his edition of great value for the study of medieval Jewish ethics as well. Goldin is also the editor and translator of *The Fathers According to Rabbi Nathan* (New Haven, 1955 and New York, 1974), another text from the period of the Mishnah which parallels *Avot.* The translation is distinguished, the notes scholarly and helpful. For a selection of other Talmudic texts on moral subjects, one may consult Montefiore and Loewe (eds.), *A Rabbinic Anthology* (New York, 1974), pp. 382-399. The secondary literature on rabbinic ethics *per se* (as opposed to studies of contemporary ethical problems which draw upon rabbinic materials) is not large. Among the most accessible and helpful studies are the following: A. Cohen, *Everyman's Talmud* (New York, 1949) pp. 210-237; David Daube, *Collaboration With Tyranny in Rabbinic Law* (London, 1965); Max Kadushin, "Introduction to Rabbinic Ethics," *Yehezkel Kaufman Jubilee Volume* (Jerusalem, 1960), pp. 88-114; Max Kadushin, *Worship and Ethics: A Study in Rabbinic Judaism* (Chicago, 1964); and George Foot Moore, *Judaism in the First Centuries of the Christian Era,* Vol. 2 (Cambridge, 1927 and New York, 1971), pp. 79-197. On Biblical ethics generally, see I. Efros, *Ancient Jewish Philosophy* (New York, 1964 and 1976), part II, "The Philosophy of Biblical Ethics."

9. See David Feldman, "The Structure of Jewish Law" (chapter one below) for a discussion of what Mishnah and Talmud are.

pound upon morals and human conduct. The literature of the period seems to fall rather naturally into four different and widely recognized categories: philosophic, rabbinic, pietistic, and kabbalistic. Joseph Dan points out[10] that medieval Jewish ethics appeared in many literary forms beyond what might be called the classical ethical literature of books and treatises on specific ethical issues. Among the many forms which ethical literature took, we find homiletical works, ethical wills[11] and letters, moralistic storybooks and collections of ethical fables, poetry, and commentaries on the Biblical book of Proverbs and on Tractate Avot. There were also concrete and specific manuals of behavior, the so-called *hanhagot*.

Jewish philosophy in the medieval period was deeply concerned with the question of the proper relationship between faith and reason. The literature of the Jewish philosophical ethics of the period reflects this concern in its emphasis on the problem of the proper relationship between religious and ethical perfection. The earliest of the Jewish philosophers to write on ethics, Saadia Gaon[12] and Solomon ben

---

10. In his excellent article on "Ethical Literature" in the *Encyclopaedia Judaica* (Jerusalem, 1972), Vol. 6, cols. 922-932. Dan is also the author of many of the other articles in the *Encyclopaedia* relating to Jewish ethical literature. See Vol. 1 (Index), p. 438, *s.v.* "Ethical Literature" and "Ethics." There are two histories of Jewish literature which contain material relevant to medieval Jewish ethics. These are Meyer Waxman, *A History of Jewish Literature, 4 vols. (New York, 1938-41)* and Israel Zinberg, *A History of Jewish Literature*, Vols. 1-3 (Cleveland 1972-73), Vols. 4-9 (New York, 1974-76). Two anthologies which contain selections from medieval Jewish ethical texts are Curt Leviant, *Masterpieces of Hebrew Literature* (New York, 1969) and Louis Jacobs, *Jewish Ethics, Philosophy, and Mysticism* (New York, 1969).

11. See Israel Abrahams' collection, *Hebrew Ethical Wills* (Philadelphia, 1948 and 1976).

12. Saadia ben Joseph (892-942) initiated the tradition of medieval Jewish philosophy. He was a Gaon, head of one of the Talmudic academies in Babylonia. His major work, the *Book of Beliefs and Opinions (Emunot veDeot)* is available in two English translations. The first, under the title just given, is by Samuel Rosenblatt (New Haven, 1948). The second, a partial translation, was published by Alexander Altmann under the title *Book of Doctrines and Beliefs* (Oxford, 1956). This translation was republished together with selections from Philo and Judah Halevi under the title *Three Jewish Philosophers* (New York, 1960). Saadia's views on ethics are included in Treatise Ten of his book, on "proper conduct." The standard study of Saadia is Henry Malter's *Saadia Gaon: His Life and Works* (Philadelphia, 1921). On his philosophy generally, see Isaac Husik, *A History of Medieval Jewish Philosophy* (New York, 1930 and 1969), pp. 23-47, and Julius Guttmann, *Philosophies of Judaism* (New York, 1973), pp. 69-83. On Saadia's ethics, see I. Efros, "Saadia's General Ethical Theory and its Relation to Sufism," *JQR 75th Anniversary Volume*, pp. 166-177, and Marvin Fox, "On the Rational Commandments in Saadia's Philosophy: A Re-examination," in M. Fox (ed.), *Modern Jewish Ethics* (Columbus, Ohio, 1976), pp. 174-187.

Judah ibn Gabirol,[13] simply took over systems of secular philosophic ethics whole and made no serious attempt to root them in Judaism. The situation was considerably changed by the appearance of *Duties of the Heart* (*Hovot haLevavot*) by Bahya ben Joseph ibn Paquda, a Spanish thinker of the 11th century.[14] Bahya sought not only to instruct the Jew in religious and moral behavior, but to develop an ethical system rooted in Judaism. In his book, Bahya distinguishes between the (halakhic) obligations of the body, which directly involve behavior, and inner obligations, the "duties of the heart" of his book's title. There are many halakhic works, he says, devoted to an elucidation of the outward duties of the Jew, but none devoted to his inward obligations, and it is this gap that he seeks to fill. Bahya's emphasis on inward disposition (*kavanah*) was perhaps the first expression of a motif which was to characterize and even dominate much of Jewish ethical literature and which was to blossom forth much later in the *Musar* movement. This is the idea that proper moral behavior could best be attained through the religious perfection of the individual. This may possibly reflect the fact that the availability of halakhic guidelines for most moral problems made their analysis by ethicists superfluous. Whatever the reason, however, it is certainly the case that Jewish ethical texts tend to emphasize character development and personal virtues over social ethics. The latter are seen as depending upon the former.[15]

---

13. Solomon ben Judah ibn Gabirol (c. 1021-1058) was a neoplatonist philosopher and poet. On Gabirol generally, see Husik, pp. 59-79 and Guttmann, pp. 101-116. Gabirol is the author of an ethico–psychological work (*Tikkun Middot haNefesh*) called, in I. M. Wise's translation, *On the Improvement of the Moral Qualities* (New York, 1901). This is analyzed in D. Rosin, "The Ethics of Solomon ibn Gabirol," *JQR* (OS), Vol. 3 (1891), pp. 159-181. *Choice of Pearls* (*Mivhar haPeninim*), a collection of ethical maxims and proverbs heavily influenced by Arabic literature, is also attributed to Gabirol, although that attribution is doubted by many scholars. It was translated by B. Ascher (London, 1859) and A. Cohen (New York, 1925). Alexander Marx analyzes the problem of Gabirol's authorship of this work in "Gabirol's Authorship of the 'Choice of Pearls' and Two Versions of Joseph Kimchi's *Shekel HaKodesh*," *HUCA* 4 (1927), pp. 433-448.

14. Bahya's work has appeared in two English versions. Moses Hyamson translated the book from a medieval Hebrew version of the Arabic original (Jerusalem, 1965). Menahem Mansoor's version, translated directly from the original Arabic, is called *The Book of Direction to the Duties of the Heart* (London, 1973). On Bahya generally, see Husik, pp, 80-105, and Guttman, pp, 117-123.

15. Mention ought to be made here also of the work of Abraham bar Hiyya of Barcelona (12th cent.), author of the *Meditation of the Sad Soul* (*Hegyon haNefresh haAzuvah*) translated by Geoffrey Wigoder (London, 1969). Leon Stitskin analyzed bar Hiyya's contribution to Jewish philosophical ethics in his *Judaism as a Philosophy: The Philosophy of Abraham bar Hiyya* (New York, 1960).

The greatest medieval Jewish philosophic ethicist was the most outstanding of the medieval Jewish philosophers, Moses Maimonides (1135-1204).[16] It was Maimonides' general position that faith and reason do not conflict,[17] and this attitude is reflected in his ethics. He adopts the basic outline of Aristotle's golden mean, rooting it, however, in Judaism and modifying it to meet the exigencies of the tradition as he understood it.[18]

Maimonides is the author, among other things, of three major works: *Commentary on the Mishnah*, the *Mishneh Torah* (or *Yad haHazakah*) and the *Guide of the Perplexed* (*Moreh Nevukhim*). The first two of these contain material directly relevant to Jewish philosophical ethics, while the *Guide* can be read as a work of which the ultimate end is ethical. The introduction to Maimonides' commentary to Tractate Avot is a self-contained ethical treatise, called *Eight Chapters* (*Shemonah Perakim*).[19] It is in this text in particular that he develops his ideas on the golden mean. The commentary to *Avot* itself is obviously also important here.[20] Maimonides' code of Jewish law, the *Mishneh Torah*, contains a number of texts in which ethics plays an important role. In particular, two parts of the first section of the work, the *Book of Knowledge* (*Sefer haMada*), are important: "Laws of Ethics" and "Laws of Repentance."[21] Maimonides' discussion of messianism at the

---

16. For a general introduction to his life and works see Isadore Twersky (ed.), *A Maimonides Reader* (New York, 1972) and the literature cited in the bibliography there. On his thought generally, see also Husik, pp. 236-311 and Guttman, pp. 172-206.

17. For the necessary qualifications on this otherwise hopelessly broad generalization, see Norbert Samuelson, "Philosophic and Religious Authority in the Thought of Maimonides and Gersonides," *CCAR Journal* (October, 1969), pp. 31-43.

18. For a very valuable study of Maimonides' modifications of the doctrine of the mean, see Steven Schwarzschild's "Moral Radicalism and Middlingness in Medieval Jewish Ethics," *Studies in Medieval Culture* XI (1977).

19. This was translated by J. Gorfinkle under the title *The Eight Chapters of Maimonides on Ethics* (New York, 1912 and 1966). Herbert Davidson subjects this work to close textual study in "Maimonides' 'Shmonah Perakim' and Al-Farabi's *Fusul al Madani*," *PAAJR* 31 (1963), pp. 33-50. See also Harry S. Lewis, "The Golden Mean in Judaism," *Jewish Studies in Memory of Israel Abrahams* (New York, 1927), pp. 283-295, and Eliezer Schweid, *Studies in Maimonides' "Eight Chapters"*, 2nd ed. (Jerusalem, 1969).

20. *Commentary to Aboth*, translated by Arthur David (New York, 1968).

21. Volume 1 of the *Mishneh Torah*, the *Book of Knowledge*, was translated into English by Moses Hyamson (New York, 1974). In referring to "*Hilkhot Deot*" as the "Laws of Ethics" I am following the suggestion of R.L. Weiss, "Language and Ethics: Reflections on Maimonides' 'Ethics'," *Journal of the History of Philosophy* 9 (1971), pp. 425-433. On the ethical teaching of the *Book of Knowledge*, see Leo Strauss, "Notes on Maimonides' Book of Knowledge," *Studies in Mysticism and Religion Presented to Gershom Scholem* (Jerusalem, 1967), pp. 269-283; R. L. Weiss, *Wisdom and Piety: The Ethics of Maimonides*

end of the *Mishneh Torah* contains material which played an important role in Jewish ethics in the modern period.[22]

Mention should be made here also of the philosophical commentary to the Pentateuch of Levi ben Gerson (Gersonides, 1288-1344). At the end of each Torah portion, Gersonides listed those *to'aliyot* or advantages to be derived from the portion. Many of these are explicitly mentioned as being of an ethical character.[23]

The tradition of medieval Jewish philosophy reached its apogee with the work of Maimonides; its descent thereafter was quick and precipitous. Certainly none of the philosophers who followed Maimonides, Gersonides included, had anything significant to add to his philosophic analysis of Jewish ethics. Indeed, given the general opposition to Jewish philosophy which followed upon the apostasy of so many Jews in Spain and Portugal in the fourteenth and fifteenth centuries (which was blamed, in part, on their devotion to philosophical pursuits), it is hardly surprising that there arose a trend in Jewish ethics in direct opposition to philosophical ethics. Writers identified with this category of Jewish ethical literature sought to demonstrate that rabbinic Judaism and its texts provided all that one

---

(Chicago, 1966); A. Cronbach, "The Maimonidean Code of Benevolence," *HUCA* 20 (1947), pp. 471-540; and H.I. Levine, "The Experience of Repentance: The Views of Maimonides and William James," *Tradition* 1 (1958), pp. 40-63. On the *Mishneh Torah* generally, see chapter one by David Feldman below.

22. Maimonides' most important statements about the messiah are found at the very end of his *Mishneh Torah,* in his "Laws of Kings," (*Hilkhot Melakhim*) the last section of the *Book of Judges,* translated by A.M. Hershman (New Haven, 1949), and in his commentary to the tenth chapter of Mishnah *Sanhedrin.* This commentary was translated by A.J. Wolf in *Judaism* 15 (1966), pp. 95-101, 211-216 and 337-342. This translation is included in Twersky's *A Maimonides Reader,* pp. 401-423.

Many of Maimonides' ethical writings are collected conveniently in Weiss and Butterworth (eds.), *Ethical Writings of Maimonides* (New York, 1976), as well as in Twersky's anthology. Further studies on the subject include B.Z.Bokser, "Morality and Religion in the Theology of Maimonides," in J.L. Blau (ed.), *Essays on Jewish Life and Thought* (S.W. Baron Festschrift) (New York, 1959), pp. 139-158; Marvin Fox, "Maimonides and Aquinas on Natural Law," *Dine Yisrael* 3 (1972), pp. 5-36 and reprinted in J. Dienstag (ed.), *Studies in Maimonides and St. Thomas Aquinas* (New York, 1975); and Steven S. Schwarzschild, "Do Noachites Have to Believe In Revelation?" *JQR* 52 (1961-62), pp. 297-308 and 53 (1962-63), pp. 30-65.

23. Although a 17th century Yiddish translation of the *To'aliyot* exists, they were never translated into any other language. Published independently of the Bible commentary in their original Hebrew, they achieved widespread popularity. Further on the *To'aliyot* see Zinberg, Vol. 3, pp. 138-139. On Gersonides generally, see Husik, pp. 328-361, Guttman, pp. 236-253 and M. M. Kellner, "Rabbi Levi ben Gerson: A Bibliographical Essay," *Studies in Bibliography and Booklore,* forthcoming.

required in order to generate a full-fledged ethical system. There was no need, they felt, to turn to the Greeks for ethical instruction. This literature contains little innovation, and seeks rather to apply rabbinic ethics directly to the conditions of the medieval world. The two most influential texts in this genre are Jonah ben Abraham Gerondi's *Gates of Repentance* (*Sha'arei Teshuvah*) (13th century), and Isaac Aboab's *Candelabrum of Illumination* (*Menorat haMa'or*)(14th century).[24]

The third generally recognized category of medieval Jewish ethical literature is that associated with the Hasidei Ashkenaz, a pietistic movement in 12-13th century Germany. The major work in this category is the *Book of the Pious* (*Sefer Hasidim*), an extensive compilation attributed to Judah ben Samuel heHasid of Regensburg (d. 1217).[25] German pietistic literature is concerned largely with specific problems and actual situations. It is marked by deep piety and superstition, and by an emphasis on the effort involved in a deed; the more difficult an action, the more praiseworthy it is. The *Book of the Pious* introduces the distinction between the law of the Torah and the much stricter law of Heaven. The pietist is marked by his adherence to the law of Heaven which demands greater devotion and involves more difficulty than the law of the Torah which applied to all. This general attitude was to have tremendous influence on the development of European Jewry and its effects are still felt strongly today.

---

24. Gerondi's *Gates of Repentance* was and is a book of wide influence and has been published repeatedly in the centuries since it was written. It was translated by S. Silverstein (Jerusalem, 1967). On Gerondi see Waxman, Vol. 2, pp, 273-274.

The *Candelabrum of Illumination* is actually the name of two fourteenth-century ethical compilations. Aboab's book became one of the standard Jewish religious texts of the middle ages, going through over seventy editions. It has been translated into Spanish, Ladino, Yiddish and German. See Waxman, Vol. 2, pp. 282-287 and I. Efros, "The Menorat Ha-Maor," *JQR* 9 (1918-19), pp. 337-357. The other book of the same name, which remained in manuscript until the present century, was written by Israel ben Joseph al-Nakawa of Toledo (d. 1391). On this book see Waxman, Vol, 2, pp. 279-280 and Israel Davidson, "Enelow's edition of Al-Nakawa's Menorat HaMeor," *JQR* 21 (1930-31), pp. 461-468.

25. Portions of the *Book of the Pious* were published in English translation by S. Singer under the title *Medieval Jewish Mysticism — Book of the Pious* (Northbrook, Illinois, 1971), and by A. Cronbach, "Social Ethics of 'Sefer Hasidim'," *HUCA* 22 (1949), pp. 1-148. On the Hasidei Ashkenaz see Waxman, Vol. 1, pp. 360-364; Zinberg, Vol. 2, pp. 35-56; Gershom Scholem, *Major Trends in Jewish Mysticism* (New York, 1961), pp. 80-118; S. Kramer, *God and Man in the Sefer Hasidim* (New York, 1966); A. Rubin, "Concept of Repentance Among Hasidei Ashkenaz," *Journal of Jewish Studies* 16 (1965), pp. 161-176; and Haym Soloveitchik, "Three Themes in the *Sefer Hasidim*, " *AJS Review* 1 (1976), pp. 311-358.

Two other works in the tradition of German pietism deserve mention. These are the anonymous *Ways of the Righteous (Orḥot Ẓaddikim)*²⁶ and Rabbi Asher ben Jehiel's *Ways of Life (Orḥot Ḥayyim)*²⁷. The *Ways of the Righteous* was probably composed in Germany in the fifteenth century. It has had great influence and has been published over eighty times. Although its author was clearly influenced by Jewish philosophical ethics, there is no doubt that the book was written by one of the German pietists as it is permeated with the attitudes and values of that movement.

Rabbi Asher ben Jehiel (Asheri or Rosh), c. 1250-1327, was one of the leading halakhists of his generation. A refugee from Germany (where his father, his first teacher, was active in the pietist movement and was himself a student of Judah ben Samuel), R. Asher settled in Spain. His *Ways of Life,* often called *Ethical Manual of the Rosh (Hanhagot haRosh)* or *Testament of the Rosh (Ẓavva'at haRosh)*, consists of ethical sayings arranged for daily recitation.

One of the major developments in the history of medieval Judaism was the rise of Kabbalah (Jewish mysticism).²⁸ This had definite impact on Jewish ethics, stimulating the development of a fairly well-defined class of kabbalistic-ethical texts. This literature is permeated with the kabbalistic idea that the actions of human beings have a profound impact on the very structure of the universe. There is a definite interdependence between the deeds of human beings and the mystical development of the world.

Of the many works in this category two of the most important are *Palm Tree of Deborah (Tomer Devorah)* by Moses ben Jacob Cordovero (1522-1570),²⁹ and *Beginning of Wisdom (Reshit Ḥokhmah)* by Elijah ben Moses de Vidas (sixteenth century), a student of Cordovero's.³⁰ Cordovero's work is a detailed guide to ethical behavior, relating moral perfection on the one hand to mystical union with aspects of the deity on the other. He seeks to unfold the mystical and ethical

---

26. Translated under that title by S.J. Cohen (New York and Jerusalem, 1974).

27. Published as *Orchos Chayim LehawRaush or The Pathways of Eternal Life* by K.S. Orbach (Israel, 1968).

28. On the Kabbalah, see Scholem's *Major Trends,* the standard work in the field. His articles on the major figures, works and issues of the Kabbalah from the *Encyclopaedia Judaica* have been collected and published under the title *Kabbalah* (New York, 1974). He is also the author of *On the Kabbalah and its Symbolism* (New York, 1969).

29. Translated by Raphael Ben Zion (Jacob Cohn) in *The Way of the Faithful: An Anthology of Jewish Mysticism* (Los Angeles, 1945), pp. 11-80, and by Louis Jacobs (London, 1960).

30. On de Vidas, see Waxman, Vol. 2, pp. 288-289, and Zinberg, Vol. 4, pp. 56-62.

significance of God's thirteen attributes of mercy (enumerated in Exodus 34:6-7 and Micah 7:18-20) and to explain how it is possible to imitate them, as the *halakhah* demands. De Vidas makes explicit use of kabbalistic texts and develops the idea that the cosmic struggle between good and evil is affected by the moral behavior of individual human beings.

What may be the most important work in the field of kabbalistic ethics, *The Path of the Upright* (*Mesillat Yesharim*), is rarely considered to be in that category at all. This may simply reflect the fact that by the close of the Jewish middle ages (mid-18th century), Kabbalah had so permeated all aspects of Jewish life that no one took special notice of a kabbalistic-ethical work. In addition to this, and more importantly, this work of Moses Hayyim Luzzatto made relatively little use of explicit kabbalistic texts, while still being overwhelmingly kabbalistic in tone.[31] Luzzatto (1707-1746), an Italian mystic, playwright and ethicist, leads the reader of his book along the way or path of the upright, which begins with the forsaking of sin and culminates in mystical contact with God. *The Path of the Upright* develops the mishnaic concept of the world as a corridor leading to the world to come; human life must be devoted to preparation for the ultimate end.[32] Luzzatto's book became enormously influential and popular; to this very day it is considered by many traditionalist Jews to be the Jewish ethical text *par excellence*.

Before turning to a discussion of contemporary developments in Jewish ethics, we must consider one important and still-influential outgrowth of medieval Jewish ethics, the *Musar* movement. Jewish life in Eastern Europe (specifically Poland and Russia), at the end of the Jewish middle ages, was characterized by a marked religious, cultural and social decline. Eastern European Jewry suffered what can only be called a "failure of nerve" as a consequence of the Chmielnicki massacres of 1648, the collapse of effective government in Poland which followed shortly thereafter in the face of the Ukrainian and Swedish wars, and the remarkable and pervasive despair and degradation of spirit engendered by the apostasy of the false messiah, Shabbetai Zevi (1666).[33] In the face of these calamities,

---

31. Luzzatto's book was translated by Mordecai M. Kaplan under the title *Mesillat Yesharim: The Path of the Upright* (Philadelphia, l936 and 1964). On Luzzatto, see Simon Ginzburg, *The Life and Works of M.H. Luzzatto* (Philadelphia, 1931), and Zinberg, Vol. 6, pp. 186-187.

32. *Avot* 4:16.

33. On Sabbateanism, see Gershom Scholem's *Sabbatai Sebi* (Princeton, 1973).

Jewish education suffered terribly; Talmud study became cold, rigid and formalistic; the democracy and sense of mutual responsibility which had formerly characterized the Jewish communal organizations degenerated; and there arose a huge mass of ignorant and only nominally observant Jews.[34]

The most well-known reaction to this situation is to be found in the ḥasidic movement, which sought to regenerate Jewish life and spirit. The ḥasidic teachers, evangelical and charismatic religious leaders, tried to inject mysticism into everyday life and emphasized, as did the earlier pietists of medieval Germany, the importance of inwardness and intention as opposed to the formalistic obedience to law. The Musar (ethical reproof) movement may be seen as a non-ḥasidic response to the same degradation of spirit which engendered Ḥasidism. The musarniks sought to bridge the gap between rabbinic training on the one hand and religious-ethical fervor on the other. The Musar movement was founded for the training of Jews in strict ethical/religious behavior. It emphasized character development (echoing one of the earliest and most consistent themes in medieval Jewish ethics) and concerned itself strongly with the psychological health of the individual. Followers of the Musar movement often organized themselves into small groups which met regularly to read ethical texts and to engage in mutual criticism and spiritual strengthening. By the early years of the present century, the musar ideal had been adopted by most of the great European rabbinical academies (yeshivot), almost all of which set aside a portion of each day for the study of ethical texts and many of which had individuals on their staffs specifically devoted to the ethical guidance of the students.[35]

---

34. For the historical background, see Howard M. Sachar, The Course of Modern Jewish History (New York, 1958), pp. 25-35.

35. The literature on the Musar movement in English is extensive. Two general works which ought to be consulted are Zalman F. Ury, The Musar Movement (New York, 1970), and Lester S. Eckman, The History of the Musar Movement (New York, 1975). The notes in Hillel Goldberg, "Toward an Understanding of Rabbi Israel Salanter," Tradition 16 (1976), pp. 83-119, constitute an annotated bibliography of recent writings on the subject. At least one musar text is available in English: Rabbi Joseph Hurwitz of Nevardok's Mezake HaRabim: To Turn the Many to Righteousness, translated by S. Silverstein (New York and Jerusalem, 1972). Mention ought to be made here of the work of Rabbi Israel Meir haKohen (Kahan, Kahana, Kagan), 1838-1933. Universally known as the "Hafez Ḥayyim," he is the most distinguished modern expositor of traditional rabbinic ethics. Many of his writings have appeared in English translation. Among them are: Leonard Oschry (trans.), Ahavath Hessed: Kindness as Required by God (Jerusalem, 1967); A. Kagan (trans.), The Dispersed of Israel (New York, 1951); S. E. Brog (trans.), Fortress of

The distinction between contemporary and medieval Jewish ethics reflects the great difference that obtains between pre-modern and contemporary Judaism. Up until the end of the 18th century there was no country in Europe (and, outside of the United States, no country in the world at all) which recognized its Jews as full-fledged citizens possessed of normal civil rights. The spread of Enlightenment ideals, however, led to the gradual emancipation of European Jewry. But the call of emancipation was often couched in terms such as: "To the Jew as Frenchman, everything; to the Jew as Jew, nothing!" Emancipation was predicated in almost every case on assimilation. The Jews of Western Europe were faced with a situation unique in their experience and were confronted with a wholly new problem: how to remain Jewish while simultaneously participating in Western civilization. It was largely by way of response to that problem that the various religious movements of contemporary Judaism — Orthodoxy, Conservatism, Reform — developed and defined themselves.

Contemporary Judaism is distinguished from medieval Judaism, therefore, in that it is faced with an entirely new problematic and in that it presents a multiplicity of answers to that complex of problems. With respect to the subject at hand, we may say that contemporary Jewish ethics is distinguished from medieval Jewish ethics in that the problems it faces are largely those it shares with the surrounding culture (e.g., the problem of relating morality and religion, and specific questions like political obedience and medical ethics). In short, Jews and Judaism have become part of the modern world and, to a significant degree, the modern world has become a factor which cannot be ignored by both Jews and Judaism. Contemporary Jewish ethics is further distinguished from its medieval counterpart by the fact that it speaks with a divided voice. One must not ask today, "What is the Jewish position on such and such?" but rather, "What is the Orthodox, Conservative, or Reform interpretation of the Jewish position on such and such?" Although many writers persist in presenting the Jewish position on various subjects, it very often ought more correctly to be characterized as a Jewish position.

In order to understand fully the differences between Orthodox, Conservative and Reform Judaism one ought to examine them in terms

Faith (New York, 1964); and I. Aryeh and J. Dvorkes (eds. and trans.), Hafetz Hayyim on the Siddur (Jerusalem and New York, 1974). Mendel Weinbach has collated and translated some of the Hafez Hayyim's ethical teachings in Who Wants to Live (Jerusalem, 1968), and Give us Life (Jerusalem, 1969). Biographical studies include M. M. Yosher, Saint and Sage (New York, 1935), and Lester Eckman, Revered by All (New York, 1974).

of their historical development.[36] For our purposes, however, it should be sufficient to sketch out their basic theological differences. This can be done conveniently by examining their varying conceptions of revelation. Briefly put, Orthodoxy follows the traditional rabbinic claim that the Torah represents the direct, conclusive revelation of God's will. *Halakhah*, which derives directly from that revelation, is the will of God. It is normative for all Jews in all places and at all times. Although Orthodoxy recognizes the fact of halakhic change, it insists that such change has come about and may come about only within the context of well-recognized halakhic mechanisms. The basic Orthodox contention with respect to the *halakhah* is that it is a divine, not a human system, and that as such it is not subject, in essence, to the sort of historical development which is characteristic of human institutions.

Reform Judaism, on the other hand, in both its classic and modern positions, entirely rejects the claim that the *halakhah* represents the revealed will of God. Revelation, it maintains, is progressive, akin to inspiration, and is ultimately concerned with ethics. This emphasis is summed up in the famous motto of early Reform, that Judaism is nothing more than ethical monotheism. While contemporary Reform thinkers have largely given up the classic Reform claim that Judaism took a quantum leap from the time of the prophets (in whose call for social morality early Reform thinkers saw God's revelation most clearly embodied) to the nineteenth century and the rise of Reform, it is still the case that Reform Judaism rejects the *halakhah* as a norm and still looks to the prophetic tradition for the "essence" of Judaism.

The Conservative[37] position is roughly midway between that of Orthodoxy and Reform. Conservative Judaism does not view revelation as God "talking" to the Jewish people, as it were, revealing to them exactly what it is He wants them to do. Rather, Conservative Judaism maintains that the Jewish people have had what may be called "revelatory" experiences of God, to which they reacted by creating the Torah. *Halakhah*, then, is the way in which Jews have sought to preserve their experiences of God. Although taking its source in the Jews' experience of God, it is basically a human institution and undergoes change and historical development like all

---

36. This is admirably done in David Rudavsky, *Modern Jewish Religious Movements* (New York, 1967).

37. The reader should be careful to differentiate between our use of the word "Conservative," denoting the movement, and "conservative," in its usual adjectival meaning.

human institutions. It is normative in the conditional sense that one ought to obey the *halakhah* if one wants to preserve the insights and experiences of the Jewish people as a whole and of those Jews in particular who have confronted God directly in their own lives. Conservative Judaism thus sees the *halakhah* as the Jewish vocabulary for approaching God. It does not see the *halakhah* as normative in the absolute sense, however, which would imply that obedience to *halakhah* is explicitly demanded of every Jew by God.[38]

These three different interpretations of revelation and *halakhah* give rise to different emphases within Jewish ethics. Generally speaking, Orthodox thinkers will approach questions of ethics by seeking to determine the teachings of the *halakhah* on the issues at hand. That is not to say that they do not recognize a super–halakhic realm of Jewish ethical teaching. The article by Aharon Lichtenstein below shows the extent to which an Orthodox thinker can recognize such a realm. But no Orthodox thinker will admit the possibility of there being a Jewish ethical teaching which might contradict *halakhah*. [39] That possibility, however, is explicitly stated by at least one important Conservative thinker, Seymour Siegel. "It is my thesis," he writes, "that according to our interpretation of Judaism, the ethical values of our tradition should have power to judge the particulars of Jewish law. If any law in our tradition does not fulfill our ethical values, then the law should be abolished or revised."[40] This position would most likely be rejected by Orthodox thinkers on the grounds that it sets human beings up as judges of God's law.

Generally speaking, at least until very recently, the Reform approach to ethics has been to identify Jewish ethics with prophetic teachings which, in turn, were usually interpreted in terms of contemporary liberalism. Of late, however, Reform thinkers have shown new sensitivity to the teachings of the post–Biblical Jewish tradition

---

38. On the contemporary situation with respect to the three main interpretations of Judaism, see Eugene B. Borowitz, "The Prospects for Jewish Denominationalism," *Conservative Judaism* 30 (1976), pp. 64-74.

39. For an Orthodox perspective on this problem see Emanuel Rackman, "Jewish Law in the State of Israel; Reflections from History," *Dine Yisrael* 6 (1976), pp. vii-xxiv, esp. pp. xxi-xxiv. The essay by Eliezer Berkovits below in this volume [see Kellner, pp. 355-pp. 374], however, shows how far a thinker of impeccably Orthodox credentials is willing to go in judging *halakhah* by ethical norms (which norms, however, he assimilates into *halahkah* itself).

40. Seymour Siegel, "Ethics and the Halakhah," *Conservative Judaism* 25 (1971), pp. 33-40, see pp. 33-34.

and generally seek to ground their ethical judgments in the Jewish tradition as a whole.[41]

Summing up, we may say that the contemporary Jewish approach to ethical problems is distinguished from the medieval approach in at least two important ways. It is no longer informed by the basic unanimity of spirit which underlay medieval Jewish ethics in all its various styles and forms. Further, and as a result of the Jew's unprecedented level of integration into the surrounding world, Jewish ethics today faces an entirely new complex of problems. Although there are elements of continuity between medieval and modern Jewish ethics, the discontinuities are more important. This is one of the many ways in which the wrenching changes which accompanied the Jewish entry into the modern world are reflected. It is basically the confrontation with that world which sets the theme for the essays collected in this volume, exploring the new problems facing contemporary Judaism and the novel approaches taken to solve them.

---

41. For a general view of Reform ethical thinking today, see the various essays in D.J. Silver (ed.), *Judaism and Ethics* (New York, 1970).

RELIGION, LAW AND MORALITY

1.

The Structure of
Jewish Law

DAVID M. FELDMAN

The Talmud

Supreme in authority—the "fundamental law"—is the Torah in its narrower sense, which means the Pentateuch, the Five Books of Moses. In its broader sense, the "Torah" encompasses all of developed Jewish religious law and lore. From the legal standpoint, even the remainder of the Bible serves as an auxiliary basis; when the Rabbis speak of a "biblical law," they are referring to commandments or ordinances that derive from the Pentateuch alone. The word "derive" here is used advisedly, for ordinances not found literally in the Pentateuchal text but which the Rabbis deduced therefrom by agreed-upon rules of interpretation are also called *d'oraita* [from the Torah]. Amplification of biblical law to include safeguards—a "fence around the law"—or ordinances, observances, or even new enactments *(takkanot)* instituted by classic rabbinical authority, are called *d'rabbanan* [from the Rabbis].[1]

The conventional division is between *Torah shebikh'tav*, the Written Torah, and *Torah sheb'al peh*, the Oral Law. "By the side of Scripture there had always gone an unwritten tradition, in part interpreting and applying the written Torah, in part supplementing it," says George Foot Moore in his study of Talmudic Judaism.[2] This oral interpretation is, in turn, divisible into two essential forms: In defining what the Torah requires in the matter of practice ("the way wherein they should walk and the thing which they should do" [Exodus 18:20]), the *halakhah*

(from *halokh,* to go, to walk) was devised. The detailed application of Torah law was systematically formulated, and the ordinances and observances were defined and regulated in accordance, again, with agreed-upon rules or canons of legal decision. Hence, *halakhah* is the law or a particular law. Where, on the other hand, the oral law yielded extralegal teaching such as moral maxims, legends, philosophical and historical speculation, theological observations, and the like, these became known as *aggadah* [the narrative]. *Halakhah* and *aggadah* are the two great currents in the oral tradition.[3]

The earliest widely accepted reduction to writing of the legal matter of the oral law was the work of R. Judah the Patriarch (*HaNasi,* known simply as "Rabbi," d. 219) and was called the *Mishnah* [the *disciplina,* or manual of study]. Before his time, R. Akiva (d. 132) and his pupil R. Meir had essayed earlier compositions of the *Mishnah,* but that of "Rabbi" promptly became the canonical one. The word *Mishnah* derives from a root meaning "to study"; hence its definition as a manual or the repository of relayed teaching. It is indeed the cornerstone of all later law, for the Talmud, with all its vast size, is primarily a commentary and exposition of the Mishnaic nucleus. Traditional material formally omitted from the Mishnah, moreover, is given due consideration by the Talmud. Described by the general term *baraita* [outside], this material becomes an aid to explaining the Mishnah and stands alongside it in the Talmud's discussions. The word *baraita* covers other definitive corpora of law as well, though they have individual names, such as the *Tosefta* [Supplement] which is now a separately printed collection of remnants of earlier compilations of halakhah that found no place in Rabbi's official *disciplina.* Also, the *Mekhilta, Sifra,* and *Sifrei* are included in this general term, although they are works of *Midrash* rather than Mishnah.

Midrash is an important term for our purposes: The word means "exposition" and refers to large extra-Talmudic collections of biblical interpretation. Like the Oral Law itself and unlike the Mishnah, there are Midrash collections of both halakhah and aggadah. The three mentioned above are halakhic *Midrashim* on books of the Pentateuch and are largely contemporaneous with the Mishnah. On the other hand, the *Rabbah* collection of Midrash comprises aggadic elaboration of, and homilies upon, the Five Books of Moses as well as the Books of Ruth, Song of Songs, Ecclesiastes, and so on, which date anywhere from the sixth century to the eleventh. But these, like the *Tanhuma,* another cycle of *aggadic* Midrash, are based on material of much earlier vintage.

Since the Mishnah is the fundament of the Talmud, its six divisions, called Orders, are the divisions of the Talmud itself. The Six Orders are further divided into sixty-three tractates called *massekhtot*. The word's root is akin to that of the Latin *textus*, both meaning, a weaving together, hence a text or treatise.[4] The third of the Six Orders, for example, is *Nashim*, meaning Women, and contains seven tractates, the first of which is *Y'vamot*, literally "Sisters-in-law" or Levirate Wives. Because this tractate contains the pivotal *baraita* about contraception, as well as references to the duty of procreation, it is referred to frequently in this study. Other tractates in the Order *Nashim*, such as *Kiddushin* [Betrothals] and *K'tubot* and *Gittin* [Writs of Marriage and of Divorce] also contain much material relevant to our subject, as does *Niddah* [The Menstruant] from the sixth Order *Tohorot* which deals with ritual purities. Since the Talmudic discussion of any subject within the tractates, however, follows not a logical but an organic sequence, and since all of Jewish law is interconnected, with analogies adduced from one sphere to the other, references from the whole of the Talmud are brought to bear on the subject at hand in the relevant literature. Source texts from tractate *Shabbat* of the second Order [*Moed*, "Appointed Times"], or from tractate *Sanhedrin* [The High Court] of the fourth Order [*N'zikin*, "Torts"], or from any number of other tractates, necessarily figure in our discussion as well.

Infinitely more voluminous than the Mishnah itself, the large body of analysis, discussion, dissection, and commentary on the Mishnah is called *G'mara*, meaning, in Aramaic, "the study."[5] In Hebrew "the study" is the "Talmud." By usage, Talmud refers to both Mishnah and *G'mara* together and hence, leaving to one side the great collections of Midrash, "the Talmud" is the comprehensive term for the large corpus of official formulations of oral law and lore. The Talmudic period, if it is said to begin with early Mishnaic times, comprises a span of at least six centuries. The ongoing argumentation, commentary, and refinement continued for at least three centuries after the redaction of the Mishnah and was brought to a close about the year 500. This scholastic activity took place primarily in the academies of Babylonia—Sura, Nehardea, and Pumbedita—where the Sages lived under Zoroastrian rule. Back in Palestine, a parallel development was taking place: the comments and interpretive teaching of the Sages there were sifted and set down in writing about a century earlier than was the case in Babylonia. The Talmud of Babylonia is much more exhaustive than the Palestinian Talmud and, for many and various reasons, predominated throughout subsequent Jewish history as the object of intensive study and as the reigning authority in Jewish law.[6] Hence, "the Talmud" means the Babylonian recension thereof, although *TB* as opposed to *TP* is used for accurate footnote reference.

Post-Talmudic Codes

The first important stratum of interpretation after the period of the Talmud is that of the Geonim. With Babylonia still the center of the Jewish world, the heads of its higher academies bore the title of *Gaon* [Excellency] and taught the Torah to students from near and far. In addition to the Responsa which they wrote as answers to queries in matters of law and faith, they were the first to compose systematic codes of halakhah by summing up in logical arrangement the conclusions of Talmudic discussion. The first of these is the *She'iltot* of R. Ahai Gaon (d. 760), a leading scholar of Pumbedita. The book contains 191 discourses, arranged according to the sections of the Torah as read in the synagogue, and seeking to explain the commandments therein in the light of the Talmud and other halakhic works.[7] The *Halakhot G'dolot* by R. Simon Kaira of the ninth century is another early example of an ambitious attempt to arrange topically the material of Jewish law and offer the decisions. After him, the estimable R. Hai Gaon and others produced some important partial codes in the next century and a half.

The scene shifts to North Africa where Talmudic studies flourished at the beginning of the second millennium. Chief among the commentators of this school was R. Hananel of Kairawan, who combined three convergent streams of learning: the Palestinian, the Babylonian, and the European. His annotations are of the greatest importance and appear alongside the text in printed editions of the Talmud.

For our purposes, the important product of the North African school is the work of R. Isaac of Fez, Isaac Al Fasi (1013—1073). Like the *Halakhot G'dolot* on which it was modeled, this "Alfasi" is a codex which closely follows the Talmud but which omits when it can all the discussion leading up to the legal conclusions. By including an opinion of one of the Sages, Al Fasi stamps it as the norm (halakhah); by simply ignoring another opinion he shows it to be rejected. His greatest influence lies in this, his role as decisor [*posek*] of the halakhah, for in the Talmud the debates on doubtful points often leave a matter undetermined. Al Fasi helps us to understand the meaning of the text as well: "We have, therefore, in the Alfasi, a work which is a commentary and a code at the same time. The commentary is implied; the code is manifest. And both are in the form of an abridged Talmud."[8]

Rashi and Tosafot

The commentary par excellence on the Talmud was, however, being composed by Al Fasi's younger contemporary on a different continent. Rashi, the acronym for R. Sh'lomo Yitzhaki (1040–1105) of the French province of Champagne, lived in an era of thriving Talmudic study in Europe after its decline in Babylonia. It was the century when R. Samuel HaNaggid of Granada in Spain had composed his systematic *Introduction to the Talmud* and when the pupils of the illustrious Rabbenu Gershom of Mayence—among whom Rashi's teacher is to be counted—founded many schools. From his teacher Rashi had learned the value of keeping written notes. Out of his classroom explanations to his disciples, there came the great Commentary on the Talmud. Based on earlier notes of R. Gershom's school, his Commentary is largely the result of his own keen insight, comprehensive mastery of all of Talmudic literature, awareness of the pupil's difficulty, and an unrivaled felicity of style. Here, too, however, we deal not with a "dictionary," with commentation which merely explains obscure passages—although that it does magnificently—but with a legally decisive presentation of the essence and applicability of the Talmudic argument.[9]

In the several schools that rose up under the influence of Rashi's popular intellectual activity, his notebook came to serve as a text. Known as the *konteros*, after the Latin *commentarius*, it was and is formally studied along with the Talmud and has opened to great numbers what had been virtually a sealed book.

Among the most eminent teachers of the next generation utilizing this companion text, were members of Rashi's own family. The central debate on the birth control *baraita* in this study has as its principals Rashi on one side and his grandson R. Jacob ben Meir of Rameru on the other. The latter is known as *Rabbenu Yaakov Tam*, "Our Rabbi Jacob the Unblemished," after the biblical description of Jacob as *tam*, meaning whole, simple, unblemished. To Rabbenu Tam pupils flocked in large numbers, some from countries as distant as Bohemia and Russia, and he was consulted by Rabbis from near and far. Rabbenu Tam "possessed a remarkably original, broad yet subtle intellect, and his writings display keen penetration and singular vigor of thought."[10] These words apply as well to the other masters of the new species of Talmudic literature initiated by Rabbenu Tam. Under the general heading of *Tosafot* (literally, "Supplements"), this type of commentation does much more than supplement the *konteros*, which served as its point of departure. The *Tosafot* aim at profounder depths, dissecting a Talmudic passage or Rashi's accepted commentary with the scalpel of subtle and forceful logic, against the background of an all-embracing mastery of the principles and content of the Talmud. Rabbenu Tam in particular "took pleasure," a modern biographer of Rashi puts it, "in raising ingenious objections to Rashi's explanations and in proposing original solutions," as did the other Tosafists. He continues,

> Yet, it would be a mistake to see in the *Tosafot* nothing but the taste for controversy or the love of discussion. . .the Tosafists even more than Rashi sought to deduce the Halakhah. . .and to discover analogies permitting the solution of new cases.[11]

A large part of Rabbenu Tam's contribution is contained in his *Sefer HaYashar*, but his pupils quote him in the *Tosafot* on just about every other page of the Talmud. Another prolific writer of Tosafot, a nephew of Rabbenu Tam, was R. Isaac of Dampierre, known as "Ri". In all standard editions of the Talmud since the first Bomberg (printed) edition of 1523, the text is flanked by Rashi and Tosafot facing one another and lending it their respective modes of illumination. Many Tosafot, other than those appearing in editions of the Talmud, were composed during this time and later published separately. The Tosafot of R. Isaiah da Trani of thirteenth-century Italy—known as *Tos'fot RiD*— is an important example.

Maimonides' Code

While such commentation proceeded apace, the work of proper and systematic codification awaited a successor to Al Fasi. It found one in the son of a disciple of his disciple—R. Moses ben Maimon, "Rambam" (1135-1204) of Cordova in Spain, deservedly the most famous Jew of the Middle Ages. Not the least of many achievements of Maimonides was the greatest single work of halakhah ever produced—a monumental code of Jewish law. He called it the *Mishneh Torah*, the "Second Torah," because thenceforth no other book "would be needed" in determining the law. He states his purpose in the Introduction as that of offering the student the developed law conveniently accessible, making it unnecessary to consult any intervening work. Arranged in architectural orderliness and written with brilliant lucidity, the Code comprises all of Talmudic and Geonic law in fourteen grand divisions, or books, which total one thousand chapters. (In the Hebrew numerical system, 14 is *Yad*, which gave the book its more popular name *Yad HaHazakah*, the "Strong Hand.") This marvel of structure, scope, and clarity commands the awesome respect of scholars to this day and must be reckoned with in any analysis of the halakhah. Yet it suffered from the defects of its virtues: Intending it as a single, complete, practical handbook, Maimonides chose to exclude even the minimum of Talmudic discussion and, of course to omit the citation of authorities for his decisions. Less understandable is his omission of the views of the Franco–German scholars. Dogmatically, in clean but categoric propositions, Maimonides laid down the law. His work thus became the target of the strictures of R. Abraham ben David of Posquieres in Southern France, and subsequent editions of the Code have Ben David's demurrals printed on the margin or as a kind of inset within the text. Other scholars of that and later generations endeavor to supply the missing source references (as in the Commentary, *Maggid Mishneh*) and the Franco–German material (*Hagahot Maimuniyot*), as well as to meet the objections of Ben David (*Migdal Oz*), or elucidate the material generally (*Mishneh LaMelekh*). Several of these commentaries are likewise printed with the Code itself, so that the regal masterpiece, with *nos'ei kelav*, its "armament bearers," now reigns supreme, unique and impregnable.

Ben David himself, despite his opposition to Maimonides' method of code-making, contributes a small work to this genre—a partial code. He collected the laws of *Niddah*, the treatment of which he concluded with a compact discourse on proper marital relations; hence the importance to our subject of this work, which he called *Ba'alei HaNefesh*. An earlier work of Maimonides, his *Commentary to the Mishnah*, is also relevant.

The Thirteenth Century Scholars and Asheri's Code

Some sort of a union between the Spanish and the French–German schools is exemplified by the mid-thirteenth-century Code, called *Sefer Mitzvot Gadol* (*SMaG*). Here the material is grouped around the 613 biblical commands, divided into positive and negative ones, under which are given the Talmudic deductions therefrom and other material less closely connected. The views of the Tosafists of the Rhineland are given a hearing along with those of Maimonides, serving as a bridge of acquaintance between the two. A generation later Rabbi Isaac of Corbeil wrote his compendium called *Sefer Mitzvot Katan* [*SMaK*], which proved highly popular among laymen and scholars alike and which, too, figures in our treatment here. So does an important thirteenth–century Code called the *Mord'khai* by R. Mordecai ben Hillel of Nuremberg (d.1298). Actually less of a code in the usual sense than a digest of opinions, decisions, and Responsa, the *Mord'khai* is held in high esteem by scholars to whom it served as a comprehensive source book.

Another code–like commentary from this period, or commentary that offers a digest of Talmudic debate, is the *Beit HaB'hirah* of R. Menahem HaMeiri (1249–1315) of Perpignan, Southern France. Written in the lucid style of his model Maimonides, this work is a running commentary to most of the tractates of the Talmud, many of which, unfortunately, were not published until the nineteenth century when the work quickly became a popular study companion. His ability to interpret, distill, and set forth the essence of the Talmud and of other authorities had instant appeal among students. His own newly coined phrases in referring to these authorities became well known: Al Fasi was the "Greatest of Decisors"; Rashi, the "Greatest of Teachers," and Maimonides the "Greatest of Systematizers."[12]

The "great reconciler" between the two schools was the foremost Talmudic scholar of his age, R. Moses ben Nahman—Nahmanides, ("Ramban," 1195–1270) who lived in Spain but who had learned his Talmud from French masters. He esteemed their method, the analytic method of subtle dialectic, and blended it with the local Spanish approach, the method of synthesis, of erudite systematization. Much more important than his partial Code, *Torat HaAdam*, on mourning customs, are Nahmanides' analytic commentaries and *novellae* on the tractates of the Talmud, where his genius yields new insights and resolutions of difficulties. Of course, his superb Commentary to the Bible itself, which is ample in both erudition and keenness, must be mentioned. Also, a small tract, important for our study, the *Iggeret HaKodesh* on the subject of sexual relations, has been ascribed to him as well.[13]

Nahmanides' most outstanding pupil was R. Solomon ben Adret ("Rashba," 1215–1310), who compiled codes of particular sections of the halakhah and who, too, is better known for his incisive *novellae* on the Talmud, to say nothing of his Responsa. Three thousand of his Responsa have been published.

As the famous Rabbi of Barcelona, Ben Adret was host one day to R. Asher ben Yehiel (1250-1327), who had fled there from the pillage and persecution visited upon the Jews of medieval Germany. Rabbenu Asher (Asheri or, better, "Rosh") was appointed Rabbi at Toledo and achieved renown as a scholar, teacher, and judge. His fame for our purposes rests upon his Abstract of the Talmud which followed the example of Al Fasi (and like it, was called "*Halakhot*"), but was enriched by the opinions of the later authorities, Maimonides and the Tosafists. His Abstract was marked by scholastic acumen and met with a ready reception in his old and new homes. Some parts of the Talmud itself were the object of a running commentary by Asheri; he has, moreover, authored separate Tosafot of his own to many tractates. All of these, together with one of his Responsa, figure prominently in our study. Rabbenu Y'ruham (d. 1340), author of a significant code not infrequently consulted, is reckoned among the pupils of Asheri.

The Tur Code

The next landmark code was that of Asheri's son, Jacob, who, next to Maimonides, is the most resourceful of all codifiers. He took the *Mishneh Torah* as his model, but his work is the independent creation of an original mind. He gives neither sources nor proof but generally cites the post-Talmudic authorities by name. Rabbinic studies had developed rapidly since the period of Maimonides two centuries earlier and, as R. Jacob says in the Introduction to his work, there was then hardly a point of law on which there were no differences of opinion.

Like that of his father and Nahmanides, the work of R. Jacob combined the French-German dialectics with Spanish systematics, and answered all the requirements of a code for the next two centuries. Even then, the new codices adopted his system and arrangement, about which more must be said: His book is called *Tur*, short for *Arba'ah Turim*, the Four Rows (after Exodus 28:17, the four rows of stones on the High Priest's breastplate). The first of the Four is called *Orah Hayyim* [Way of Life] and comprises the laws of Sabbath, festivals, daily prayers, and so on. The second is *Yoreh Deah* and deals with forbidden and permitted foods, as well as vows and purity regulations. The third is *Even HaEzer*, which treats of marriage, divorce, sexual relations, and the like. The fourth is *Hoshen HaMisphat*, collating civil and criminal law, inheritance, property, etc. The name of the third of the Four Rows, that of *Even HaEzer*, alludes to the phrase *ezer k'negdo* in Genesis, where the woman is called man's "helpmeet." Later codes adopted this highly serviceable arrangement, and even the section numbers within each of the Four Rows became standard. Hence, *E.H.* appears frequently in our footnotes, with *E.H.* I and *E.H.* 23 signifying the same relevant section in either the *Tur* or the later codes or commentaries thereon. Responsa books, too, have designated either sections or entire volumes accordingly: Vol. *E.H.*, Vol. *O.H.*, etc. R. Jacob's *Tur* succeeded as the standard Code even in his own lifetime and, on account of its conciliatory yet definitive nature, displaced many similar works of before and after.

The two centuries that elapsed between the *Tur* and the *Shulhan Arukh* saw little that was novel in the field of complete codes. Some partial efforts, such as a work on the liturgy alone, called *Sefer Abudarham*, of R. David Abudarham of Seville (d. 1345) may be mentioned, as well as *Maharil*, the custom compilation on the authority of R. Jacob Halevi Mollin of the Rhineland (d. 1427). A highly popular work, translated into many European languages, was the *Sefer HaHinnukh* of R. Aaron Halevy of thirteenth- and fourteenth-century Barcelona. This is a catalog of the commandments according to the weekly Torah reading, accompanied by much legal definition and moral edification. While significant new codes may not have been produced, the study of Talmud was far from neglected. This was the period of the great *Rishonim*, the Early Authorities, so called because they date from before the *Shulhan Arukh*. In addition to Nahmanides, Ben Adret, and Asheri mentioned above, these include R. Nissim, Ritva, R. Aaron Halevi, R. Isaac bar Sheshet—even R. Yosef Habib, whose *Nimmukei Yosef* Commentary to Al Fasi's Abstract is an important source—and many others. A work called *Shittah M'kubetzet* of the seventeenth century preserves some of the literary fruit of these *Rishonim*, much of it not otherwise available in their volumes of *novellae*.

The Shulhan Arukh

After the expulsion of the Jews from Spain and Portugal towards the end of the fifteenth century, they found themselves scattered throughout many lands—Turkey, Holland, Asia Minor, Palestine, and so on. This upheaval undermined the power of the "custom of the country"; in some places mixed communities arose, made up of Spanish, Italian, German, and other Jews. Only one who had mastered the immense material gathered since the *Tur* and whose prestige was commensurate could meet the challenge of dislocation and reestablish legal and customary order. R. Joseph Karo, scholar and mystic of Safed, qualified; moreover, he possessed the literary capacity necessary to reduce the existing codices to one Code. He began by writing his *Beit Yosef*, ostensibly a commentary to the *Tur*, but actually an independent, self-contained work. This was the result of twenty years of painstaking examination and study of every line and phrase in the *Tur*, supplying analysis and sources. After spending twelve more years in revision, he set out the conclusions of *Beit Yosef* in brief and called them the *Shulhan Arukh* [the "Set Table"], where the student could find what he wanted prepared and accessible. His ranking pillars of authority are Al Fasi, Maimonides, and Asheri; he usually adopts an opinion held by any two of the three. Some determination independent of antecedent authority is also evident in his great Code. Along with an insufficient acquaintance with the Ashkenazi (Polish-German) practice, this feature invited opposition—which might very well have been fatal to his Code were it not that the lack was overcome by R. Moses Isserles of Poland. The latter's *Glosses*, reflecting Ashkenazic differences in accepted practice, became the *Mappah* ["the Table Cloth"] to the *Shulkan Arukh*. Still, acceptance was far from won. It took a while before Karo's Code, even thus augmented, could triumph over another code of that time, or overcome the criticism of R. Solomon Luria.

Luria found much to criticize in the *Shulhan Arukh* and brought forth his own competing Code-Commentary in its place. He maintains that his own is closer to the original Talmud and, therefore, more authoritative. Since, after all, the Talmud is the final "court of appeal," and all subsequent literature must be judged in terms of its faithfulness to the original Talmudic law,[14] his claim could not be ignored. The other competing Code was that of R. Mordecai Jaffe, who had been preparing a comprehensive code before the *Beit Yosef*, then the *Shulhan Arukh*, and then the *Mappah* had appeared. In each case, he welcomed news of these efforts only to find them lacking as far as he was concerned. His own Code, called *L'vush*, paraphrases rather than quotes the earlier authorities, which makes for a highly readable work. It follows the divisions of the *Tur* and *Shulhan Arukh*, except that the first of the Four Rows, *Orah Hayyim*, is divided into two. Also contemporaneous is a small code–like tract, emanating from Karo's circle of mystics in Safed, called the *Sefer Haredim*.

The Later Authorities

The commentators and decisors after the *Shulhan Arukh* are known by the inclusive term *Aharonim*, the Later Authorities. Some of them helped make the *Shulhan Arukh* the accepted standard work it became. R. David ben Samuel HaLevy (author of *Turei Zahav*, the *"Taz"*) and R. Shabb'tai ben Meir HaKohen (*Siftei Kohen*, the *"Shakh"*) offered their Commentaries to Karo's Code, in the middle of the seventeenth century, questioning or defending its decisions and adding refinements and new "case law."

In keeping, however, with what was stated above, that the Talmud is really the final authority, the *Aharonim* are formally considered inferior to the earlier masters. In the Talmud itself, none of the Amoraim (Sages of the *G'mara*) may contradict the words of the *Tannaim* (Mishnaic Sages). Every exponent of the Law is—in the phrase of a medieval Commentator to the Mishnah—superior "as a matter of assumption" (*min ha-s'tam*) to those of succeeding generations.[15] Where faithful transmission of authentic tradition is involved, such retrospective deference is proper. Less proper but quite understandable is the sentiment expressed by a contemporary of the above two expositors of the *Shulhan Arukh*. R. Aaron Kaidanover (d. 1676) wrote to a colleague:

> You have given attention to the later authorities (*Shakh* and *Taz*). My studies are limited, thank God, to the Talmud and older authorities. Why should we nibble at the bones of later teachers when we can feast on the meat spread

upon the golden tables of Talmud, Al Fasi, Maimonides, Asheri. . .on which everything depends. The later writers confuse a man's mind and memory. You would, therefore, do better to sell their books and buy an edition of the *Tur* with Joseph Karo's commentary.[16]

But the hierarchy here is one of learning, rather than of authority. According to the canons of rabbinic decision, the latter-day master— assuming his awareness of earlier rulings which he may show to be inadequate or inapplicable—is, by virtue of that cumulative knowledge, to be deferred to. The principle is then *halakhah k'batra'ei*—the law follows the latest ruling.[17]

Competent in logic and learning and cumulative in legal precedent and refinement, the writings of *"Shakh"* and *"Taz"* gained their merited acceptance and were printed alongside the text of the *Shulhan Arukh*. So were many others—such as *Beit Sh'muel* of R. Samuel ben Uri on the *Even HaEzer* section—far too numerous to mention; they will be identified as they enter our discussion. The result was that Karo's Code became the new citadel, after Talmud, Maimonides and Tur, around which there clustered commentaries and glosses. The incomparable Elijah, "Gaon" of Vilna in the eighteenth century, chose the medium of commentation upon the *Shulhan Arukh* for his magnum opus in rabbinical writing.

In 1863, R. Solomon Ganzfried compiled a laymen's handbook of some everyday laws; he called it the *Kitzur* (abridged) *Shulhan Arukh*. It remains in wide use and high usefulness, and has been translated into English—but under the extravagant title, "Code of Jewish Law."[18] Unabridged digests of one or more of the Four Rows of the *Shulhan Arukh* also were composed, distilling again the continuing legal development. The overarching achievement in this realm is the *Arukh HaShulhan*, a grand restatement of the entire Code and of subsequent legislation, not without independent judgments, in most felicitous language. The work of R. Yehiel M. Epstein at the turn of this century, it enjoys widespread popularity and esteem.

Works based on the *Shulhan Arukh*, or even volumes of Responsa, were not at all the only literary media for the *Aharonim*. Some have their say, in the present treatment, through the instrumentality of Commentaries to the Talmud, which continue to be authored up to the present time. Some, such as the colorful R. Jacob Emden (d. 1776), utilize all three of these categories and several more as well.

The Extralegal Tributaries

Our subject draws heavily on the mainstream of Codes and Code Commentaries, of course. But if the authoritativeness of works in the legal complex is a function of their sequence or position in a framework, or of their fidelity to basic Talmud law, such is not the case with the extralegal tributaries. Even the Bible Commentaries, so many of which contribute to the picture presented in this study, would not, by the mere fact of being attached to the Bible, be able to overrule official interpretation of scripture. The latter properly finds its elaboration in Commentaries to the Talmud and to the Codes. Philosophic works of the Middle Ages partake of the same status: they are extralegal and, as elements in the "Jewish mind," help shape the picture, but are only auxiliary to the legal process. They require no sequential sketch at this time; when introduced in this study, they are briefly characterized in the body or the footnotes.

Some are in a special category and do merit mention here. The *Sefer Hasidim*, for one, contains the literary testament of three leading spirits of Hasidism (Pietism) in medieval Germany (five centuries before the Hasidic movement of R. Israel Ba'al Shem Tov, in the eighteenth century), and, in particular, of the writings of R. Judah the Hasid. The book often resembles a mass of casual jottings, with numbered paragraphs, yet is

. . .undoubtedly one of the most important and remarkable products of Jewish literature. No other work of the period provides us with so deep an insight into the real life of the Jewish community. . .in the most intimate connection with every day life.[19]

The author's "historical position," according to a modern scholar, is akin to that of Francis of Assisi.[20] The book became popular in many circles and is even quoted in legal contexts by some Responsa.

Menorat HaMaor ["The Lamp of Light"] is the name of two separate but similar books, both worthy of special mention here. The first is by R. Israel Ibn Al Nekawa of Toledo, who died in 1391. The book is a fine example of popular ethico–philosophic writing, although not very original. It is primarily a compilation of hundreds of beautiful maxims regarding the practice of virtue and of various virtues, garnered from all corners of Talmudic literature and skillfully woven together. The second is by R. Isaac Aboab of the same city, who died in 1492. It resembles the method and content of its namesake work but surpasses it in intellectual level and narrative competence. Both of these frequently reprinted classics contain a section on proper conjugal relations.

Another literary creation in a special category is the Zohar, which book, or group of books by that name, is the Bible of Kabbalah, of Jewish mysticism. It is the very cornerstone of the entire mystic movement, which became a substantial factor in Jewish life for six centuries after the Zohar's appearance in the thirteenth century. All later mystical works merely use its passages as a basis for further development.

Its mode of appearance was rather quaint and is still a matter of debate: The Zohar is ascribed to the Tanna (of the Mishnah) R. Simon ben Yohai with the assistance of an assembly of Sages initiated into the secrets of mysticism. It made its appearance at the end of the thirteenth century through the Kabbalist, Moses De Leon. This "Book of Splendor" was accepted by his contemporaries, though it did not lack for those who doubted its antiquity. After the Zohar's authority grew, voices of challenge to its antiquity or genuineness became louder, and, by the nineteenth century, a fair-sized literature on the subject had grown up with scholars taking various positions as to how much and which, if any, elements were of ancient origin.[21]

The mystic orientation was a dominant influence in the lives of many. The term mystic in this connection refers to a wide gamut of attitudes or motifs: from a dark, theurgic occultism to an enlightened, romantic suprarationalism, or an inwardness of religious experience. The author of the *Shulhan Arukh* was a mystic, but he intended his Code to be a bare statement of the inherited law, uninfluenced and unadorned.[22] Something of the role that mysticism did play in the development of our subject will become evident [later in this book]. This includes the contribution of the Zohar's spiritual descendants as well, such as *Sefer Haredim*, already mentioned, and the estimable *Sh'nei Luhot HaB'rit* (The *"ShLaH"*) of R. Isaiah Hurwitz (d. 1628).

The Responsa Literature

Because the pivotal baraita on the birth control question was not included by the major Codes the door was opened to its extensive consideration by another body of literature. The Responsa are formal replies to legal queries addressed to the scholars of all generations. We have already referred to some, from as soon after the Talmud as the Geonic period. As Jewish life developed in the various countries of sojourn, historical, political, and economic changes raised many new legal problems. The Tosafists and *Rishonim*, too, had authored Responsa and, after the dislocation caused by the Spanish expulsion, much literature of this type emanated from Turkey, Poland, and Palestine. Most of the great codifiers and commentators mentioned above are also authors of Responsa. The period of the *Aharonim* saw the issuance of a huge number of Responsa, and the process continues to this very moment.

In the main, Responsa are replies to queries submitted by Rabbis to their more learned colleagues concerning questions not specifically dealt with in the *Shulhan Arukh* or other Codes. They are characterized by personal attention to a specific case at hand. The data are given and the Respondent analyzes the legal literature bearing upon the case, cites analogies and the rulings of previous authorities, and comes up with an answer of "forbidden" or "permitted" or with advice on steps to be taken to resolve the issue or problem.[23] Highly individual, the question and the answer appertain primarily to the person involved, although they become part of "case law" and enter the legal mainstream as precedent authority. But further characterization of this unique literature, or even identification of the leading Respondents, is best not undertaken at this time.[24]

Notes

1. In Maimonides' Introduction to his *Commentary on the Mishnah*, he defines biblical laws as (1) laws expressly stated in the Torah; (2) laws derived from the Torah by interpretation; and (3) certain laws not derived from the Torah but regarded as *"halakhot* to Moses from Sinai."* This last phrase is understood by Asheri (in *Rosh* to *Hilkhot Mikvaot*, Ch. 1) to include laws as clearly accepted or as anciently established as if they were derived from Moses on Sinai.

2. G. F. Moore, *Judaism* (Cambridge, 1927), I, 251. The tradition is referred to in the New Testament as *paradosis ton presbyteron*, the "tradition of the Elders." Mark 7:2–13. See also Hermann L. Strack, *Introduction to the Talmud and Midrash* (Philadelphia, 1931), Part I, Ch. 2.

3. See, e.g., Strack, *op. cit.*, Part I, Ch. 1.

4. See, e.g., George Horowitz, *The Spirit of Jewish Law* (New York, 1953). Appendix I, for contents of the Six Orders of the Mishnah; also Ben Zion Bokser, *The Wisdom of the Talmud* (New York, 1951) for much informative material.

5. Strack, *op. cit.*, p. 5.

6. See Ch. I, "An Introduction to the Palestinian Talmud," in Louis Ginzberg, *On Jewish Law and Lore* (Philadelphia, 1962).

7. See, e.g., Meyer Waxman. *A History of Jewish Literature* (second ed.), I. 281 ff. S.K. Mirsky, in the Introduction to his edition of *She'iltot d'Rav Ahai Gaon*, maintains that this work incorporates material of Talmudic times.

8. Samuel Daiches. *The Study of the Talmud in Spain* (London, 1921), quoted by Horowitz, *op. cit.*, p. 50. See also Ch. 5, "The Codification of Jewish Law," in Ginzberg, *op, cit.* On medieval rabbinic studies generally, see S.W. Baron, "The Reign of Law" in *A Social and Religious History of the Jews*, second ed. (Philadelphia, 1958), VI, Ch. XXVII.

9. See the fine biography by M. Liber, *Rashi* (Philadelphia, 1926).

10. Liber, *op. cit.*, p. 188.

11. *Ibid.*, pp. 191–192.

12. He refers to them respectively as *g'dolei ha–pos'kim, g'dolei ha-rabbanim, g'dolei ha-m'habb'rim.*

13. On the question of the authorship of *Iggeret HaKodesh*, see David M. Feldman, *Birth Control, etc.*, Ch. 4, Note 89.

14. See, I.H. Weiss, *Dor Dor V'Dor'shav*, III, 215 ff. See also Feldman, *op. cit.* Ch. II, p. 213, on Luria's *Introduction to Bava Kamma.* Cf. Note 17, below.

15. *Tos'fot Yom Tov to Eduyot*, I, 5. Cf. *TB Shabbat* 112b: "If the Early Ones were as angels, we are as humans, etc."

16. *Resp. Nahalat Shivah* (Warsaw, 1884), No. 50. See N. H. Dembitzer, *K'lilat Yofi*, p. 62.

17. The principle is Geonic (*see Iggeret R. Sh'rira Gaon*, ed. Levin, p.38); it is explained by, e.g., Alfasi to *Eiruvin* (end); Asheri to *Sanhedrin* (IV, 6); and by R. Joseph Kolon (d. 1480) in his *Responsa*, Nos. 84 and 94, the latter relayed by Isserles to *Hoshen Mishpat*, 25,2 (end). See also *Pri M'gadim, K'lalim* No. 8, Preface to *Yoreh Deah.*

18. For significant variations in phraseology, with respect to sexual matters, in *Shulhan Arukh*, the *Kitzur*, and their antecedents, see Feldman, *op. cit.* pp. 70 ff.

19. Gershom Scholem, *Major Trends In Jewish Mysticism* (Schocken, 1941), p. 83.

20. F.I. Baer, quoted by Scholem, *loc. cit.* The two men lived at about the same time and had similar pietistic influences upon their communities.

21. See Scholem, *op. cit.* Chs. 5 and 6; Waxman, *op. cit.*, II, 392 ff.

22. See "The Shulhan Arukh: Enduring Code of Jewish Law," by Isadore Twersky, in *Judaism: A Quarterly Journal* (Spring, 1967), pp. 146, 149, 153.

23. Partial collections of references to the Responsa have been appended to the *Tur* or to the *Shulhan Arukh* in the form of Commentaries thereto. The *K'neset HaG'dolah* of 17th-century R. Hayyim Benvenisti is an example of the first; *Sha'arei T'shuvah* to *Sh. Ar. Orah Hayyim* and *Pit'hei T'shuvah* to the other three sections, the latter by 19th-century R. Zvi Hirsch Eisenstadt, are examples of the second. Far more exhaustive is *Otzar HaPoskim*, a monumental project recently undertaken by a collegium of scholars in Jerusalem. The initial volumes, on the opening *simanim* of *Even HaEzer*, have already appeared.

24. See Solomon Freehof, *The Responsa Literature* (Philadelphia, 1955), esp. Chs. 1 and 2.

Morality and Religion

In his dialogue *Euthyphro,* Plato posed a question which has exercised the intellects of theologians and philosophers ever since. Do the gods love the good, he asked, because it is good, or is it good because the gods love it? Rephrasing the question in modern terms, we might put it as follows: Does there exist some standard of morality independent of God's will? Do God's commands define morality, or can they themselves be judged in terms of some independent standard?

Neither of these apparently exclusive alternatives is attractive. If God's commands define morality, then, theoretically, were God to command us to torture young children it would be the morally correct thing to do. *Not* to torture them in such a situation would be the grossest immorality. But this clearly offends our strongly held prephilosophical notion that some things are inherently evil. Alternatively, if we assert that there is some standard of good and evil by which God's commands can be judged, then what do we need God's commands for? Theoretically, we should be able to discover the nature of right and wrong without them. Furthermore, and more importantly, there would be no such thing as obedience to God in the strict sense: we would act in accordance with His commands, not because they are His commands, but because they are right. Indeed, God Himself would be *obligated* to obey those standards which are independent of Him.

Immanuel Kant (1724-1804), arguably the greatest moral philosopher since Plato, clearly adopted the second alternative, insisting that there is an absolute standard of morality. He further maintained that obedience to commands, whatever their source, cannot count as moral behavior. Moral behavior, in Kant's terminology, must be autonomous (from the Greek words *auto* [self] and *nomos* [law]) or self–legislated. That is to say, it must be free and unconditioned. Moral actions are distinguished from all others by the fact that they are prompted by no ulterior motives at all, but are done simply for the principle they embody.

39

This position would have no particular importance for religious thinkers were it not for the fact that it is very widely perceived as being, in fact, correct. Many theologians and philosophers feel forced to admit that Kant has hit the nail squarely on the head and has isolated a crucial and defining element of moral behavior. The problem is that if Kant is right, then no divinely revealed morality can really count as moral. This problem dominates contemporary discussions of religion and morality and must be confronted in any discussion of religious ethics. (See for example the essays collected in Outka and Reeder (eds.), *Religion and Morality* [New York, 1975].) It is important to consider it in the present context for it makes no sense to study Jewish ethics if there can be no such thing as religious ethics generally.

There would seem to be three avenues of approach available for anyone trying to solve this problem. One can attempt to show that religion really preaches an autonomous ethic after all. In such a case, one accepts the truth of Kant's position and tries to demonstrate that religion conforms to it. This very common approach is the one taken by Louis Jacobs in the selection presented here. However, the tendentious reading of the sources, which is apparently necessary to support such a position, is subjected to incisive criticism by Sid Leiman.

If Judaism cannot be made to cohere with Kantian philosophy, as Leiman insists that it cannot, there is still the possibility that some compromise can be effected between the two. Emil Fackenheim seeks to bridge the gap between the Kantian demand for moral autonomy and the religious affirmation of the significance of God's command. He does this by arguing that man adopts God's will as his own, as it were. In the "pristine commanding moment," God's will is revealed and freely affirmed by man as his own. The Jew accepts the "yoke of the commandments" as his own.

There is yet a third way of solving the problem: one can reject Kant altogether. This is the position of Norbert Samuelson. He attempts to show that the difficulty is a psuedo–problem since, in the final analysis, the Kantian ethic is unacceptable. It makes possible duties to oneself, a notion which Samuelson insists is incorrect. Furthermore, the claim that we accept God's will as our own makes disputing God's will impossible. But Abraham and Moses each disputed that will on at least one occasion. Fackenheim's position is therefore inconsistent, Samuelson urges, with some basic Jewish views.

The Relationship Between Religion and Ethics in Jewish Thought

LOUIS JACOBS

This essay seeks to explore the relationship between religion and ethics as conceived of in the Jewish tradition. As in every other investigation of a great Jewish theme it must begin with the Bible, the source book of the Jewish faith, but the biblical writers were not systematic philosophers, so that it would be futile to examine the Bible in order to discover any kind of direct treatment of the relationship between religion and ethics. There are, in fact, no words for these concepts in classical Hebrew. What Zangwill said of the Rabbis of the Talmud is true of the biblical authors—they were the most religious of men but had no word for religion. Nor had they a word for ethics. The ethical injunctions in the Bible are numerous but nowhere in this book, or, better, collection of books produced over a long period, is there any consideration in abstract of the nature of ethics. Just and righteous conduct is urged with passion but Socratic-like discussions as to how justice is to be defined are totally absent. Yet, indirectly, the biblical viewpoint of the relationship between religion and ethics is stated clearly enough and can be detected without any attempt at reading into the texts ideas they do not contain.

It is as well to begin with the Decalogue. In six of the ten commandments ethical conduct is enjoined as a divine imperative: "Honour thy father and thy mother"; "Thou shalt not murder"; "Thou shalt not commit

Reprinted by permission of Doubleday & Company, Inc. from *Religion and Morality*, Gene Outka and John P. Reeder (Eds.), Copyright © 1973 by Gene Outka and John P. Reeder, Jr.

adultery"; "Thou shalt not steal"; "Thou shalt not bear false witness"; "Thou shalt not covet." (In the Bible and in the Jewish tradition generally the Decalogue is called the "ten words" not the "ten commandments" but this is irrelevant for our purpose since they are obviously put forward as divine commands.) Although God commands them it is not implied that the command is the reason for their observance, so that if God had commanded man to steal or to murder this would have been the right thing to do. On the contrary, the commands are announced in such a way as to suggest that they are already fully comprehensible to man as the basis for living the ethical life. It is implied that man by his nature knows that it is wrong to steal and right to honor his parents, so that what God is ordering him to do is to be true to himself, to be a man, to be fully human. God, being God, so it is implied, could not have commanded him to do wrong. Once God has commanded, however, the command itself is, of course, an additional reason for its observance.

The Covenant Code is introduced with the words: "These are the rules that you shall set before them" (Ex. 21:1). The famous modern biblical exegete Ehrlich understands the words "that you shall set before them" to mean "for their approval," i.e., that God wishes the people to see that the laws He gives are fully in accord with human nature and humans are bound to say "Amen" to them. But even if Ehrlich's comment is too fanciful it remains true that nowhere in the whole of the biblical record is there the faintest suggestion that God imposes upon man arbitrary rules which must be obeyed purely on the grounds that God so desires. The Deuteronomist states it explicitly: "Behold, I have taught you statutes and ordinances, even as the Lord my God commanded me, that ye should do so in the midst of the land whither ye go in to posses it. Observe therefore and do them; for this is your wisdom and your understanding in the sight of the peoples, that when they hear all these statutes, shall say: 'Surely this great nation is a wise and understanding people' " (Deut. 4:5-6). The "peoples," without the benefit of revelation, are quite capable of acknowledging the "wisdom" and "understanding" inherent in the precepts. "And what great nation is there, that both hath statutes and ordinances so righteous as all this law, which I set before you this day?" (Deut.4:8). The statutes and ordinances are not recommended because they are in the law but, so it is suggested: they are in the law because they are "righteous." (This is not to say, of course, that the Deuteronomic authors held that the *sole* purpose of the observance of the laws was for the "nations" to acknowledge Israel's wisdom.) An

Abraham can even plead with God Himself to practice justice: "That be far from Thee to do after this manner, to slay the righteous with the wicked, that so the righteous should be as the wicked; that be far from Thee; shall not the Judge of all the earth do justly?" (Gen. 18:25). The similar plea is put into the mouth of Moses: "O God, Source of the breath of all flesh! When one man sins, will you be wrathful with the whole community?" (Num. 16:22).

Writing at the end of the twelfth century, Moses Maimonides was close to the meaning of the above passages when he remarks:

> There is a group of human beings who consider it a grievous thing that causes should be given for any law; what would please them most is that the intellect would not find a meaning for the commandments and prohibitions. What compels them to feel thus is a sickness that they find in their souls, a sickness to which they are unable to give utterance and of which they cannot furnish a satisfactory account. For they think that if those laws were useful in this existence and had been given to us for this or that reason, it would be as if they derived from the reflection and the understanding of some intelligent being. If, however, there is a thing for which the intellect could not find any meaning at all and that does not lead to something useful, it indubitably derives from God; for the reflection of man would lead to no such thing.[1]

For the group Maimonides attacks it is an offense to suggest that the laws of God are "reasonable," for if they are then they are all too human. Only a law which humans would never arrive at by their own understanding has a right to be called divine. Maimonides attacks this as folly, as a sickness of the soul. "It is as if, according to these people of weak intellects, man were more perfect than his Maker; for man speaks and acts in a manner that leads to some intended end, whereas the deity does not act thus, but commands us to do things that are not useful to us and forbids us to do things that are not harmful to us." Maimonides relies on the verse in Deuteronomy we have quoted. Moreover, he applies the idea to all the precepts including the ritualistic taboos for which there is no evident reason. For Maimonides there is reason behind all these and it is man's task to discover what the reason might be, because the notion of God ordering man to carry out purposeless acts is abhorrent to Maimonides' religious sensibilities.

According to the critical view, the Pentateuchal laws which "God spoke to Moses, saying," are the fruit of the people's sustained reflection on ethical conduct and of their ripe ethical experience. Thus, to give one example among many, when the older laws regarding inheritance were seen to be unfair to women, the "test case" of the daughters of Zelophehad (Num 27:1-11) was constructed and read back into the times of the great lawgiver since this development of just legislation was seen as God's command: " 'Why should the name of our father be done away from among his family, because he had no son? Give unto us a possession among the brethren of our father.' And Moses brought their cause before the Lord. And the Lord spoke unto Moses, saying: 'The daughters of Zelophehad speak right: thou shalt surely give them a possession of an inheritance among their father's brethren; and thou shalt cause the inheritance of their father to pass unto them. And thou shalt speak unto the children of Israel, saying: If a man die, and have no son, then ye shall cause his inheritance to pass unto his daughter' " (vs. 4-8). In these instances the right course for man came to be seen as God's will for him and hence "given" to Moses by God.

In many of the Pentateuchal laws the reason for their observance is stated, a reason which appeals to man's innate ethical sensibility. "And a stranger thou shalt not oppress; for ye know the heart of a stranger, seeing ye were strangers in the land of Egypt" (Ex. 23:9). "If thou at all take they neighbour's garment to pledge, thou shalt restore it unto him by the time that the sun goes down; for that is his only covering, it is the garment for his skin, wherein shall he sleep? And it shall come to pass, when he crieth unto Me, that I will hear; for I am gracious" (Ex. 22:25-26). "Thou shalt not have in thy bag diverse weights, a great and a small. Thou shalt not have in thy house diverse measures, a great and a small. A perfect and just weight shalt thou have; a perfect and just measure shalt thou have; that thy days may be long upon the land which the Lord thy God giveth thee. For all that do such things, even all that do unrighteously, are an abomination unto the Lord thy God" (Deut. 25:13-16). "Thou shalt not abhor an Edomite, for he is thy brother; thou shalt not abhor an Egyptian, because thou wast a stranger in his land"(Deut. 23:7).

The same theme is found constantly in the prophetic writings. If the good were simply identified with the will of God it would be tautologous to say, as the prophets do, that man should obey God's will *and do good.* "Will the Lord be pleased with thousands of rams, with tens of thousands of rivers of oil? Shall I give my first-born for my transgressions, the fruit of my body for the sin of my soul? It hath been told thee, O man, what is good, and what the Lord doth require of thee: only to do justly, and to love mercy, and to walk humbly with thy God" (Mic. 6:7-8). "Wash you, make you clean, Put away the evil of your doings from before Mine eyes, Cease to do evil; Learn to do well; seek justice, relieve the oppressed, Judge the fatherless, plead for the widow" (Isa. 1:16-17). The prophet Amos castigates Damascus, Gaza, Tyre, Edom, Ammon, and Moab for atrocities they have perpetrated, even though these peoples had received no divine law, the implication being that man is capable of discerning right from wrong by the natural light within him (see Amos, chaps. 1 and 2). Indeed, nowhere in the prophetic writings are the "nations" condemned for worshiping their gods, only for the ethical abominations such as child sacrifice associated with the worship. The very detailing of separate ethical offenses in prophetic admonition is itself proof of the contention that for the prophets each of these offenses is wrong in itself and they are consequently not covered by the blanket condemnation of disobedience of God's will.

> Oh that I were in the wilderness, In a lodging-place of wayfaring men, that I might leave my people, and go from them! For they are all adulterers, An assembly of treacherous men. And they bend their tongue, their bow of falsehood; And they are grown mighty in the land, but not for truth; for they proceed from evil to evil, And Me they know not, saith the Lord. Take ye heed every one of his neighbour, And trust ye not in any brothers; For every brother acteth subtly, And every neighbour goeth about with slanders. And they deceive every one his neighbour. And truth they speak not: They have taught their tongue to speak lies, They weary themselves to commit iniquity. [Jer. 9:1-4]

The autonomy of ethics is similarly adumbrated in the Rabbinic literature. It is implicit in the very classification by the Rabbis of the precepts into the two groups, "between man and God" (e.g., prayer, study of the Torah, wearing phylacteries) and "between man and his neighbor."

> For transgressions that are between man and God the Day of Atonement effects atonement, but for transgressions that are between a man and his fellow the Day of Atonement effects atonement only if he has appeased his fellow. This did Rabbi Eleazar ben Azaria expound: *From all your sins shall ye be clean before the Lord* (Leviticus 16:30)—for transgressions that are between man and God the Day of Atonement effects atonement; but for transgressions that are between a man and his fellow the Day of Atonement effects atonement only if he has appeased his fellow. [Mishnah, Yoma 8:9]

The idea is found in the Rabbinic literature that God Himself keeps His laws. The Greek saying that the law is not written for the king is quoted and it is said that a human king decrees laws for others but need not keep them himself, whereas God orders man to rise in respect before the aged and He did this Himself, as it were, out of respect for Abraham (Jerusalem Talmud, Rosh Ha-Shanah 1:3). The Rabbis give as examples of commandments "which if they had been written in Scripture should by right have been written": the laws concerning idolatry, immorality, bloodshed, robbery, and blasphemy (Babylonian Talmud, Yoma 67b). The third-century Palestinian teacher Rabbi Johanan said: "If the Torah [the law] had not been given we could have learnt modesty from the cat, honesty from the ant, chastity from the dove, and good manners from the cock who first coaxes and then mates" (Babylonian Talmud, Eruvin 100b). Gentiles, to whom the Torah was not given, could still be righteous and the righteous of all nations have a share in the World to Come (Tosefta, Sanhedrin 13:2). Stories are told of Gentiles who observe such obligations as honoring parents in a manner superior to that of the Jews (Babylonian Talmud, Kiddushin 31a). In this Talmudic passage the late second-century teacher Rabbi Hanina observes that if Gentiles who are not commanded to honor parents are so heavily rewarded for honoring them, Jews who are *commanded* to do so will be rewarded all the more since one who does that which he is commanded to do is greater than one who does it without being commanded. The idea here seems to be that by a natural human propensity that which is commanded awakens rebellion. There is a need to kick against the traces. The verboten has its subtle allure. Man finds it easy to do the most difficult things except when these are in response to the call of duty. In any event it is clearly acknowledged that the moral life needs no religious spur to be effective. When God, it is further said in the same passage, began the ten commandments with "I am the Lord thy God" and "Thou shalt have no other gods," the nations of the world declared that He was "expounding for His own glory." But when they heard Him say: "Honor thy father and thy mother," they acknowledged the earlier commandments, i.e., they saw that even the first two were not for God's sake but for the benefit of man.

The nearest a strongly ethically orientated religion like Judaism comes to a complete separation between religion and ethics is in the following remarkable Talmudic comment (Babylonian Talmud, Kiddushin 40a):

"Say ye of the righteous, when he is good, that they shall eat the fruit of their doings" (Isaiah 3:10). Is there then a righteous man who is good and a righteous man who is not good? But he who is good to Heaven and good to man, he is a righteous man who is good: good to Heaven but not good to man, that is a righteous man who is not good. Similarly, you read: "Woe unto the wicked man that is evil; for the reward of his hands shall be given unto him" (Isaiah 3:11). Is there then a wicked man that is evil and one that is not evil? But he that is evil to Heaven and evil to men, he is a wicked man that is evil: he who is evil to Heaven but not evil to man, he is a wicked man that is not evil.

Somewhat misleadingly, this is rendered by Montefiore and Loewe as: "One who is good towards God and good towards men is a good righteous man: and one who is good towards God but bad towards men is not a good righteous man. Similarly: one who is bad towards God and bad towards man is a bad bad man; one who is bad towards God but not bad towards man is not a bad bad man."[2] Montefiore remarks:

In these strange words, the Talmud seeks to distinguish between the commands in the Law which are ordered by God, but which do not relate to our fellow-men, and those commands which do relate to our fellow-men. The former set of commands are less weighty than the latter. Thus one might say, from this point of view, the Jew who violates the Sabbath, does not observe the Day of Atonement, etc. but who honours his parents, and is charitable, just and kind towards his fellows is "not a bad bad man," whereas he who does just the reverse, is "a not good righteous man."[3]

Loewe admits that the difficulty is a real one but suggests that the cause of it might be the deficiency in Hebrew of abstract terms. Actually, the Rabbis here use the terms "wicked" (rasha) and "righteous" (tzaddik) in the technical sense of what we would today call a man with religious feeling. They are, in fact, calling attention to the phenomenon that it is quite possible for a man to have a strongly developed religious or "numinous" sense but to be at the same time a thorough scoundrel so far as his ethical conduct is concerned. The passage contains no ethical judgment as Montefiore suggests it does. The meaning is brought out more clearly if, instead of "bad bad man," "good bad man," etc., we paraphrase: "bad irreligious man"; "good irreligious man"; "good religious man"; "bad religious man." At all events it is suggested here that one can speak of a man as having a strong moral character without him having any use for religion and the Rabbis are saying that such an assessment of human character need not be wrong since religion is one thing and ethics another, though, of course, for the Rabbis, Judaism demands both.

Before leaving the Rabbis it is perhaps worthwhile referring to Moritz Lazarus' rejection, in the name of the Rabbinic attitude, of von Hartmann's reproach that "theism may not suffer a moral principle above or beside the Divine Being." Lazarus quotes the Targum (the Old Aramaic translation of the Bible), which renders Genesis 3:22 as: "See, man is unique, knowing of himself good and evil" and he concludes:

> The moral principle is, indeed, not above and not beside the Divine Being; it is *in itself.* Precisely for that reason it is at the same time *in God*—in God in as much as He is the prototype of morality. To repeat: not because the principle is in God is it the moral principle, but because it is the moral principle, in itself and absolutely, therefore it is necessarily in God.[4]

The medieval Jewish thinkers, influenced by Greek philosophy in its Arabic garb, began to think systematically about their religion. In the year 933 the great Babylonian teacher Saadia Gaon compiled his *Beliefs and Opinions,* in which he has a classification of the precepts of the Torah into the *rational* and the *revealed,* a classification much utilized by subsequent thinkers.[5] The rational precepts, which include the ethical, would be recognized as binding even without revelation. Revealed precepts (such as the Jewish dietary laws) are not irrational, there is a reason for them (a view which Maimonides followed, as above) but here obedience to God's will is more prominent. Obviously man would not know the revealed precepts without revelation. He would not wear phylacteries or refrain from eating pork if he were not *commanded* to do so, for how would he otherwise know that this is what God would have him do? But what need is there, asks Saadia, for revelation in connection with the rational precepts? If man can know them without revelation, if, in the terminology we use nowadays, they are autonomous and are to be kept because it is right to do so, not because they are enjoined in Scripture, why are they, in fact, revealed through the prophets? His basic answer is that revelation is required to avoid all uncertainty and for the precise details of how the rational precepts are to be carried out. Thus, for example, it is true that man would know by his own reason that it is wrong to steal but revelation is required in order to inform man how property is to be acquired. Saadia seems to be saying that without religion's precise teachings man's moral sense would still function but it would be confused in application. In Saadia's own words:

A further example is that, although reason considers stealing objectionable, there is nothing in it to inform us how a person comes to acquire property so that it becomes his possession. It does not state, for instance, whether this comes about as a result of labor, or is effected by means of barter, or by way of inheritance, or is derived from what is free to all, like what is hunted on land or sea. Nor is one informed by it as to whether a sale becomes valid upon the payment of the price or by taking hold of the article or by means of a statement alone. Besides these, there are many other uncertainties pertaining to this subject which would take too long and would be too difficult to enumerate. The prophets, therefore, came along with a clear-cut decision for each instance. Another example is the question of the expiation of crime. Reason considers it proper, to be sure, that whoever commits a crime should expiate it, but does not define what form this expiation ought to take: whether a reprimand alone is sufficient, or a *malediction* should go with it, or flogging too should be added. In the event that the punishment take the form of flogging, again, the question is how much, and the same applies to the malediction and the reprimand. Or it is possible that no satisfaction will be obtained except by the death of the criminal. And again it might be asked whether the punishment should be the same for whoever commits a certain crime, or whether it should vary from person to person. Then the prophets came and fixed for each crime its own penalty, and grouped some of them with others under certain conditions, and imposed monetary fines for some. For these considerations, then, that we have enumerated and other such reasons, it is necessary for us to have recourse to the mission of God's messengers. For if we were to defer in these matters to our own opinions, our views would differ and we would not agree on anything. Besides that, we are, of course, in need of their guidance on account of the precepts prescribed by revelation, as we have explained.[6]

Strictly relevant to our theme is the acute analysis of Moses Maimonides (1135-1204) of Greek and Hebraic ethical ideals where these seem to be in conflict.[7] Who is the better man, asks Maimonides, the one who has no desire to do wrong or the one who wishes to do wrong or the one who wishes to do wrong but refrains by exercising constant self-control? The Greek thinkers appear to be saying that the better man is the one who has no desire to do wrong, no murder in his heart, no urge to take that which does not belong to him, no hateful or harmful thoughts. The Talmudic Rabbis, on the other hand, seem to be saying the exact opposite. The Rabbis seem to maintain that man should have a desire to sin and a man should not say that he would not do this thing even if it were not forbidden. For instance, the Rabbis maintain that a man should not say that it is impossible for him to eat forbidden food but he should rather say that he would like to eat it and wants to eat it, only his Father in heaven had commanded him not to do so. Maimonides resolves the conflict by a neat (some have felt an over-neat) distinction between religious and ethical laws. The Rabbis are thinking of purely religious laws and here the element of obedience is paramount. The man who has no desire to eat forbidden food because, for example, he dislikes its taste does not abstain out of religious conviction and since the act itself is ethically neutral his abstention has no religious value. But the Greeks are thinking of ethical demands and the Rabbis would agree that to refrain from murder by exercising self-control is to fall short of the purpose of the ethical laws, which is to produce the good character the possessor of which has no wish to harm others.

Also relevant to our theme is the medieval discussion of the purpose of divine worship. Moses Nahmanides (1194-1270), for instance, in his *Commentary to the Pentateuch,* considers whether divine worship is for God's sake or for man's.[8] Nahmanides first quotes the Midrash (Genesis Rabbah 44:1) on the verse: "The word of the Lord is tried" (Ps. 18:31). The third-century Babylonian teacher Rab is quoted in the Midrash as taking the Hebrew word (*tzerufah*) translated as "tried" to mean "refining." Hence Rab understands the psalmist to be saying that the word of God refines, it has a purifying effect, and he concludes: "The precepts were given for no other purpose than to refine people. For what difference does it make to God whether the act of slaughtering animals for food is done at the neck or from the back of the neck? But the precepts were given only for the purpose of refining people." The meaning of Rab's teaching would seem to be that it is absurd to imagine that the deed in itself can have any significance for God but that it is the effect of the deed on the human character that God wants. The command to kill animals for food in this way rather than that, at the neck rather than from the back of the neck, has as its aim the inculcation of kindliness and compassion. By slaughtering the animal in the most painless way rather than by cruel methods, man's character becomes refined. Nahmanides quotes this passage because he sees in it the key to the Rabbinic understanding of the purpose of worship. By worshiping God, by obeying His laws, which all have the effect of benefiting man and encouraging virtue, man becomes more perfect, more God-like. God does want us to worship Him, as it were, but it is not the act of worship in itself that He requires but the effect it has on the human character. In Nahmanides' words:

> The benefit which comes from the observance of the precepts is not to God Himself, may He be exalted, but the benefit is for man himself, to keep him far from injury or from evil beliefs or from ugly traits of character or to remind him of the miracles and wonders of the Creator, blessed be He, so that man might come to know God. This is the meaning of "to refine people," that they should be as refined silver. For the silver-refiner does not carry out his task without purpose but does it in order to remove all the dross from the silver. So it is with regard to the precepts. Their aim is to remove every evil from our hearts, to make the truth known to us, and to remind us of it at all times.[9]

It goes without saying, continues Nahmanides, that God does not need for Himself the light provided by the lampstand in the Temple or the meat of sacrifices or the fragrance of incense, but even when He commands us to remember the wonders He wrought in Egypt and that He created the world it is not for His benefit or advantage only that we should know the truth, for our words and our recalling these things mean nothing to Him.

Thus both Maimonides and Nahmanides from different angles, and they are typical of medieval Jewish philosophical thought in general, refuse to identify the good with the will of God. If God's will can be spoken of at all in this connection, it is, according to these thinkers, that man should strive to improve his character to be a good man in the ethical sense.

Maimonides' discussion on the negative side found an echo centuries later on the positive side among the followers of the nineteenth-century Lithuanian Musar movement, a movement whose aim was to promote greater inwardness in the religious life but with profound ethical concern. The Musar teachers encouraged severe self-scrutiny; every one of man's deeds should be carefully weighed to see if it accorded with the highest ideals of Judaism. The opponents of the movement, and they were many, view this emphasis on introspection with suspicion, arguing that it cannot be wholesome for a man always to be taking his spiritual temperature. Be that as it may, the leaders of the movement considered the following question. The devout Jew prefaces the performance of a religious obligation with the declaration that he does it for the sake of God. (The actual formula for this is very late and is mystical in content but for the Musar teachers its mystical aspect was not primary. The important thing for them was attention was being called to the performance of the obligation as an act of divine worship. The mystical formula is: "I am about to do this for the sake of the unification of the Holy One, blessed be He, and His *Shekhinah*" [Divine Presence]. It is recited, for example, before donning the prayer shawl or the phylacteries.) Would this apply to the performance of acts of benevolence, to the precept: "Love thy neighbor"? The Musar teachers were divided on this point. Rabbi Zalman Dolinsky used to recite the declaration before he carried out any act of mercy. But Rabbi Simhah Züssel of Kelm argued that "one should fulfill precepts of this order out of natural feelings; they should stem from the natural benevolence of a kind heart," i.e., to invoke the concept of a religious duty here is to frustrate the purpose of the command of love. Rabbi Simhah Züssel gives an interesting turn to the verse: "Love thy neighbour as *thyself*": "Just as self-love is natural to man, requiring no calculations or special intentions, so should be his love for his fellows."[10] The man who has to have the intention of performing a religious duty before he can love others will never progress beyond the *I-It* relationship, to use Martin Buber's terminology, when what is called for is the *I-Thou*. The religious command to love others should be seen as a ladder to be kicked away once it has served as the means by which man attains to the heights to which it is directed.

One of the most powerful protests in modern times against the identification of religion with "human morality" in which the question of God and His commands have no place, is that of Søren Kierkegaard. Kierkegaard's *Fear and Trembling* is a commentary on the story of the binding of Isaac (the *Akedah*, "binding," as it is known in Jewish thought) told in the twenty-second chapter of the book of Genesis. Abraham is bidden by God to sacrifice to Him his only beloved son Isaac. Abraham, in Kierkegaard's interpretation of the story, cannot be sure that God really wants this dread thing from him but, if He does, Abraham is prepared to carry it out. If it is really God's will then there must be a "teleological suspension of the ethical" and the deed must be done, but of this Abraham cannot be sure. And so he goes in "fear and trembling," ready to obey if need be but haunted all the time by the fear that he may be embarked on an act of sheer murder.

The chutzpa of a Gentile, Jews might protest, to write a midrash on "our" biblical narrative, but what a midrash it is! Only so gifted a writer as Kierkegaard could call attention so effectively to the heart of the ancient tale missed by both the philistine and the pious.

We read in those holy books: "And God tempted Abraham, and said unto him, Abraham, Abraham, where art thou? And he said, Here am I." Thou to whom my speech is addressed, was such the case with thee? When afar off thou didst see the heavy dispensation of providence approaching thee, didst thou not say to the mountains, Fall on me, and to the hills, Cover me? Or if thou wast stronger, did not thy foot move slowly along the way, longing as it were for the old path? When a call was issued to thee, didst thou answer, or didst thou not answer perhaps in a low voice, whisperingly? Not so Abraham: joyfully, buoyantly, confidently, with a loud voice, he answered, "Here am I." We read further: "And Abraham rose early in the morning"—as though it were to a festival, so he hastened, and early in the morning he had come to the place spoken of, to Mount Moriah. He said nothing to Sarah, nothing to Eleazar. Indeed who could understand him? Had not the temptation by its very nature exacted of him an oath of silence? He cleft the wood, he bound Isaac, he lit the pyre, he drew the knife. My hearer, there was many a father who believed that with his son he lost everything that was dearest to him in the world, that he was deprived of every hope for the future, but yet there was none that was the child of promise in the sense that Isaac was for Abraham. There was many a father who lost his child; but then it was God, it was the unalterable, the unsearchable will of the Almighty, it was His hand took the child. Not so with Abraham. For him was reserved a harder trial, and Isaac's fate was laid along with the knife in Abraham's hand. And there he stood, the old man, with his only hope! But he did not doubt, he did not look anxiously to the right or to the left, he did not challenge heaven with his prayers. He knew that it was God the Almighty who was trying him, he knew that it was the hardest sacrifice that could be required of him; but he knew also that no sacrifice was too hard when God required it—and he drew the knife.[11]

A distinguished Jewish theologian, the late Milton Steinberg, writes in fierce opposition to Kierkegaard's interpretation:

From the Jewish viewpoint—and this is one of its highest dignities—the ethical is never suspended, not under any circumstance, and not for anyone, not even for God. *Especially not for God.* Are not supreme Reality and supreme Goodness one and co-essential to the Divine nature? If so, every act wherein the Good is put aside is more than a breach of His will; it is in effect a denial of His existence. Wherefore the Rabbis define sin as constituting not merely rebellion but atheism as well. What Kierkegaard asserts to be the glory of God is Jewishly regarded as unmitigated sacrilege. Which indeed is the true point of the *Akedah*, missed so perversely by Kierkegaard. While it was a merit in Abraham to be willing to sacrifice his only son to God, it was God's nature and merit that He would not accept an immoral tribute. And it was His purpose, among other things, to establish that truth.[12]

Steinberg has misunderstood Kierkegaard. To be sure, the story has a "happy ending"; the angel bids Abraham stay his hand. And Steinberg is right that God, being God, could not have commanded a man really to murder his son. Kierkegaard is fully aware of the "dread" in the whole episode. His point is rather that if Abraham had been convinced that it was God's will he would have done it because as "knight of faith" his ultimate aim, unlike that of "ethical man," is not subservience to the universal ethical norm but his individual relationship with God. Abraham is "ethical man" as well as "knight of faith." That is why he goes in "fear and trembling." In terms of our analysis we might put it that God wants man to be "ethical man" but this is because to be "ethical man" is part of that which is involved in the relationship the "knight of faith" has with his God.

This leads to a possible solution to the question which now must loom very large. We have tried to examine how the tension between religion and ethics manifests itself in a particular religious tradition—the Jewish. If, as we have seen, it is a dominant theme in Judaism that religious motivation is not essential for leading the good life in the ethical sense, and if ethics is really independent of religion, what, then, is the connection between religion and ethics? The fundamentalist thinker might follow up the hint thrown out by Saadia that in revealed Scripture we have the precise details of how ethical norms are to be applied in concrete situations. But such a solution is not open to anyone who, under the influence of biblical criticism, cannot see the biblical laws as direct divine guidance of this kind. It might still be argued, as it should be, that there is sufficient wisdom in the religious classics of Judaism to provide help in the inquiry, but even so a subjective element enters into the picture to make Saadia's suggestion less convincing. What then are the religious associations of ethics? The answer is surely that for the believer religion provides life with an extra dimension, as it were. The religious man sees his ethical concern as part of his total relationship with his God. This should not be taken to mean that there is a conflict between love of God

and love of man as George Orwell did, for instance, when he pronounced that you cannot love both God and man. On the contrary, the
love of man is part of what is meant by the love of God. In theological
language, it is the will of the Father of mankind that all His children
should love one another. But this in itself imparts a different quality to
man's ethical strivings. Man has no need for the God hypothesis in order
to appreciate the claims of the ethical side of human life. If he has to
invoke his religion here he is remote from the good as religion sees it. But
the religious man believed that God *is* and that His nature is such that
every act of love and compassion makes for the fulfillment of His purpose, every act of cruelty and oppression for its frustration. Man is to
live both horizontally and vertically, open to earthly needs and
responding to them as any other ethical man would do, but with his
religious beliefs to add to the scene the infinite glories of heaven.

This idea was emphasized especially by the Jewish mystics. There is,
for example, a detailed treatment of our theme in the gigantic compendium of Jewish piety known as *Shenei Luhot ha-Berit* (The Two
Tablets of the Covenant) by the German Kabbalist Isaiah Horowitz
(c.1555-c.1630) At the beginning of the book under the heading
"Creatures," Horowitz discusses the obligation to love all God's
creatures and its connection with the other great command to love
God.[13] The Babylonian Talmud (Sabbath 31a) tells a well-known tale of
the master Hillel. A prospective convert to Judaism approached Hillel
requesting the sage to teach him the Torah while he stood on one leg.
Hillel replied: "That which is hateful unto thee do not do unto thy
neighbor. This is the whole of the Torah. All the rest is commentary, go
and learn!" The medieval commentators were puzzled by the tale. What
of Judaism's purely religious obligations? The eleventh-century French
commentator Rashi, whose commentary is printed in most editions of
the Talmud, remarks that Hillel was either referring solely to the ethical
precepts or that by "thy neighbor" he meant God. Horowitz uses this as a
basis for his contention that in fact both loves—of the neighbor and of
God—are really one since God is One and all is from Him. The love of
the neighbor is part of the love of the God who created the neighbor. By
loving one's neighbor one fulfills God's purpose. Horowitz adds a more
mystical note. Since there is a divine spark in the soul of man, who is
created in God's image, the love of one's fellow is quite literally the love
of God.

Horowitz sums it up as follows:

In the truth if you examine the matter carefully, you will find that the majority of the precepts depend for their fulfilment on the command to love one's neighbour. First there are all the precepts regarding alms-giving, leaving the forgotten sheaf and the corners of the field to the poor, tithing, honesty in business, the prohibition of usury and many others of a like nature. Then there are all the virtuous traits of character: compassion, kindliness, patience, love, judging others charitably, running to help them when they are in danger, not slandering them or bearing tales, not scorning them or hating them or feeling envious of them, not flying into a rage, not being over-ambitious, these and thousands of other virtues depend on loving one's neighbor and only thus can one become perfect by keeping both the positive and negative precepts. And even with regard to those precepts which have no connection with one's neighbour—the prohibition, for example of forbidden food and of eating leaven on Passover—a man will keep them *a fortiori*. For if he loves his neighbour as himself how much more will he love God Who loves him with an unqualified and true love, Who is Lord of the universe and to Whom all belongs, blessed be He. So you see that the command "and thou shalt love thy neighbor as thyself" is the leg upon which the whole world stands. [There is possibly a hint at the Hillel story here in which there is a reference to "standing on one leg."] So you see that "and thou shalt love thy neighbor as thyself" brings about "thou shalt love the Lord thy God."[14]

Something of the kind would seem to be implied in the normative Jewish approach to this question. The love of other human beings and the ethical life in general are autonomous in that they justify themselves, requiring no support from religion. But there is a religious dimension to life and it has its effect on the whole of life. On the religious view it is God's concern, as it were, how man behaves towards his fellow and the love of the neighbor is the love of God.

Notes

1. Moses Maimonides, *Guide of the Perplexed*, trans. S. Pines (Chicago: Univ. of Chicago Press, 1963), pp.523-24.

2. Claude Montefiore and H. Loewe, *A Rabbinic Anthology* (London: Macmillan, 1938), pp.285-86.

3. Ibid.

4. Moritz Lazarus, *The Ethics of Judaism* (Philadelphia: Jewish Publication Society of America, 1900), pp.130-31.

5. Saadia Gaon, *Beliefs and Opinions*, trans. S. Rosenblatt (New Haven: Yale Univ. Press, 1948), Pt. III, chaps. 1-3.

6. Ibid., p.146.

7. Moses Maimonides, *Eight Chapters* (New York: Columbia Univ. Press, 1912), chap. 6.

8. Moses Nahmanides, *Commentary to the Pentateuch*, II (Jerusalem: Mosad Harav Kook, 1960), pp.448-51.

9. Ibid., p.451.

10. On the views of these teachers see Dov Katz, "The Musar Movement," *Tenuat Ha-Musar*, V (Tel Aviv: Tzioni, 1963), pp.138-39.

11. Søren Kierkegaard, *Fear and Trembling*, trans. Walter Lowrie (Princeton: Princeton Univ. Press, 1969), pp.35-36.

12. Milton Steinberg, *Anatomy of Faith* (New York: Harcourt, 1960), p.147.

13. Isaiah Horowitz, *The Two Tablets of the Covenant* (Jerusalem edition, 1963), pp.44b-45b.

14. Ibid.

3.

Critique of Louis Jacobs

SID Z. LEIMAN

Clearly, the most articulate Jewish ethicist in recent years has been Louis Jacobs, whose ethical concerns have found expression in the numerous books, anthologies, studies, and scholarly editions of classical texts he has edited and published.

In a recent study ("Relationship. . ."), Jacobs explores the relationship between religion and ethics in the Jewish tradition. Moving chronologically from the biblical through the modern periods, Jacobs adduces a variety of proof-texts in support of his claim that the autonomy of ethics is presupposed by all of Judaism. Specifically, he argues that in Judaism ethics is independent of religion so that "religious motivation is not essential for leading the good life in the ethical sense." Indeed, Jacobs is sufficiently persuaded by his own argument that at the close of the study he is forced to confront a new, more troubling question: "If ethics is really independent of religion, what, then, is the connection between religion and ethics?" His somewhat anemic solution that religion provides life (and, hence, ethics) with an extra dimension is not likely to win many adherents.

More disturbing is the methodology Jacobs employs in arriving at his conclusions. By means of a highly selective choice and interpretation of materials, Jacobs has imposed his view on the classical texts, and in the process he may have raised more problems than he solved. When discussing the biblical period, for example, Jacobs states that "nowhere in the whole of the biblical record is there the faintest suggestion that God imposes upon man arbitrary rules which must be obeyed purely on the grounds that God so desires"—conveniently overlooking Genesis 22

Reprinted from *Religious Studies Review*, Vol. 2 no. 2 (April 1976). Copyright © 1976 by the Council on the Study of Religion.

(from Abraham's perspective, if not God's) and Ezekiel 20:25. As part of the biblical evidence, Jacobs adduces the view of modern Bible scholarship that certain egalitarian laws (such as the right of women to inherit property) were inserted into the Pentateuch in the post-Mosaic period. These instances prove that "the right course for man came to be seen as God's will for him and hence 'given' to Moses by God." Jacobs may be right; but this, then, would be the view of modern Bible critics and Jacobs. It is certainly not the view of the biblical authors or of classical Judaism, despite Jacobs' claim that this is what he set out to present.

Turning to the rabbinic evidence, Jacobs conveniently makes no mention of passages such as Mishnah Berakhoth 5:3 and its explanation in the Babylonian Talmud (Berakhoth 33b) to the effect that God's commandments are to be obeyed precisely because they are divine fiat, and not because they are ethically charged. (Cf. Rashi, *ad loc.*, for a medieval elaboration of this view.) As proof of ethical autonomy in rabbinic literature, Jacobs cites a teaching ascribed to a third-century Palestinian teacher, which reads: "If the Torah had not been given we could have learned modesty from the cat, honesty from the ant, chastity from the dove, and good manners from the cock who first coaxes and then mates." But what does this passage really prove? How many Jews (or Gentiles, for that matter) have learned modesty from a cat? And if one could learn modesty from a cat, why not promiscuity from a dog? In short, it does not suffice merely to marshal evidence for a moral realm separate and distinct from God's commandments as prescribed in the Torah. The vitality of that realm needs to be examined, and specifically, its potency when in conflict with God's commandments. Jacobs does not discuss moral *obligation* or *accountability* outside of God's commandments, a crucial oversight in any discussion of the relationship between religion and ethics. Indeed, the distinctions he introduces between religion and ethics (in the Jewish tradition) appear to be artificial. At one point, Jacobs remarks that "the nearest. . .Judaism comes to a complete separation between religion and ethics is in the following remarkable Talmudic comment. . ."—and then proceeds to cite from the Talmud an exegetical *midrash* on Isaiah 3:10-11!

In sum, the Jewish tradition speaks in many more voices than Jacobs is willing to concede. William of Ockham's "God the Commander" is as prominently displayed in Judaism as Aquinas' "God of Virtue." Jacobs' rationalist bent colors his view of traditional Judaism, rendering it difficult, if not impossible, to distinguish the descriptive from the normative in his writings. Despite its faults, Jacobs' study is informative and provocative.

4

The Revealed Morality of Judaism and Modern Thought

A Confrontation with Kant

EMIL FACKENHEIM

Preface: On Jewish Philosophy Today

This preface is in the nature of an afterthought, written after the essay itself. Its purpose is to state the method which the essay itself uses, and to clarify the reasons for the use of this method, a clarification which will show that this essay means to fall into the discipline of modern Jewish philosophy.

First, while the essay is throughout concerned with the revealed morality of Judaism, it nowhere categorically affirms the reality of revelation. This is not because I am not prepared to make such an affirmation but rather because, in my view, to do so would transcend the scope of philosophy, Jewish philosophy included. For I hold the affirmation of revelation to presuppose a commitment, which in turn permeates the religious thinking which springs from it. Philosophical thinking, however, both presupposes, and stays with, objective

---

Reprinted by permission of Quadrangle/The New York Times Book Co. from *Rediscovering Judaism*, Arnold J. Wolf (Ed.) Copyright © 1965 by Quadrangle Books, Inc.

detachment, which is why both a religious commitment and the religious thinking flowing from it are, as such, extraphilosophical. I hasten to add that they are not for that reason antiphilosophical.

This is enough to indicate that the very concept of a Jewish philosophy is gravely problematical. How can thinking be at once truly philosophical and yet essentially Jewish? To say that it must be *essentially* Jewish is to dismiss, as deserving no further thought, that a philosophy might become Jewish by virtue of the accidental Jewish origin of its author. How then can it at once have the objectivity and universality which is required of it as philosophy, and yet be essentially committed to a content which has Jewish particularity? To judge by many contemporary samples of Jewish philosophizing, it must sacrifice either one or the other. If it is a rational endorsement of "values" found in Jewish history and literature, the very endorsement—which, being rational, is universal—makes these values essentially human, because universally valid, thus reducing their Jewishness to a historical accident. But if it remains bound to specifically Jewish goals, such as the survival of Jewish life, this limitation deprives it of the radical detachment and the radical universality required of philosophy. This is not to say, incidentally, that either of these pursuits is useless or illegitimate.

Can there be a Jewish philosophy, then, which is at once genuinely philosophical and yet essentially Jewish? This was possible at least under the special intellectual conditions which prevailed in the Jewish Middle Ages. Jewish philosophy then was the *confrontation between philosophy and Judaism.* This confrontation presupposed that philosophy and Judaism were different from each other and irreducible to each other; that it was necessary to confront them; and that it was possible to confront them in a manner which would compromise neither.

In the Middle Ages, all these conditions were accepted by those who engaged in Jewish philosophy. They accepted, first, the existence of two independent sources of truth, of which one was human reason, and the other a divine revelation embodied in the sacred Jewish Scriptures. On the basis of this fundamental assumption, they accepted these additional ones: that reason and revelation cover at least in part the same ground; that there is at least some apparent conflict between them; and that the conflict is apparent only—that it can be resolved without violence to either reason or Judaism. Without the first and third of these additional assumptions, there would have been no possibility of a Jewish philosophy, and without the second, no necessity for it.

It is noteworthy that, although there was a continuous tradition of Jewish philosophy in the Middle Ages, Jewish philosophy has appeared only sporadically in the modern age, and then unsure of its status. This is no accident. First, it has not been easy—to put it mildly—for modern philosophers to accept revelation as a source of truth, over and above reason itself. Reason, in the modern world, is apt to take itself as autonomous and all-encompassing. It is evident that, on such an assumption, philosophy cannot *confront* Judaism. If taking note of Judaism at all, it can only *absorb* it. Judaism then turns out to be, essentially, a "religion of reason," which is Jewish only by accident.

But even when philosophic reason does not make such radical claims a modern philosophic confrontation with Judaism is beset with difficulties unknown in the Middle Ages. At that time, it was assumed that there was at least one common basis for argument, in principle acceptable to both philosophers and religious believers. Revelation at Sinai—or revelation anywhere else—if actual, was an objective historical fact exactly like any other historical fact. If its acceptance as fact depended on the acceptance of authorities, this was true of *any* historical fact. Judah Halevi could argue, *both* as a philosopher and a believing Jew, that the testimony of the six hundred thousand present at Mt. Sinai could not have been mistaken.

But this view concerning revelation and authority is no longer acceptable either to modern philosophers or to thoughtful modern believers. Modern analysis has disclosed that it is not authority which is the source of faith but rather faith which is the source of acceptance—if any—of authority. An agnostic, had he been present at Mount Sinai, would have heard only the thunder and no voice of God. Revelation, as an objective event of communication, is hearable only to those already listening; and the listening is a listening in faith. This is a view accepted alike by modern philosophers and the best of modern religious thinkers. At any rate, it is my view.

It is on this view that the question arises whether, under modern circumstances, there can be a Jewish philosophy at all. For if that view is correct, then religious thinking—at least Jewish religious thinking vis-a-vis revelation—is from beginning to end *committed* thinking, which stands in dialogical relation to the God of Israel. But, as has been said, philosophical thinking must be from beginning to end *detached* thinking. It may thus seem that there is now no basis for meeting, as there was under medieval assumptions, since revelation is accessible, if at all, only to a commitment which is *ipso facto* non-philosophical. At best there could be only an attempt to show the compatibility of modern reason with a modern acceptance of revelation; and even such an attempt, unlike its medieval precursors, would be more concerned with keeping the two apart than with binding them together.

It is in this precarious situation that the following essay seeks, nevertheless, to contribute to a revival of Jewish philosophy. Although insisting both on the detachment of philosophic thought and on commitment as the condition of the accessibility of revelation, I nevertheless assume that revelation is not *wholly* inaccessible to philosophic reason. Under what conditions can this be possible?

As has already been said, this requires, in the first place, that the philosopher, *qua* philosopher, should suspend judgment as to the actuality of revelation. The essay which follows confronts the revealed morality of Judaism with certain modern philosophical standards of morality. It does not commit itself to the actuality of a revealed morality.

But how, without such a commitment, can there be a philosophical understanding of the *nature* of a revealed morality? The essay undertakes such an understanding through what may be called a *sympathetic phenomenological re-enactment*. This remains bound to the limits of philosophical detachment, while at the same time seeking a sympathetic understanding of truths accepted only on the basis of a commitment. Such an understanding will obviously have certain limits. One cannot, for example, remain a detached philosopher and yet ask—let alone find an answer to—the authentic Jewish question, "What does the God of Israel demand of *me?*" At the same time, it would seem that to deny in principle the possibility that detached thinking might understand some of the meaning of committed faith is impossible, for it is to be led to absurd consequences, such as that unless one shares the faith of a religious literature it must be wholly unintelligible; or that a leap from detachment to commitment, if and when it occurs, must be wholly blind. It would also be to imply that a Jewish philosophy is impossible in the present age.

The argument for the possibility of such a philosophy, as presented in this preface, is obviously fragmentary. It is hoped that the reader may find less fragmentary the example of Jewish philosophizing given in the following pages.

I

Can a law be at once moral and the will of God? Can one accept it as at the same time a moral duty and divinely revealed? Or is, perhaps, a revealed morality, radically considered, nothing less than a contradiction in terms?

At one time, such questions would have seemed preposterous to uncritical religious believers, and even critically minded philosophers would have seen no need to ask them. Today, they have become part of the fabric even of popular religious thought. This is due, more than to anything else, to the influence of one single philosopher. Present-day academic moral philosophy may not pay much attention to Kant; most popular moral or religious tracts may not so much as mention his name. But on the topic of revealed morality, moral and religious thought at both levels is still much influenced—consciously or unconsciously—by Kant's moral philosophy.

A Jewish philosopher concerned with that topic does not therefore engage in a mere antiquarian academic exercise if he seeks a confrontation of Kant and Judaism; that is if, investigating this topic, he takes Judaism as his example of a revealed morality, and Kant as his main guide in moral philosophy. This is the undertaking of the present essay which, under double guidance, asks whether the moral characteristics of a religious law or commandment must clash with the way in which it is revealed. We say: "must clash." For that a clash is *possible* must be taken for granted, and one need not be either modern or a philosopher to know it. Rabbinic teachers, for example, knew well enough that human behavior falls short of true morality if it is motivated solely by fear of heavenly punishment or the hope of divine reward.[1]

II

Philosophy has always questioned revelation in general and revealed morality in particular. But no philosopher prior to Kant found it necessary to question all revealed morality as being less than truly moral simply by virtue of being revealed. The question whether all revealed morality might be a contradiction in terms is a question which was not asked.

This may be shown by a brief review of the most radical objection to revealed morality made by pre-Kantian philosophy on grounds of morality alone. Theologians often claim that revelation is the sole source of our knowledge of moral law. Philosophy has almost always been forced to reject this claim. For to be obligated to any law, a man must be able to know that law; and to qualify as moral, a law must be universally obligatory. But, on the admission of theologians themselves, revealed moral law is accessible only to those who possess the revealed Scriptures.

It will be noted that this objection by no means amounts to a rejection of revealed morality. It is merely a threat of rejection, unless a certain demand is met. The demand is for an independent, universally human access to moral law, in addition to revelation.

Can Judaism meet this philosophical demand? One's first resort would be to the general Noachidic revelation which, unlike the revelation at Mount Sinai, is given to all men. But this can satisfy the philosopher only if he can exact a further concession. The Noachidic "revelation"—if one chooses to retain this term—must be accessible without a Scripture: for the Noachides have no Scripture. It must be, that is, a universal human capacity; in short, just what the philosopher has called reason all along.

Traditional Judaism may have misgivings about this concession. If pressed, however, it will nevertheless concede. For it must then, itself, distinguish between *moral* revealed laws which, "had they not been written by God, would have had to be written by men," and *non-moral* revealed laws, "to which Satan and the Gentiles object."[2] But if, except for divine action, men would have *had* to write moral law, they must be *able* to write it. And if the Gentiles—who object to non-moral revealed law—do *not* object to moral revealed law they must, in fact, have written or be able to write at least some of it.

This clarifies sufficiently for the present purpose the relation between Jewish revealed morality and philosophical rational morality, as set forth prior to Kant. However loudly and lengthily the two moralities may quarrel about the *content* of moral law, they have no necessary quarrel concerning its *foundations*. The philosopher has no moral reason for objecting in principle to a morality resting on revelation. And the Jewish theologian has no religious reason for objecting in principle to a morality resting on reason. What is more, this mutual tolerance concerning the foundations of morality produces opportunities for settling conflicts concerning its content as well. This is attested to by a long line of Jewish rationalists who believed that, since the same God was the creator of human reason and the giver of the Sinaitic revelation, the discoveries of reason and the teachings of Judaism could be in no genuine conflict.

III

This peaceful coexistence was upset by a thesis advanced by Immanuel Kant, first prominently stated in his *Fundamental Principles of the Metaphysics of Morals* (1785). Kant himself recognized that his thesis was both crucial and revolutionary; he held that previous moral philosophy did not contain it, and that, because of this failure, it had failed as a whole. Kant also recognized the revolutionary implications of his thesis for revealed morality. Indeed, this is a theme to which he kept returning, as if unable to leave it alone.

In a passage exemplary for our purpose Kant writes:

> [If the will is moral] it is not merely subject to law, but subject in such a way that it must also be regarded as imposing the law on itself, and subject to it for that reason only . . . . All past efforts to identify the principle of morality have failed without exception. For while it was seen that man is bound by his duty to laws, it was not seen that he is subject only to his own, albeit at the same time universal legislation, and obligated to act only according to his own, albeit universally legislating will. So long as one thought of man as merely subject to a law, whatever its content, without this law originating in his own will, one had to think of him as impelled to action by something other than himself. The law had to carry with it some interest which induced or impelled him to action. But in this way all labour to discover the supreme ground of duty was lost beyond recovery. For one could thus never arrive at duty, but merely at the necessity of acting for some interest.[3]

But this, Kant concludes, is at best only an impure morality. An externally compelling or cajoling law must necessarily be heteronomous or impure so far as moral motivation is concerned. To be pure, a moral law must be autonomous, or self-imposed.

We must be sure to grasp the essence of the Kantian thesis. It is by no means the mere assertion—as we have seen, far from new—that in order to be morally obligatory, a law must have a universality enabling all men to know it. Kant would have thought this condition satisfied by those ancient moralists who identified the moral law with the law of the universe, or by their present-day heirs who identify it with the laws of mental health. The essence of the Kantian thesis is that neither of these laws, however universal, can by itself *obligate* a man to obedience; they can do no more than promise happiness or mental health as the reward of obedience, and threaten unhappiness or neurosis as the punishment of defiance. This is because both laws confront man only from without. They are not imposed on man by man himself. A law which cannot unconditionally obligate may be prudent, wise, or beneficial. It cannot be moral.

According to Kant, then, there may be much that can induce us or force us to obey. But no law in heaven or on earth can obligate us to obey unless we *accept ourselves* as obligated to obey. And unless we can accept ourselves as obligated we cannot *be* obligated. Once clearly identified, the Kantian thesis seems very nearly irresistible.

It poses, however, an unprecedented challenge to every revealed morality, regardless of content, and simply by virtue of its being revealed. *If in order to be moral a law must be self-imposed, not imposed from without, then how can a law given or imposed by God have genuine moral qualities?* Pre-Kantian moral philosophy, as was seen, could accept revealed morality conditionally. Kant's moral philosophy threatens it radically. It does so because revelation is either a gift to man from without—the gift of a God *other* than man—or else it is not revelation at all.

IV

According to one widely popular interpretation of Kant's thesis, the will, in imposing moral law on itself, *creates* that law. Moral law is the collective creation of the human spirit; and only because it is such a creation is it moral at all. In rising to the life of morality, man actively transforms his own being in the light of ideals which are themselves a creative human product. All true morality is creative simply by virtue of being truly moral. And all passive submission, no matter to whom or what, is less than truly moral simply *because* it is passive submission.

Philosophers who accept this version of the Kantian thesis must reject in principle all revealed morality, radically, unequivocally, and immediately. To them, such a morality must be at worst a mere passive submission to the whims of an alien Deity. Even at best, it is just a creative morality which fails to recognize itself for what it is, for it mistakes its own creation for a passively received gift. And by virtue of this mistake it still falls short in some measure of the ideal morality.

But it is a matter of great importance that this version of the Kantian thesis is decidedly not Kant's own.[4] Kant does not assert that the human spirit creates moral law; he emphatically denies it. And his denial dramatizes his conviction—often stated by Kant himself but frequently overlooked by his interpreters—that in order to impose moral law on himself, man need be neither its individual nor collective creator. He need be capable only of *appropriating* a law, which in fact he has *not* created, *as though* he had created it. The attacks of "creative morality" philosophies on revealed morality, whatever their merits, we may thus ignore.

Unlike these, Kant's own doctrine does not rule out revealed morality from the start. For if the moral will need only appropriate, and not create, moral law, why might it not be *prima facie* possible for it to appropriate a law given by God? This, however, seems possible only *prima facie;* while not ruling out revealed morality from the start, Kant's doctrine deeply threatens it in the end. Indeed, this threat may be described as far more dangerous than that of "creative morality" philosophies. These latter—which reject revealed morality on the basis of criteria external to it—invite a like treatment from the defenders of revealed morality. This is not true of Kant, who takes revealed morality in its own right with a considerable degree of seriousness before he questions it radically.

Kant does not rule out revealed morality from the start; his moral will does not create moral law. Yet he threatens that morality in the end: for his moral will must act as though it were the creator of moral law. This Kantian assertion confronts the believer in a revealed morality with a grave dilemma: *Either he concedes that the will can and must impose the God-given law upon itself; but then its God-givenness becomes*

*irrelevant in the process of self-imposition and appropriation; or else he
insists that the God-givenness of the law does not and cannot at any
point become irrelevant; but then the will cannot impose the law on itself—it can only submit to it for such non-moral reasons as trust in
divine promises or fear of divine threats.*[5]

Kant himself perceives this dilemma with the utmost clarity; only for
him it is not a dilemma. In his view, the religious man must choose between what Kant terms, respectively, "theological morality" and "moral
theology." But to choose moral theology is to gain everything and to lose
nothing.

The religious man chooses theological morality when he accepts laws
as moral because they are the will of God. In so doing he not only submits to an alien law, but he submits to it because it is alien. Hence he cannot impose that law upon himself; and he can obey it—if he does obey
it—because of its external sanctions only.[6] "Theological morality" is, and
must be, heteronomous morality.

The religious man can rise above this only if he embraces "moral
theology." He must not accept laws as moral because they are the will of
God, but he must ascribe laws to God because they are intrinsically
moral, and known to be so, quite apart from the will of God. It is
because the will is capable of recognizing their intrinsic morality that it
can impose laws upon itself, thus achieving moral autonomy. But this
achievement is bought at a price. In imposing moral laws on itself, the
will need not and, indeed, cannot pay heed to their God-givenness. The
same act which appropriates the God-given moral law reduces its God-
givenness to irrelevance.

One might therefore well ask why Kant's religious man, when
achieving moral autonomy, should still *be* a religious man. Why should
he end up with "moral theology" rather than with morality pure and
simple? What necessity is there for ascribing the moral law to divine
authorship, and what is the function of this ascription? This is a question
of some complexity. But so long as we move in a purely moral context—
asking ourselves what our duty is and why we should do it—the question
does not arise at all. In that context, the question of the authorship of the
moral law may be, or possibly even must be, left open. Kant writes:

The veiled goddess before whom we bend our knees is the moral law within
us . . . To be sure, we hear her voice and clearly understand her com-

mandments, but are, in hearing them, in doubt as to who is speaking: whether man, in the self-sufficient power of his own reason, or Another, whose nature is unknown, and who speaks to man through the medium of his reason. Perhaps we would do better to refrain even from inquiring. For such a question is merely speculative, and our duty remains the same, whatever the source from which it issues.[7]

V

Such, then, is the challenge of Kant to revealed morality. The student who in its light considers the revealed morality of Judaism makes two extraordinary discoveries. One is that this morality cannot be classified as either autonomous or heteronomous in the Kantian sense. The other is that, in the nearly two hundred years since the Kantian doctrine first appeared to challenge them, Jewish religious thinkers have noticed this fact but rarely, and, when they have noticed it, only dimly.

Apologetic tendencies have marred at least all the standard Jewish responses to the Kantian challenge. Thus, orthodox thinkers can certainly never have forgotten that, according to a central traditional Jewish doctrine, the commandments are not truly performed until they are performed for their own sake. Yet when faced with the Kantian challenge they have tended to behave as though they had indeed forgotten that Jewish doctrine. Rightly concerned to rescue the divine Law-giver from irrelevance, they have been prone to argue that, but for the divine sanctions behind the commandments, the latter would remain universally and necessarily unperformed. They should have insisted that the revealed morality of Judaism is not heteronomous. What they did insist all too often was that all human morality must be so. But thereby they not only put forward a false doctrine but pleaded Judaism guilty to a mistaken charge.

Liberal responses to Kant have suffered even more gravely from apologetic bias. While orthodox thinkers argued that the morality of Judaism is revealed but heteronomous, their liberal colleagues have often acted as though it were autonomous but not revealed. They would have prophets and rabbis speak with the Kantian voice of self-legislating reason.

This can be done in one of two ways; but both are foredoomed to failure. One can say that prophets and rabbis taught an autonomous morality, as it were, unconsciously: for they still gave conscious fealty to a revealing God. But then their morality stood, after all, still in need of liberal purification which finally eliminated the revealing God. Or one can picture prophets and rabbis teaching an autonomous morality for what it is—but this picture is a scandalous distortion of historical fact.

Because of the haste with which they resorted to apologetics, both these standard reactions to Kant failed to bring to light the authentic revealed morality of Judaism, which takes it out of the realm of both autonomous and heteronomous morality. One group of apologists saw that the revealed morality of Judaism is not autonomous, because it stands in an essential relation to a commanding God. The other saw that it is not heteronomous because, bidding man to perform commandments both for their own sake and for the sake of God, it rises above all blandishments and threats. But neither group was able to perceive the essential togetherness of these two elements. And yet the source and life of the revealed morality of Judaism lies precisely in that togetherness; a divine commanding Presence which never dissipates itself into irrelevance, and a human response which freely appropriates what it receives. The Jewish thinker does not respond adequately to the Kantian challenge until he brings this togetherness to philosophical self-consciousness, in order to ask a question which Kant literally forces upon him: *How can man appropriate a God-given law or commandment, accepting and performing it as though it were his own, while yet remaining, in the very act of appropriation, essentially and receptively related to its divine Giver? How can man morally obey a law which yet is, and never ceases to be,* essentially revealed? According to Kant, this is clearly impossible. Puzzlement and wonder arise for the Jewish philosopher because—if he is to believe the testimony of both Jewish life and Jewish thought—what Kant thought impossible is real.

VI

We must take care above all lest what is essential in this remarkable togetherness slip from notice. This would happen if one were to attend now to the divine commanding Presence in its otherness, and then to the human response in its power of free appropriation, but not to the two together. This togetherness is essential. In displaying it, we shall find that it exists in Judaism from its beginnings and throughout its history. Only in periods of spiritual decay can the one element seem capable of existence without the other. And this *is* the decay. With the exception of such periods, there is no age in the spiritual history of Judaism so "primitive" as to manifest—in the style of "theological morality"—only a divine commanding Presence but "not yet" an act of human appropriation. Nor is there an age "advanced" enough to manifest—in the style of "moral theology"—only a free human appropriation but "no longer" a commanding God who can be present in all His otherness.

At no moment in the spiritual history of Judaism is the otherness of the divine commanding Presence so starkly disclosed as in that pristine one in which the Divine, first reaching out to the human, calls him to His service. For in that moment there are as yet no specified commandments but only a still unspecified divine commanding Presence. Abraham is commanded to go to another country without being told of the country, nor of the purpose which his migration is to serve. Prophets are called as messengers, without as yet being given a specific message. Israel as a whole is challenged, knowing as yet no more of the challenge than that it is divine. In the pristine moment, the divine commanding Presence does not communicate a finite content which the human recipient might appraise and appropriate in the light of familiar standards. On the contrary, it calls into question all familiar content, and, indeed, all standards. Whatever may be true of subsequent history, there can be, at any rate, no mistaking this initial voice for one already familiar, such as conscience, reason, or "spiritual creativity."[8]

It may therefore seem that, whatever the nature of the human response to this pristine challenge, it cannot, at any rate, be free appropriation. There can certainly be no appropriation of specific commandments in the light of commensurate human standards; for there are as yet no such commandments. And how could there be an appropriation of the unspecified divine commanding Presence itself, when in the pristine moment it discloses itself as wholly other than human? It may thus seem that, if there is human freedom at all in the pristine moment, it can at most be only heteronomous freedom; the kind, that is, which is conditioned by fear or hope.

And yet a freedom of this sort could not survive the touch of the divine

Presence. Such freedom might survive, perhaps, in moments of divine distance which, giving rise only to finite fear or hope, could leave room, as it were, for a freedom conditioned by them. But a fear or hope produced by the touch of divine Presence would of necessity be an absolute Fear or Hope; and as such it would of necessity overwhelm the freedom conditioned by them. If in relation to God man is capable of heteronomous freedom only, then the event of divine Presence would reduce him, while that event lasts, to a will-less tool of a blind fate.

Such a reduction is indeed the primordial experience of some religions. But it is not the primordial experience of Judaism. For here the Divine manifests Itself as *commanding*, and in order to do so it requires real human freedom. And since the Divine is *Presence* as well as commanding, the required human freedom cannot be merely conditional; it must be unconditional and absolute. Finally, this unconditional and absolute freedom must be more even than the freedom to accept or reject, for their own sake and on their own merit, specific commandments: there are as yet no such commandments. The freedom required in the pristine moment of the divine commanding Presence, then, is nothing less than *the freedom to accept or reject the divine commanding Presence as a whole, and for its own sake—that is, for no other reason than that it is that Presence.* It is such freedom that the prophet displays when he responds, "Here I am, send me"; or the people as a whole, when they respond, "we shall do and hearken."⁹

This pristine human freedom of choice is not autonomous. Without the Other, man might have the self-sufficient power for all kinds of choice, but the power of choice to accept or reject the divine commanding Presence he would not have. How could he accept God, unless God had become present to him, for him to accept? How could he reject Him, unless He had become present to him, for him to reject? The divine commanding Presence, then, may be said to *give* man choosing power. It may even be said to *force* the actual choice upon him. For in being present, It *singles out*; and in singling out It rules out every escape from the choice into some spurious third alternative.

And yet this pristine choice most decidedly *is* a choice. The divine commanding Presence may force the choice on singled-out man. It does not force him to choose God, and the choice itself (as was seen) is not heteronomous; for it accepts or rejects the divine commanding Presence for no other reason than that it *is* that Presence. But this entails the momentous consequence that, *if and when a man chooses to accept the divine commanding Presence, he does nothing less than accept the divine Will as his own.*

But how is this humanly possible? We have already asked this question, in a general form. But it may now be given a sharper form which states in full clarity what is at stake: *How can man, in the very moment which starkly discloses the gap between him and God, presume to bridge that gap, by accepting God's will simply because it is God's, thus making it his own? How can man presume to act out of love for the sake of God?* It is perhaps no wonder that a philosopher, when first coming upon this decisive question, should shrink from it in thought. Even prophets shrank from it, when first confronted with it in life.[10]

VII

It may therefore seem prudent for a philosopher to suspend if not to avoid that question, by turning from the pristine moment which initiates the revealed morality of Judaism, to the developed life of that morality itself. Here revelation has become a system of specified laws and commandments; and at least insofar as those are moral in nature they possess in Judaism undoubted permanence and undoubted intrinsic value.[11] A Jeremiah may believe that whereas in one situation God demands resistance to the enemy, in another He demands submission.[12] But one cannot conceive of him as saying that concerning justice or love and injustice or hatred. Just how moral law can assume permanence and intrinsic value within the framework of a revealed morality is indeed a deep and weighty question, which requires treatment in its own right.[13] The fact of its doing so, in Judaism at any rate, can be in no serious doubt.

This may suggest to the philosopher that, once permanent law of intrinsic value has made its appearance in Judaism, the divine commanding Presence of the pristine moment has vanished into an irrelevant past. What could be the function of His Presence? If it contradicted moral standards already in human possession, its voice would surely have to be rejected, as a voice of temptation. And if it confirmed these standards, it would only tell what is already known. In short, once revelation has become specified as a system of laws, new and revealing immediacy is either false or superfluous.[14]

If this were the full truth of the matter, then revealed moral law in Judaism would allow of only two human responses: One obeys it for its own sake, by recognizing and appropriating its intrinsic value. Then, however, one obeys it for its own sake *only*, and the divine Giver of the law becomes irrelevant in the process of appropriation and so does the revealed quality of the law itself. Or one obeys it *because* it is revealed. But then one could not obey it either for God's sake or for its own; not the former because the Divine, having lost commanding presence—immediacy—after the rise of law, would have reduced itself to the mere external sanction behind the law; and not the latter, because the law would then need such sanctions. In short, one would be driven back to the Kantian alternative between a "moral theology" which is essentially unrevealed, and a "theological morality" which is less than fully moral.

But must the divine Presence pass into irrelevance once revealed moral law has appeared? To ask this question is to recognize that the Kantian alternative contains a hidden premise. This premise, to be sure, is hard to reject, but Judaism implicitly rejects it. According to the testimony of Jewish life and teaching, the divine commanding Presence does *not* pass into irrelevance once moral law has assumed permanence and intrinsic value. The Torah is given whenever men are ready to receive it,[15] and the act of receiving Torah culminates in the confrontation with its Giver. The prophet, to be sure, has a specific message; yet the words "thus saith the Lord" are not an empty preamble but an essential part of the message itself. Kant holds that, mediating between man and God, moral law rules out or renders irrelevant an immediate divine commanding Presence. Judaism affirms that, despite the mediating function of the revealed moral law, the Divine is still present in commanding immediacy. The Kantian premise is that moral law is a *bar* between man and its divine Giver. The premise of Judaism is that it is a *bridge*.

How can the law be a bridge? Only by making a most startling demand. For Kant, all morality, including religious morality, demands a two-term relationship between man and his human neighbor. The revealed morality of Judaism demands a three-term relationship, nothing less than a relationship involving man, his human neighbor, and God

Himself. If it demanded a human relationship only, then the God in Whose name it was demanded would indeed reduce Himself to mere external sanction behind the demand. The startling claim of the revealed morality of Judaism is, however, that God Himself enters into the relationship. He confronts man with the demand to turn to his human neighbor, and in doing so, turn back to God Himself. Micah's celebrated summary of the commandments does more than list three commandments which exist side by side. It states an internally related whole. For there is no humble walking before God unless it manifests itself in justice and mercy to the human neighbor. And there can be only fragmentary justice and mercy unless they culminate in humility before God. Here lies the heart and core of Jewish morality.[16]

What human response is adequate to this divine demand? The response remains fragmentary until the commandments are performed, on the one hand, for *their* sake, and on the other, for *God's* sake. And each of these must point to the other.

Moral commandments, to be moral, must be performed for *their* sake. For unless so performed they do not realize a three-term relationship which takes the human neighbor in his own right seriously; they function merely within an attempted two-term relation between man and God. We say "attempted." For such a relationship is rejected by God Himself. It is God Himself Who bids man to take his neighbor in his own right seriously. To obey God, man accepts both his neighbor, and the commandment concerning him, as possessing intrinsic value. He performs the commandment for its own sake.

And yet the commandment remains fragmentary if performed for its own sake *alone*. For if such performance discloses the human neighbor, and ourselves, too, as beings of intrinsic value, it is ultimately *because the divine commanding Presence so discloses them*. This is why, even if beginning with the acceptance of the disclosure only, a man is finally led to confront the divine Discloser; why performance of the commandment for *its* sake points to its performance for *God's* sake. Both are certainly part of Jewish teaching. And they exist not contingently side by side, but in an internal and necessary relation. God is not barred from direct human access by the intrinsic value of man, or by the intrinsic value of the commandment which relates to man. On the contrary, *He discloses Himself through all intrinsic value, as its ultimate Source*. And the man who accepts this disclosure acts for the sake of God. In the hour of his martyrdom, Rabbi Akiba knew that the love of God is not one commandment side by side to others. It is the life of all.[17]

Thus, the territory in which we have sought philosophic refuge from the decisive but bewildering question raised by the pristine moment of divine commanding Presence, while no doubt safer, is by no means absolutely safe, if by "safety" is meant the comfortable distance, and hence the irrelevance, of the Divine. We first saw that in the pristine moment of divine commanding Presence there is already the possibility of free human appropriation, and we have now seen that, once human freedom can appropriate specific laws and commandments endowed with permanence and intrinsic value, the divine commanding Presence will still confront it. Divine commanding Presence and appropriating human freedom still point to each other. And the philosophical question raised by their togetherness can no longer be suspended or avoided. In the light of the foregoing, we may reformulate that question, to read as follows: *how can man presume to participate in a three-term relationship which involves not only his human neighbor but also God Himself? How can he—as he must, in order to participate in such a relationship—act out of love for the sake of God, when God is God while man is only man?* In Kantian language, what is the condition of the possibility of such action?

VIII

It is a testimony to Kant's genius as a religious thinker that he should not have wholly ignored this question. He even supplied it with an answer. But Kant's answer is not and cannot be the Jewish answer. Instead, we come to a final parting of ways.

Kant writes:

> The virtuous man fears God without being afraid of Him. This is because he is not worried lest he himself might wish to resist Him or His commandments. God is awe-inspiring to him because such resistance, while unthinkable in his own case, is not in itself impossible.[18]

For Kant's virtuous man, it is "unthinkable" that he might not will the will of God. For a prophet when first singled out, it is unthinkable how he *could* will it. To fear God at all, Kant's virtuous man must imagine himself as willing what he is in fact incapable of willing. The rabbis need no such strategy in order to stand in fear of God. Their impossible possibility is not the fear but rather the love of God.[19] For Kant, the oneness of the human with the divine will is automatic once virtue is achieved. For prophets and rabbis, such oneness is very far from automatic even for the virtuous man, and, in a sense, for him least of all. For prophets and rabbis, there is a radical gulf between God, Who is God, and man, who is only human. How then is a oneness of wills possible at all?

It is possible if God Himself has made it possible. Man can appropriate divine commandments if they are handed over for human appropriation. He can live by the Torah in the love and for the sake of God, if the Torah itself is a gift of divine love, making such a life a human possibility. He can participate in a three-term relationship which involves God Himself if God, Who in His power does not need man, in His love nevertheless chooses to need him.

The belief in the reality of such a divine love is as pervasive in Judaism as is the belief in revealed law itself. For here divine commandment and divine love are not only coeval, they are inseparable. The Torah manifests love in the very act of manifesting commandment; for in commanding *humans* rather than angels, it accepts these humans in their humanity.[20] Hence in accepting the Torah, man can at the same time accept himself as accepted by God in his humanity. This is why to attempt to perform the commandments, and to do so both for their sake and for the sake of God, is not to attempt the humanly impossible. At least in principle, the commandments *can* be performed in joy.[21]

This belief in divine love manifest in the divine commandment is present in Judaism from its pristine beginnings and throughout its history. From its beginnings: having first shrunk from the divine commanding Presence, the prophet ends up accepting it because he has experienced the divine love which makes acceptance possible.[22] Throughout its history: our daily prayer renders thanks for the divine love in which God has given the commandments.

If this faith permeates Jewish life so universally and so obviously, one may well ask why Jewish thought, when confronted with the Kantian challenge, should have failed to bring it clearly to philosophical self-consciousness. Had it done so, it would not have accepted so meekly the terms of the Kantian dilemma between a morality which, because genuinely moral, cannot be essentially revealed, and a morality which, because essentially revealed, must be less than truly moral. It would have repudiated this dilemma, recognizing—and clearly stating—that, if divine love is manifest in the revealed commandments, the dilemma does not arise.

Perhaps it is not far-fetched to identify as the cause of failure, in the case of non-Jewish philosophers like Kant, an ancient prejudice against Judaism bolstered by ignorance of Judaism; and, in the case of Jewish philosophers, uncritically assimilated reliance on non-Jewish modes of philosophical thought.

An ancient prejudice contrasts Jewish law with Christian love; and this is only slightly modified by the concession that love "evolves" in later stages of Judaism as well. Against this prejudice, it is by no means enough to insist that divine love is as ancient in Judaism as is divine commandment. For such love might still be confined, in Pelagian style, to the remission of sins which strict justice would condemn; and this would still leave law itself prior to love, and in itself loveless. In Judaism the primordial manifestation of divine love is not subsequent to but *in* the commandments; primordial human joy is not in a future subsequent to the life of the commandments but in that life itself.

Now it is precisely this technique which Paul either could not comprehend or could not accept. Paul did not merely assert that the commandments cannot be performed wholly, which to the rabbis was not new. He asserted that they cannot be performed at all. This was because, while accepting one aspect of Jewish teaching he did not accept the other. He saw man commanded to act for God's sake, by a God incommensurate with all things human. But he did not see, or was personally unable to experience, the divine love which, handing the commandments over for human appropriation, makes their performance a human possibility. Hence he thought man was obligated to do the humanly impossible.

Kant's moral philosophy may be regarded, among many other things, as a protest against this Pauline conclusion. It rightly insisted that man can be morally obligated to do only what he is able to do, and hence that, if an unbridged gap exists between the human and the Divine, divine commandments cannot be moral commandments. It also properly refused to divorce the Divine from the moral. But this compelled it to deny the gap between the Divine and the human. And the result was that the divine will became a moral redundancy.[23] In all this, Kant's anti-Pauline protest shares one assumption with Paul's own position; the denial of divine love manifest in the God-given commandment. From the standpoint of the revealed morality of Judaism, Kant may therefore be viewed as the nemesis of a tradition which begins with Paul.

IX

Throughout our essay, the term "Judaism" has meant classical Judaism which finds literary expression in the Hebrew Bible and in rabbinic literature. Re-enacting this Judaism in thought, we have rejected the Kantian dilemma between a morality which, if autonomous, is not essentially revealed, and, if essentially revealed, must necessarily be heteronomous.

But can the Jewish philosopher of today do more than give a phenomenological re-enactment of the classical faith? Can he accept it himself? It is all too obvious that faith in a divine love manifest in revealed commandments, always under much pressure in life, is subject to pressures of the gravest kind not only in modern life but in the realm of modern thought as well.

This is a question for separate inquiry, the results of which one cannot anticipate. One can only be certain that the Jewish philosopher who conducts it must not, at any rate, surrender quickly to modern pressures. For if there is anything that makes him a *Jewish* philosopher, it is precisely the duty to confront, and take seriously, his own Jewish tradition. He would fail in his duty if he were ever to forget that his ancestors could often live by the belief that "when the Torah came into the world, freedom came into the world."[24]

Notes

1. Cf., e.g., the famous passage in *Pirke Abot*, I, 3.

2. *Bab. Talmud, Yoma,* 67 b.

3. *Fundamental Principles of the Metaphysics of Ethics,* translated by Abbott (London, 1926), pp. 59, 61. I have revised Abbott's translation. When possible, readily available English translations of Kant are quoted; otherwise, the Prussian Academy edition, 23 vols., 1900-56, is the source, and the translation is my own.

4. The "creative morality" interpretation of Kant, given by thinkers from Fichte to Hermann Cohen, has affected quite un-Kantian philosophies, such as those of Nietzsche and Dewey, as well as much popular moral and psychological thinking. Instead of documenting the view that it is not Kantian, which I intend to do elsewhere, I refer only to G. Krüger, *Philosophie und Moral in der Kantischen Kritik* (Tübingen, 1931).

5. A remarkable nineteenth century Jewish thinker neatly illustrates this dilemma. Samuel Hirsch subscribed to Kantian autonomous morality. Yet he also believed quite literally in revelation. Aware of the possibility of conflict, he sought to resolve it by interpreting revelation (following Lessing) as divine education toward moral autonomy. Hirsch's ingenuity in developing this doctrine does not save it from ultimate failure. Revelation here is a divine guidance the sole purpose of which is to emancipate man from the need for guidance, and hence from revelation itself. Cf. my article "Samuel Hirsch and Hegel" in *Studies in Nineteenth-Century Jewish Intellectual History,* ed. A. Altmann (Cambridge, Mass., 1964), pp. 171-201.

6. Kant returns to this theme on countless occasions. We confine ourselves to quoting one representative passage: "so far as practical reason has the right to guide us, we shall not regard actions as obligatory because they are divine commandments. We shall regard them as divine commandments because we are inwardly obligated to them." *Critique of Pure Reason,* b. 847.

7. Prussian Academy edition, VIII, 405.

8. Cf., e.g., Gen. 12:1 ff.; Exod. 3:4 ff., and 19:5 ff.; Isa. 6:1 ff.; Jer. 1:1 ff. When bidden to become a holy nation (Exod. 19:5-6), Israel is, of course, already in possession of *some* commandments in terms of which the content of holiness may be specified. Still, it is of the greatest importance that the bulk of revealed commandments are yet to come.

9. Isa. 6:8; Exod. 24:7. We follow the traditional interpretation of the last passage.

10. Cf., e.g., Isa. 6:4; Jer. 1:6.

11. Whether or not *all* the 613 commandments of traditional Judaism may be regarded as having permanence and intrinsic value is a large question, and one transcending the scope of this essay.

12. Jer. 27.

13. Our brief remarks on the topic (*infra*, section VII) are not, of course, meant to be an adequate treatment of this subject.

14. It is interesting to note that Kant and Kierkegaard use the same Biblical tale— Abraham's sacrifice of Isaac—for opposite purposes: Kant to argue that, since we must judge the claims of supposed divine voices in the light of our moral standards, such voices must be *a priori* either false or superfluous (Prussian Academy edition. VIII, 63 ff.; *Religion within the Limits of Reason Alone,* translated by Greene and Hudson [New York, 1960], p. 175); Kierkegaard to argue that, if revelation is to be a present possibility, there must be, in an extreme situation, the possibility of a teleological suspension of the ethical (*Fear and*

Trembling [New York, 1954]). Any Jewish interpreter of the Abraham story will surely be dissatisfied with both the Kantian and the Kierkegaardian accounts. But one must face the fact that if, as Kant argues, a revealed morality is necessarily heteronomous, there is no third possibility.

15. Cf., e.g., *Midrash Tanhuma*, Yitro, and many other passages, in hasidic as well as rabbinic literature.

16. Mic. 6:8. The point made in this section is perfectly expressed in a Midrash in which God is made to say, "Would that they had deserted Me, and kept My Torah; for if they had occupied themselves with the Torah, the leaven which is in it would have brought them back to Me" (*Pesikta Kahana*, XV). Liberal writers are fond of quoting the first half of this Midrash only, thereby perverting a profound statement of the morality of Judaism into a humanistic platitude.

17. *Bab. Talmud, Berakhot* 61b.

18. *Critique of Judgment*, tr. Meredith (Oxford, 1952), p. 110. The translation is mine.

19. According to one Midrash (*Tanhuma, Hukkat*), the righteous do not cease to fear God even though they have received His assurance. According to another (*Sifre Deut.*, *Wa'ethanan*, No. 32), while everywhere else love drives out fear, this is not true of the love and fear of God.

20. In *Tanhuma, Behukkotai*, God is made to reject the offer of the angels to observe the Torah, on the ground that the Torah is appropriate only for human observance.

21. Cf., e.g., *Bab. Talmud, Berakhot* 31a, *Shabbat* 30b.

22. Isa. 6:6-7; Jer. 1:7-8.

23. As already indicated (*supra*, section IV), for reasons which are beyond the scope of this essay, Kant does not regard the divine will as an *absolute redundancy*. He does, however, regard it as redundant within a purely moral context.

24. *Midrash Genesis Rabba, Wayyera* LIII, 7.

5.

Revealed Morality and Modern Thought

NORBERT SAMUELSON

Within the classical or mediaeval tradition of Jewish philosophy the study of man centered around two questions, how is man a knowing agent, and how is man a moral agent. This paper is an attempt to answer the latter question.

Many contemporary American intellectuals are caught in a strange ethical dilemma. On one hand they unqualifiedly assert through their public actions that civil rights are good and the war in Viet Nam is bad. They are equally convinced that Nazi hate was bad but (at least in some circles) love is good. On the other hand these same intellectuals are as committed conceptually to one or more of the various forms of ethical subjectivism that are current today. When, not on the picket line but in their studies, they are asked, What does it mean to say that something is good or that something is bad? they will offer either of the following answers: (a) Good and evil are culturally determined; there is no such thing as absolute good or evil (Moral Relativism or Contextual Ethics). (b) Good and evil are emotive terms; if you say that something is good you have given information about yourself (your tastes and likes), but you have told me nothing about the thing (Emotivism).

Rarely is there any realization that the ethical theory stands in direct opposition to the moral practise. No one risks his life, or even his future, for mere matters of taste. Yet on any of these ethical theories moral judgments are ultimately no different than matters of taste. One or the other must be wrong. Either the moral theory is inadequate, in which case the behavior may be justified, or if the theory is correct the behavior is foolish. I personally find the behavior to be sound and the theory to be nonsense.

I am convinced that our concrete moral judgments are as founded in experience and hence as objectively justifiable as any other judgments that we make about experienced states of affairs. In this paper I will attempt to defend this conviction. What I propose to do is offer a conceptual model of what is involved in making the judgment, ". . . is good." Then I will use this model to examine briefly two dominant positions in contemporary ethical theory, viz., Kant's Deontology and Contextual Ethics.[1] Since I am committed to moral judgments being founded on experience, I will have to show in what ways these two positions are sound. Similarly, because of this presupposition, I must also show how it is possible for there to be errors in moral judgments. Finally, I will make some comments on how my model is relevant to Jewish religious thought in general and I will apply my model to a specific issue, viz., Emil Fackenheim's presentation of the dilemma of autonomous and revealed morality in his article "The Revealed Morality of Judaism and Modern Thought."[2]

I

Definition of Terms

A. VALUES

A1. The terms "good" and "evil" are used in many ways. Sometimes they are used as emotive expressions, e.g., "the chicken soup is good." More often they are used to express excellence or skills. For example, the judgment "this is a good knife" involves the following claims; (a) a knife has certain functions insofar as it is a knife, e.g., cutting. (b) to fulfill well these functions proper to a knife the knife must possess certain properties, e.g., to cut, the knife must be sharp. (c) this knife possesses these properties.

A2. Neither of the above uses of the terms "good" and "evil" are moral uses. We will consider in this model only moral uses.

A3. The terms "good" and "evil" are value terms.

A4. There are different kinds of value terms. Four such kinds are, mathematical, aesthetic, truth, and moral values.

A5. Mathematical values;

A5a. Values cannot be defined. Rather they can be enumerated and it can be shown how they are used.

A5b. Mathematical values consist of an infinite list of natural numbers. For example, the value of 2^2 is 4; the value of 4^2 is 16, etc.

A5c. In the statement "2^2 is 4," "2" is the term or object which has the value, "$\ldots^2$" is the context, and "4" is the value. Contexts are functions of terms. Only terms in context take specific values. Objects alone have no values. Functions alone have a range of values, i.e., a list of all of the possible values that may be assigned to a function depending on its term. (A term is an object in context.) For example, 2 alone has no value, but $\ldots^2$ can have any number of values (4 for 2^2, 16 for 4^2, 36 for 6^2, etc.)

A6. The description of what is a particular kind of value consists in the following: (a) Enumerating a list of these values. (b) Specifying their range. For example, mathematical values are natural numbers which range over mathematical propositions which consist of mathematical functions and natural numbers as their objects. (c) Providing criteria for the application of these values to that over which they range, i.e., enumerating rules by which applications can be judged to be correct or incorrect. For example, part of understanding what mathematical values are is to be able to say that "2^2 is 4" is correct whereas "2^2 is 5" is not correct.

A7. The aesthetic values are "beautiful" and "ugly." The truth values are "true" and "false." Neither aesthetic nor truth nor mathematical values should be confused with moral values.

A8. That the mathematical, truth, aesthetic, and even moral values have no existence of their own outside of value judgments in no way means that these judgments are not objective.

B. MORAL VALUES

B1. The moral values are "good" and "bad."

B2. The moral values range exclusively over (a) relations (b) between persons. In other words, if something is not a relation between persons it makes no sense to say that it is morally good or bad. However, sometimes by analogy the value terms are extended to apply to the persons themselves.

B2i. Persons are conscious beings.

B2ii. "Consciousness" may not be definable but its range in use is intelligible. Generally, humans fall into the class of conscious beings, whereas stones do not; whether or not animals do is problematic. More specifically the distinction between persons and non-persons or conscious and non-conscious beings can be characterized as follows: At one level we may say that a conscious being is able to be the immediate cause or agent of some of its actions. (Such acts are called "voluntary.") At another level, imagine two entities both self movers in the sense that each is the immediate agent of some of its actions where one of the entities is an automaton of the other. Imagine that the automaton is programmed so that its actions and the actions of that of which it is a copy are overtly the same. It still is conceivable that the original is in the class of conscious beings and its copy is not. So far as this distinction is intelligible the notion of "consciousness" is exact.

B2iii. Persons in relation have moral values. Persons alone have not. Relations whose terms are persons have a moral value range.

B3. Every relation between persons involves obligations, i.e., responsibilities arising out of the relation upon each participant in the relation. These responsibilities need not be symmetrical, i.e., given a relation between two persons the responsibilities of one of the participants in the relation may be very different from the responsibilities of the other. For example, consider the responsibilities of a student and a teacher in a student-teacher relation.

B4. Success and failure in fulfilling the obligations that arise in morally judged relations are the criteria by which particular moral values are determined. In this sense judgments of moral right and wrong are judgments about obligations.

B5. Actual success and failure are the criteria of judgment and not intended success and failure. Intention is a sign that an agent is conscious, and moral relations are limited to relations between conscious beings. Hence intention enters the moral situation only as a precondition for moral judgment.

B6. The obligations themselves are not morally judged. Rather these provide the criteria by which moral judgments are made. However not all obligations are admissible. Some obligations are morally self-contradictory.

B7. A self-contradictory moral obligation is an obligation whose fulfillment destroys the relationship. For example, if A demands that B kill him, he makes a self-contradictory demand. If B fails to fulfill the demand the relation ends, i.e., it is unsuccessful. However if B fulfills the demand and kills A, the relationship also ends. This is what it means to say that the obligation is morally self-contradictory. It is not logically self-contradictory.

B7a. Relations involving only self-contradictory obligations are morally neutral. In cases involving choice where the contrary choices are all morally bad, the relations themselves are morally neutral. Hence cases of mercy killing are not moral contexts.

B8. The terms or participants in moral relations are either individual persons or collective persons. Collective persons are simply classes of persons consisting of their members only. Nations are examples of collective persons.

B9. Moral relations involve a minimum of two persons. A person has relations to himself and obligations to himself. But these are not moral contexts. One consequence of this is that while I may be the source of your moral obligations and you may be the source of mine, neither of us can be the source of our own moral obligations. Hence whereas I may impose moral worth on you in your context and you may impose moral worth on me in my context, neither of us may impose any moral worth on ourselves. Alone we have no value. (The word *nachas* is an expression of this moral state-of-affairs where one may bestow value on another through his acts but not on himself.)

B10. The terms or participants in moral relations may be individuals with individuals, collectives with collectives (e.g., relations between nations), collectives with individuals, or individuals with collectives.

C. GENERAL CHARACTERISTICS

C1. The statement "R is good" resembles the statement "P is true" where P is a proposition about some experienced state-of-affairs, e.g., "the table is blue." That P is true is not given in experience, but the judgment is nonetheless objective and based on experience. All that is needed to make the judgment is the experience of P. The same may be said for the proposition that R is good.

C2. The contexts discussed here are only simple in that they involve single relations between two or more terms. We have not considered complex contexts involving two or more relations between two or more terms. As there is a moral logic for simple contexts, so there is in principle a moral logic for complex contexts. However, the criteria for judgment in the latter logic may be radically different from the criteria in the former. An example of a question involving a logic of complex contexts is, "Am I morally responsible to be loyal to my country concerning matters in which I judge my country to be morally wrong?"

II

Kant's Deontology

A. INSIGHTS

1. Kant clearly recognized the different senses of the term "good," and he saw that in none of the senses in which "good" was used to express excellence of function was the term being used morally (A1,2)[3]. He offered the following proof: If good is reducible to any set of characteristics of a thing, then the statement, "X is good" and the statement, "X has such and such characteristics" would be equivalent. However, where the word "good" is used with moral significance this equivalence does not hold. The question "Ought X to have such and such characteristics?" is perfectly intelligible in a way that the question "Ought X to be good?" is not.

2. Good is not identical with anything in the world. The good may or may not exist. If it does it is something supremely good (whatever that means). However, even then that thing and good are not the same. Good functions only as a predicate term (A8).

3. The terms "good" and "evil" are simple terms and therefore not definable (A5b). All that can be shown is how to use them. Thus the major task of moral philosophy is not to provide definitions but to develop a logic of moral judgments (A6). Towards this end Kant developed his various formulations of the Categorical Imperative.[4] Unfortunately Kant thought that this one rule was sufficient to make all moral judgments.

4. If moral judgments are to be moral they must be objective (A8). Kant's Categorical Imperative provided a necessary condition for such objectivity. However, Kant thought that it was sufficient as well as necessary.

5. Kant recognized that moral value judgments are possible only when persons are involved in what is judged. This led Kant to assume that moral values reside in the will (B2).[5] However, what is a necessary condition for moral judgments, viz., the will, Kant judged to be a sufficient condition.

6. All moral judgments involve expressions of obligations. A sign of this fact is that the statement, "X is good" more resembles in its logical form the imperative "Do X!" than it does the explicative "X is F." This linguistic feature misled others (not Kant), such as C. L. Stevenson, to conclude that moral judgments are not statements about facts (C1). Kant himself was also misled by his insight in that he confused the criteria for moral judgments with the judgments themselves. It is an easy "slip" to make. (For example, the behaviorist identification of color percepts with light waves.)

7. Kant recognized that not all obligations are morally admissable. His Generalization Argument[6] is a sufficient criterion to exclude such obligations. It is the sound insight of the Utilitarians that, at least within this context, arguments from consequences are morally admissible. However, this argument is not a sufficient criterion to make all moral judgments (B5).[7]

B. MISTAKES

1. From Kant's recognition that moral values are neither things nor in things (B2), and that where persons are not involved moral judgments cannot be made, he concluded that moral values range over the intentions of acts rather than over the acts themselves (B5). As a consequence of this it follows that overt acts do not enter into moral judgments. But this is clearly false. To unintentionally kill someone is not as bad as intentionally killing someone, but manslaughter properly is as much a crime as is murder. The recognition of this moral fact is a strength of Utilitarianism over Kant's Deontology.

2. Since Kant thought that intentions alone are what is good and evil and that the will is a sufficient condition to determine moral judgments, he concluded that persons are the source of their moral values (B9). This is difficult to imagine. I certainly am the source of some of my obligations, but as I was free to originate them I remain free to end them. If this is so, such obligations differ radically from moral obligations. In

his *Treatise of Human Nature* David Hume asks us to imagine a desert island on which a single person is living in a situation in which there is no chance that any other person will ever find the island. If we further exclude God from the imagined situation, is it the case that this unfortunate person has any moral obligations? Hume said that he could not imagine any. Neither can I. That moral obligation demands a social context is a sound insight of those who defend either Utilitarianism or Contextual Ethics.

3. A number of problems arise from Kant's claim that the Categorical Imperative and the Generalization Argument are sufficient rules for moral judgment. One problem is that it becomes impossible to identify morally neutral contexts in relations between persons. But certainly not all obligations are morally admissable (B7a). Equally important is that while these rules provide negative tests, i.e., ways by which we can decide that some maxims are bad, they do not provide a positive test, i.e., a way by which we can decide that some maxims are good. Of course this criticism presupposes that there are morally neutral obligations. Finally, these rules are not able themselves to account for exceptions to the rules which in fact there always are.[8]

C. CONTEXTUAL ETHICS

The soundness of Contextual Ethics is its realization that general formulae are not in themselves absolutely good or bad. Moral judgments depend on contexts. If nothing else the study of anthropology teaches us this (A5, B2). The problem with this position is that it concludes from the above fact that moral judgments are thus not absolute. But this is wrong. Squaring has no definite mathematical value, although it has a determinate range of values. But there is nothing indefinite about the judgment that two squared is four. Similarly, killing has no definite moral value, for sometimes killing is at least morally neutral. But that in no way means that the killing of six million Jews by the Nazis is not an absolute moral judgment. One of the major insights of Thomas of Aquinas in his *Summa Theologica* is that all moral judgments contain circumstances as an essential aspect of what is being judged, but that this fact of moral judgment in no way relativizes the concrete decision. Moral judgments are relational but they are not relative.

III

Jewish Religious Thought

1. For those of us who understand Judaism primarily in religious terms Judaism is fundamentally a form of historical relation between God and a particular people, Israel. Following our model, this relationship, whose terms are an individual person (God) and a collective person (Israel), is characterized by the obligations which arise in this relation. Insofar as these obligations are the obligations of Israel they may be called "Torah." This understanding of Judaism is common to all religious groupings within the Jewish people. The issue between them involves the determination of which obligations are not proper in this relationship. The model outlined above both characterizes this situation in Jewish religious thought and provides a framework in which the differences between the various Jewish religious groups, insofar as they are theoretical and not institutional, may be discussed.

2. The model also sheds light on a particular puzzle that has plagued the philosophy of religion since the days of Plato. There is certainly a close and intimate relation between religious and moral values, but the characterization of that relation has always been considered perplexing. In the *Euthyphro* Plato's Socrates asks, Is piety willed by the gods because it is pious or is it pious because it is willed by the gods? Saadia Gaon in his *Beliefs and Opinions* attempts to explain the difference between rational and nonrational commandments. Many Jewish college students ask, Am I concerned with moral issues because I am Jewish or because I am a human being? All of these questions are ultimately the same question, viz. How are religious and moral values alike yet distinct? Our model suggests an answer to this problem.

Religious values are a species of moral values. Moral values are the values of relations between persons. Where one of those persons is God they are called religious values. Religious values are thus a subspecies of moral values whose range is personal relations where one of the persons is God. They are determined by the success or failure of persons in fulfilling the obligations which arise in relationship with God.

On this model the mediaeval conception of good and evil as accepting and rejecting respectively the commandments of the will of God becomes intelligible. However, to say that God is the source of these values is to speak metaphorically. Literally the values arise in the relationship of God and other persons.

3. Also on this model the peculiar notion of chosenness in which a single God makes different demands upon different people becomes intelligible. In any relation R the nature of that relation in the particular is determined by its terms. Hence the determination of the relation aRb and the relation aRc, where "a" and "R" remain constant, will be different because the second term of that relation is different. Thus it is quite intelligible that whereas eating pork may be morally neutral for a Christian, it may not be morally neutral for a Jew. The reason is that the source of the commandment is the relation with God and not simply God.

4. That this model fits the religious language of Martin Buber is obvious.

IV

Dilemma of Autonomous and Revealed Morality

1. Emil Fackenheim has raised the following dilemma for modern Jewish philosophy:[9] Kant argued that a duty is moral only if it is done for no reason other than itself and that this condition can be fulfilled only if the source of the duty is the moral agent himself and not someone else. Now if Kant is right then it follows that if a given duty has its source in someone other than the moral agent, even if that someone else is God, then the imposed duty is not moral; and if it is moral then it originates in the will of the moral agent himself, and the revelation of the particular duty by the other, even where that other is God, is superfluous. In Fackenheim's own words:

> Either he [Kant] concedes that the will can and must impose the God-given law upon itself; but then its God-givenness becomes irrelevant in the process of self-imposition and appropriation; or else he insists that the God-givenness of the law does not and cannot at any point become irrelevant; but then the will cannot impose the law on itself—it can only submit to it for such non-moral reasons as trust in divine promise or fear of divine threats.[10]

Thus one seems to be driven by the principle of autonomy, i.e., the doctrine that any moral duty if it is moral is self-imposed, into one of two alternatives both of which are inadmissible. Either divine law ought to be obeyed because God commanded it, in which case it is not moral, or because it is moral, in which case the commanding by God is superfluous. The problem is how to find a way to demonstrate that the commandments are moral and that their divine origin is a relevant feature of their being moral.

Fackenheim himself proposes the following solution to this problem:

> The freedom required in the pristine movement of the divine commanding Presence, then, is nothing less than the freedom to accept or reject the divine commanding Presence as a whole, and for its own sake—that is, for no other reason than that it is that Presence. . . . The divine commanding Presence may force the choice on a singled-out man. It does not force him to choose God, and the choice itself (as was seen) is not heteronomous; for it accepts or rejects the divine commanding Presence for no other reason than that it *is* that Presence. But this entails the momentous consequence that *if and when a man chooses to accept the divine commanding Presence, he does nothing less than accept the divine will as his own.*[11]

The duty that a man freely imposes upon himself is the duty to make God's will his will. In doing this those duties which originate in the will of God also have the force of originating in his own will. In this way the principle of autonomy is not violated in claiming that divine commandments are moral and the necessity of divine revelation to the moral situation is preserved. To will what God wills one must know what God would will. Revelation is the source of that knowledge.

2. The style of the above discussion, as Fackenheim explains in the introduction to that discussion,[12] is a style common to the Jewish Middle Ages. It consists, in Fackenheim's own words, in a "confrontation between philosophy and Judaism." Presupposed in this confrontation are two independent affirmed sources of truth, one religious and the other secular, which appear to be in conflict with each other. In the Middle Ages the two sources were the Torah, as understood in the light of rabbinic interpretation, and a particular understanding of philosophy whose source was Plato and Aristotle. The areas of conflict centered around physics. (For example, is the universe created or eternal? The Torah seemed to say that it was created, whereas physics seemed to claim that it is eternal.) The two sources of conflict in this present case are the Torah[13] and Kant's ethics.

Given the apparent conflict of the two affirmed sources of truth one may resolve the conflict in one of three ways: (a) One may argue that the conflict is merely apparent by not real. This approach is characteristic of the greater part of Maimonides' *A Guide for the Perplexed*, and it is the approach that Fackenheim follows in this case. (b) One may argue that the conflict is real and in the light of that conflict one may modify the claim that originates in the religious authority. This is Gersonides' approach in Book III of *The Wars of God*, and I have followed it in my article "On Knowing God."[14] Or (c) one may argue that the conflict is real and in the light of that conflict one may modify the claim that originates in the secular authority. This approach is characteristic of Hasdai Crescas' *The Light of God* and it is the approach that I would propose in the present dilemma.

It must be noted that in following either of the latter two approaches the argument for modifying an authority must arise purely from within that authority itself and not from without. To propose a modification of religious authority solely because of its conflict with secular authority and conversely to propose a modification of secular authority solely because of its conflict with religious authority are illegitimate moves. To do so is to deny the authenticity and/or the independence of the two affirmed authorities. In this case the conflict would not be solved; it would be abandoned. In other words our goal is to avoid losing the game by winning, and not by quitting.

3. I object to Fackenheim's solution to the proposed dilemma on two grounds, one religious and the other philosophic. My religious objection is that if Fackenheim's characterization of the moral situation involving divine commandments is correct then there ought not to be dissent from divine will. I believe that this is not the case and, what is more, I believe that it is not an accurate or satisfactory portrayal of the accounts that we read in Scripture about the situations in which man meets God. Let me briefly mention two of many Biblical cases that I have in mind in making this accusation: The first is the account given in Exodus, chapters 32 and 33, where God wills the destruction of the children of Israel because of the golden calf incident and Moses asserts his will against God's will on behalf of Israel. I would want to approve of Moses' action. But given Fackenheim's solution to the autonomy dilemma, I believe that he would be required to disapprove. The second is the account given in I Samuel, chapter 15 in which God condemns Saul for not killing Agag, the king of the Amalekites. While I would agree that Saul's motives for his act of

mercy may not have been the noblest, and that Agag himself was far from being the noblest of men, I believe that Saul did the morally right thing, even though in this case, unlike the former, he could not convince God that his dissent from God's command was morally justifiable.

4. My philosophic objection, which in this case is more important (for the reasons stated above in (2) of this section), is that I do not think that the principle of autonomy is correct. To refer specifically to my proposed model of what it means to say that ". . .is good," I deny the principle of autonomy for the following reasons:

(B2a) Moral values range over relations between persons and not over persons themselves, as Kant is here asserting.

(B7) A self-contradictory moral obligation is an obligation whose fulfillment destroys the relationship. For this reason to kill anyone, except in cases of self-defense or possibly in cases where the one to be killed is no longer a person (as someone might argue who defends mercy killing), is not morally justifiable no matter who wills it and no matter if the conditions under which the act is willed conform to Kant's Generalization Argument. This follows because the Generalization Argument is a necessary but not a sufficient condition for moral judgment. (Cf. Kant, Insight 7.) However, given the principle of autonomy there is no reason why the Generalization Argument would not be a sufficient test for moral judgment.

Finally (B9), moral relations involve a minimum of two persons, whereas if the principle of autonomy were admissible then there could be moral obligations where, both actually and in principle, one person is involved. (Cf. Kant, Mistake 2.)[15]

5. Furthermore, I can think of no good reason why Kant himself, given the premises on which he constructed his formulations of the Categorical Imperative, would have posited the principle of autonomy other than the following (which in my opinion is not a good reason): Kant's assertion of the principle of autonomy follows logically from his claim that the will is the only thing that is good in itself. This proposition is the first axiom of his moral theory as that theory is presented in his *Groundwork of the Metaphysic of Morals.*[16] Kant argues that the only candidates for what is good in itself are the will, what he calls "gifts of fortune," and what he calls "talents of the mind." The "gifts of fortune" consist of those things which, according to Aristotle, the undisciplined mind would call happiness, e.g., having fame and fortune. The "talents

of the mind" consist in what traditionally one called virtues, e.g., intelligence and courage. Kant then argues that the latter two candidates do not qualify as being good in themselves because if they are combined with other factors their moral worth is either increased or decreased. For example, wealth, a gift of fortune, increases in moral value when it is used for desirable ends, e.g., eliminating poverty; but when that wealth is used for undesirable ends, e.g., oppressing the poor, its value decreases. Similarly, conscientiousness, a talent of the mind, is to be valued in a physician, but it does not have the same value when applied to a thief. Thus, since one of these three candidates must be good in itself and neither the talents of the mind nor the gifts of fortune qualify, the will must be good in itself.

I would like to raise two specific objections to Kant's argument in this case: (1) The objections raised against the other two candidates apply against the will as well. It is certainly desirable that a person should "act only on that maxim through which he can at the same time will that it should become a universal law." However, when that maxim is that all persons who are Jews should be sent to concentration camps, the value of the agent's consistency diminishes (cf. footnote 7). Similarly it is desirable to have a governor of a state whose motives are to serve the people rather than to advance his own political future. However, given a governor who believes that universities ought to be suppressed but that to suppress them is not politically wise, I would prefer a governor whose motives were not so pure. (2) Given any three candidates for moral worth, "a," "b," and "c," "a" may have value in itself, whereas "b" and "c" do not. Yet it may further be the case that "a" combined with "b" and/or "c" is more valuable than "a" itself, or that the combination of "b" and "c" is more valuable than "a" alone.[17] Even if we overlook the first objection the force of this claim is that even if the will is the only thing that is good in itself it does not follow that there are not other things more valuable than the virtues of an isolated will. (3) Kant's argument shows that where no will is involved no moral judgment is possible. But it does not show that the will itself is what is good. (Cf. Kant, Mistake 1.)

There are some who may object to this approach to moral issues on the ground that it is too formal, and moral life, after all, is an emotional matter. To such a charge I can only say that moral life is certainly emotional but the evaluation of that life need not be. If it be replied that it is impossible to rationally conceive moral life, the answer is that a schema has been provided for doing just that. If the schema is inadequate, show how it is inadequate. However, that, too, is a rational assertion. And if it cannot be shown to be inadequate, then the objection seems to be unimportant.

Notes

1. I will follow this approach because the proposed model largely expresses those features of these two ethical systems which I find to be cogent. Ideally the model should appear only at the end of a discussion of every factor that is involved in my positing the model. However, the demands of time force me to be selective in my discussion. Consequently I will follow this inherently less desirable method.

2. *Rediscovering Judaism,* edited by A. J. Wolf, Quadrangle, Chicago: 1965, pp. 51-76. [See Kellner, pp. 61-83.]

3. The numbers that appear in parentheses in this section are references to the propositions in the model presented in Section I.

4. "Act only on that maxim through which you can at the same time will that it should become a universal law." This imperative was to be used to judge all moral acts in the following way: (a) Take the act and express it as a demand (maxim). (b) Universalize the maxim, i.e., make it generally applicable. "Shoot John" is generalized either to "Shoot everyone" or "Shoot anyone like John." (c) If it is possible to will this generalized maxim (universal law), then the act following from the maxim is good. Otherwise it is evil.

5. Kant's "will" is what we have called "consciousness," i.e., that which is the distinguishing mark of persons.

6. "If the consequences of everybody doing X are undesirable then nobody ought to do X."

7. For example, the case of the consistent Nazi in Hare's *Freedom and Reason.* You are speaking with a Nazi who says that all Jews ought to be sent to gas chambers. You then convince him that, unknown to him, he also is a Jew. By Kant's test alone if he is willing to send himself to a gas chamber—and some would have been willing—his position is not morally objectionable.

8. On this problem see G. M. Singer, *The Generalization Argument in Ethics.*

9. Fackenheim, *op. cit.*

10. *Ibid.,* p. 61. [Kellner, p. 69-70.]

11. *Ibid.,* p. 67. [Kellner, p. 74-75.]

12. *Ibid.,* pp. 52-53 [Kellner, pp. 62-63.]

13. The Torah in this case is not understood by Fackenheim in precisely the same way that it was understood by the mediaeval Jewish philosophers, but nonetheless the resemblances between the two are sufficient to call both rabbinic interpretations.

14. *Judaism,* Winter 1969, pp. 64-83.

15. For current discussions of the question of whether or not there can be moral duties to oneself see the following:

George Marcus Singer, "On Duties to Oneself," *Ethics*, Vol. 69, 1959, pp. 202-5.

— "Duties and Duties to Oneself," *Ethics*, Vol. 73, 1962-63.

Paul D. Eisenberg, "Duties to Oneself: A New Defense Sketched," *The Review of Metaphysics*, Vol. 20, 1967, pp. 602-34.

I call particular attention to the Eisenberg article. If his arguments are correct and there can, in fact, be moral duties to oneself, then I would be forced to modify my claim that (B9) morally judged relations involve a minimum of two persons, which in turn would force me to abandon most of the objections to the principle of autonomy that I am here considering. I do not believe that Mr. Eisenberg's argument is successful but the discussion of those arguments here would be too technical and too lengthy for the purposes of the present paper.

16. See the H. J. Paton translation entitled *The Moral Law*, Barnes and Noble, New York: 1950, pp. 17 and 61ff.

17. See G. E. Moore's discussion of what he calls "organic unities" in *Principia Ethica*.

Ethics and *Halakhah*

Having discussed the question of whether or not religious ethics is possible we may now turn to the narrower but for our purposes equally important question: is Jewish ethics possible? This question must be raised, at least for those Jews who accept the normative character of *halakhah*, Jewish law, since that law is not limited to religious law alone. Much of *halakhah* is indeed given over to religious or ritual law, but it encompasses civil, criminal and moral law as well. Since *halakhah* contains an ethical component, we must ask whether it recognizes an ethical realm beyond itself. It is to this question that Aharon Lichtenstein brilliantly addresses himself. He asks whether, "for the contemporary Jew, an ethic independent of the Halakha can be at all legitimate and relevant at an operative level."

Lichtenstein answers that in its broadest sense — as a legal system as opposed to a collection of concrete laws or *dinim* — *halakhah* does not recognize an ethic beyond itself. This is so because it incorporates, as *halakhah,* demands to go beyond (literally, "within") the letter of the law (*lifnim meshurat hadin*). The duty to go beyond the letter of the law is not itself law in the narrow sense, since its application is more flexible and more defined by context than is the application of ordinary law. But it is definitely *halakhah* and is even legally actionable according to some authorities.

Lichtenstein's position — hardly surprising in a context which views the *halakhah* as the concrete expression of God's all-embracing revelation — is in practice adopted at least by most Orthodox interpreters of Judaism. In seeking to establish the position of Judaism on moral issues, such thinkers will typically identify the Jewish position with the halakhic position. Whereas they might base their answer on some of the broadest ethico-legal principles of the *halakhah* (e.g., the duty to go beyond the letter of the law, the duty to imitate God, the duty to love one's neighbor, etc.) they will not generally base their answers on principles independent of the *halakhah* itself.

6.

Does Jewish Tradition Recognize An Ethic Independent of Halakha?

AHARON LICHTENSTEIN

"Does the tradition recognize an ethic independent of Halakha?" My subject is a simple factual question presumably calling for a yes-or-no answer. But what kind of Jew responds to salient questions with unequivocal monosyllables? Certainly not the traditional kind. Moreover, as formulated, this particular query is a studded minefield, every key term an ill-defined boobytrap. Who or what represents the tradition? Is the recognition de facto or de jure? How radical is the independence? Above all, what are the referents of ethic and Halakha? A qualified reply is obviously required.

Before presenting it in detail, however, I must confess that, at one level, an unequivocal response could be easily mounted. If the issue be reduced to natural morality in general, it need hardly be in doubt. "Rabbi Yohanan stated," says the Gemara in *Erubin*, "'If the Torah had not been given, we would have learnt modesty from the cat, [aversion to] robbery from the ant, chastity from the dove, and [conjugal] manners from the cock.'"[1] The passage implies, first, that a cluster of logically ante-halakhic virtues exists; second, that these can be inferred from natural phenomena; and, probably, third—with Plato and against the Sophists—that these relate to *physis* rather than *nomos*, being not only observable through nature but inherent within it. Nor does the passage

---

stand alone. The wide-ranging concept of *derekh eretz*[2]—roughly the equivalent of what Coventry Patmore called "the traditions of civility"—points in the same direction. Its importance—again, not as descriptively synonymous with conventional conduct but as prescriptive *lex naturalis*—should not be underestimated. The Mishna cites Rabbi Eleazar b. Azaria's view that "without Torah, there is no *derekh eretz*, and without *derekh eretz*, there is no Torah";[3] and the Midrash goes beyond this dialectical reciprocity, stating that "*derekh eretz* preceded Torah."[4] In context, the primary reference is to chronological priority. Nevertheless, one senses that the common tendency—especially prevalent among the *mussar* masters—to include logical if not axiological precedence as well is a response to clearly present undertones; and, in this sense, the two texts are of course closely related. As the Maharal put it, "From this [i.e., the Mishna], we learn that *derekh eretz* is the basis of Torah which is," as explained by the Midrash, "'the way of the tree of life.'"[5] Their link reinforces our awareness of the Rabbis' recognition of natural morality.

There is, however, little need to adduce proof texts. Even if one assumes that the Rabbis' awareness of natural law as an explicit philosophic and historical doctrine was limited—a point that Baer and Lieberman[6] have debated—this would be, for our purposes, quite irrelevant. Indeed, even if one accepts the thesis, recently advanced by Marvin Fox,[7] that the concept of natural law, in its classical and Thomistic sense, is actually inconsistent with rabbinic and *rishonim*'s thought, our problem is very little affected. The fact remains that the existence of natural morality is clearly assumed in much that is quite central to our tradition. Discussion of theodicy is predicated upon it. As Benjamin Whichcote,[8] the seventeenth-century Cambridge Platonist, pointed out, one cannot ask, "Shall, then, the judge of the whole earth not do justice?"[9] unless one assumes the existence of an unlegislated justice to which, as it were, God Himself is bound; and which, one might add, man can at least apprehend sufficiently to ask the question. Or again, any attempt at rationalizing Halakha—an endeavor already found in *Hazal*, although much more fully elaborated by *rishonim*—presupposes an axiological frame of reference, independent of Halakha, in the light of which it can be interpreted. It makes no sense to say, with Abaye, that "the whole of the Torah . . . is for the purpose of promoting peace,"[10] unless the ethical value of peace can be taken for granted. The same holds true with respect to suggesting reasons for specific *mitzvot*.

The intensity of Maimonides' efforts on this front is consistent with the position—advanced by Rav Saadia Gaon[11] and, in broad outline, adopted by Rabbenu Bahya[12] and probably by Maimonides[13]—that, given sufficient time, ability, and interest, the bulk of revealed Torah could have been naturally and logically discovered.

Any supposed traditional rejection of *lex naturalis* cannot mean, therefore, that apart from Halakha—or, to put it in broader perspective, that in the absence of divine commandment—man and the world are amoral. Nor does it entail a total relativism or the view (evidently ascribed to Maimonides by Professor Fox[14]) that social convention and/or utility are the sole criteria for action. At most, the Rabbis rejected natural law, not natural morality. They may conceivably have felt one could not ground specific binding and universal rules in nature but they hardly regarded uncommanded man as ethically neutral. They could have accepted, at the natural plane, the position summarized by Whitehead: "There is no one behaviour-system belonging to the essential character of the universe, as the universal moral ideal. What is universal is the spirit which should permeate any behaviour-system in the circumstances of its adoption. . . . Whether we destroy or whether we preserve, our action is moral if we have thereby safeguarded the importance of experience so far as it depends on that concrete instance in the world's history."[15] But they would surely have gone no further. One might contend, maximally, that natural morality is contextual rather than formal. It does, however, exist.

Inasmuch as the traditional acceptance of some form of natural morality seems to me beyond doubt, I could, were I literally minded, simply answer our original question in the affirmative and close up shop. I presume, however, that its framers had something more in mind. If I read their concern rightly, the issue is not whether the tradition accords a nonhalakhic ethic some theoretical standing by acknowledging its universal validity and provenance. Rather, it is whether now that, in *Hazal*'s phrase, "Torah has been given and Halakha innovated,"[16] that standing is of any practical significance to us; whether, for the contemporary Jew, an ethic independent of Halakha can be at all legitimate and relevant at an operative level.

At this plane, the issue resolves itself, in turn, into the problem both historical and analytic, of the relation of the pre- and post-Sinai orders, something akin to the question of the relation of nature and grace that has exercised so much Christian theology. On this score, traditional thought has focused upon two complementary points. The first is that natural morality establishes a standard below which the demands of revelation could not possibly fall. Thus, in proving that the killing of a gentile constitutes proscribed murder (although the Torah at one point speaks of a man killing "his fellow" [Exod. 21:14], i.e., a Jew), the *Mekhilta* explains: "Issi b. Akiba states: Prior to the giving of the Torah, we were enjoined with respect to bloodshed. After the giving of the Torah, instead of [our obligation's] becoming more rigorous [is it conceivable] that it became less so?"[17] Moreover, this limit does not just reflect a general attitude but constitutes a definitive legal principle to be applied to specific situations. "Is there, then, anything," the Gemara asks, "which is permitted to the Jew but prohibited to the Gentile?"[18] And it uses the implicit rhetorical denial to clinch a fine point in the course of intricate discussion.

The second point is most familiarly associated with a statement—frequently quoted and never, to the best of my knowledge, seriously challenged—made by Maimonides in his *Commentary on the Mishna*. Taking his cue from a Mishna in *Hullin* concerning the prohibition against eating the sciatic nerve (*gid hanashe*), he goes on to postulate a general principle: "And pay attention to this great principle conveyed by this *mishna* as it states that it [i.e., the sciatic nerve] was 'proscribed from Sinai.' What you must know is that [as regards] anything from which we abstain or which we do today, we do this solely because of God's commandment, conveyed through Moses, not because God had commanded thus to prophets who had preceded him. For instance . . . we do not circumcise because Abraham circumcised himself and the members of his household but because God commanded us, through Moses, to become circumcised as had Abraham . . . Take note of their [i.e., the Rabbis'] remark, '613 *mitzvot* were stated to Moses at Sinai'—and all of these are among those *mitzvot*.' "[19] On this view, although the substance of natural morality may have been incorporated as a floor for a halakhic ethic, it has nevertheless, as a sanction, been effectively superseded.

At another level, however, we are confronted by an issue of far wider scope. The question is not what vestiges of natural morality continue to bind the Jew or to what extent receiving the Torah abrogated any antecedent ethic. It is rather whether, quite apart from ground common to natural and halakhic morality, the demands or guidelines of Halakha are both so definitive and so comprehensive as to preclude the necessity for—and therefore, in a sense, the legitimacy of—any other ethic. In translating my assigned topic into these terms (so strikingly familiar to readers of Hooker's *Ecclesiastical Polity*[20]), I am of course taking two things for granted. I assume, first, that Halakha constitutes—or at least contains—an ethical system. This point has sometimes been challenged—most notably, in our day, by Professor Yeshayahu Leibowitz; but I do not think the challenge, albeit grounded in healthy radical monotheism, can be regarded seriously. The extent to which Halakha as a whole is pervaded by an ethical moment or the degree to which a specific *mitzva* is rooted, if at all, in moral considerations are no doubt debatable. If evidence were necessary, we need only remember conflicting interpretations of the Mishna concerning "he who says, may your mercies encompass the bird's nest"[21] and the attendant controversy[22] over the rationalization of *mitzvot* en bloc. As for the outright rejection of the ethical moment, however, I cannot find such quasifideistic voluntarism consonant with the main thrust of the tradition. One might cite numerous primary texts by way of rebuttal but a single verse in Jeremiah should suffice: "But let him that glorieth glory in this, that he understandeth and knoweth Me, for I am the Lord who exercise mercy, justice, and righteousness, in the earth; for these I desire, saith the Lord."[23] The ethical element is presented as the reason for seeking knowledge of God, or, at the very least—if we translate *ki ani* as "that I am" rather than "for I am"[24]—as its content. In either case, the religious and the ethical are here inextricably interwoven; and what holds true of religious knowledge holds equally true of religious, that is, halakhic, action. This fusion is central to the whole rabbinic tradition. From its perspective, the divorce of Halakha from morality not only eviscerates but falsifies it.

Second, I assume that, at most, we can only speak of a complement to Halakha, not of an alternative. Any ethic so independent of Halakha as to obviate or override it, clearly lies beyond our pale. There are of course situations in which ethical factors—the preservation of life, the enhancement of human dignity, the quest for communal or domestic peace, or the mitigation of either anxiety or pain—sanction the breach, by preemptive priority or outright violation, of specific norms. However, these factors are themselves halakhic considerations, in the most technical sense of the term, and their deployment entails no rejection of the system whatsoever. Admittedly, advocates of such rejection are no strangers to Jewish history; but they are hardly our present concern.

However elastic the term *tradition* to some, it does have its limits, and antinomianism, which for our purposes includes the rejection of Torah law, lies beyond them. As a prescriptive category, the currently popular notion of *averah lishmah* (idealistic transgression) has no halakhic standing whatsoever.[25]

Essentially, then, the question is whether Halakha is self-sufficient. Its comprehensiveness and self-sufficiency are notions many of us cherish in our more pietistic or publicistic moments. For certain purposes, it would be comfortable if we could accept Professor Kahana's statement "that in Jewish civil law there is no separation of law and morals and that there is no distinction between what the law *is* and what the law *ought* to be."[26] If, however, we equate Halakha with the *din;* if we mean that everything can be looked up, every moral dilemma resolved by reference to code or canon, the notion is both palpably naive and patently false. The *Hazon Ish,* for one—and both his saintliness and his rigorous halakhic commitment are legend—had no such illusions. "Moral duties," he once wrote, "sometimes constitute one corpus with Halakhic rulings, and it is Halakha which defines the proscribed and permitted of ethical thought."[27] Sometimes—but not, evidently, always. There are moments when one must seek independent counsels. Recognition of this element rests upon both textual and practical evidence. In this setting, I presume little need be said with reference to the latter. Which of us has not, at times, been made painfully aware of the ethical paucity of his legal resources? Who has not found that the fulfillment of explicit halakhic duty could fall well short of exhausting clearly felt moral responsibility? The point to be emphasized, however—although this too, may be obvious—is that the deficiency is not merely the result of silence or ambiguity on the part of the sources. That may of course be a factor, requiring, as it does, recourse to inference and analogy to deal with the multitude of situations that, almost a priori, have not been covered by basic texts. The critical point, however, is that even the full discharge of one's whole formal duty as defined by the *din* often appears palpably insufficient.[28]

Lest this judgment appear excessively severe, let me hasten to add that it is precisely this point that is stressed by the second source of evidence: the textual. "Rav Yohanan said," the Gemara in *Baba Mezia* cites, "'Jerusalem was but destroyed because they [i.e., its inhabitants] judged [in accordance with] Torah law within it.' Well, should they rather have followed the law of the Magians?! Say, rather because they based their judgments solely upon Torah law and did not act *lifnim mishurat hadin* [i.e., beyond the line of the law]."[29] Nahmanides was even more outspoken. In a celebrated passage, he explains that the general command, "Ye shall be holy" was issued because, the scope of the Torah's injunctions regarding personal conduct notwithstanding, a lustful sybarite could observe them to the letter and yet remain "a scoundrel with Torah license." The same holds true, he continues, with respect to social ethics. Hence, there, too, the Torah has formulated a broad injuction: "And this is the Torah's mode: to detail and [then] to generalize in a similar vein. For after the admonition about the details of civil law and all interpersonal dealings. . .it says generally, 'And thou shalt do the right and the good,' as it includes under this positive command justice and accommodation and all *lifnim mishurat hadin* in order to oblige one's fellow."[30] This position is further elaborated in Nahmanides' explication of the phrase, "the right and the good." He suggests, initially, that it may refer to the collective body of specific *mitzvot*, but then presents an alternative:

> And our Rabbis[31] have a fine interpretation of this. They said: "This refers to compromise and *lifnim mishurat hadin*."[32] The intent of this is that, initially,[33] He had said that you should observe the laws and statutes which He had commanded you. Now He says that, with respect to what He has not commanded, you should likewise take heed to do the good and the right in His eyes, for He loves the good and the right. And this is a great matter. For it is impossible to mention in the Torah all of a person's actions toward his neighbors and acquaintances, all of his commercial activity, and all social and political institutions. So after He had mentioned many of them such as, "Thou shalt not go about as a tale-bearer," "Thou shalt not take vengeance nor bear any grudge," "Thou shalt not stand idly by the blood of thy fellow," "Thou shalt not curse the deaf," "Thou shalt rise up before age,"[34] and the like, He resumes to say generally that one should do the good and the right in all matters, to the point that there are included in this compromise, *lifnim mishurat hadin,* and [matters] similar to that which they [i.e., the Rabbis] mentioned concerning the law of the abutter[35]—even that which they said, "whose youth had been unblemished,"[36] or, "He converses with people gently,"[37] so that he is regarded as perfect and right in all matters.[38]

These passages contain strong and explicit language and they answer our question plainly enough. Or do they? Just how independent of Halakha is the ethic that ennobles us above the "scoundrel with Torah license"? If we regard *din* and Halakha as coextensive, very independent. If, however, we recognize that Halakha is multiplanar and many dimensional; that, properly conceived, it includes much more than is explicitly required or permitted by specific rules, we shall realize that the ethical moment we are seeking is itself an aspect of Halakha. The demand or, if you will, the impetus for transcending the *din* is itself part of the halakhic corpus. This point emerges quite clearly from the primary rabbinic source for the concept of *lifnim mishurat hadin*:

> " 'And thou shalt show them the way'—this is the study of Torah; 'and the action they should take'—good conduct"—these are the words of Rabbi Yehoshua. Rabbi Eleazar of Modi'im says: " 'And thou shalt show them'—teach them their life's course; 'the way'—this alludes to visiting the sick; 'they shall walk'—to burying the dead; 'therein'—to exercising kindness; 'and the action'—to *din* proper; 'which they shall do'—to *lifnim mishurat hadin*."[39]

Regardless of whether we accept Rabbi Yehoshua's generalization or Rabbi Eleazar's more specific catalogue, the conjunction of either "good conduct" or *lifnim mishurat hadin* with thoroughly mandatory elements clearly indicates it is no mere option.

The obligatory character of *lifnim mishurat hadin* stands revealed in the verses Nahmanides saw as related to it—"And thou shalt do the right and the good" and "Ye shall be holy." Neither was expressed in the indicative or the optative. With respect to the degree of obligation, however, *rishonim* admittedly held different views. Perhaps the most rigorous was held by one of the Tosafists, Rabbi Isaac of Corbeille. In his *Sefer Mitzvot Katan*, one of the many medieval compendia summarizing and enumerating *mitzvot*, he lists "to act *lifnim mishurat hadin*, as it is written, 'which they shall do'"[40] as one of the 613 commandments; and he goes on to cite the Gemara in *Baba Mezia* 30b as a proof text. Nahmanides did not go quite this far, as he does not classify *lifnim mishurat hadin* as an independent *mitzva*, as binding as *shofar* or *tefillin*. However, he does clearly posit it as a normative duty, incumbent upon—and expected of—every Jew as part of his basic obligation. Failure to implement "the right and the good" would obviously not be regarded as mere insensitivity to music of spiritual spheres. It is villainy—with the Torah's license—but villainy nonetheless.

Maimonides, however, does apparently treat *lifnim mishurat hadin* within a more rarefied context. After presenting his account of the golden mean in the opening chapter of *Hilkhot De'ot*, he concludes: "And the early pietists would incline their traits from the median path toward either extreme. One trait they would incline toward the farther extreme, another toward the nearer; and this is *lifnim mishurat hadin.* "[41] On this view, supralegal conduct appears as the hallmark of a small coterie of *hasidim.* Postulated as an aristocratic rather than as a popular ideal, *lifnim mishurat hadin* thus represents a lofty plane whose attainment is a mark of eminence but whose neglect cannot be faulted as reprehensible.

This is, of course, drastically different from Nahmanides and may be construed as indicating—contrary to my earlier statement—that, according to Maimonides, *lifnim mishurat hadin* is purely optional; that it constitutes a kind of supererogatory extra-credit morality rather than an obligation, strictly speaking. Even if the argument is accepted, it would not render *lifnim mishurat hadin* wholly voluntary. It would merely shift it, to use Lon Fuller's[42] distinction, from the "morality of duty" to the "morality of aspiration." But a Jew is also commanded to aspire. More important, however, this point has little impact upon our present broader purposes. The semantics and substance of the term *lifnim mishurat hadin* aside, Maimonides most certainly does not regard character development, ethical sensitivity, or supralegal behavior as non-halakhic, much less as optional, elements. He simply subsumes them under a different halakhic rubric, the demand for *imitatio dei.* "And we are commanded," he writes, "to walk in these median paths, and they are the right and the good paths, as it is written, 'And ye shall walk in His ways.' "[43] The command refers, of course, to the golden mean rather than to *lifnim mishurat hadin,*[44] but we are confronted by the same normative demand for "the right and the good." The difference in terminology and source is significant, and were my present subject *lifnim mishurat hadin* per se I would discuss it in detail. For our purposes, however, Maimonides' and Nahmanides' views point in the same general direction: Halakha itself mandates that we go beyond its legal corpus. Were I to follow Fuller's[45] example and chart a spectrum running from duty to aspiration, I think that, on Maimonides' view, so-called non-halakhic ethics would be a couple of notches higher than for Nahmanides. Even after we have taken due account of the imperative of pursuing "His ways," we are still imbued with a sense of striving for an ideal rather than of satisfying basic demands. Nevertheless, the fundamental similarity remains. The ethic of *imitatio* is not just a lofty ideal but a pressing obligation. The passage previously cited from Maimonides explicitly speaks of our being "commanded" (*u'mezuvim anu*) to pursue the golden mean; and subsequent statements are in a similar vein. Thus, he asserts that Scripture ascribes certain attributes to God "in order to inform [us] that they are good and right ways and [that] a person is obligated [*hayav*] to guide himself by them and to resemble Him to the best of his ability." Or again, he speaks of the attributes as constituting collectively "the median path which we are obligated [*hayavim*] to pursue."[46] Furthermore, it is noteworthy that in describing this ethic, Maimonides uses the very adjectives fastened upon by Nahmanides: "right and good." It can be safely assumed that, in principle, both recognize the imperative character of supralegal conduct.[47]

This exposition is admittedly partial. It rests upon two assumptions: first, that Maimonides recognizes an elitist ethic of the *hasid*, which though grounded in *din* nevertheless transcends it; second, that even the universal median ethic demands much that has not been specifically legislated and that according to Nahmanides' definition would be subsumed under *lifnim mishurat hadin*. I think both points emerge unequivocally from the account in *Mishneh Torah*; but in the earlier *Shemonah Perakim*[48] we do get a distinctly different impression. There, action *lifnim mishurat hadin* is not described as inherently superior to the golden mean but as a propaedeutic technique for attaining it. As in Aristotle's familiar example of straightening the bent stick,[49] one excess is simply used to correct another, this corresponding to standard medical practice. Second, Maimonides suggests that adherence to *din* proper produces the ideal balance so that deviation in any direction—except when dictated by the need to "cure" the opposite deficiency—becomes not only superfluous but undesirable. The brunt of this argument is directed against asceticism, and the excesses decried by Maimonides all concern material self-denial.[50] However, the list of examples adduced to prove the sufficiency of Torah law includes *mitzvot* which relate to a whole range of virtues and vices; munificence, anger, arrogance, timidity. The net impact of the passage is therefore clearly to diminish somewhat the role of an independent ethic. Nevertheless, I am inclined to regard the later and fuller exposition in *Hilkhot De'ot* as the more definitive. The difference between Maimonides and Nahmanides, though significant, does not therefore strike me as radical.

The variety of *rishonim*'s conceptions of a supralegal ethic may be judged from another perspective—in light of a very practical question: Is *lifnim mishurat hadin* actionable?[51] The Gemara records at least one instance in which it was enforced. It tells a story of some porters who had been working for Rabba the son of Rav Huna and who had broken a barrel of wine while handling it. Inasmuch as they had evidently been somewhat negligent, the strict letter of the law would have held them liable for the damage; and since they had been remiss in performing their assigned task, it would have allowed them no pay. By way of guaranteeing restitution, Rabba held onto their clothes—which had apparently been left in his possession—as surety; whereupon

> they came and told Rav [who in turn], told him, "Return their clothes to them." "Is this the *din?*" he asked. "Yes," he answered, " 'That thou mayest walk in the way of good men.' " He then returned their clothes, whereupon they said to him, "We are poor, we have labored all day, and [now] we are hungry and left with nothing!" [So] he said to him, "Go and pay their wages!" "Is this the *din?*" he asked. "Yes," he answered, " 'And keep the path of the righteous.' "[52]

Moreover, in a similar passage in the Palestinian Talmud,[53] the story is not told with reference to an *amora*—from whom a higher ethical standard could presumably be exacted—but of an ordinary potter. However, the pathetic circumstances as well as the omission of the term *lifnim mishurat hadin*[54] suggest this may have been an isolated instance. In any event, *rishonim* divided on the issue. The Rosh held that "we do not compel to act *lifnim mishurat hadin*";[55] and inferring *de silentio*, I think it is safe to assume this was the prevalent view of the Spanish school. However, a number of Tosafists—notably, Ravya and Ravan[56]—held such action could indeed by compelled. Of course, such a position could not conceivably be held with reference to all supralegal behavior. *Din* has many ethical levels; and so, of necessity, must *lifnim mishurat hadin*. Surpassing laws grounded in, say, the concept that "the Torah has but spoken vis-a-vis the evil inclination"[57] is hardly comparable to transcending those with a powerful moral thrust. Nevertheless, the fact that some *rishonim* held *lifnim mishurat hadin* to be, in principle, actionable, indicates the extent to which it is part of the fabric of Halakha.

The possibility of such compulsion arises in yet another—and possibly surprising—context. *Hazal* state that *kofin al midat Sodom*, "we coerce over a trait of Sodom." [58] as defined by most *rishonim*, the term refers to an inordinate privatism that leaves one preoccupied with personal concerns to the neglect of the concerns of others; a degree of selfishness so intense that it denies the others at no gain to oneself. There need be no actual spite. Simple indifference may suffice. Nor is *midat Sodom*— despite the severity of the term—confined to what popular morality might regard as nastiness or mindless apathy. One view in the Mishna— the definitive view according to most *rishonim*—subsumed under it the attitude that "mine is mine and yours is yours."[59] It thus broadly denotes obsession with one's private preserve and the consequent erection of excessive legal and psychological barriers between person and person.

This posture the Rabbis both condemned and rendered actionable. To the best of my knowledge, however, *Hazal* nowhere explicitly formulated the basis of this *halakha*. I would therefore conjecture that it is most likely subsumed under *lifnim mishurat hadin*; and if this be so, we have here a striking instance of its scope and force. Admittedly, most of us do not instinctively associate the two concepts. However, this is simply another manifestation of our failure to grasp the full range of supralegal obligation. So long as *lifnim mishurat hadin* is regarded as the sphere of supererogatory extracredit morality, it can hardly include rejection of actions so reprehensible as to earn the opprobrium of *midat Sodom*. However, once we appreciate its true scope—from rigorous obligation to supreme idealism—we should have little difficulty with the association.

The Maharal, at any rate, had none—precisely because he emphasized the centrality and force of *lifnim mishurat hadin*. This emphasis was clearly expressed in the course of his discussion of *gemilut hasadim* (loosely translatable as "benevolent action"). "The anitithesis of this trait," he writes, "is [a person] who does not want to do any good toward another, standing upon the *din* and refusing to act *lifnim mishurat hadin*." This virtual equation of *hesed* and *lifnim mishurat hadin* then becomes the basis for an explanation of the Gemara's comment regarding the destruction of Jerusalem. This was not, the Maharal explains, retributive punishment. It was a natural consequence, as a wholly legalistic community simply cannot exist. Supralegal conduct is the cement of human society. Its absence thus results in disintegration: "Standing upon *din* entails ruin." Likewise, excessive commitment to law invites disaster on a broader scale, for, by correspondence, it both recognizes and enthrones natural law as cosmic sovereign, thus rejecting the providential grace of miracles that deviates from it. Finally, rejection of *lifnim mishurat hadin* is defined as the hallmark of Sodom whose evil, although it issued in corruption, nevertheless was grounded in total fealty to legal nicety: "For this was their nature, to concede nothing, as the Rabbis o.b.m. said, 'Mine is mine and yours is yours—this is the trait of Sodom.' And they have where said, *kofin al midat Sodom.*"⁶⁰ Identification of *lifnim mishurat hadin* as the source of such coercion is here fairly explicit; and the conjunction of its denial with the biblical apotheosis of malice reflects the importance that the Maharal attached to supralegal conduct.

This exposition is open to two obvious objections. First, if *lifnim mishurat hadin* is indeed obligatory as an integral aspect of Halakha, in what sense is it supralegal? More specifically, on the Ravya's view, what distinguishes its compulsory elements from *din* proper? Secondly, isn't this exposition mere sham? Having conceded, in effect, the inadequacy of the halakhic ethic, it implicitly recognizes the need for a complement, only to attempt to neutralize this admission by claiming the complement had actually been a part of Halakha all along, so that the fiction of halakhic comprehensiveness could be saved after all. Yet, the upshot of this legerdemain does not differ in substance from the view that the tradition does recognize an ethic independent of Halakha—so why not state this openly?

These are sound objections; but they do not undermine the position I have developed. They only stimulate its more precise definition. As regards the first question, a comment made, interestingly, by the Ravya, points toward the solution. In explaining why Rav Nahman had not compelled the finder of a lost object whose owner had despaired of its recovery to return it—legally, he is free to retain it but the Gemara⁶¹ notes that it is returnable, *lifnim mishurat haddin*—he suggests that, in this instance, "perhaps the finder was poor while the object's owner was well-to-do."⁶² Within the framework of *din*, this would of course be a startling distinction. Powerful as is the obligation of the affluent to help the relatively disadvantaged, it is a general responsibility to a group and enforceable only through a third party, the community and its *beth din*. Although many *poskim*⁶³ regard charity as a legal and collectible debt rather than a mere act of grace, an individual pauper certainly has no right—except with respect to one type of *ma'aser ani* (tithe for the poor)⁶⁴—to seize his more affluent neighbor's property. That such a point could be made with reference to *lifnim mishurat hadin* suggests its crucial distinction from *din*. It is less rigorous not only in the sense of being less exacting with respect to the degree and force of obligation—and there are times, as has been noted, when it can be equally demanding—but in the sense of being more flexible, its duty more readily definable in light of the exigencies of particular circumstances. This has nothing to do with the force of obligation. Once it has been determined that, in a given case, realization of "the right and the good" mandates a particular course, its pursuit may conceivably be as imperative as the performance of a *din*. However, the initial determination of what moral duty requires proceeds along different lines in the respective sphere. *Din* consists of a body of statutes, ultimately rooted in fundamental values but which at the moment of decision confronts the individual as a set of rules. It is of course highly differentiated, numerous variables making the relevant rule very much a function of the situation. Yet the basic mode is that of formulating and defining directives to be followed in a *class* of cases—it is precisely the quality of generality that constitutes a rule—and applying them to situations marked by the proper cluster of features. Judgments are essentially grounded in deductive, primarily syllogistic reasoning. Metaphors that speak of laws as controlling or governing a case are therefore perfectly accurate.

Lifnim mishurat hadin by contrast, is the sphere of contextual morality. Its basis for decision is paradoxically both more general and more specific. The formalist is guided by a principle or a rule governing a category of cases defined by *n* number of characteristics. The more sensitive and sophisticated the system, the more individuated the categories. Whatever the degree of specificity, however, the modus operandi is the same: action grows out of the application of class rules to a particular case judged to be an instance of that class or of the interaction of several classes, there being, of course principles to govern seemingly hybrid cases as well. The contextualist, by contrast, will have nothing to do with middle-distance guidelines. He is directed, in theory, at least, only by the most universal and the most local of factors—by a minimal number, perhaps as few as one or two, of ultimate values, on the one hand, and by the unique contours of the situation at hand, on the other. Guided by his polestar(s), the contextualist employs his moral sense (to use an outdated but still useful eighteenth-century term) to evaluate and intuit the best way of eliciting maximal good from the existential predicament confronting him. A nominalist in ethics, he does not merely contend that every case is phenomenologically different. That would be a virtual truism. He argues that the differences are generally so crucial that no meaningful directives can be formulated. Only direct ad hoc judgment, usually—although this is logically a wholly separate question—his own, can serve as an operative basis for decision. Between ultimate value and immediate issue, there can be no other midwife.

It goes without saying that Judaism has rejected contextualism as a self-sufficient ethic. Nevertheless, we should recognize equally that it has embraced it as the modus operandi of large tracts of human experience. These lie in the realm of *lifnim mishurat hadin*. In this area, the halakhic norm is itself situational. It speaks in broad terms: "And thou shalt do the right and the good"; "And thou shalt walk in His ways." The metaphors employed to describe it—"the ways of the good" or "the paths of the righteous"—denote purpose and direction rather than definitively prescribed acts. And the distinction from *din* is, finally, subtly recognized in the third source we have noted: " 'And the action'—this is the line of *din*; 'that they shall take'—this is *lifnim mishurat hadin"*—the reified static noun being used in relation to one and the open-ended verb in relation to the other. In observing *din*, the Jew rivets his immediate attention upon the specific command addressed to him. His primary response is to the source of his prescribed act. With respect to *lifnim mishurat hadin*, he is, "looking before and after," concerned with results as much as with origins. His focus is axiological and teleological.

Quite apart from the severity of obligation, therefore, there is a fundamental difference between *din* and *lifnim mishurat hadin*. One, at a more minimal level, imposes fixed objective standards. The demands of the other evolve from a specific situation; and, depending upon the circumstances, may vary with the agent.

This point was clearly recognized by a late *rishon*, author of a fourteenth-century commentary on the *Mishneh Torah*. In explaining why Maimonides both expanded and differentiated the concept of *dina debar mezra*, making it legally enforceable in some cases but only obligatory *ante facto* in others,[65] the *Maggid Mishneh* both echoes Nahmanides and goes beyond him. "The point of *dina debar mezra*," he comments,

> is that our perfect Torah has laid down [general] principles concerning the development of man's character and his conduct in the world; as, in stating, "Ye shall be holy,"[66] meaning, as they [i.e., the Rabbis] said, "Sanctify yourself with respect to that which is permitted you"[67]—that one should not be swept away by the pursuit of lusts. Likewise, it said "And thou shalt do the right and the good," meaning that one's interpersonal conduct should be good and just. With regard to all this, it would not have been proper to command

[about] details. For the Torah's commands apply at all times, in every period, and under all circumstances, whereas man's characteristics and his behavior vary, depending upon the time and the individual. The Rabbis [therefore] set down some relevant details subsumed under these principles, some of which they made [the equivalent of] absolute *din* and others [only] *ante facto* and by way of *hasidut*[68]—all [however] ordained by them. And it is with reference to this that they said, "The words of consorts [i.e., the Rabbis] are more beloved than the wine of Torah, as stated, 'For thy love is better than wine.' "[69]

The *Maggid Mishneh* is certainly not espousing an exclusively relativistic or situational ethic. No conscientious halakhist could even countenance the possibility. He is, rather, defining the character of *dina debar mezra*, specifically, and of "the right and the good" generally; and, beyond this, noting that, from a certain perspective, the greater flexibility and latitude that characterize this class of rabbinic legislation gives it an edge, as it were, over the Torah's absolutely rigorous law. The concluding remark is of considerable interest in its own right. Comparisons aside, however, the passage clearly reveals the respective characters of *din* and *lifnim mishurat hadin*.

The second objection—that I am either playing games or stalking a Trojan horse, and possibly both—can likewise be parried. Whether supralegal behavior is regarded as an aspect of—and in relation to—Halakha does matter considerably. The difference, moreover, concerns not so much the prestige of Halakha as the substance of that behavior. And this in three respects. First, integration within Halakha helps define the specifics of supralegal conduct. One of its principal modes entails the extension of individual *dinim* by (1) refusal to avail oneself of personal exemptions; (2) disregard of technicalities when they exclude from a law situations that morally and substantively are clearly governed by it; and (3) enlarging the scope of a law by applying it to circumstances beyond its legal pale but nevertheless sufficiently similar to share a specific telos. All three, however, constitute, in effect, the penumbra of *mitzvot*. To this end, relation to a fundamental law, which posits frontiers and points a direction, is obviously essential.

Not all supralegal conduct bears this character, however. It may, alternatively, either fill in a moral lacuna at a lower level—*kofin al midat Sodom* is an excellent example—or, at a higher plane, aspire to attainments discontinuous with any specific practical norm. Even within these nether and upper reaches, however, relation to the overall halakhic system is important both for the definition of general goals and by way of molding orientation, context, and motivation. Even while closing an interstice or reaching for the stars, one does not move in a vacuum. The legal corpus is here, to adapt Ben Jonson's remark about the ancients, more guide than commander; but it is vital nonetheless.

Finally, the halakhic connection is relevant at a third level, when we are concerned with an ethic neither as decisor of specific actions nor as determinant of a field of values but as the polestar of life in its totality. Halakhic commitment orients a Jew's whole being around his relation to God. It is not content with the realization of a number of specific goals but demands personal dedication—and not only dedication but consecration. To the achievement of this end, supralegal conduct is indispensable. Integration of the whole self within a halakhic framework becomes substantive rather than semantic insofar as it is reflected within the full range of personal activity. Reciprocally, however, that conduct is itself stimulated by fundamental halakhic commitment.

Let me emphasize that in speaking of the investiture of an independent ethic with a halakhic mantle, I hold no brief for terminology per se. I would readily concede that we can, if we wish, confine the term *halakha* to *din* and find some other term to cover what lies beyond. Moreover, such limitation would probably be consonant with the use of the term *halakha* by *Hazal*. In classical usage, the term *halakha*—properly lowercase and commonly used without the definite article—generally denotes a specific rule (hence, the frequent appearance of the plural, *halakhot*) or, in broader terms, the body of knowledge comprising Torah law. It does not convey the common contemporary sense in which it is roughly the equivalent of halakhic Judaism—the *unum necessarium* of the Jew committed to tradition, in which, as a commanding presence, magisterial to the point of personification, it is regarded as prescribing a way of life; in which, as with the term *Torah* in *Hazal*, Halakha and its Giver frequently become interchangeable. Hence, we ought not be surprised if we find that *Hazal* did differentiate between *halakhot* and other normative elements. Thus, in commenting upon the verse, "If thou wilt diligently hearken to the voice of the Lord thy God, and wilt do that which is right in His eyes, and wilt give ear to His commandments, and keep all his statutes,"[70] the *Mekhilta* notes:

> " 'And wilt do that which is right in His eyes'—these are wonderful *agadot* which hold every one's ear; 'and wilt give ear to His commandments'—these are orders; 'and keep all His statutes' these are *halakhot*." . .These are the

words of Rabbi Yehoshua. Rabbi Eleazar of Modi'im says. . ." 'And wilt do that which is right in His eyes'—this is commercial dealing. [The verse thus] teaches [us] that whoever deals honestly and enjoys good relations with people is regarded as having realized the whole Torah. 'And wilt give ear to His commandments'—these are *halakhot* 'and keep all His statutes'—these are [prohibitions concerning] forbidden sexual relations."[71]

This exposition I understand readily and, semantics apart, find fully consistent with the view I have outlined above. At most, it requires that we adjust our customary terminology somewhat and then issue with the thesis that traditional halakhic Judaism demands of the Jew both adherence to Halakha and commitment to an ethical moment that, though different from Halakha, is nevertheless of a piece with it and in its own way fully imperative.[72] What I reject emphatically is the position that, on the one hand, defines the function and scope of Halakha in terms of the latitude implicit in current usage and yet identifies its content with the more restricted sense of the term. The resulting equation of duty and *din* and the designation of supralegal conduct as purely optional or pietistic is a disservice to Halakha and ethics alike.

In dealing with this subject, I have, in effect, addressed myself both to those who, misconstruing the breadth of its horizons, find the halakhic ethic inadequate, and to those who smugly regard even its narrower confines as sufficient. In doing so, I hope I have presented my thinking clearly. But for those who prefer definitive answers, let me conclude by saying: Does the tradition recognize an ethic independent of Halakha? You define your terms and take your choice.

Notes

1. *Erubin* 100b. Soncino translates "we could have learnt, " but I think "would" is more accurate. Rabbenu Hananel, it might be noted, has *lamadnu*.

2. In the passage cited from the Gemara in *Erubin*, the term has a rather narrow meaning, referring, in context, to proper conjugal gallantry. Elsewhere, however, it clearly denotes far more, sometimes civility or culture generally. The *Mahzor Vitry*, commenting on *Abot*, 3:17 (ed. Horowitz, p.517), renders it as *nourriture*, and the Maharal of Prague spells out its latitude quite clearly: "The things that are *derekh eretz* are all ethical matters included in *Abot*, those mentioned in the Talmud, and all other ethical matters. It is that conduct which is right and fitting toward (possibly, "in the eyes of") people; and failure to pursue some of its elements is sinful and a great transgression" (*Netivot Olam*, "Netiv Derekh

Eretz," chap. 1). See also N. S. Greenspan, *Mishpat Am Haaretz* (Jerusalem, 1946), pp. 1-5; the references cited in Boaz Cohen, *Law and Tradition in Judaism* (New York, 1959), p. 183n.; and *Encyclopedia Talmudit*, Vol. 7, pp. 672-706. One might add that the flexible range of *derekh eretz* parallels those of curteisie and manners in their Middle English and Elizabethan senses.

3. *Abot,* 3:17. Cf. also ibid, 2:2, and *Tosafot Yeshanim, Yoma* 85b, s.v. *teshuva.*

4. *Vayikra Rabba,* 9:3 (*Tzav*); cf. *Tanna Debei Eliyahu Rabba,* chap. 1.

5. *Netivot Olam, "Netiv Derekh Eretz,"* chap. 1.

6. See Saul Lieberman, "How Much Greek in Jewish Palestine?," in *Biblical and Other Studies,* ed. A. Altmann (Cambridge, Mass., 1963), pp. 128-29.

7. M. Fox, "Maimonides and Aquinas on Natural Law," *Dine' Israel* 3 (1972):5-27. Cf. also Ralph Lerner, "Natural Law in Albo's *Book of Roots,"* in *Ancients and Moderns,* ed. Joseph Cropsey (New York, 1964), pp. 132-44.

8. The statement appears in one of his *Discourses* but the exact reference eludes me at present.

9. Gen. 18:25.

10. *Gittin* 59b. This passage was cited by Maimonides in the concluding lines of *Sefer Zemanim:* "Great is peace, as the whole Torah was given in order to promote peace in the world, as it was stated: 'Her ways are the ways of pleasantness and all her paths are peace' " (*MT, Hannuka,* 4:14). There may be a shift in focus, however, as Maimonides dwells upon the reason for giving the Torah while the Gemara may conceivably refer to its content and the telos to which its inner logic leads. In either case, Torah is regarded as serving the interests of peace and therefore, presumably, as axiologically ancillary to it. In the *Guide* (III: 27; and cf. III: 52), this nexus is reversed. Peace and social stability are subsumed under the welfare of the body that is merely a condition for attaining man's ultimate perfection via the soul's intellectual apprehension. There is no contradiction, however, as the passage in *Mishneh Torah* probably refers to the specific corpus of revealed Torah and the regimen prescribed by it rather than, as in other contexts, to the full range of spiritual perception.

11. See *Ha'emunot Vehadeot,* "Introduction," sec. vi; and cf. III;iii.

12. See *Hovot Halevavot,* III:i-iii.

13. This point is not explicitly developed in Maimonides' discussions of prophecy, which focus upon its nature rather than upon the need for it. However, it is implicit in the substance and tone of numerous passages concerning the Torah's revelation and dovetails with Maimonides' faith in the spiritual capacity of singular individuals, on the one hand, and his conviction about the average person's indolence, on the other.

14. See Fox, "Maimonides and Aquinas on Natural Law," pp. 15-17.

15. Alfred North Whitehead, *Modes of Thought* (New York, 1938), p. 20.

16. *Shabbat* 135b.

17. *Mishpatim, Massekhta Dinezikin,* iv (ed. Horowitz-Rabin), p. 263.

18. *Hullin* 33a; cf. *Sanhedrin* 59a.

19. *Perush Ha-Mishnayot, Hullin,* 7:6. The talmudic citation is from *Makkot* 23b.

20. See, especially, Book 2.

21. *Berakhot* 5:3 and *Megilla* 4:9.

22. See Maimonides, *Guide,* III:26, III:31, and III:48; Nahmanides' comment on Deut. 22:7; and Maharal, *Tiferet Israel,* chaps. 5-7. See also Yitzhak Heinemann, *Taamei Ha-Mitzvot Besafrut Yisrael* (Jerusalem, 1954), Vol. 1, pp. 46-128.

23. Jer. 9:23.

24. The J.P.S. translation, following A.V., has "that I am," an interpretation implicitly supported by *Ikkarim,* 3:5. However, Radak is closer to "for I am," which I am more inclined to accept. The Septuagint's *hoti* is inconclusive but the Vulgate's *quia* parallels "for."

For a discussion of the verse, see Maimonides, *Guide*, III:54.

25. The term *avera lishma* does, of course, appear in the Gemara that cites a statement by Rabbi Nahman b. Yitzhak that "an *avera lishma* is greater than a *mitzva* performed with an ulterior motive" (*Nazir* 23b and *Horayot* 10b). However, this apparent priority of telos and motivation over formal law has no prescriptive or prospective implications. At most, it means that, after the fact, we can sometimes see that a nominal violation was superior to a licit or even required act; but it gives no license for making the jump. Moreover, in the case at hand—Yael's sexual relations with Sisera—most likely there was no formal violation. Most *rishonim* assume that a woman, inasmuch as she can be regarded as passive during coitus, is not obligated to undergo martyrdom rather than engage in incest or adultery (see *Sanhedrin* 74b). This is true even when she is threatened but not assaulted, as it is the element of willful involvement that defines her sexual participation as a human action. Hence, when motivated by the need to save her people, Yael's relations with Sisera, even though she may have initially seduced him, may very well be regarded as passive and therefore no formal violation whatsoever; see *Tosafot, Yebamot* 103a, s.v. *veha* and *Yoma* 82b, s.v. *ma*. The term *avera* refers, then, to an act which is proscribed under ordinary circumstances and yet, its usual sinful character notwithstanding, here becomes superior to a *mitzva*. Likewise, Raba's remark that the verse, "In all thy ways know Him and He will direct thy paths" (Prov. 3:6), is to be understood "even with regard to a matter of *avera*" (*Berakhot* 63a), may refer to acts that are ordinarily forbidden but in certain cases have formal dispensation. See, however, Maimonides, *Shemonah Perakim*, chap. 5.

26. K. Kahana, *The Case for Jewish Civil Law in the Jewish State* (London, 1960), p. 28n (his italics).

27. *Hazon Ish: Emunah Uvitahon* (Jerusalem, 1954), p. 21. The point is illustrated by a discussion of economic competition, aspects of which are very differently evaluated, depending upon their being regarded as aggressive or defensive; and this, in turn, is a function of legal right. Of course, in such a case, the moral duties include many outright *dinim*. However, the implication of the sentence stands and is clearly accepted in the following chapter, pp. 44-46. Cf., however, p. 49.

28. Many of the leaders of the *mussar* movement, who criticized what they regarded as the ethical shortcomings of their contemporary Torah community, often ascribed many of these failings to the fact that the relevant halakhot had been insufficiently developed. They therefore urged the fuller analysis and exposition of these categories as a remedy; see J. D. Epstein, *Mitzvot Ha-bayit* (New York, 1966), pp. 34-57. I am inclined to think that while such neglect could be a factor in causing the alleged failings, its importance—and the potential for resolution via fuller halakhic exposition—has been exaggerated by the *mussar* movement.

29. *Baba Mezia* 30b.

30. Lev. 19:2.

31. In his edition of Nahmanides' commentary, *Perush Ha-Ramban al Ha-Torah* (Jerusalem, 1960), II, 376n., C. B. Chavel notes that no extant source of this comment is known.

32. Rashi, Deut. 6:18, comments, "This is compromise *lifnim mishurat hadin*." This reading—he is presumably quoting the same source as Nahmanides—narrows the scope of the remark considerably.

32. In the preceding verse, 6:17.

33. The verses cited are from Lev. 19:16, 18, 16, 14, and 32, respectively.

34. A Rabbinic ordinance that requires a seller to give first option to any prospective customer who already owns property adjacent to that to be sold; see *Baba Mezia* 108.

35. *Ta'anit* 16a.

36. *Yoma* 86a.

37. *Deut.* 6:18.

39. *Mekhilta, Yithro, Massekhta D'Amalek,* ii (ed. Horowitz-Rabin), p. 198. The phrase I have rendered as "their life's course" is *bet hayehem.* Rashi interprets it variously as "the study of Torah" (*Baba Kama* 100a, s.v. *bet*) and as "a trade from which to derive a livelihood" (*Baba Mezia* 30b. s.v. *zeh*).

40. *Semak,* 49.

41. *MT, Hilkhot De'ot,* 1:5.

42. See his *The Morality of Law* (New Haven, 1964), pp. 5-9; cf. also A. D. Lindsay, *The Two Moralities* (London, 1940), passim.

43. *De'ot,* 1:5.

44. Maimonides thus distinguishes here between "the right and the good" and *lifnim mishurat hadin.* Elsewhere, however, he seems to identify them. See Rabbi M. Krakowski's commentary, *Avodat Hamelekh* (Vilna, 1931), *ad loc.,* and S. Rawidowicz, *Iyyunim Bemahashevet Yisrael* (Jerusalem, 1969), I, 430-31.

45. See Fuller, *The Morality of Law,* pp. 9-13.

46. *De'ot,* 1:6 and 1:7, respectively.

47. See, however, *Avodat Hamelekh, De'ot* 1:5, who expresses some uncertainty on this point.

48. See chap. 4; cf. also *Perush Ha-Mishnayot Abot* 4:4.

49. See *Nic. Eth.,* 1109b.

50. Most involve actual physical deprivation so that the passage largely anticipates *MT, De'ot,* 3:1. However, it also criticizes excessive munificence; cf. *MT, Arakhin* 8:13.

51. There is of course no question about practices such as *dina debar mezra* (i.e., "the law of the abutter") that were instituted by Hazal on the basis of the principle of "the right and the good;" see *Baba Mezia* 108. The question concerns situations that have not been singled out for rabbinic prescription.

52. *Baba Mezia* 83a. The citations are from Prov. 2:20.

53. *P. T., Baba Mezia* 6:6.

54. However, Rashi, *ad loc.,* does use the term.

55. *Pesakim, Baba Mezia* 2:7.

56. This view was advanced by the author of the *Mordecai, Baba Mezia,* sec. 327, who cites his predecessors, the Ravan and the Ravya as support, but it is usually associated with the latter and cited in his name by *Hagahot Maimuniyot, Hilkhot Gezela,* 11:3. The Ravya's original text is no longer extant, however. The reference to the Ravan is presumably to *Sefer Ravan* (ed. Ehrenreich), II: 198, but that passage, while it unequivocally states that the finder, in the case in question, is fully obligated to return the lost object, says nothing of juridic coercion. Perhaps the *Mordecai* drew upon another, more explicit source. See also Z. Y. Meltzer, "*Lifnim Mishurath Hadin,*" in *Mizkeret: In Memory of Rabbi I. H. Herzog* (Jerusalem, 1962), pp. 310-15.

57. *Kiddushin* 21b.

58. *Ketubot* 103a. For an analysis of this *halakha,* see my "*Leverur kofin al midat Sodom,*" in *Hagut Ivrit Be'Amerika,* ed. M. Zohori et al. (Tel Aviv, 1972), Vol 1, pp. 362-82.

59. *Abot* 5:10.

60. *Netivot Olam,* "*Netiv Gemilut Hasadim,*" chap. 5.

61. See *Baba Mezia* 24b.

62. Quoted in *Mordecai, Baba Mezia,* sec. 327.

63. See *Ketzot Ha-Hoshen,* 290:3.

64. See *Tosafot, Yebamot* 100a, s.v. *ma'aser* and Maimonides, *Matnot Aniyim,* 1:8.

65. The *halakha* in question concerns criteria for assignment of priorities among various prospective purchasers, none of whom is an abutter. In such cases, Maimonides states that while "this, too, is included within the good and the right," the priority is not enforceable, "for the Rabbis only commanded regarding this by way of *hasidut*, and it is a virtuous soul which acts thus" (*Shekhenim*, 14:5).

66. Lev. 19:2.

67. *Yebamot* 20a.

68. I know of no satisfactory English equivalent for this term. It suggests a blend of spiritual elevation and refinement with scrupulousness and pietism. Perhaps "saintliness" comes closest, though more in the Jamesian than in the popular sense, of total selflessness or other-worldiness; but that too, has too ethereal a ring.

69. *Shekhenim* 14:5. The concluding talmudic quotation is from *Avoda Zara* 34a, the verse from Cant. 1:3.

70. Exod. 15:26.

71. *Beshalah, Massekhta D'Vayissa,* i (ed. Horowitz-Rabin), pp. 157-58; see also the notes there.

72. This is pointed up by the fact that Nahmanides (Exod. 15:26) quotes Rabbi Eleazar's statement and yet, in the same passage, refers the reader to his subsequent discussions of "the right and the good."

Foundations of Jewish Ethics

J ewish ethics has no universally accepted "first principle" or "ground-norm" such as is often found in systems of philosophical ethics (e.g., Kant's categorical imperative, or Mill's principle of utility) and religious ethics (e.g. the principle of *agape*). It does, however, have a number of basic teachings or doctrines to which regular appeal is made by Jewish ethicists. Here, these will be termed "foundations" of Jewish ethics. Among the most important of these are the command "to walk in the ways of the Lord" (*imitatio dei* or imitation of God), and the command to love one's neighbor as oneself.

A number of authorities count *imitatio dei,* like the obligation to go *lifnim meshurat hadin* (beyond the letter of the law), as a positive commandment of Judaism. They thus import what might otherwise be considered supra–legal moral considerations into the *halakhah* itself. The Talmud, as David Shapiro points out, uses the doctrine of *imitatio* to derive specific ethico–legal obligations from the Bible. In fulfilling those obligations (such as visiting the sick or clothing the naked) one obeys the command "to walk in the ways of the Lord," whatever other halakhic imperatives one might be fulfilling at the same time. Shapiro traces the doctrine of *imitatio* throughout Jewish literature, while Martin Buber, in his essay, sharpens our understanding of the doctrine of *imitatio* in Judaism by comparing it to the parallel teaching in Christianity.

The command to love one's neighbor as oneself was used by Rabbi Akiba to summarize, in an ethico–homiletical fashion, all the teachings of the Torah. In his essay, Chaim Reines links the obligation to love one's neighbor to the fact that the neighbor is made in the image of God. He argues that love, however, which can be "blind and selfish," is not enough, and must be linked with concern for one's neighbor's dignity as well. The main thrust of the essay is an attempt to reconcile the obligation of neighborly love with what Judaism has always recognized as the legitimate demands of self-interest and self-respect.

A practical question involving the command to love one's neighbor as over against the demands of self-interest involves the extent to which one is expected or commanded to sacrifice one's life on behalf of one's neighbor. Louis Jacobs examines that question in his essay on self-sacrifice, throwing the entire issue into sharp relief.

7

The Doctrine of the Image of God and Imitatio Dei

DAVID S. SHAPIRO

I

The biblical doctrine of man is based on the presumption that man is the creature of God, and as such must acquire the proper perspective of his place in the world. While the uniqueness of man in the Divine order is constantly emphasized, it is equally made clear that the besetting sin of man is pride. Man the creature forgets his status and arrogates for himself the prerogatives of his Creator.

The Scriptures express their estimate of man by affirming that he was created in the image of God (Gen. 1:27; 5:1; 9:6). This judgment implies that there is a similarity, in some profound sense, between man and his Maker. Yet ultimately man resembles God no more than a shadow resembles a real person.[1] In the first chapter of Genesis the creation of man in God's image is narrated. The second chapter relates how man succumbed to the temptation of striving to be like God. The serpent persuades man that God is envious of him, for if he were to eat of the forbidden fruit he would become like God, knowing good and evil (*ibid.* 3:5). Man is enjoined to walk in God's ways (Deut. 10:12; 11:22; 26:17) and to be like Him: "Holy shall ye be, for holy am I the Lord your God" (Lev. 19:2). But the path trodden by those who aspire to holiness is fraught with grave hazards and disastrous pitfalls.[2] This paradox constitutes the terrible predicament of man's life and the tragedy of his history.[3]

Reprinted from *Judaism*, Vol. 13, no. 1. Copyright © 1963 by the American Jewish Congress.

The doctrine of man as created in the image of God is the ground for the mandate of *imitatio Dei*. Simultaneously, *imitatio Dei* defines the extent to which the doctrine of the *image of God* can be applied. While the *image of God* describes the essential nature of man, its relevance is restricted to the sphere of action. Man is not God, he cannot become God, but his behavior can be Godlike. It is thus clear that holiness to which man is called is not so much a holiness of essence as a holiness of conduct. This distinction clarifies the chasm that obtains between Judaism's imitation of the ways of God and pagan concepts of apotheosis and identification with, and absorption in, Deity.[4]

That *imitatio Dei* is a genuine Jewish concept is evident from the fact that the imperative of holiness, whether applied to Israelites or to priests, is consistently motivated by the holiness of God (Lev. 11:44; 19:2; 20:26; 21:8). God loves the stranger; therefore the children of Israel are to love the stranger (Deut. 10:18-19). God, Who executes justice for the orphan and the widow *(ibid.)*, Who loves justice and hates robbery with iniquity (Is. 61:8), the father of the fatherless and the judge of widows (Ps. 68:6), is the exemplar for human conduct. What He abominates man must abominate. What He hates men should hate (Deut. 12:31). The mercy, justice, and righteousness in which He delights should give delight to the hearts of human beings (Jer. 9:23). That in which He finds displeasure should be reprehensible to them (Is. 66:4). The graciousness of God is the implicit ground for the humane treatment of the poor (Ex. 22:26).[5] For He Who dwells in the high and holy place looks upon him who is poor and of a contrite spirit, to revive the spirit of the humble, and to revive the heart of the contrite ones (Is. 57:15). Righteousness is to be practiced in judgment because judgment is a function of the Deity (Deut. 1:17), and the court-of-justice is denominated "God."[6] Because the Almighty is the paradigm of justice, He may not tolerate any deviation therefrom that may lead to its distortion on earth: "Shall not the Lord of all the earth do justly?"[7]

A number of commandments prescribe a kind of conduct which duplicate Divine activity at certain crucial moments of history, activity which is reflective of Divine character. The children of Israel are not to be sold as bondmen, because the Lord brought them forth out of the land of Egypt so that they should not be bondmen (Lev. 25:42). The Sabbath is to be kept by the children of Israel as a sign that the Lord made heaven and earth in six days and ceased from His work and rested on the seventh (Ex. 20:10–11).[8] The man-servant and maid-servant are to be granted rest on the Sabbath because God granted rest to His people from Egyptian slavery (Deut. 5:14–15). God's vindication of justice in redeeming bondmen from Egypt is to serve as an examplar of justice and compassion towards the stranger and the widow (*ibid.* 24:17–18). The sacrifice upon the altar of the first-born males of the beasts reflects the power of the Lord in slaying the first-born of Egypt, while the redemption of the first-born sons reproduces the redemptive grace of God which saved the children of Israel from disaster.[9] All the commandments of God are guides to the achievement of holiness, the supreme goal of *imitatio Dei*.[10] But those associated with God's entrance into history concretize for us the Divine concern, a measure of which it is our duty to make our own.[11]

The genuineness of the Jewish character of *imitatio Dei* is, moreover, corroborated by the Biblical expression "to walk in the ways of God," which means nothing other than modelling one's life on the attributes of God. While the phrase "the way of the Lord" (in singular) may refer to *a way designated or indicated by the Lord*,[12] the same phrase in the plural[13] means walking in His footsteps, as can be confirmed from parallel usages.[14] During his days of intercession on Mount Sinai, Moses asked the Almighty to show him "His ways" (Ex. 33:13). The prophet's request was granted when the Lord passed before him and proclaimed: "The Lord, the Lord, God, merciful and gracious, long-suffering, and abundant in goodness and truth; keeping mercy unto the thousandth generation, forgiving iniquity and transgression and sin; and that will by no means clear the guilty; visiting the iniquity of the fathers upon the children, and upon the children's children, unto the third and unto the fourth generation."[15] That the *ways of the Lord* were revealed to Moses in the theophany at Sinai was clearly understood in very ancient times. Thus the Psalmist explicitly asserts:

> The Lord executeth righteousness,
> And acts of justice for all that are oppressed.
> *He made known His ways unto Moses,*
> *His doings unto the children of Israel.*
> *The Lord is full of compassion and gracious,*
> *Slow to anger, and plenteous in mercy.*
> *He will not always contend;*
> *Neither will He keep His anger forever.*[16]

The *ways* of the Lord and His *paths* are defined in an identical manner:

> All the paths of the Lord are mercy and truth
> Unto such as keep His convenant and His testimonies
>
> (Ps. 25:10).

Those who reject God's covenant have, of course, another conception of Deity and practice the *imitatio Dei* in their own way:

> These things hast thou done, and should I have kept silence?
> Thou hadst thought that I was altogether such a one as thyself
>
> (Ibid. 50:21).

The concept of *imitatio Dei* as "walking in the ways of the Lord" looms large in the prophetic vision of the end of days. All nations shall flow to the house of the Lord and they shall say:

> Come ye, and let us go up to the mountain of the Lord,
> To the house of the God of Jacob;
> And He will teach us of *His ways*,
> And we will walk in His paths (Is. 2:3).

The "knowledge of the Lord" of which the Scriptures speak so often refers primarily to the knowledge of the attributes of mercy and justice upon which men are called to model their lives (Jer. 9:23; 22:16 cf. Is. 58:2).

II

In rabbinic literature, the doctrine of *imitatio Dei* is clearly enunciated. The Tanna Abba Saul emphasized the significance of this principle by deriving it from two separate passages in the Pentateuch. On the verse: "Holy shall ye be, for holy am I the Lord your God," Abba Saul comments: "The household attendants of the king cannot but follow in the footsteps of the king."[17] The verse in Exodus (15:2): "This is my God and I will glorify Him" elicited from him the following comment: "Be like unto Him; just as He is merciful and gracious, so be thou likewise merciful and gracious." [18] There is an obvious difference in emphasis in the two passages. The attainment of holiness may mislead a person into self-deification.[19] In striving for holiness one must, therefore, remember that he is merely a servant, a member of the household, who can only walk in the footsteps of the Divine Master Whose "holiness is superior to yours."[20] The achievement of compassion is less likely to tempt a man to grandiosity, even while aspiring to be merciful like God.

An Amora, Rabbi Hama bar Hanina, derived the principle of *imitatio Dei* from the verse in Deuteronomy: "After the Lord your God ye shall walk" (13:5):

How can man walk after God? Is He not a consuming fire? What is meant is that man ought to walk after the Divine attributes. Just as the Lord clothes the naked, attends the sick, comforts the mourners, and buries the dead, do thou likewise.[21]

That the Lord is a consuming fire (Deut. 4:24) means that He is a righteous judge and by no means will clear the guilty. Rabbi Hama's question apparently intends to exclude the qualities of judgment from the sphere of *imitatio Dei*. Other Midrashim do so explicitly. Thus we read in Tanhuma:[22]

When Moses told the children of Israel: "After the Lord your God ye shall walk," and when again he commanded them to walk in the ways of the Lord, they asked him: "Who can walk in His ways? Is it not written: 'The Lord, in whirlwind and in the storm is His way, and the clouds are the dust of His feet' (Nah. 1:3)? Is it not further written: 'Thy way was in the sea; and Thy path in the great waters, and Thy footsteps were not known' (Ps. 77:20)? Is it not also written: 'A fire devoureth before Him, and round about Him it stormeth mightily' (*ibid.* 50:3)." Moses answered his questioners: "I was not speaking of these ways. His ways are lovingkindness, truth, and the works of charity, as it is written: 'All the paths of the Lord are mercy and truth' (*ibid.* 25:10). The Torah opens with an act of lovingkindness and closes with an act of lovingkindness.[23]. So do you follow after the qualities of God."

These Midrashic passages make it clear that God's stern judgment and wrath are in themselves aspects of His mercy and concern (*"All* the paths of the Lord are mercy and truth"), for only through the exercise of justice can the world be maintained. Nevertheless, the application of retributive justice as the guide for normal, daily behavior is rejected *a priori*. Man cannot follow God Who is a consuming fire. Man cannot emulate the vengeance and anger of the Lord (the fire, the whirlwind, the clouds, and the storm). Four Divine attributes are specifically excluded, by another

Midrash, as norms for human conduct. These are jealousy (Ex. 20:5; Deut. 6:5), vengeance (Deut. 32:35; Is. 63:4; Nah. 1:2; Ps. 94:1), grandeur (Ex. 15:1; Is. 12:5; Ps. 94:1), and circuity (1 Sam. 2:3; Ps. 66:5). Only God knows how to employ these means for beneficent ends. In this vein another Midrash formulates the doctrine of *imitatio Dei*.[25]

"And thou shalt walk in His ways." This passage refers to the ways of Heaven (God). Just as the ways of Heaven are compassion upon the transgressors and restoration to God's favor when they repent, so be you merciful to one another. Just as the ways of Heaven are graciousness and the bestowal of undeserved favors both to those who know Him and to those who do not know Him, so do you bestow kindness upon one another. Just as the ways of Heaven are patience with the wicked and their rehabilitation after repentance, so do you be patient with one another for your welfare's sake, but do not be patient (indifferent) in the presence of each other's troubles. Just as the ways of Heaven are an abundance of mercy and an inclination towards mercy, so do you incline yourselves towards mercy rather than towards vindictiveness.

That the emphasis of *imitatio Dei* should be on the attributes of mercy, patience, and forbearance is implied in the enumeration of the Divine attributes revealed to Moses at Sinai.[26] The "thirteen qualities of mercy,"[27] which throughout the Biblical period,[28] as well as later, served as the source of the "knowledge of God" are heavily weighted towards lovingkindness and compassion. Even the stern pronouncement that the Lord visits "the inquity of the fathers upon the children, and upon the children's children, unto the third and fourth generation"[29] is set up in contrast to the Lord's goodness which "keeps mercy unto the thousandth generation,"[30] thereby establishing a five-hundred-fold preponderance of mercy over justice.[31]

The declaration that the Lord visits the sins of parents upon their children was included by some sages among the attributes of mercy. This visitation was said to mean that if within three generations or four a righteous man will arise from the descendants of a transgressor, the ancestor will be spared in God's judgment.[32] While this interpretation was not universally accepted, the infliction on progeny of the sins of ancestors was, without exception, regarded as limited to those instances where the children follow in the footsteps of their forbears.[33] It goes without saying that this judgment can be executed only by the Divine court and not by human judges.[34] Moreover, this visitation was abrogated by the decree of the prophet Ezekiel.[35]

The statement of the decalogue that the Lord is a jealous God (Ex. 20:5), while taken by some sages in the sense of *stern* and *ruthless* (to those who worship other gods),[36] was purported by others to mean "a Lord of jealousy," a phrase that was interpreted as signifying that He is God and Master over jealousy and not that jealousy has control over Him.[37] Likewise, the passage in Nahum: "The Lord avengeth and is full of wrath" (1:2; literally, "the Lord of wrath") was explained as meaning that God is Master of wrath and not that wrath has mastery over Him.[38] Terms descriptive of God's power and strength are taken as referring to His overwhelming goodness and His suppression of the stern quality of justice.[39] While God does not clear the guilty and allowance must be made in the Divine economy for the administration of justice, yet God never acts tyrannically,[40] autocratically,[41] and certainly not arbitrarily. Retribution is exacted only when there is no other recourse for the governance of the world, where all other possibilities have been exhausted, and when no hope for the future arrests the hand of Divine vengeance.[42] Even then, justice is dispensed without vindictiveness, for "the Lord grieves over the blood of the wicked which is shed."[43]

Justice has to be administered in human society, but only by the properly ordained agencies, upon whom the name of God is called.[44] While no human being or agency can attain Divine omniscience or even Divine compassion,[45] those whose duty it is to stand in judgment over their fellow-men must seek to emulate the Lord in their patience,[46] their search for the "side of merit,"[47] their pity and love,[48] and their sympathy with a human being in suffering even though condemned for a crime.[49]

God is described in the "attributes of mercy" as plenteous in lovingkindness (Ex. 34:6). This lovingkindness is the term that, more than any other, expresses God's essential character and His relationship to the world that He has created. This world is established upon lovingkindness (Ps. 89:3).[50] The world was created by the quality of mercy.[51] All the earth is full of His lovingkindness (*ibid.* 33:5; 119:64). The compassions and the kindnesses of the Lord are from eternity (*ibid.* 25:6) and they endure forever (*ibid.* 136:22 ff.). He conducts the world with lovingkindness and His creatures with mercy,[52] and because His lovingkindness is eternal He renews the work of creation daily.[53] Hence lovingkindness above all is the goal of all human action and by practicing it man becomes like his Creator and fulfills the *imitatio Dei*.[54]

God is also described in the register of attributes as "abundant in truth" (Ex. *ibid.*). God's truthfulness is synonymous with His faithfulness (Deut. 32:4). He is not a man that He should lie; neither the son of man that he should repent (Num. 23:19; 1 Sam. 15:29). The seal of the Lord is truth.[55] As the God of truth He demands truthfulness from human beings (Ex. 23:6; Zech. 8:16). Nevertheless, as the One Who makes peace in His high places (Job. 25:2), He prizes peace above all. He Whose name is Peace[56] has by His own example demonstrated that peace must be given precedence over scrupulousness for exactitude,[57] or even over the reverence due to His own name.[58] God is not like man who repents, yet He repents of the evil which He has decreed (Ex. 32:14; Joel 2:13; Jonah 3:9,10; 4:2). Hence, while a prophecy of peace cannot be rescinded, a prophecy of doom can be nullified (Jer. 28:9).[59] God has indicated by example that man should not permit himself to be bound by oaths or vows made in anger or haste and that disrupt normal human relationships. He has instituted the release from verbal commitments made without due consideration by demonstrating that Divine compassion undoes the judgment decreed in wrath.[60]

That God serves as the ideal pattern of righteousness and goodness provides the sages with a good reason to extol His scrupulous observance of the Law which He gave to His children. Kings of flesh and blood, they tell us, write laws for others, but disregard these laws themselves. The Holy One, however, sets an example of observance.[61] He commanded that one should rise before the hoary head (Lev. 19:32), and He was the first to comply with this law.[62] He teaches men to pray by praying Himself.[63] He puts on the phylacteries.[64] He studies Torah and He teaches little children.[65] God Who is high and exalted is the paragon of humility. His concern is primarily for the lowly and the humble. He is omniscient and omnipotent. Yet He consults with His angels and His prophets. The ascription of humility to God is intended to serve as an example for the rulers and the mighty among men.[66]

The Rabbinic passages which dwell upon the differences between normal human behavior and the conduct of the Holy One, with stress on His humility, His joy in the triumph of His creatures over His measure of judgment, His freedom from vindictiveness, His approachability, and His compassion, are all meant to stimulate human beings to choose the more Godly path.[67] Unlike human rulers who reserve all glory for themselves, the Holy One is eager for His creatures to share the qualities of Divinity, which are their rightful possessions as creatures made in His image, so that they can be like Him. Like God, human beings can attain Godliness, wisdom, love, friendliness, uniqueness (chosenness), right-eousness, and holiness.[68]

III

The attainment of *imitatio Dei* is not merely a pious desideratum. It is an imperative of the Halachah, and as such is embodied in Jewish Law. Thus, in enumerating the positive commandments of the Torah, Maimonides places the commandment to emulate the Almighty to the best of our ability as the eighth in the list.[69] The fact that the second of the treatises of the sage's great Code (the *Mishneh Torah*), which follows the one dealing with the theological principles of Judaism,[70] opens with a for-mulation and an analysis of the *imitatio Dei*[71] testifies to the great significance that he attached to this principle.

The manner in which Maimonides has handled the doctrine of *imitatio Dei* has been subjected to serious criticism.[72] It appears that Maimonides identified *imitatio Dei* with the Aristotelian *doctrine of the mean*.[73] As has correctly been pointed out, the sage's own formulation of *imitatio Dei*: "Just as He is gracious so be thou gracious, just as He is merciful so be thou merciful, just as He is holy so be thou holy"[74] seems to be com-pletely incongruous with the ethical theory of a "golden road" between two vices.[75] Nevertheless, it appears to this writer that a more careful reading of the text will reveal that the *mean* of the Jewish philosopher and the Stagirite are not at all identical. The former, building upon the *imitatio Dei*, recognized the Divine attributes as the basic virtues. Within each of the attributes he discerns two extremes—such as e.g., a maximum of compassion (a totally indiscriminate compassion) and a minimum of compassion (compassion restricted only to the undeniably deserving). Between these two extremes within the confines of the imitable qualities the *mean* is declared to be the proper objective of man's moral strivings,[76] except in the case of humility and patience where the extremes (humility without reservations and total restraint from anger) are the proper norms.[77]

It is noteworthy that among the attributes applied to God which man is to emulate, Maimonides also includes *strength* and *might*. Possibly he had in mind bravery and courage in the struggle against both evil and temptation.[78] None of the commentators of the Code, however, indicate any Rabbinic source for the inclusion of *strength* and *might* in the *imitatio Dei*. It might here be suggested that the preservation and well-being of the physical organism may be implied in these attributes, for the maintenance of the body in good health is the prerequisite for the perfect ethical life,[79] and is thus a propaedeutic to walking in the "ways of God."[80] Moreover, the preservation of bodily health is a corollary of God's mercy and concern for everything that He has created.[81]

In the Halachah, *imitatio Dei* is the source of man's duty to exercise compassion towards the brute creation,[82] towards slaves,[83] towards heretics,[84] and towards idolators.[85]

According to the Halachah, *imitatio Dei* means doing that which is *good in the eyes of the Lord*. Not only must man refrain from doing that which is evil in His sight (Deut. 4:25), he must seek also that which is *right and good* in His eyes (*ibid.* 6:18). In his search he will discover higher goals and ideals that go beyond the normal requirements of the Law.[86] *Going beyond the strict line of duty*[87] man will approach the goal of holiness towards which the people of Israel must strive.[88]

The relationship of Halachah to the concept of *imitatio Dei* seems to be so close that the very word *Halachah* (from the root *haloch*) may be nothing other than the technical term for *walking in the ways of God*, which is *imitatio Dei*.

IV

The doctrine of *imitatio Dei* also plays a very important role in the philosophy of Maimonides as in his Halachah. To him it is the goal of all creation:

> . . .God is the final purpose of everything. Again, it is the aim of everything to become, according to its faculties, similar to God in perfection.[89]

The thirteen attributes revealed by God to Moses represent virtues for all men to follow, but, above all, they apply to the rulers of men.[90] When the ruler is a prophet, he may also employ the Divine attribute of vengeance, which means the administration of retributive justice in human society.[91] All the perfections which man is capable of achieving, including the moral and intellectual, find their fulfillment in the knowledge of God as the source of lovingkindness, justice, and righteousness in the earth:

> The perfection in which man can truly glory is attained by him when he has acquired—as far as this is possible for man—the knowledge of God, the knowledge of His providence, and of the manner in which it influences His creatures in their production and continued existence. Having acquired this knowledge he will then be determined always to seek lovingkindness, justice, and righteousness, and thus to imitate the ways of God.[92]

In the Kabbalah, *imitatio Dei* occupies a central position. Since even the physical organism of man, according to the mystical teachings, reflects the *Sefiroth*, the diverse channels of Divine grace, through whose irradiations everything was created and is maintained, and as the organism is the embodiment of their spiritual potencies, the sanctification of the entire personality, spiritual, intellectual, and physical, including every phase of one's life and every limb of one's body, constitutes the true meaning of *imitatio Dei*. It is, of course, not the *En-Sof* (God as the limitless and unrevealed) Who is the object of imitation, but the *Sefiroth* (just as in the Bible it is the "ways" and the "paths" which are imitated, and in the Rabbinic and philosophic literature, it is the "measures," the "qualities" [*middoth*], and the "attributes"). By implementing, in all aspects of his life, the total implication of his spiritual powers and moral qualities, man's life becomes not only Godlike, but man thereby truly enhances the life of the *Sefiroth* with whom his own is inextricably bound, and he activates and enriches their life-giving and beneficent powers.[93]

The outstanding work of Kabbalistic ethics, *Tomer Deborah*, of Rabbi Moses Cordovero of Safed (16th century), is based upon the final verse of Micah in which the thirteen attributes of mercy are embodied:

> Who is a God like unto Thee, that pardoneth iniquity and passeth over the transgression of the remnant of his heritage? He retaineth not His anger forever, because He delighteth in lovingkindness; He will again have compassion upon us. He will suppress our iniquities; yea, Thou wilt cast all their sins into the depths of the sea. Thou wilt show truth unto Jacob, lovingkindness unto Abraham, as Thou hast sworn to our fathers in the days of old (7:18).

The unfoldment of the meaning of each of the attributes and their application to human life result in a work which "both in its clearness and loftiness of conception is beyond doubt the most outstanding system of mystic ethics ever formulated in any language," to quote the evaluation of a late Jewish mystic.[94]

No summary can do justice to any book, much less a book of the nobility and beauty of *Tomer Deborah*. An inkling of its contents can, however, be gained from the following resume by the great Anglo-Jewish scholar, Israel Abrahams:[95]

> Thus, man must bear insult; must be limitless in love, finding in all men the objects of his deep and inalienable affection; he must overlook wrongs done to him, and never forget a kindness. Cordovero insists again and again on this Divine patience and forbearance, on God's passing over man's many sins and on his recognition of man's occasional virtues. So must man act. And he must temper his justice with mercy, must be peculiarly tender to the unworthy. His whole being must be attuned to God's being. His earthly eye must be opened to the good in all men, as is the Heavenly eye; his earthly ear must be deaf to the slanderers and the foul, just as the Heavenly ear is receptive only of the good. For God loves all men, whom He made in His very image, and how shall man hate where God loves.

V

In the light of the preceding it is evident that *imitatio Dei* (or more precisely, *imitatio viarum Dei*) is not merely a genuine, but a central, doctrine of Judaism. One modern Jewish thinker, Professor Leon Roth, in a lecture delivered at the Hebrew University in 1931,[96] has attempted to deny *imitatio Dei* a place in Jewish religion and thought. Roth argues that Judaism could not possibly teach this doctrine for three reasons: (1) The ideal of holiness as a Divine attribute which we are asked to emulate has a completely negative character, since it signifies the total separation from everything lowly and ignoble.[97] (2) How can man imitate God Who is transcendent, indescribable, and devoid of any form? (3) We are exhorted to imitate only certain attributes of God, not all of them, the implication being, Roth maintains, that it is not the concept of imitation as such which is the decisive factor.[98]

These arguments may be countered as follows: (1) Even if holiness were only of a negative character, the abstention of man from everything that is unworthy and ungodly would still be *imitatio Dei*. (2) God as He is in His sublime and transcendent majesty is indescribable, but the Bible does constantly refer to His attributes. The Jewish *imitatio Dei* is not an imitation of God Himself but of the virtues by which His relationship to the world and His activity are described. (3) It *is* the imitation of God's way that is Israel's religious and ethical ideal; however, the criterion whereby we determine which of the attributes are to serve as models for man's conduct is man's ability to follow them wisely and constructively. The exercise of jealousy and wrath by man is exceedingly hazardous and can be entrusted only to the properly ordained agencies who are fully aware of human limitations and will exercise their powers with extreme care and scrupulousness. Only those who, like God, in wrath remember compassion (Hab. 3:2), can be entrusted with the dispensation of justice.

VI

Most interestingly, the doctrine of *imitatio Dei* is also found in Plato, Aristotle, and the Stoic philosophers. Thus we read in Plato's *Thaeatetus*[99] the words of Socrates:

> Evils, Theodorus, can never pass away; for there must always remain something which is antagonistic to good. Having no place among the gods in heaven, of necessity they hover around the mortal nature, and this earthly sphere. Wherefore we ought to fly away from earth to heaven as quickly as we can; and to fly away is to become like God, as far as this is possible; and to become like Him, is to become holy, just, and wise. . . Whereas the truth is that God is never in any way unrighteous—He is the perfect righteousness;[100] and he of us who is most righteous is most like Him.

This noble passage is duplicated in the Laws (IV, 717), in the words of the Athenian:

> Then what life is agreeable to God, and becoming in all His followers? One only, expressed once for all in the old saying that "like agrees with like, with measure measure" . . . Now God ought to be the measure of all things, and not man . . . and he who would be dear to God must, as far as is possible, be like Him and such as He is. Wherefore the temperate man is the friend of God, for he is like Him; and the intemperate man is unlike Him, and different from Him.

In these passages Plato has reached the peak of his philosophy.

Aristotle likewise operates with the concept of *imitatio Dei.* Thus he says in his *Nicomachean Ethics:*[101]

> But such a life [self-sufficiency, leisureliness, unweariedness] would be too high for man; for it is not insofar as he is man that he will live so, but insofar as something Divine is present in him; and by so much as this is superior to our composite nature is its activity superior to that which is the exercise of the other kind of virtue. If reason is Divine, then, in comparison with man, this life according to it is Divine in comparison with human life. But we must not follow those who advise us, being men, to think of human things, and, being mortal, of mortal things, but must, as far as we can, make ourselves immortal, and strain every nerve to live in accordance with the best thing in us; for even if it be small in bulk, much more does it in power and worth surpass everything.

Aristotle further states:

> But that perfect happiness is a contemplative activity will appear from the following consideration as well. We assume the gods to be above all other beings blessed and happy; but what sort of action must we assign to them? Acts of justice? Will not the gods seem absurd if they make contracts and return deposits, and so on? Acts of a brave man, then, confronting dangers and running risks because it is noble to do so? Or liberal acts? To whom will they give? It will be strange if they are really to have money or anything of the kind. And what would their temperate acts be? Is not such praise tasteless since they have no bad appetites?[102] If we were to run through them all, the circumstances of action would be found trivial and unworthy of gods. Still everyone supposes that they live and therefore that they are active; we cannot suppose them to sleep like Endymion. Now if you take away from a living being action, and still more production, what is left but contemplation? Therefore the activity of God, which surpasses all others in blessedness, must be contemplative; and of human activities, therefore, that which is most akin to this must be most of the nature of happiness. . . For if the gods have any care for human affairs, as they are thought to have, it would be reasonable both that they should delight in that which was best and most akin to them (i.e. reason) and that they should reward those who love and honor this most, as caring for the things that are dear to them and acting both rightly and nobly. And that all these attributes belong most of all to the philosopher is manifest. He therefore is dearest to the gods.[103]

Without doubt, the *imitatio Dei* of Plato is much closer to the outlook of Judaism than that of Aristotle. To Plato being like God means, in words that are so strangely reminiscent of the Bible and the Rabbinic sources, to become holy, just, and wise like God in Whom there is no unrighteousness.[104] Aristotle's conception of passivity, leisureliness, and contemplation as the embodiment of Godlikeness has little in common with the historic Jewish ideal. Contemplation and study, at least in this life, are the major instruments, according to Judaism, for the attainment of a knowledge of God and the discovery of His will whereby man is enabled to implement the *imitatio Dei* in his life in its abundant richness. A life of contemplation alone, without fulfillment in action and holy conduct, is not *imitatio Dei*.[105] Aristotle's inability to associate God with acts of justice is, of course, altogether incomprehensible to a Jew.[106] Nevertheless, it appears that even Plato's *imitatio Dei*, in addition to the fact that it never emanates as an imperative to man from God Himself to walk in His ways, is heavily tinged with otherworldliness ("wherefore we ought to fly away from earth to heaven as quickly as we can; and to fly away is to become like God"). The grandeur of Plato's vision transcends our earthly life. The fulfillment of his *imitatio Dei* belongs to another realm of existence, for our own earth must forever remain unredeemed ("evil can never pass away"). The *imitatio Dei* of Judaism is to be fulfilled in this world and in this life, for God is on earth as He is in heaven.

The closest approximation to the Jewish conception of *imitatio Dei* in the Greek world that this writer has been able to find is in Epictetus. This gentle Stoic writes thus:

> The next thing is to learn what is the nature of the gods; for such as they are discovered to be, he, who would please and obey them, must try with all his power to be like them. If the Divine is faithful, man also must be faithful; if it is free, man also must be free; if beneficent, man also must be beneficent; if magnanimous, man also must be magnanimous; as being then an imitator of God, he must do and say everything consistently with this fact.[107]

VIII

It has been suggested that the Platonic *imitatio Dei* was derived from the teachings of Pythagoras, one of whose precepts was: "Follow God."[108] While this phrase is identical with the Biblical "walking after God," it is noteworthy that the Scriptures do not use this expression prior to the Sinaitic Revelation. The accounts of the lives of the antediluvians and the patriarchs of Israel use the expression "to walk with God" and "to walk before God."[109] Neither of these phrases explicitly refers to the imitation of God or His ways. "To walk with God" implies a close companionship with Him (and the reflexive form *mithalech* perhaps indicates the intense efforts exerted to achieve this goal), such as may have led its subject to try to sever ties with earthly existence in the manner described by Plato.[110] "To walk before God" may denote either walking before Him to be scrutinized or to herald His coming.[111] Those who walk before the Lord serve by their lives as an exemplar of the Divine attributes before the attributes are revealed. When God made His attributes known, the commandment to "walk after the Lord" became an exhortation to *imitatio Dei*.[112] The Divine promise that God will walk in the midst of Israel so that He will be a God unto them and they a people unto Him (Lev. 26:12) may mean just this, that God will once again reveal His attributes to Israel in all their resplendent glory, so that Israel will truly be His people who embody in their collective and individual lives the exalted ideals of *imitatio Dei*.

It is quite apparent that the Pythagorean admonition to "follow God" had a high ethical connotation and was undoubtedly a survival of the pristine religious traditions of the very ancient schools of thought known to our sages as the "Academies of Shem and Eber."[113] "Walking with God" which appears in Hinduism may likewise be a vestige of these ancient, pre-Sinaitic teachings. The preachments of Buddha concerning the inanity of existence and the striving of bliss through Nirvana (a doctrine which is basically refined Hinduism) may hark back to the extreme views of the ancient sages represented by the Biblical Enoch.[114] These early doctrines had become corrupted by the substitution of *deification* for *imitatio Dei*. Instead of striving to be like God by walking in His ways, men sought to become gods. The sin of Adam became the rule of the day. Against this self-deification of kings, rulers, and nobles the sages and prophets of Israel fought. In Plato's dialogues, the doctrine of *imitatio Dei*, in the wake of the Pythagoreans, once more approximates that of the ancient monotheistic teachers. In Aristotle there is a straying from it. In Epictetus (except for the polytheistic phraseology which very likely is only stylistic), the Jewish and the Stoic *imitatio Dei* become identical.

The Alexandrian Jewish philosopher, Philo, who recognized the great importance of the Biblical *imitatio Dei*, and refers to it in a number of passages,[115] also alludes to Plato's doctrine as expounded in the *Thaeatetus* and comments on it with admiration.[116] Perhaps Philo's eagerness to create a synthesis between Moses and Plato made him fail to see the very significant distinction between the *imitatio Dei* of one and that of the other.

At this juncture, this writer would venture the recrudescence of a theory believed in strongly by the Jewish-Hellenistic writers as well as by the medieval Jewish scholars,[117] and perhaps also intimated in the Talmud,[118] to the effect that the Greek philosophers were subject to Hebraic influences. This theory has long been discarded as untenable, even fantastic and ludicrous. Surprisingly, Biblical evidence in support of this conjecture has never been brought forward. But the Scriptures do speak of Judean captives being sold into slavery in Ionia.[119] The prophet refers to refugees who will find their way to the islands of Greece and there spread the word of God and speak of His glory.[120] There appears to have been some contact between Israel and Crete.[121] It is hardly likely that the Greeks would not have some knowledge about the Israelites through information gathered from the Phoenicians, or perhaps even from the Philistines, who were Israel's neighbors. Is it at all possible that Israelites or Judeans were found in the Aegean area without exerting some influence or exciting some interest? Perhaps the study of the relationship of Israel and Greece ought to be opened anew.[122]

It has been indicated that Buddhism also developed a doctrine of *imitatio Buddhae*.[123] While there is great emphasis in Buddhism on compassion, and *imitatio Buddhae* undoubtedly entails great compassion on all creatures, nevertheless, the doctrine of *imitatio Buddhae* has a different meaning from *imitatio Dei* of Judaism. The former is closer to the pagan concept of apotheosis, insofar as striving for Buddhahood, which is the ideal of Buddhism, means more than imitating the attributes and virtues of Buddha. It imports striving to be a Buddha—which means, the attainment of Nirvana or complete enlightenment. Every human being is destined to overcome his individual self and become a Buddha (again, another version of the Hindu reabsorption into Brahman). "Look within; thou art Buddha."[124] Imitation of Buddha is thus not a way of being like Buddha, but of becoming a Buddha. Moreover, as suggested above in connection with Plato, Buddhism, not being a religion of obligation, but a system whereby one voluntarily or fatefully seeks liberation from Karma and its effects, does not make its ethical principles mandatory, since they do not flow from a lawgiver.

In Christianity the central figure, of course, is Jesus of Nazareth, and it is his life that serves as a model for emulation. In the classic work of Christian piety, *Imitatio Christi*, the emphasis is upon the passion of Jesus and the faithful's glorying in tribulation (II, 6), and bearing the Cross (*ibid.* 11, 12). "He went before thee bearing his cross and died for thee upon the cross, that thou also mayest bear thy cross and mayest love to be crucified upon it" (ibid. 12).[125] While the search for pain of body and tribulation of spirit as a medium for salvation may sometimes be awe-inspiring, and may at times even be necessary for the purification of the soul,[126] the judgment of the Jewish people—which has, as a people suffered more than any other, and whose register of saints and martyrs exceeds that of any faith on earth—is that suffering as an established mode of the religious life is contrary to the will of God,[127] that self-mortification as a spiritual goal, except for special disciplinary purposes, is debasing and brutalizing,[128] and that man may reach God through joy rather than through self-inflicted pain and sadness.[129] The imitatio Dei of Judaism and the imitatio Christi of Thomas a Kempis have little in common.

Because the religious and ethical ideal of Judaism is grounded on God Whose perfection cannot be emulated, and Whose attributes can only be adumbrated in human life, it presents us with an everlasting goal which man must endeavor to reach, but which he can never fully attain. A religion based on imitatio Dei can never remain ethically static. It aspires towards greater and nobler goals of love, compassion, and holiness.[130] It constantly strives heavenward. It seeks nothing less than the establishment of the Heavenly Kingdom upon earth. More than any other faith Judaism has succeeded in teaching a doctrine of Godlikeness which affirms the value of all existence, in its manifold and variegated forms, transfigured and sanctified by man created in the image of God who lives by the light of the attributes of the Holy One, Blessed Be He.

Notes

1. The Hebrew word tzelem is derived from tzel ("shadow"). Cf. Mandelkern's Concordance, s.v. tzelem. See, however, the Lexicon of Gesenius-Brown (Oxford, 1959), where tzelem is derived from a root meaning "to cut out." Cf. also Commentary of Samson Raphael Hirsch to Gen. 1:26 who derives the word from salmah, meaning an external frame or cover.

2. See Mahsheboth Harutz by Rabbi Tzadok ha-Kohen of Lublin, No. 1.

3. Cf. Reinhold Niebuhr, The Nature and Destiny of Man, passim and his other works.

4. The attempt to relate the imitatio Dei of Judaism to pagan notions, as is done by Israel Abrahams (Pharisaism and the Gospels, II, pp. 138-139), appears to this writer to be

misleading. The imitation of the ways of God is the very antithesis of man's striving to be God. The first is man's greatest virtue, the second his greatest blasphemy. See the direct contrast in Ex. Rabbah 8:1-2: God shares His greatness with man; but there have been men who, because they have been divinely endowed with great gifts, proclaimed themselves God! It is just as likely that man's striving to become God is a distortion of the *imitatio Dei* which enjoins man to follow in the ways of God as that *imitatio Dei* is an emergent of the former. See also below, sections VI and VII.

5. Cf. Tanhuma, Mishpatim 16.

6. Ex. 21:6 (cf. Mechilta); cf. Ps. 82 (see Midrash Tehillim, Rashi, and other commentators *ad locum*).

7. Gen. 18:25. God reveals His intentions towards Sodom and Gomorrah to Abraham because Abraham was destined to be a teacher of righteousness and justice to his descendants and followers (*ibid.* 18:19). Any departure from the perfect standard will therefore vitiate Abraham's effectiveness as a teacher. Cf. Nahmanides to Gen. 18:18, who sees in the "way of God" of verse 19 a reference to *imitatio Dei*.

8. Cf. Sheeltoth, quoted in Tanhuma, Bereshith, 2.

9. Ex. 13:14-15. Cf. also Ex. Rabbah 15:12 in reference to the Paschal sacrifice.

10. Ex. 22:30 (cf. Mechilta); Lev. 11:44; 20:26; Deut. 14:2,21. Cf. *Yisrael Kedoshim* by Rabbi Tzadok ha-Kohen of Lublin, No. 1.

11. The festivals are occasions of bringing joy to the orphan, widow, stranger, and Levite. See Deut. 16:11.

12. Gen. 18:18; see, however, above, note 7. Cf. also Ex. 18:20: "And thou shalt show them the way wherein they must walk." Also *ibid.* 32:8; Deut. 9:12; Jer. 7:22. The "way" here is definitely the way pointed out by God. See, however, Baba Metzia 30b and Targum Jonathan to Ex. 18:20 which seem to interpret this "way" as referring to *imitatio Dei*. Cf. Rabbi Samuel Edels (Maharsha), Baba Metzia, *ibid.* See also the two Mechiltas *ad locum*.

13. Deut. 26:17; *et passim*.

14. Cf. 2 Chr. 17:3; 22:3; *et passim*. It should be noted that while the Book of Kings always uses the singular (*derech*), e.g. 1 Kings 15:26,34, the Book of Chronicles uses the singular and plural interchangeably; see 2 Chr. 11:17. It appears that the Chronicler understood the singular as likewise signifying "following an example." Cf. Deut. 32:4: "For all His ways are justice"; Hosea 14:10: "For righteous are the ways of the Lord." Perhaps the conjunction *ekeb* used in Gen. 26:5, and Deut. 7:12 is also to be understood as "walking in the footsteps of God," which is *imitatio Dei*. Cf. S. Kierkegaard, *Training in Christianity*, p. 32, on "footsteps."

15. Ex. 34:6-7. On the visitation of the sins of the fathers upon their children, see below, section II.

16. Ps. 103:9; cf. Kaminka, *Mehkarim*, I, 124-129. The last phrase: "He will not always contend, neither will He Keep His anger forever," appears to be a commentary on the passage which speaks of the visitation of the sins of fathers upon their children unto the third and fourth generation. The Psalmist tells us that this means *only* to the third and fourth generation. This fact is an indication that He does not contend forever. See below.

17. Sifra, Lev. 19:2. The verb *mehakeh* is generally translated "to imitate." See Hullin II, 9 (40b). It would be more meaningful from the standpoint of the Hebrew to translate *mehakeh* as "enclosed within the limits set." Cf. Job 13:27. See also Nahmanides to Gen. 26:5 who takes the noun *hukkah* (generally translated as "statute") to refer to *imitatio Dei*. See the note of Rabbi Charles B. Chavel in his edition of Nahmanides' Commentary to the Pentateuch (Jerusalem 5719), p. 151. How Nahmanides applies this concept to the suprarational commandments known as *hukkim* is not made clear by the great sage. See, however, above, note 10. The function of sanctification applies to the *hukkim* as well.

18. Mechilta and Mechilta de-Rabbi Simeon ben Johai *ad locum;* Shabbath 133b. The attempt by M. Friedmann, quoted with approval by Abrahams, *op. cit.,* 174-5, to create a dispute between Abba Saul and R. Ishmael on the basis of an impossible reading in the Yalkut, is without grounds. R. Ishmael takes *ve-anvehu* in its literal sense and simply asks how one can beautify God. But there is no dispute as to the validity of the concept of *imitatio Dei.*

19. See above, notes 2 and 3. Rabbi Tzadok ha-Kohen attributes the grandiosity which contributed to the fall of Jesus and Shabbetai Zebi to their extreme asceticism whereby they were deluded into believing that they had attained a degree of sanctity equivalent to that of God Himself. See work cited in note 2.

20. Lev. Rabbah 24:9.

21. Sotah 14a. That God performs these services is proved from Gen. 3:21; 18:1; 25:11; Deut. 34:6. Rabbi Hama is very likely citing an ancient *Boraita.*

22. Va-Yishlah, 10.

23. Gen. 3:21; Deut. 34:6.

24. Midrash ha-Gadol (ed. Schechter), Gen. Chap. 37, Va-Yesheb; cf. S. Schechter, *Aspects of Rabbinic Theology,* pp. 204-5.

25. Tanna debe-Eliyahu (ed. Friedman), p. 135. Cf. *ibid.,* p. 65. Cf. Midrash Shir ha-Shirim Zuta 1,15..

26. Ex. 34:6-7.

27. Pesikta Rabbati, 16; Nu. Rabbah 21:16. On the importance of the "thirteen attributes of mercy" in Jewish liturgy see Rosh ha-Shanah 17b. The "thirteen attributes" are a very important component of the liturgy of the High Holy Days from the Selihot to Neilah. In some rituals they are recited twice every day when Tahanun is read. As pointed out by R. Jacob Reischer in his commentary to the En-Yaakob, Rosh ha-Shanah, *ibid.,* the importance of the recital of the attributes is that they inspire us to live by them. See also Etz-Yoseph to En-Yaakob, *ibid.,* in the name of R. Moses Alshech.

28. See Z. Jawitz, *Toledoth Yisrael,* Appendix to Vol. I.

29. Ex. *ibid.,* 7.

30. *Ibid.* On the enumeration of the attributes see Tosafoth to Rosh ha-Shanah 17b, and Asheri, *ibid.* See also Meiri, *ibid.,* on whether the visitation of the sins of fathers upon children should be included (ed. Sofer, p. 43).

31. Tosephta Sotah IV, 1. Cf. G. F. Moore, *Judaism,* I, 393 ff.

32. Mishnath Rabbi Eliezer (ed. Enelow) p. 95; Midrash Hashkem cited in M. Kasher, *Torah Shelemah,* to Ex. 20:5 (Vol. XVI, pp.44-5).

33. Berachoth 7a.

34. See Sanhedrin 27b; cf. Novellae of Rabbi Nissim (Ran) *ad locum.* The case discussed in Jebamoth 79a, in allusion to 2 Sam, 21:6, is apparently regarded as a case of punishment by the hand of heaven, since the sentence was not executed, only acquiesced in, by the courts of Israel. The exclusion of the Gibeonites from the right to marry Israelites, as a result of their cruelty to the grandchildren of Saul, demonstrates the revulsion with which this act of transfer of guilt to children was regarded. David acquiesced only because the sanctification of God's name was involved, as a failure to yield to their demands would have meant to them that Israel's God has no concern for strangers (see Jebamoth, *ibid.*).

35. Makkoth 24a. The statement in Ezekiel referred to is 18:4: "The soul that sinneth it shall die." Very likely the declaration concerning Ezekiel's abrogation signifies that the visitation of sins unto the fourth generation is not an attribute that describes the eternal relationship of God with men. This measure applied only under certain conditions in the history of the human race. In Ezekiel's time it was no longer warranted. (Cf. similarly Jer. Tal. Sotah VII, 5; Sanhedrin 43b). According to R. Jacob Reischer (in his commentary to

En-Yaakob to Makkoth), the punishment of little children, at the hand of God, for the sins of their parents (see Maim. Teshubah 6,1; Sifre to Deut. 24:16; Rashi, *ibid.*) was repealed by Ezekiel. That decrees of doom in general are abrogable, see below, note 59. See also the comments of R. Samuel Edels (Maharsha), to Makkoth, *ibid.*

36. Mechilta de-Rabbi Simeon ben Johai to Ex. 20:5.

37. Mechilta, *ibid.*

38. Gen. Rabbah 49:8.

39. Sifre to Nu. 27:12; Rashi to Deut. 3:23.

40. Abodah Zarah 3a.

41. Rashi to Gen. 1:26; 11:7.

42. Baba Kamma 38b; see Gen. 15:16; Sotah 9a.

43. Sanhedrin 46a.

44. See above, note 6. Cases involving compulsion, penalties, corporal and capital punishment require a court whose members are ordained judges (*musmachim*) who are known as *Elohim* (God). See Gittin 88b; Sanhedrin, first chapter.

45. Sanhedrin 39b; cf. Pesikta Rabbati (ed. Friedmann), 195-6; *et passim.*

46. Aboth I, 1.

47. Sanhedrin 32 ff.

48. *Ibid.*, 45a. The commandment of love (Lev. 19:18) applies even to the criminal. See also Sanhedrin 36b, and Maimonides, Sanhedrin 2:3.

49. Sanhedrin 63a.

50. That *olam* in this verse may mean "world" is accepted by our sages (see Sanhedrin 58b; Targ. Jon.). H. P. Chajes in his critical commentary (*Beur Madai*, ed. A. Kahana) gives preference to this interpretation. Cf. Ps. 66:7, and comment of Chajes.

51. Mechilta to Ex. 22:26; *et passim.*

52. Nishmath of Sabbath Service; cf. Birchat ha-Mazon, first benediction.

53. Daily Prayer Book, Morning Service.

54. See above, section I. The king's throne likewise is established in lovingkindness (Is. 16:5; Prov. 20:28). Cf. Maim., Melachim 2:6 on the king's duty to be gracious and merciful, as well as humble and long-suffering. See also Maim. Teshubah 3:13; Sanhedrin 92a; Zohar II, 21b. Cf. below, section IV.

55. Sanhedrin 64a.

56. Jud. 6:24; Shabbath 10b.

57. Jebamoth 65b.

58. Sukkah 53b.

59. See Maim., Yesodei ha-Torah 10:4. On the problem of Jer. 18:9-10, see Kimhi *ad locum* and comment of R. Jacob Emden in notes to Maim., Intro. to Commentary on the Mishna. However, the contradiction is only apparent. The prophet in Jer. 13:7 ff. is referring not to a prophetic pronouncement, but to God's plans prior to their publication. Such plans represent possibilities, not final decrees.

60. Hagigah 10a; Sanhedrin 110b. See, however, Rosh ha-Shanah 18a on the decree accompanied by an oath.

61. Jer. Tal. Rosh ha-Shanah I, 3.

62. *Ibid.*

63. Berachoth 7a.

64. *Ibid.*, 6a.

65. Abodah Zarah 3b. These imaginative and seemingly fantastic representations of God's activities are, of course, not to be taken literally, and have a profound religious and ethical meaning. See Otzar ha-Geonim (ed. B. M. Levin) to Berachoth *ad locum*, and the commentaries to the En-Yaakob. Cf. also H. Zeitlin, *Be-Fardes ha-Hassiduth ve-ha-*

Kabbala, Tel-Aviv 1960, p. 98. They are, nevertheless, rendered in such a way as to serve the interests of *imitatio Dei* as well. The statement of A. Cohen, quoted in *Pharisaism and the Gospels*, II, 171, requires modification on this account. S. Schechter's statement in *Aspects of Rabbinic Theology*, p. 37 (also quoted by Abrahams, *op. cit.* p. 172), that "a great number of Scriptural passages, when considered in the light of Rabbinic interpretation, represent nothing else but a record of a sort of *imitatio hominis* on the part of God" should be qualified. It is, after all, not man who is being imitated by God, but admirable virtues are ascribed to God, Who is thus represented as their source and exemplar. An *imitatio hominis* would hardly offer an idealized representation of God's activities, from the viewpoint of the Rabbis.

66. Sanhedrin 38b; Gen. 18:17; Am. 3:7; Megillah 31a; cf. above, note 41. Cf. also Hermann Cohen's *Religion der Vernunft*, 494 ff. On Cohen's conception of *imitatio Dei* as *Vereiferung* (emulation) rather than as *Nachahmung* (imitation), see op. cit. p. 188, also p. 109 ff. See also J. B. Agus, *Modern Philosophies of Judaism*, p. 104, and p. 363 ff. on the difficulties of Cohen's theory of the attributes.

67. Shabbath 127a; Erubin 19a; Pesahim 119a; Yoma 75a; Baba Bathra 10a, 88b; cf. Mishnath Rabbi Eliezer (ed. Enelow) pp. 205-221; see *op. cit.* note to line 12 ff. for other references. Cf. Yoma 86b and *Tosafoth Yom ha-Kippurim* (by R. Moses Ibn Habib), *ibid.*

68. Tanhuma, Kedoshim, 5; Ex. Rabbah 8:1; Nu. Rabbah 14:3; 15:13. See also A. Marmorstein, *Studies in Jewish Theology*, p. 116, on the concept of man's partnership with God in the Aggada as a derivative of *imitatio Dei*.

69. Sefer ha-Mitzvoth, 8. All codes list *imitatio Dei* as a positive commandment: *Hinuch* (ed. C.B. Chavel, p. 726ff.); *Yeraim* (Comm. 3); *Semag* (Pos Comm. 6), etc.

70. Hilchoth Yesodei ha-Torah.

71. Mishneh Torah, Deoth 1.

72. M. Lazarus, *Ethik des Judenthums*, 386 ff. See also the more recent study of S. Rawidowicz in the *Mordecai M. Kaplan Jubilee Volume* (Hebrew), p. 205 ff., esp. 235-6.

73. Deoth 1:4; see *Nicomachean Ethics*, 1107a. The references to Aristotle in this paper are from Richard McKeon, *The Basic Works of Aristotle*.

74. Deoth 1:6.

75. M. Lazarus, *op. cit.* Aristotle, however, is aware of godlike virtue (*Nic. Eth.* VII, 1145b).

76. Deoth 1:5.

77. *Ibid.* 2:3.

78. *Ibid.* 1:6; cf. Jos. 1:6; cf. Yesodei ha-Torah 7:1 and Aboth 4:1.

79. Deoth 4:1.

80. *Ibid.*; Yesodei ha-Torah, *ibid.*

81. Cf. Taanith 11a-b; 22b; *et passim.*

82. Baba Metzia 85a, based on Ps. 145:9: "The Lord is good to all; and His tender mercies are over all His works." See also notes of *Hatham Sofer* to Baba Metzia 32b. The disputation found in the Talmud as to whether *tzaar baale-hayim* (the suffering of animals) is proscribed Biblically or Rabbinically (Baba Metzia, *ibid.*) can refer only to a specific prohibition. The general principle of *imitatio Dei*, of course, always applies, except when human interests must take precedence. On this aspect of *de-oraitha* and *de-rabbanan* see my work *Midrash David*, p. 218.

83. See Maim., Abadim, end. Cf. Gittin 12a.

84. Berachoth 7a. On the duty of dealing even with transgressors beyond the strict measure of justice, see Targum Jonathan to Ex. 18:20.

85. Maim., Melachim 10:12. While the strict letter of the law may demand that kindness be not extended to those who violate the seven commandments of the children of Noah and

who themselves are far from mercy (Maim., Abodah Zarah 10:1), yet the law of imitatio Dei which demands the welfare of all creatures as a Biblical principle (Gittin 59b; Maim. Megilah 4:14) necessarily supersedes the discriminatory law, and renders it purely theoretical, in the same manner as the Divine measure of mercy suppresses the stern measure of justice (above, note 39). Cf. R. A. I. Kook, Igroth Hareiyah, I, 305.

86. Baba Metzia 108a; Nahmanides to Deut. 6:18; Maggid Mishneh to Maim., Schechenim, end.

87. Baba Metzia 35a.

88. Nahmanides to Lev. 19:2.

89. Guide to the Perplexed (tr. M. Friedlander) I, 69.

90. Ibid. I, 54.

91. Ibid. The right of the king to punish rebels is derived from Jos. 1:18. See Sanhedrin 49a, Maim., Melachim 3:8. It appears from the passage cited in the Guide that only a king who is a prophet can exercise this prerogative. Nevertheless, the condition of prophecy in a king is not specifically stated in the Mishneh Torah. See Friedlander's note to his translation, I, p. 196. On the quality of mercy in a king see above, note 54. Cf. also Hinuch (ed. Chavel), p. 632. On the reputation of the kings of Israel as merciful kings, see 1 Kings 20:31. See also Ez. 34.

92. Guide III, 54.

93. See R. Isaiah Horowitz, Schne Luhoth ha-Berith, 384b (ed. Amsterdam); et passim. Abrahams' statement (op. cit., p. 170) that in the Kabbalah imitatio is of God Himself is altogether incorrect.

94. Raphael Ben Zion (Rabbi Jacob Cohn), The Way of the Faithful, 1945, pp. 12-13. The late Jacob Cohn translated the Tomer Deborah into English. While this is being written, there has appeared an announcement that a new translation of this work by Dr. Louis Jacobs of London has been published.

95. Op. cit., 145.

96. Ha-Hidamuth la-El ve-Raayon ha-Kedusha, A memorial lecture in honor of Ahad ha-Am, Jerusalem 5691.

97. The concept of holiness will be discussed separately.

98. See above, Notes 44-49.

99. P. 176. The quotations are from Jowett's translation. M. Buber, in Israel and the World, p. 68 [See Kellner, p. 154], makes the following statement: "However 'insensuous' Platonism, especially later Platonism, thought to make its god, it cannot pry him loose from the sensuous world of Phidias, wherein form and shape are brought to perfection. The exemplary character of the god, the god in his character as a model to be imitated, remains founded on his figurative character, his character as a plastic representation of the desired. The Greek can only imitate the wish that he himself has given a visible form." How this judgment applies to Plato, Aristotle, or Plotinus, I am unable to see.

100. Cf. Ps. 92:16, based on Deut. 32:4.

101. 1177b.

102. Cf. Shabbath 89a what is said about the angels who demanded the Torah for themselves.

103. Nic. Eth. 1178b. Plotinus' conception of imitatio Dei (Ennead I, Tractate 2) is much closer to that of Aristotle than to that of Plato.

104. The striving to be wise like God is strangely nowhere, to my knowledge, included, in Jewish sources, among the virtues of God to be emulated. Perhaps because the true wisdom of man, Biblically speaking, is the knowledge of God which leads to imitatio Dei (see above, end of Section I. Cf. Deut. 4:6). While God inspires man with wisdom (Gen. 31:39; Ex. 31:3; Is. 11:2), yet the true wisdom of God is forever closed to man (Job 28).

Perhaps the meaning of Gen. 2:17 consists just in this, that man sought to be like God by attempting to appropriate for himself that wisdom which is not his and to which he can never have access. Man's life is shortened (Gen. 3:22) so that he will not devote himself to the fulfillment of a vain ambition.

105. See Abodah Zarah 17b. On Maimonides' view, see my article in *Hadoar*, Vol. XXXVI, 38; cf. also S. B. Auerbach, *Ammude ha-Mahshabah ha-Yisrealith* II, 178ff. On this problem in medieval philosophy see A. O. Lovejoy, *The Great Chain of Being*, p. 82 ff.

106. On Maimonides' view, see *Guide* III, 17 ff.

107. *Discourses of Epictetus* (tr. George Long), Book II, 14. Cf. M. Aurelius, *Meditations X*, 8. See also Plato's *Phaedrus*, 248.

108. Quoted by J. Burnet in *Encyclopedia of Religion and Ethics* X, 526 (also quoted by Abrahams, *op. cit.* p. 155; M. Buber, *Israel and the World*, p. 66 [See Kellner, p. 152]). Cf. M. Aurelius, *op. cit.* VII, 31: "Love mankind—follow God."

109. Gen. 5:24; 6:9; 17:1; 48:15. Enoch and Noah walk *with* God. The patriarchs walk *before* Him.

110. See commentary of S. R. Hirsch to Gen. 5:24. Perhaps for this reason the locution "walking *with* God" is not applied to Israel's patriarchs.

111. Gen. Rabbah 30:10.

112. The phrase "to walk *after* God" is also found in later writings, e.g., 2 Kings 20:3; Ps. 116:9. "To walk *with* God" is not found again.

113. Gen. Rabbah 63:6.

114. In *Hinduism and Buddhism* by Coomaraswamy, p. 65 and p. 75, note 163, there is reference made to *brahmacariya* ("walking with God"). In the *Khandogya Upanishad* (*Sacred Books of the East*, ed. Mueller, Vol. XV, 1884, p. 131) the term is translated as abstinence. In the *Atharva Veda* (Vol. XLII, p. 215) *brahmacariya* is used for a holy life. The term apparently goes back to hoary antiquity. If the locution "walking with God" used in reference to the antediluvian patriarchs actually means a life of withdrawal and asceticism, then Noah's planting of a vineyard after the Flood (Gen. 9:20) represents a departure from the ascetic way of life.

115. *De Opificio*, 114; *De Decalogo*, 73; *De Virtutibus*, 168; *De Spec. Leg.*, IV, 188. See in Loeb Classical Library VIII, p. 436, where the Philonic idea of assimilation to God is attributed to the *Thaeatetus*. This is, of course, erroneous.

116. *De Fuga*, 63. Abrahams' statement (*op. cit.*, 157) that Philo's metaphor of *fleeing to God* is derived from the *Thaeatetus* is highly questionable. Although Philo quotes Plato, there are Biblical precedents to the idea of fleeing to God. See 2 Sam. 22:3; Jer. 16:19. Again Abrahams' contention that Philo's constant refrain that man must strive to imitate God *as far as he can* is distinctly Platonic (*op. cit.*, *ibid.*) is likewise doubtful. I have found this expression only once in Philo (*De Virt.* 168); no constant refrain is evident. Nor need it be the product of Platonic influence. That one should imitate God *as far as he can* is inherent in the very idea of *imitatio Dei*. See Lev. Rabbah 24:9, and above, note 20. Maimonides also uses the expression "as far as possible" in connection with *imitatio Dei* (Sefer ha-Mitzvoth, 8; Deoth 1:6; see above, notes 89 and 92). Aristotle makes the same reservation (*Nic. Eth.* 1177b). Most likely the origin of the phrase in Jewish writers is Eccl. 9:10. Actually in *De Virt.*, Philo does not use the same Platonic expression that he quotes in *De Fuga*.

117. See H. Wolfson, *Philo* I, 141; cf. *Kusari* 2:66, and commentary *Kol Yehudah*. See other references in Abrahams, *op. cit.*, p. 179.

118. Sotah 35b.

119. Joel 4:6.

120. Is. 66:19; see also Zech. 9:13.

121. Jer. 2:10; Num. 24:24; Is. 23:1.

122. At this writing, newspapers are reporting the recent discoveries of Prof. Cyrus Gordon which tend to disclose a common origin for the culture of Israel and Greece.

123. See Abrahams, *op. cit.*, p. 159.

124. Cf. C. Humphreys, *The Wisdom of Buddhism*, pp. 22, 37-38.

125. Cf. also M. Buber, *op. cit.*, pp. 69-70 [See Kellner, p. 155]. See also S. Kierkegaard, *op. cit.*, p. 179, *et passim*.

126. Shabbath 83b; Tamid 32a; Aboth 6:4.

127. Baba Kamma 91b; cf. above, note 81.

128. Pesahim 49b.

129. Shabbath 30b; cf. Lev. 23:40; Deut. 16:11; Ps. 100:2; *et passim*.

130. Abodah Zarah 20b; Berachoth 64a; R. Moses Hayim Luzzato, *Mesillath Yesharim*. [In Islam the imitation of Muhammad as an ideal occupies an important place, according to L. V. Berman, in a paper published in *Studia Islamica*, Paris 1961 (called to my attention by Dr. J. Rosenthal of the College of Jewish Studies in Chicago). I do not recall anywhere in Judaism that a human being is set up as a model for imitation. The closest to such an attempt is perhaps Maimonides' statement that any man can attain the saintliness of Moses (Teshubah V, 2) or the passage in Tanna de-be-Eliyahu (Chap. 25) that every man must ask himself when his deeds will approximate those of our ancestors, Abraham, Isaac, and Jacob. See also Yoma 35b. The criticism to which all Jewish heroes have been subjected by our sages throughout the ages precludes their acceptance as models for emulation, although we study their lives to learn from them both how to practice *imitatio Dei*, as well as how to avoid the pitfalls which they encountered. See, nevertheless, Baba Bathra 17a where four individuals are said to have lived sinless lives. But even these individuals are never placed on a pedestal for emulation. The implication seems to be that no human being has yet attained his full potentialities, even if he was sinless. See also A. S. Yahuda, *Al-Hidaja Ila Fara'id al-Qulub des Bachja Ibn Josef Ibn Paquda*, Leiden 1912, p. 60 and note 1, where it is pointed out that the Muslim *imitatio prophetae* is modelled after the Christian *imitatio Domini*. On the idea of *imitatio Dei* in Islamic philosophy, see above paper by L. V. Berman. Dr. Berman, however, seems to be unaware that the idea of *imitatio Dei* is not merely a product of Greek philosophy.]

8

Imitatio Dei

MARTIN BUBER

They imitate God's mercy.
ARISTEIDES OF ATHENS, ON THE JEWS

I.

In Plato's *Theaetetus* Socrates declares that evil can never vanish from our world. Evil is needed as the opposite of good, and as it has no place with the gods it must dwell with men; this being so, we had better make haste to flee hence. The way of this flight is, however, to become as like God as we can; and that means to become just and pious through knowledge.

It is probably correct to trace this doctrine to the Pythagorean school, to which the phrase "follow after God" is ascribed by the Greek anthologist Stabaeus and of whose founder Jamblichus said that the whole of his and of his disciples' lives was directed toward this "following after God." Plato too repeatedly uses the conception of "following after," as for instance when he says in the *Phaedrus* that only the soul which best follows after God and assimilates to him shall see true being.

We can only fully understand what is meant here by "following after God" and "becoming his likeness" when we recall the Pythagorean conception of metempsychosis as developed by Plato. The soul is a fallen godlike being, which as a punishment for its guilt has been enclosed in the tomb of the body and must migrate through the bodies of animals and men; when the souls purify themselves in the course of their transmigrations and win back their likeness to God, they free themselves from the compulsion to re-enter the corporeal life and enter anew the world of the gods. God is, then, the model of the soul that purifies itself in order to return home.

God—but what kind of God is this? When these philosophers from Pythagoras to Plato say "God," or "the god," what do they mean and whom do they mean? In order to imitate God one must know him—who is he? "Zeus, the great leader in heaven," says Plato in the section of the *Phaedrus* from which I have already quoted. But who is Zeus?

When we put this question to ourselves, the first thing that comes to mind is the gold and ivory statue by Phidias of Zeus with the olive wreath on his head, the goddess of victory standing in his right hand, in his left the many-metalled scepter surmounted by an eagle, and on his mantle animal figures and flowers; the statue which, as Pausanias tells us, the god himself ratified by a roar of thunder in answer to Phidias' prayer.

But whence did Phidias take his conception? Tradition has him answer this question by saying that he kept to the model given in the famous verses of the Iliad (I.527) in which the sovereign is depicted with his dark brows raising and lowering and the ambrosial locks falling in waves down his immortal head. When one thinks of all the tales in this same Iliad in which Zeus behaves like a raving prehistoric giant rather than like the majestic Olympian, one feels the full power that artistic selection exercised in classical statuary. And one further understands from this that Zeus is the wishful creation of the Greek longing for perfection, accomplished by the elimination of everything inadequate. The imagination, in its struggle to achieve the final shape, tears away from him his original demonic character, such as has survived in the snake-bodied Zeus Ktesios, and, by sloughing off all which does not conform to the desired picture, makes the pure image stand forth clearly. Even before this happened, it is true, the longing for the ideal, finding no fulfilment in plastic forms, expressed itself in the sublime phrase of Aeschylus' *Heliades*, a phrase that utterly dissolves all form and shape: "Zeus is all, and that which rules over all"; and from here the way leads irresistibly on to that complete dissolution of the person, even of the substance itself, which we find in the prayer which Euripides in his *Trojan Women* put into the mouth of the queen of the Trojans, "Whoever you are, O Zeus, you who are hard to espy—necessity of nature or spirit of man, to you I cry!" But sculpture, the truest taskmaster of the Greek idea, defies its destiny, and troubled by what the tragic poets have done, makes the form conclusively visible, and with that imitable. Only then can the Platonic mimesis arise out of the Pythagorean "following after." However "insensuous" Platonism, especially later Platonism, thought to make its god, it cannot pry him loose from the sensuous world of Phidias, wherein form and shape are brought to perfection. The exemplary character of the god, the god in his character as a model to be imitated, remains founded on his figurative character, his character as a plastic representation of the desired. The Greek can only imitate the wish that he himself has given a visible form.

2.

"Be ye therefore followers of God, as most dear children; and walk in love, as Christ also hath loved us," says the Epistle to the Ephesians (V.1f.) ascribed to the apostle Paul. The imitation of God is for Christianity identical with the imitation of its Founder, who represents to it the Deity in the image of a human being and a human life: so the Gospel of John (XIV.9) has the Founder himself say: "He that seeth me seeth the Father also." These words, taken together with the repeated call, "Follow me," give the inner meaning of the tendency which is called *imitatio Christi*. It arose in the early days of Christianity, to reach its height more than a thousand years later; it did not however find its mature literary expression until the fifteenth century, and since then its influence has continued only in isolated and solitary lives.

One instance may suffice to illustrate the beginning and one the climax of this tendency. Polycarp, bishop of Smyrna in the first half of the second century, was a man without any outstanding intellectual gifts, but his strength of character and trustworthiness made him appear so important that the great Ignatius wrote to him that the age needed him to reach to God. In his Letter to the Philippians (VIII.2) Polycarp urges them to be imitators of the patience of Jesus, or rather of his readiness to suffer. The written tradition was not the sole source of Polycarp's knowledge of this quality of Jesus and the deeds that had flowed from it, which he now desired the Philippians to imitate; he had received the knowledge in his youth by mixing with people who had been eyewitnesses of how his Master lived and died.[1] This knowledge did not merely transform itself in him into a demand on the Philippians—it determined his own living and dying. Of his conduct before his martyrdom we are told[2] that when the populace in the amphitheater clamored for him to be thrown to the lions, he neither fled nor gave himself up, but proceeded to a farm and waited there "to be betrayed," as he had been told that Jesus did. It is thus not surprising that in describing his death one of his fellow Christians counted him among "the witnesses and imitators."[3]

This tendency reached its consummation in Francis of Assisi. "The imitation of Christ's life of poverty" is the watchword of his order. In the introductory section to the first rule he wrote down for his order, he states that its aim is to follow in the footsteps of Jesus. From the time of his conversion he devoted his own person entirely to this aim, sympathetically participating in the acts and sufferings of Jesus in an utterly immediate way. But the account of his life given in legend shows clearly what had grown out of the tendency to imitation during these thousand years and more. Legend describes the similarity in the appearance of Francis of Assisi and Jesus; it pursues the similarity through great things and small, often to the point of discovering "correspondences" that border on the trivial, finally to culminate in the miracle-stories connected with the stigmatization, in which the imitation of Jesus is bodily expressed. In ways such as these, legend made Francis the *signaculum similitudinis vitae Christi.*[4] In place of the ethico-religious urge to imitate Jesus, we have here a miraculous metamorphosis, a mystical state of "conformatancy" with Jesus is achieved which indeed in individual cases almost verges on the magical; in place of the *Christo conformiter vivere* of Bonaventura, a hundred years later we have the register of the miraculous *conformitates* of Bartholomew of Pisa, whose book *Liber conformitatum* Luther introduced as "the Barefooted Monks' Eulenspiegel and Alcoran."

The core of all Christian imitation is however after all a memory, a remembrance handed down from one generation to the next; the core is in no way damaged by the accretion of myth deposited in the course of the process of transmission. Moreover, it is a question of the remembrance of a life, a human life. This double fact—life and remembrance—makes Christian imitation a complete contrast to Greek imitation. In spite of Plato's indignant remark[5] about the men of Crete who "follow" Zeus in his more questionable habits, it never occurred to the Greeks to incorporate what their myths told them about their supreme deity into the ideal form which they imitated; indeed, everything mythical had to fall away that the form might become a model; and this was possible, just because the Greeks were not linked to Zeus by a memory. For the Christian that one human life which established him a Christian is the standard and pattern; he does not imitate an image, he imitates a life-history.

This, to be sure, raises a great question all the more insistently: How far can this imitation of a human life be said to be an imitation of God? The Church answers this question with the dogma of the Incarnation. Other voices answer us from out of the early Christian communities. The clearest among these seems to be that of Ignatius of Antioch to whom reference has already been made. He writes in his Epistle to the Philadelphians (VII.2): "Be ye followers of Jesus Christ, as he was a follower of his Father." This reminds one strangely of Paul's words in the First Epistle to the Corinthians (XI.1): "Be ye followers of me, even as I also am of Christ." The imitation is made easier and possible by intermediary links. We need only transfer ourselves from mediacy to immediacy, from the imitation of Jesus to his imitation of our Father, and we are standing on Jewish soil.

3.

The imitation of God, and of the real God, not of the wishful creation; the imitation, not of a mediator in human form, but of God himself—this is the central paradox of Judaism.

A paradox, for how should man be able to imitate God, the invisible, incomprehensible, unformed, not-to-be-formed? One can only imitate that of which one has an idea—no matter whether it be an idea springing from the imagination or from memory; but as soon as one forms an idea of God, it is no longer he whom one conceives, and an imitation founded on this conception would be no imitation of him.

On what can the imitation of God be based?

The answer given in the Jewish teaching, insofar as we can draw it from the words of the Haggadah, is this: The Jewish teaching is founded on the fact that we are destined to be like Him.

The Midrash[6] interprets the saying of Moses, "Ye are this day as the stars of heaven for multitude" (Deut.1:10), by taking the word *rov*, here translated "multitude," in the sense of "Lord," "Master," and reads, "Today are ye like the stars, but in the time to come ye are destined to be like your Lord." And the Midrash[7] completes another passage of Deuteronomy (4:4) in still stronger language: "But ye that did cleave unto the Lord your God are alive every one of you this day," is interpreted as: "In this world Israel cleaves unto the Lord, but in the time to come they will be like him."

But has then the world to come, "the world of fulfilment," become so divided from the present world, the world of want, that no bridge of thought can any longer lead from here across to there? It is plainly impossible for us to comprehend that we should be like God; and it is really most comprehensible to us that we are unlike him, in just the way in which such a figurine kneaded out of "the dust of the earth" must be unlike the Creator of all things. How can human effort even in part fill the abyss between that "being like" and this unlikeness?

The teaching, however, does not remain content with the bare promise.

Rabbi Aha was a contemporary of the Emperor Julian; he was that astounding man who at weddings used to set the bride on his shoulder in order that he might thus dance the holy dance with her, and at his death it was said that the stars shone by day. It was this Rabbi Aha who commented on the verse of Psalm 100, "Know ye that the Lord He is God; it is He that hath made us, and we are His" by saying: "He hath made us, and toward Him we perfect our souls."[8]

We perfect our souls "toward" God. "Being like" God is then not something which is unconnected with our earthly life; it is the goal of our life, provided that our life is really a perfecting of our soul "toward" God. And this being so, we may well add that the perfection of a soul is called its being like God, which yet does not mean any equality, but means that this soul has translated into reality that likeness to God which was granted it. We perfect our souls "toward" God; this means that each of us who does this makes perfect *his* likeness to God, his *yehida*, his soul, his "only one," his uniqueness *as* God's image.

"For in the image of God made He man." It is on this that the imitation of God is founded. We are destined to be like Him, this means we are destined to bring to perfection out of ourselves, in actual life, the image in which we were created, and which we carry in us, that we may—no longer in this life—experience its consummation.

Judaism, which more than any other religion has grasped the seriousness for actual life of the fact that God created man, has also most unequivocally recognized the importance for the life of man of that phrase "in His image." To this fact the saying of Rabbi Akiba bears witness, that saying which we are still far from understanding in all its profundity: "Beloved is man, in that he was created in the image of God. But it was a special act of love that *made it known* to him that he was created in the image of God."[9] The fact that it has been revealed to us that we are made in His image gives us the incentive to unfold this image, and in doing so to imitate God.

God said, "Let us make man in our own image, after our likeness"; but of the creative act itself it is said, "And God created man in His own image"; the image alone is mentioned here, without the likeness. How are we to understand that? A haggadic interpretation answers our question thus: "In His image alone and not also after His likeness, because the likeness lies in the hand of man."[10] The "likeness" is the process of becoming like.

The Fall of the first human being consisted in his wanting to reach the likeness intended for him in his creation by other means than by perfecting "the image."

"The fundamental reason for the creation of man," says a hasidic book,[11] "is that he is to make himself as much like his Creator as he can." The book further cites the beautiful saying of Rabbi Hizkiah, the son of Rabbi Hiyya: "Happy are the pious prophets who liken what is formed to him who forms and what is planted to him who plants,"[12] and explains it in the following manner: "They make themselves like their Creator by unifying all their limbs to resemble His unity, and driving all share of evil out of themselves that they may be perfect with the Lord their God. . . That is why God said, 'Let us make man to our image and after our likeness'—out of His love for man He created him in His own image, so that man should be able to make himself like his Creator."

Again the question which we seemed to have mastered rises up before us: How can we imitate God? True, His image has been placed in us, has been outlined in us, and therefore we can be sure that the goal exists, and that it is possible to walk "in the way." But what is "the way"? Have we to fasten our attention on our soul alone, on its hidden image, which we have been commanded to unfold? Or have we a model of what we should unfold and perfect our image into? Is God our model? And yet again: How can He, the unimaginable, be that?

Again the answer is given us by one of the masters of the Talmud, by one who lived after the death of Hadrian and who was a still more astounding man than Rabbi Aha—Abba Shaul. He was a giant in stature, by profession a baker in the house of the Patriarch; he devoted himself beyond everything else to the fulfilment of the religious duty to bury the dead, and he could tell of strange observations he made in this work; he was withal a man of prayer, and interpreted, obviously from very personal experience, the sentence of the Psalm (10:17)—"Lord, Thou hast heard the desire of the humble: Thou wilt strengthen their heart, Thou wilt cause their ear to attend"—by saying that the granting of the prayer became manifest in the strengthening of the heart. It was he who used to comment on the word of God, "Ye shall be holy; for I the Lord your God am holy," by explaining: "It behooves the royal retinue to imitate the King."[13] But another of his sayings leads us even deeper into what he conceives *imitatio Dei* to be. He begins with a verse of the song which Moses and all Israel sang when they had passed through the sea: *Zeh eli veanvehu*, which has been rendered: "This is my God, and I will glorify Him." But Abba Shaul takes the contested word *veanvehu* in a different sense: "I will become like unto Him," or "I will make myself like unto Him."[14] Rashi[15] explains the reason for this interpretation thus: Abba Shaul resolved the word *veanvehu* into its two component parts, *ani vehu*, and accordingly understood it as "I and He," and said: "I will become like unto Him," or as Rashi expresses it, "I will form myself after Him, I will cleave to his ways." And in fact, Abba Shaul continues: "As He is merciful and gracious so be thou merciful and gracious."

To imitate God means then to cleave to His ways, to walk in His ways. By these are meant not the ways which God has commanded man as man to walk in, they are really God's own ways. But, yet again, the old question comes back in a new form: How can we walk in His ways? They are past finding out, and we are told that they are not like our ways!

Abba Shaul already indicates the answer in his last words; it is amplified in two explanatory comments on the words of Deuteronomy, which Schechter once called "Israel's book of *imitatio dei*." It says: " 'To love the Lord your God, to walk in all His ways.' What are the ways of God? Those which He himself proclaimed to Moses: 'God, merciful, gracious, long-suffering, abundant in lovingkindness and faithfulness.' "[16] Another saying[17] still more explicit: "After the Lord your God shall ye walk" (Deut.13:5); how should man be able to walk in the footsteps of the Divine Presence? Is it not written (Deut.4:24): "The Lord thy God is a devouring fire"? But the meaning is: Follow after the *middot*, the "attributes," still better, the modes in which God works as far as these are made known to man. As He clothed the nakedness of the first human beings, as He visited the sick Abraham in the grove at Mamre (where according to tradition Abraham suffered the pangs of circumcision), as He comforted Isaac with his blessing after Abraham's death, until the last act of God in the Pentateuch, when He Himself buried Moses—all these are enacted *middot* visible patterns for man, and the *mitzvot*, the commandments, are *middot* made human. "My handicraft," as the Midrash has God say to Abraham, "is to do good—you have taken up My handicraft."[18]

The secret of God which stood over Job's tent (Job 29:4), before it grew fearfully into his suffering and questioning, can only be fathomed by suffering, not by questioning, and man is equally forbidden to question and to imitate these secret ways of God. But God's handicraft, His revealed way of working, has been opened before us and set up for us as a pattern.

Thus it was not vouchsafed to Moses to see God's "face," but he learned his "ways," which God Himself proclaimed, when he passed by before him; and this proclamation God calls the proclamation of His "Name."

But where are the revealed ways of God's working revealed?

Just at the beginning of the wandering through the desert; just at the height of Job's trial; just in the midst of the terror of the other, the incomprehensible, ununderstandable works; just from out of the secret. God does not show mercy and grace alone to us; it is terrible when His hand falls on us, and what then happens to us does not somehow find a place *beside* mercy and grace, it does not belong to the same category as these: the ultimate does not belong here to the attribute of righteousness—it is beyond all attributes. It is indeed the secret, and it is not for us to enquire into it. But just in this quality of God's is His "handiwork" manifested to us. Only when the secret no longer stands over our tent, but breaks it, do we learn to know God's intercourse with us. And we learn to imitate God.

Notes

1. Irenaeus' account in Eusebius, *Church History*, V. 20.
2. *Martyrdom of Polycarp*, I. 2.
3. Eusebius, *Church History*, IV. 15.
4. Ubertinus de Casali, *Arbor vitae crucifixae*.
5. *Laws*, 636 D.
6. Deut. Rabbah on 1:10.
7. Pesikta Rabbati, ed. Friedmann 46 b.
8. Gen. Rabbah on 49:29.
9. Sayings of the Fathers III, 18.
10. Yalkut Reubeni on Gen. 1:27.
11. Beer Mayyim Hayyim on Gen. 1:26.
12. Midrash Tehillim on 1:1.
13. Sifra on Lev. 19:2.
14. Palestinian Talmud, Peah 15 b.
15. In his comment on Shabbat 133 b.
16. Sifre on Deut. 11:22.
17. Talmud, Sotah 14 a.
18. Gen. Rabbah on 23:19.

The Self and the Other in Rabbinic Ethics

CHAIM W. REINES

It was Judaism that posited love of fellowman as the guiding principle of ethics; in doing so it incidentally illustrated its concept of the relationship between religion and ethics. The religious attitude finds its ultimate source in an awareness of values in life and the world. It is characterized, moreover, by the effort to transcend the self-interests of the individual. The pragmatic attitude underlying science takes things to be the "objects" of the experience and "environment" of the individual. It evaluates them from a utilitarian viewpoint. Religion, on the other hand, assumes that the personality is aware of itself in relationship to that which is beyond itself and its attitude toward the latter is based on the feeling of awe. This attitude involves an absolute not a utilitarian evaluation. The basic achievement of Jewish ethics is its application of this absolute evaluation whose original setting is the religious situation — man confronting God — to the area of life where man confronts his neighbor.

On the simplest level, our fellowmen are objects of our experience and merely constitute a part of our environment. To be sure, in social life the relationship between persons takes on a specific character, one that distinguishes it from the individual's relationship to all other objects. Common interests bind people together; occasionally, so closely together that the other may even become part of one's own ego. Even on this level, the relationship to the other is still based, strictly speaking, on what may be called a higher selfishness. The emotional stance toward the

Reprinted from *Judaism*, Vol. 2, no. 1. Copyright © 1953 by the American Jewish Congress.

other may be that of affection, aversion or indifference. In each instance, the motivation is subjective and determined by relative considerations. The Biblical commandment of love of one's fellowman stands on an altogether different level. In its universalistic and normative character it demands that one's fellowman should be not merely an object of personal affection but should rather be loved for his own sake. In this paper, we propose to establish the theoretic meaning and religious basis of this universalistic and binding commandment and to define its scope and limits in the practical realm.

Ahad Ha-Am's efforts in this direction[1] were much too cursory[2] and the apologetic tendency that informed his famous essay led him to formulate the differences between Jewish and Christian ethics somewhat superficially. The Hebrew essayist saw the basis of Jewish ethics in the twin ideas of justice and the moral worth of man. Aside from the fact that he deliberately omits the religious source of these ideas, he contrasts the "objective" value of justice, native to Judaism, with the "subjective" value of love central to Christian ethics. This characterization does not, as we have already indicated, exhaust the full meaning of the Biblical commandment of love of fellowman. Hermann Cohen, in his earlier writings,[3] approached the problem from a not too dissimilar viewpoint. On religious grounds, he found the ethic of love inadequate since by its very nature it is subjective and selective and hence far too limited to express the universalism that must be the hallmark of ethics. He proposed instead that ethics orient itself towards jurisprudence where the relationship of the self and other is most characteristically expressed in the legal contract. Whatever validity this criticism of the ethic of love and its alternative may possess, it is hardly applicable to Judaism in which the two — jurisprudence and ethics — are brought into intimate relationship.

Both Ahad Ha-Am's grounding of Jewish ethics in the value of justice as opposed to love and Hermann Cohen's critique of the latter are implied in a famous Talmudic controversy between Rabbi Akiba and Ben Azzai.[4]

Rabbi Akiba declared the Biblical commandment to love one's neighbor as oneself "the great maxim of the Torah." For Ben Azzai, the central rule of the Torah is contained in the verse (Gen. 5:1) "This is the book of the generations of man, in the image of God created He him." As did Hillel before him, Rabbi Akiba followed the lead of the prophets who asserted that love was the highest demand made on man by religion.[5] With penetrating insight, Ben Azzai discerned in the verse in Genesis a broad and firm foundation for ethics — the essential unity of mankind and the dignity of the individual. The same verse elicits from a later Aggadist[6] the comment: "If you put a man to shame, know that you are putting to shame the image of God." Ben Azzai's declaration bears striking similarity to Kant's formulation of the basic principle of ethics as respect for the dignity of man. The difference in viewpoint between Ben Azzai and Akiba is more apparent than real. For elsewhere[7] the latter declares: "Beloved is man in that he was created in the image of God". Yet another Rabbinic statement — possibly that of Rabbi Akiba — [8] motivates the Biblical "love thy neighbor as thyself" by adding the words, "for I, the Lord, created him." In any case, the seemingly divergent viewpoints of Akiba and Ben Azzai lend themselves to ready reconciliation.

While the foundation of ethics is to be found in the dignity of man by reason of his creation in the image of God, the directive for concrete moral action is to be sought in the commandment of love. Ethics must have as its *leitmotif* the idea of humanity but since its actual specific concern is with the individual and his relationship to his fellow man only the love of man can serve as its generative force. The natural ground and starting point for such love of man is man's own self-love as indicated by the oft-quoted verse in Leviticus. In this commandment — thou shalt love thy neighbor as thyself — Hillel saw the essence of the Torah's teaching in regard to man's relationship to his fellowman. His paraphrase of the verse in negative terms — "What is hateful unto thee, do not do unto thy neighbor" —[9] has long been made by Christian theologians the subject of invidious contrast with the New Testament's positive formulation.[10] The case has, at the very least, been overstated. Positive formulations of the injunction to love one's fellowman are fairly abundant in Rabbinic and extra-Rabbinic Jewish sources.[11] Indeed, Hillel himself, in a passage in the Mishnah,[12] states the command in positive, universal terms. His negative formulation is hardly more than a random choice of terminology and may have been prompted by his desire to express the concept in terms of a popular proverb. The latter conjecture is supported by the fact that Hillel in speaking to the would-be proselyte phrases the maxim in Aramaic, the lingua franca of his day.

Nevertheless, the value of love of fellowman can never completely overcome the subjective nature of the emotion which is its matrix; hence, it cannot serve as the ultimate ground of ethics. The latter can only be based on the recognition and acknowledgment of the absolute worth of man. This idea is conceptually equivalent if not verbally identical with the Rabbinic doctrine of *Kevod habrioth*, the honor of man.[13] While the term honor signifies the unique and infinite value of every human being, it implies that such value does not derive from the individual as an isolated, natural being. It springs rather from the idea of mankind which the individual represents and, in religious terms, from his having been created in the image of God. While love begins with the self and only in obedience to the Biblical command does it become transitive and outgoing, honor grows out of an awareness of humankind as a whole and is incorporated in the individual in the sense of self-respect. Love alone may be blind and selfish. Honor, though it signifies the inviolability of the individual, lacks emotional depth and the sense of the personal. Rabbinic ethics therefore joins the two and declares that man's relationship to his fellowman must be based on both love and honor. The Rabbis put it succinctly when they say, "love men and respect them".[14]

The Rabbis were quick to note that the Biblical command enjoining love of fellowman implies a concern for his dignity. Rabbi Eleazar formulated the implication in the following terms: "Let the honor of your neighbor be as precious to you as your own".[15] If Scripture commands love of fellowman and not honor, it is because the former alone is wholly positive. The positive corollaries of honoring one's fellowman are limited to manifesting tokens of respect and courtesy. The true significance of the concept is to be found in its negative implication; to refrain from any assault on that most intimate sphere of the personality — its self-consciousness. The perennial human propensity towards indulging in this kind of assault — really, a form of disguised self-inflation of the ego — explains the reiteration the concept of the honor of one's fellowman receives in Rabbinic ethics. Several typical examples illustrative of the Rabbinic amplification and application of the concept may be offered.

"If with regard to the stones of the altar that are void of any understanding of good and evil, the Holy One, Blessed Be He, demands that they should not be treated in a degrading manner, then certainly one's fellowman who was created in the image of the Creator of the world should not be dealt with contemptuously".[16] Here, incidentally, one catches an echo of the prophetic denunciation of those in ancient

Israel who together with a scrupulous observance of the cultic ritual were guilty of the grossest violations of man's fundamental moral duties towards man. Another Rabbinic statement seeks to motivate and inspire the attitude of honoring one's fellowman by a realistic appraisal of recalcitrant human nature itself. "If even the angels who are not burdened with the evil impulse honor each other how much more so should men in whom the evil impulse is present."[17] Since man is inclined to deprecate and denigrate his fellowman, he should place him above himself and should not say, "I am greater than you." Great emphasis is placed in Rabbinic ethics on overcoming the outcroppings of the "evil impulse" particularly as the latter manifests itself in seeking to direct man's relation to his fellowman.[18] Native egotism and self-conceit tend both to inhibit a man from recognizing the worth of his neighbor and from showing him the respect that is his due. Addressing themselves to the members of the academy — the natural audience to whom their moral admonitions are frequently directed — the Rabbis declared: "Let the honor of your pupil be as precious to you as your own, and let the honor of your colleague be in your eyes as the reverence you owe your master, and your reverence for your master as the reverence for God."[19] Thus, to counteract the tendency of the superior (the master) to treat with disdain those inferior to him, and the tendency of the scholar to deprecate his colleague,[20] Rabbinic ethics demands that the inferior be dealt with as an equal, the equal as a superior and the superior be approached with religious awe. The same transvaluation is applied to man generally. Ethically, respect for man implies that the individual should be treated not on the basis of his social position or the actual level of his intellectual and moral achievements but in accordance with his ideal value as a human being. Such, at least, is the intent of the Rabbinic dictum, "great is the honor of man."[21]

These maxims reveal a basic tenet of Judaism. Though Judaism stamps humility a cardinal virtue and everlastingly insists on the unbridgeable distance between man and God, it nevertheless proclaims that the honor of God is reflected in man who was created in His image.[22] The Psalmist's "What is man that Thou art mindful of him?" in no way lessens the obligation of respecting the dignity of every man. The denunciation of pride is a theme common to Prophet, Psalmist and Wisdom Teacher. The latter, with their profound intuitive understanding of human nature, recognized in pride the crassest manifestation of that egotism which prevents the person from recognizing in his fellowman a being possessing worth equal to his own. The Prophets traced war, political and social oppression to the psychological root of pride; a pride manifestated in the lust for power and domination. Hence, in the coming judgment, they proclaimed that the pride of man will be broken.[23] In their recognition of the mischievous effects of egotism, the ancient Jewish moralists anticipated modern psychology.

Following the Prophets and the Wisdom Teachers, the Rabbis declared that pride is tantamount to idolatry[24] and that, per contra, humility is the crowning virtue.[25] Christianity adopted this appreciation of humility and, characteristically, carried it to extravagant extremes. Augustine and Calvin declared self-contempt to be a virtue. It was largely as a reaction against medieval monastic morality with its emphasis on self-abasement that the virtue of humility fell into disrepute in modern times. Spinoza and Kant termed it a vice rather than a virtue. Indeed, while Judaism commands humility before God and commends it as an ethical safeguard against pride, it must be joined to and limited by self-respect. It cannot be the aim of ethics to command respect of fellowman and at the same time preach self-contempt. Even in its insistence on tipping the scales in favor of one's fellow in the honor to be shown him, Rabbinic ethics cautioned against extremism.[26]

Indeed, the Rabbis emphasized the necessity and duty of self-respect. The scholar, they declared, should be particularly careful not to offend his own dignity since it is bound up with the dignity of the Torah itself. It was probably out of a recognition that exaggerated self-effacement might lead to a diminished respect for the scholar that some Rabbis advocated a modicum of self-pride as an attitude most befitting a scholar.[27]

No analysis of Rabbinic ethics can limit itself to the Agadah of the Rabbis. It is the Halakhah which is normative; its legal principles reflecting as they do the ethical views of the Rabbis bring the latter to sharp and precise focus. What is decisive, in the moral sphere, is not the broad sweeping moral injunction but rather its application to concrete life situations where conflicting interests and loyalties must be evaluated and, if possible, reconciled. How did the Rabbis apply the Biblical commandment of love of neighbor to the specifics of their time? Several illustrations borrowed from the Halakhah may serve to answer the question.

The following law is stated in the Mishnah.[28] If a man finds an object such as a sack or bundle that he would not ordinarily carry in public because of the loss of dignity involved, he is not obliged, as he otherwise would be, to pick it up and bring it to its owner. Commenting on this law, the Amora Rabba declares that if the person in question would carry the object to his own home if it were his own, he is obliged to return it to the owner. Rabba's reasoning is obviously based on the maxim that one is supposed to do for others what one is prepared to do for oneself. Consequently, since he would waive his dignity for the sake of saving his own property, he is likewise obliged to disregard it for the sake of saving his neighbor's property. Interestingly enough, Maimonides avers[29] that it is commendable in this case to go beyond the requirements of the law and return the lost object to its owner even though the finder demeans himself thereby. Indeed, no rigid line of demarcation can be drawn in Judaism between law and ethics. Frequently, the Halakhah gives legal status to what is merely moral counsel in the Bible. Our illustration serves as a case in point. By the same token, the Rabbis strongly urged[30] the kind of action that went beyond the requirements of the law. (Lifnim meeshurath ha-din, middath hassiduth). The line between the law and the higher ethical standard fluctuated and domains once governed by law became matters of the moral conscience. Contrariwise, what was once left to the decision of the individual's moral sensitivity became subject to the power of the law.[31]

Broadly conceived, the law was founded upon a justice whose source was the equal and reciprocal obligations obtaining among men. The ethical requirement, on the other hand, demanded more from the individual than the latter had the right to claim from others. This idea finds articulation in the distinction the Rabbis make between the Am Ha-Arez (the boor) and the Hassid (the pious man).[32] The former says, "What is mine is yours and what is yours is mine"; the latter says, "Mine is yours and what is yours is yours." The Am Ha-arez thinks that because he is prepared to give his neighbor a share in his property he is thereby entitled to an equal share in the property of his neighbor. The Hassid recognizes that his own generosity does not give him any claim on the generosity of his neighbor. The Hassid's acts of unselfish devotion to the welfare of his neighbor are designated by the Rabbis as Gemillath Hassadim (the doing of deeds of loving kindness).[33] Rashi succinctly sums up the Rabbinic attitude towards the duties a man owes his neighbor by describing them as the effort to fulfill the needs of every man, be they material or psychological.[34]

In stressing the individual's moral obligations to his neighbor, the Rabbis recognize at the same time that one's duty to oneself must take precedence over the duties to others. There would, at first glance, seem to be a contradiction here. Analysis, however, reveals that the contradiction is a purely formal one. Since, as we have seen, Jewish ethics is founded on the universalistic idea of duty to man as being created in the image of God, it must include the duty to oneself. Hence, the latter should not be subordinated in the name of self-denial to the obligation one owes one's fellowman. Concrete expression of this idea is given by the Rabbis when they establish the principle that in the distribution of charity relatives take precedence over strangers and the inhabitants of one's city take precedence over the needy of other cities.[35]

From the Biblical designation of one's fellowman as "thy brother" and "thy neighbor" Christian theologians have long been prone to conclude that Jewish ethics lacks universalistic scope. The true meaning of the Biblical designation is to be found in the persistent effort of ethics to extend the love which has its origin in the circle of the family and the closed social group to humanity at large. The Biblical commandment takes as its point of departure the natural beginnings of the moral attitude. The Rabbinic insistence that the duty to the self has priority over the duty to others in no way infringes upon or limits the universalism in terms of which they conceived the moral idea. The prior duty to the self they deduced from the Torah itself.[36] They found it implied in the verse, "Albeit there shall be no poor in your midst." (Deuteronomy 15:4) The injunction is taken to mean that one should not be so overly generous as to become impoverished and thus become a public charge. At the famous rabbinical synod at Usha, held in the second century, an enactment was instituted that one should not give to charity more than a fifth of one's possessions.[37]

The very Rabbi who establishes the principle that the duty to the self takes precedence over duty to the other adds the warning that he who rigidly guides his actions by this principle eventually gets what he fears, i.e. poverty. Rashi interprets the latter statement to the following effect. Though, according to the law, self-interest legitimately takes precedence, one should not consistently base his action on the law but go beyond it for the sake of piety and charity. The implication in both the original statement and Rashi's interpretation thereof come to this: self-interest enjoys precedence only when the stakes involved between the self and the other are equal. Thus, for example, where there is a choice between recovering one's own property or that of another or where the alternatives are liberating oneself from prison or liberating another, the self takes precedence even over one's father or teacher.[38] As has been said, this principle is only applicable where the alternatives are absolutely equal. But if one is in a better position to sustain the loss of the property or the risk entailed in remaining in prison is less than that involved in another's continued detention, then it is the other who is entitled to priority. Similarly, one is morally bound to rescue a drowning person even if it entails some risk for the rescuer since the former is certain to drown unless saved and the danger to the latter is problematical.[39]

While the idea of self-sacrifice may appear logically unwarranted, it nevertheless has deep roots in unreflective morality and religiosity. Its traces are to be found in Jewish ethics and are reflected in a controversy between Ben Peturah and Rabbi Akiba.[40] The case is the hypothetical one of two men wandering in a desert and in danger of dying of thirst. One of them finds a jug which contains just enough water to sustain one man. It is Ben Peturah's judgment that both should drink of it rather than the one who found it even though it must mean the death of both of them. Rabbi Akiba, however, is of the opinion that the water should be drunk by the man who found the jug. This opinion he deduces from the Scriptural verse (Leviticus 25:36) "and thy brother shall live with thee"; the saving of one's own life takes precedence. It is apparent from the phraseology of the controversy ("until Rabbi Akiba came and taught") that the opinion of Ben Peturah prevailed until it was supplanted by that of Rabbi Akiba. It may be surmised that this opinion reflected the outlook of the Hassidim who were distinguished by their piety and love of fellowman, and were extreme in their religious and ethical standards. In this particular instance, the uncritical moral sense would support Ben Peturah since equity seems to demand that in a situation where two men are sharing the same dangers they should likewise share any opportunity of preserving their lives even though the opportunity is the original possession of but one of them. This verdict, however, would lead to the strange consequence that the finder of the jug ought die out of sheer sympathy for the plight of his fellow even though his self-sacrifice must prove fruitless. Rabbi Akiba's thesis is, as we have seen, a logical extension of the principle that self-interest ought take priority over the duty a man owes his neighbor.

The primary duty of self-preservation is reflected in the unanimous opinion that one is not bound to sacrifice one's life for the sake of the fulfillment of the commandments. The commandments, the Rabbis declare, were given that man should "live by them" (Leviticus 18:5) and not die because of them.[41] Since the commandments are intended for the good of man he obviously cannot fulfill them unless he lives; hence, the duty of self-preservation takes precedence over all other duties. Thus, Rabbi Akiba's opinion in the case cited above is a logical corollary of the general principle of the priority of the duty of self-preservation, a principle from which there is no dissent among the Rabbis.

Broad and basic as the principle is, it too has its limitations. One may not save his own life at the cost of another's. The *Amora* Rabbah was once asked by a Jew whose life had been threatened by the governor unless he took another man's life whether he was permitted to do so under the circumstances. The prompt epigrammatic reply came back: "Who shall say that your blood is deeper hued than his, perhaps his blood is deeper hued than yours?"[42] Rabbah's epigram contains the basic assumption of all morality and law. The life of every man is of equal worth; consequently, one life should not be destroyed for the sake of saving another.[43]

The Tosefta discusses a case in which this principle receives vivid illustration and application.[44] A group of travellers is attacked by desperadoes who demand that one of the travellers — undesignated by them — be surrendered to them to be murdered. Unless their demand is met, they threaten to kill the entire group. The law declares that they should all surrender themselves to the murderers rather than hand over a single soul of Israel to be killed. The same holds true where the victim has been singled out by the attackers but unbeknown to them is in a position to escape. This situation which may be presumed to have faced Jewish communities more than once and in which the law demanded the self-sacrifice of the many for the sake of a single individual is the application of the principle enunciated in the Mishnah[45] that the saving of one life is tantamount to the preservation of the entire world. If, however, the victim whose surrender is demanded cannot possibly escape and is foredoomed, rabbinic opinion is divided as to what course of action the group should take. According to one view, the individual should be given up; according to another opinion, he should be surrendered only if the intended victim has committed an offense for which the penalty is capital punishment. This latter view will recall that of Ben

Peturah quoted above. There is, however, a surface distinction between the two situations. In the case of the group of travellers, the group is directly instrumental in bringing about the victim's death since they surrender him to those who intend to kill him. Yet, it may be argued, their action does not really bring about his death since in any event he would be legally put to death as punishment for the capital crime he has committed.

An actual case in which the principles here discussed were involved is reported in the Talmud.[46] A certain Ulla who was sought by the Roman authorities because of rebellious activities took refuge in the town of Lydda where Rabbi Joshua ben Levi was the head of the community. The Romans threatened to destroy the city unless the refugee was surrendered to them. Rabbi Joshua ben Levi persuaded him to give himself up. Thereupon, legend adds, the prophet Elijah ceased to reveal himself to the Rabbi as was his wont. Elijah explained that he did not reveal himself to "informers". The Rabbi argued that he had acted in accordance with the law. To which Elijah replied, "Is this a Mishnah of Hassidim?" The commentators explain Elijah's query to mean that a pious man like Rabbi Joshua ben Levi should act beyond the requirements of the law. Their explanation assumes that the law as stated and on which Rabbi Joshua ben Levi based his action is not in agreement with the teaching of the Hassidim on this point. The Elijah legend expresses the viewpoint of the Hassidim and hence the rebuke to the Rabbi. Apparently, the Hassidim were prepared to sacrifice their lives rather than transgress any aspect of the law though the law itself did not demand such sacrifice. It is therefore not surprising to find them demanding sacrifice of the self in a case where the highest ethical principle and gravest moral offense in Judaism were involved. Maimonides who invariably follows the ethical teaching found in the agadah accepts the teaching of the Hassidim in this case. Despite Maimonides' codification of the Hassidic teaching, the opinion of the Rabbis who like Rabbi Akiba rejected useless self-sacrifice in the name of love of fellow man ought to be reckoned with.

To Jewish ethics, as it seeks to guide the individual in his relationships with his fellow man, one may apply the words of the scripture: "It is not in heaven that you should say, who will go up for us to heaven and bring it to us, that we may hear it and do it. . .But the word is very near you; it is in your mouth and in your heart, so that you can do it." Its constitutive principal is the axiom, permanent and universal, that man bears the ineffaceable imprint of his Maker. Its rule of action is that natural self love which left unchecked yields the rankest egotism but directed outward produces the highest moral good. The just reconciliation of the proper claims of the self as opposed to the claims of the other is no mean task and, perhaps, never completely and perfectly achieved. But no objective student of rabbinic ethics can escape the impression that here is a sound and penetrating effort to achieve such reconciliation; one that while it reckons with the unmalleable in human nature sees man's role in terms of inescapable moral imperatives fairly balanced between himself and his neighbor.

Notes

1. In his essay, "Between Two Stools" in *Al Parashat Derakhim*, vol. IV.

2. Ahad Ha-Am was criticized for concerning himself with so "theological" a problem as the differences between Christian and Jewish ethics. In a postscript to the essay referred to above, he remarked that he wrote the essay for the enlightenment of those who still clung to the "old" (religious) outlook upon Judaism.

3. Herman Cohen, *Ethik des reinen Willens*, vol. II, pp. 116 ff. In his last works on the philosophy of religion, Cohen modified this viewpoint considerably. He sees in the orientation of religion towards the individual a necessary correction and supplement to the abstract universalism of ethics. He likewise emphasized the significance of love of fellowman which he attributed to religion rather than ethics. For a critique of this view, see Reines, *Yahid VeZibbur BeYahaduth*, pp. 12 et seq.

4. Sifra Kedoshim and parallel passages.

5. Hosea 6:6; Micah 6:8; Zachariah 7:9.

6. Genesis Rabbah ch. XXIV.

7. Mishnah Aboth, III, 2.

8. Aboth de R. Nathan, ed. Schechter, ch. 16. Some manuscripts attribute this saying to Rabbi Akiba. See L. Finkelstein's introduction to Aboth, pp. 47-49.

9. Shabbat 31a.

10. Matthew 7:12.

11. See Kaufmann Kohler's essay "Nachstenliebe in Judenthum" in *Festschrift an Hermann Cohen*, pp. 475 et seq.

12. Mishnah Aboth I:12.

13. Some ethical philosophers distinguish between "dignity" as a moral concept and honor as a strictly sociological concept which latter signifies the relative worth of the individual in society. See Eugene Terraillon's, *L'Honneur*. This sharp distinction is unwarranted since honor in an ethical sense signifies the absolute value of man. The Hebrew term "kavod"—literally, weighty—signifies worth. The corresponding terms for honor in other languages bear the same significance. See Ihering, *Der Zweck im Rechte*, II, 501.

14. Aboth de R. Nathan, ed. Schechter,52.
15. Mishnah Aboth, II,12.
16. Mekhilta Yitro, ed. Friedmann, 74a.
17. Source cited note 14.
18. Baba Meziah 32b.
19. Mishnah Aboth IV, 2.
20. The pupils of Rabbi Akiba are said to have died young because of their failure to respect one another. Yebamoth 62b.
21. Rabbi Yohanan ben Zakkai applied this dictum to a thief. Baba Qama 79b.
22. Both aspects of man, his humility and dignity, are expressed in Psalms, 8:7.
23. Isaiah 2:11. See Reines op.cit. p. 88.
24. Sotah 4b.
25. Avodah Zarah 20b.
26. Maimonides' well-known statement that one should seek the extreme in the exercise of humility, rather than the golden mean must be understood in the light of his defense of the Jewish viewpoint against that of Aristotle who deprecated humility.
27. Aboth de R. Nathan, p. 88. Though the Talmud says that a scholar may waive the honor due him (Kiddushin 32b) some decisors, among them R. Isaac bar Sheshet (Responsum No. 220) refer this as applying only to marks of deference but not to any offense to his honor.
28. Baba Meziah 29b.
29. Mishneh Torah, Hilkhot Gezelah VeAvedah XI, 13.
30. Baba Meziah 30b.
31. See Simon Federbusch, HaMusar VeHaMishpat BeYisrael.
32. Mishnah Aboth, V, 10.
33. Sukkah 49b. R. Eleazar declares that the merit of an act of charity is relative to the "chesed" it contains. Rashi interprets "chesed" in this context to mean the degree of effort expended in performing the act. More precisely, the term might be rendered here as the good intent involved in the deed.
34. Ketuboth 17a.
35. Baba Meziah 71a.
36. Baba Meziah 33a.
37. Ketuboth 50a.
38. Baba Meziah 33b.
39. See Responsa of R. David ben Zimra, Warsaw 1882, Responsum No. 1583.
40. Baba Meziah 62a.
41. Toseftah Shabbat ch.XV.
42. Sanhedrin 74a.
43. Mishnah Oholoth VII, 6.
44. Toseftah Terumoth ch. VII.
45. Mishnah Sanhedrin IV, 5.
46. Yerushalmi Terumoth 46b.

10.

Greater Love Hath No Man. . .
The Jewish Point of View of Self-Sacrifice

LOUIS JACOBS

"Greater love hath no man than this, that a man lay down his life for his friends." This teaching has long been considered as belonging to the ripest fruits of Christianity. It is believed that in a man's capacity for self-sacrifice in the interests of others, the finest flowering of Christian character is seen. What is the attitude of Judaism to the question of giving one's life that another may live? Would the act of a Sidney Carton in *A Tale of Two Cities* be allowed, or even advocated, by Jewish teaching, or would it be condemned?

Jewish teachers in modern times have been so nearly unanimous in their rejection of this doctrine in the name of Jewish ethic, that it may be forgiven if one entertains the suspicion that their repudiation is not so much the result of a careful examination of the classic sources, as the desire to defend at all costs the *ethical* distinctions between Judaism and Christianity in an age when the doctrinal and theological differences between the two faiths are treated as irrelevant or "remote." Ahad Ha'am, for example, remarks in his polemic against Claude Montefiore's espousal of some aspects of the Christian ethic to the detriment of the Jewish,[2] that while Christianity is based on the concept of love, Judaism is based on that of justice. Love demands that a man give his life for his

Reprinted from *Judaism*, Vol. 6, no. 1. Copyright © 1957 by the American Jewish Congress.

friend; justice, that his life is not his own to dispose of. Love advocates the most excessive altruism; justice, that altruism is an inverted form of egotism. Ahad Ha'am states that the difference between Jewish morality and that of the Gospels is not merely one of degree, but of the very basis of morality. The Christian ethic is "subjective"; the Jewish ethic "objective," based on absolute justice, attaching moral value to the individual as such, without any distinction between the "self" and the "other." "All men, including the self, are under obligation to develop their lives and their faculties to the limit of their capacity and, at the same time, each is under obligation to assist his neighbor's self-development, so far as he can. But just as I have no right to ruin another man's life for the sake of my own, so I have no right to ruin my own life for the sake of another's. Both of us are men, and both our lives have the same value before the throne of justice."

Ahad Ha'am quotes in support of this highly debatable thesis, the well-known passage in the earliest Halachic Midrash, the *Sifra*.[3] "If two men are travelling on a journey[4] and one has a pitcher of water, if both drink they will both die, but if only one drinks, he will reach civilization. Ben Petura taught that it is better that both should drink and die, rather than that one of them should behold his companion's death. Until Rabbi Akiba came and taught: " 'that thy brother may live *with* thee;'[5] thy life takes precedence over his life." "Little is known," concludes Ahad Ha'am, "of Ben Petura,"[6] and his view is certainly not adopted. Akiba's voice is that of authentic Judaism.

Dr. J. H. Hertz follows Ahad Ha'am. Writing in his *Commentary to the Pentateuch* on the Golden Rule in Judaism, he remarks:

Rabbi Akiba could not agree that two should perish where death demands but one as its toll. And, indeed, if the Torah had meant that a man must love his neighbor to the extent of sacrificing his life for him, in all circumstances, it would have said: "Thou shalt love thy neighbor *more than thyself*."

There are those, both in ancient and modern times, who do not agree with Rabbi Akiba, and who deem the view of Ben Petura the more altruistic, the more heroic. Such would have preferred that the words *as thyself* had not occurred in the Golden Rule. Others again preach the total annihilation of self, or at any rate, its total submergence as the basic principle of human conduct. New formulations of the whole duty of man have in consequence been proposed by various thinkers. We need examine but one of these formulations—*Live for others*. Were such a rule seriously translated into practice, it would lead to absurdity. For *Live for others* necessarily entails that others live for you. You are to attend to everybody else's concerns, and everybody else is to attend to your concerns—except yourself. A moment's examination of this or any other proposed substitute for "Thou shalt love thy neighbor as thyself" only brings out more clearly the fundamental sanity of Judaism.

While Dr. Hertz is undoubtedly correct that it would be an absurdity to expect *all* men to love others more than themselves, his denial that Judaism would expect this of *any* man is open to question. After all, the Rabbis do speak frequently of the loftier standards demanded of the saint, of the *mishnath hasidim*. It is hoped that the following observations will help refute so pedestrian a view of the Jewish ethic as that of Ahad Ha'am and Hertz. Sanity and balance are wholly admirable, but is it true that Judaism has no use for the "fool of God"?

While our problem is not dealt with explicitly in the Bible, there are a number of Scriptural passages relevant to it. That many of the Biblical characters risk their lives in war for the sake of their people, and are commended for so doing, has no real bearing on our question for they were fighting for themselves as well as for others. More to the point is Deborah's praise of Zebulon and Naphtali, who "jeoparded their lives unto the death in the high places of the field,"[7] i.e., they bore the brunt of Sisera's attack, unlike some of the other tribes who thought only of themselves.[8] Abraham, too, risks his life in order to save his kinsman Lot: "And when Abraham heard that his brother was taken captive, he armed his trained servants, born in his own house, three hundred and eighteen, and pursued them unto Dan . . . And he brought back all the goods, and also brought again his brother Lot, and his goods, and the women also, and the people."[9] Later, Lot, too, risks his life in giving shelter to the two angels.[10] On the other hand, both Abraham and Isaac adopt the subterfuge of pretending that their wife is their sister, in order to protect themselves,[11] but there is no suggestion that Scripture condones their behavior. If anything, the narratives voice an implicit condemnation of it. The Rabbis were close to the spirit of the Tamar narrative when they said[12] that Tamar was prepared to allow herself to be burnt rather than put Judah to shame.[13] Moses risks his life by smiting the Egyptian[14] and by delivering the daughters of Jethro from the shepherds.[15] When his people sinned, Moses offers his life in his prayer of intercession: "Yet if thou wilt forgive their sin; — and if not, blot me, I pray thee, out of thy book which thou hast written."[16] And when God wants to exterminate the people, and make of Moses "a greater and mightier nation," he refuses to allow it.[17] Samson kills himself in order to slay the Philistines, the enemies of his people.[18] David places his life in jeopardy when he accepts the challenge of Goliath.[19] In all these is implicit the thought that it is a natural thing for men, at times, to consider others even at the risk of their own safety. Indeed, the Gospels do not suggest that Jesus was advancing any new doctrine when he said: "Greater love hath no man than this." He mentions it to his disciples as axiomatic, as the established view of his day. If this is correct, not only was the doctrine of "Greater love. . ." part of the general Jewish attitude, but was recognized as such by the Gospel writers, who lay no claim to originality in this teaching.

To turn to the teachings of the *Halakhah*, we must first consider the general *Halakhic* attitude to self-sacrifice for the sake of a good cause. The verse: "Which if a man do he shall *live* in them"[20] is quoted[21] in support of the unanimously accepted Rabbinic teaching that it is permitted to transgress a Torah precept in order to save one's life. There are, however, certain exceptions to this rule. The Jew is expected to give his life rather than worship idols or commit adultery or incest or commit murder.[22] Later teachers decided that in times of religious persecution by the ruling power, a Jew must incur martyrdom rather than transgress even a minor precept.[23] The history of Jewish martyrdom affords sufficient evidence that these teachings were followed in practice. According to Maimonides,[24] where there is no obligation for a Jew to give his life for the Torah, he is guilty of committing suicide if he allows himself to be killed. But other authorities rule that while there is no obligation, it is an act of piety to give one's life,[25] if a Gentile compels a Jew to offend against his religion by transgressing *any* of the precepts of the Torah.[26] According to some commentators, Maimonides would concur in this if the man concerned was a renowned saint, determined to provide an object lesson for his people.[27]

There is a rather curious tale in the Talmud of a man who conceived a violent passion for a certain woman so that his life was endangered. The doctors who were consulted said that he could only be cured if she submitted to him but the Sages ruled: "Let him die rather than that she should yield." Then the doctors said: "Let her stand nude before him" but the Sages answered: "Sooner let him die." Then the doctors said: "Let her converse with him from behind a fence." "Let him die," replied the Sages, "rather than she should converse with him from behind a fence."[28] Two opinions are then recorded.[29] Some say that the woman in the case was a married woman and this would then be an extension of the rule that adultery may not be committed even to save life. But others say that she was an unmarried woman and yet the case was treated in so severe a fashion either because of "the disgrace to her family" or "that the daughters of Israel may not be immorally dissolute."

It follows, from the above-mentioned rule, that whatever the views of the Rabbis on sacrificing one's life to save another's, they agree in condemning the sacrifice of another's life to save one's own. The Talmud tells of a man who came before Raba (299–352 C.E.) and said to him: "The governor of my town has ordered me: 'Go and kill so-and-so; and if not, I will kill you.' " Raba replied: "Let him kill you rather than that you should commit murder; what reason do you see for thinking that your blood is redder? Perhaps his blood is redder."[30] As Rashi explains,[31] although it is permissible to sin in order to save one's life, this cannot apply to the crime of murder. For here, either way, a life is lost so that the commission of the crime does not save a life. From the moral point of view, the only reason there can be for preferring one's own life is that it is of greater value. But no human being can know which life is of greater value.[32] Hence, it is forbidden to save one's life by committing murder. The Talmud adduces no Scriptural proof for this, considering it to be self-evident—it is a *sabara*, "common sense." It would seem, moreover, from Raba's ruling that even a great scholar and saint would be prohibited from saving his life at the expense of the meanest member of the community, for here, too, it would be argued that, for all we know to the contrary, the life of the latter would be the worthier in God's eyes. In a fascinating Responsum on this question, Rav Kook even suggests that a number of men would be prohibited from saving their lives, at the expense of one man, for in the eyes of God the one man may count more than all the others.[33]

Talmudic literature deals not alone with the question of committing murder in order to save one's life, but with the more complicated question of handing over a man to be murdered in order to save one's life. The Mishnah[34] states concerning a parallel case, "If Gentiles said to many women: 'Give us one from among you that we may defile her, and if not we will defile you all,' let them defile all, but let them not betray to them one soul of Israel." Solomon ben Adret (1235–1310) rules that even if one of the women was of bad repute, (as in Maupassant's famous tale) the others are forbidden to save their virtue by giving her to the Gentiles.[35] The Jerusalem Talmud[36] to this section of the Mishnah adds: "It was taught: If a company of men travelling on a journey were held up by Gentiles, who said to them: 'Give us one of you and we will kill him, and if not, we will kill all of you,' let them all be killed and let them not betray to them one soul of Israel. But if the Gentiles specified one of the company, as in the case of Sheba, the son of Bichri,[37] he may be delivered to them so that the others may be saved." R. Simeon ben Lakish understands this to mean that even where one of the company had been specified by name, the others may not deliver him to the Gentiles, unless he is guilty of death as Sheba, the son of Bichri, was guilty for his rebellion against the king. R. Johanan holds that the others may have saved themselves by handing over the man, whose name had been specified, even if he is not guilty of death. The passage concludes with an account of a man who was wanted by the Romans, and who fled to the town of Lydda, where Joshua ben Levi resided. When the Romans besieged the town, Joshua delivered the man to them, whereupon Elijah, the prophet, who was a regular visitant of the Rabbi, appeared to him no longer. After Joshua had fasted for many days, Elijah eventually appeared and rebuked him for his conduct. "But I followed the ruling of the Mishnah," objected the Rabbi. "Yes," replied Elijah, "but is this a teaching that saints ought to follow (mishnath hasidim)?"[38]

To revert to the "Sidney Carton" question, it is far from certain that Ahad Ha'am's view is correct. There are, for one thing, Talmudic references to the "martyrs of Lydda" in Asia Minor, Lulianus and Papus, two brothers who took upon themselves the guilt for the death of the Emperor's daughter, so as to save the community as a whole.[39] It is said that they heard it proclaimed in Heaven that no man can stand in the celestial compartments of the martyrs of Lydda, so elevated is their station. However, it is possible, as Rav Kook suggests,[40] that had these men not confessed, they would have been executed in any case, together with the rest of the community for the murder of the princess.

Ahad Ha'am assumes that Akiba's view is accepted because of the dictum that Akiba's view is always adopted if he disagrees with only one of his contemporaries. Here, too, however, Rav Kook expresses doubts.[41] In the Talmudic discussion, in which the passage from the Sifra is quoted,[42] it is said that R. Johanan holds that interest paid illegally by a debtor to his creditor cannot be reclaimed in court, while R. Eliezar relies on the verse: "Take thou no usury of him, or increase; but fear they God; that thy brother may live with thee";[43] which implies that if interest is taken, it should be returned that "thy brother may be able to live with thee." R. Johanan, on the other hand, interprets the verse to agree with R. Akiba in the case of the two men and the water. From which, it would seem, that if the view of R. Eliezar is adopted, the verse cannot be interpreted to agree with Akiba, and Ben Petura's teaching would be followed. The Codes are strangely silent on the question of Akiba versus Ben Petura, but seeing that they do adopt R. Eliezar's ruling with regard to interest, the logic of the Talmudic passage quoted would demand that they follow Ben Petura; though, of course, this is no more than *pilpul* and is hardly conclusive.

But even if Akiba's view is adopted, this means no more than that there is no obligation for *both* to die, if one can drink the water and survive. In the ordinary way, this would mean that the one who has the water in his possession will drink, but this is not as Ahad Ha'am says it is: "because to preserve your own charge is a nearer duty than to preserve your neighbor's" but simply because there cannot be any *obligation* for one to hand over the water to the other, seeing that the other one would have the same obligation to hand it back again! Akiba would agree, however, that if the man holding the water wanted to give it to his neighbor, his would be a special act of piety—*middath hasiduth*. Ben Petura, too, would of course not object to one of the two allowing his friend to drink the water and survive. The debate between Akiba and Ben Petura concerns only the case were both want to drink; here, Akiba argues that it would be wrong for *both* to die, if one can live.

In this connection, reference should be made to a subtle distinction of *Ma–Haram Schiff* (Meir Schiff, 1605-c.1641) in his *Hakakhic* commentary to the Talmud. On the basis of the verse, "because he fareth well with thee,"[44] i.e., as thine equal, the Talmud rules[45] that if the owner of a Hebrew slave has only one cushion, he must give it to the slave, for by keeping it for himself, he would not be treating the slave as an equal. Why, asks Schiff,[46] is the verse "that thy brother may live *with thee!*" interpreted by Akiba to mean that the man in possession of the water may keep it, while the verse "because he is well *with thee,*" is taken to mean that the owner must give up his cushion to the slave? The answer is a fairly obvious one, once it is pointed out. In the case of the water, there can be no obligation for one to hand over the water to the other, for then the other would also be obliged to hand it back again. But in the case of the master and his slave, there is no such *reciprocal* obligation, for the verse "because he is well with thee" is addressed to the master, not to the slave!

Ahad Ha'am quotes the case of Raba mentioned above and argues that Raba would say that where the issue is saving the life of another by giving one's own life: "Let the other be killed, and do not destroy yourself. For do what you will, a life must be lost; and how do you know that his blood is redder than yours? Perhaps yours is the redder." This is to confuse the issue. Raba deals with murder and, as Rashi points out, it is forbidden to commit a *crime* in order to save a life, if life must be lost in committing the crime. But the sacrifice of one's life for another is no crime, for suicide is only an offense because *a* life is lost, not because *my* life is lost! Furthermore, the question of "whose blood is redder" is irrelevant here, for it could be argued that the act of self-sacrifice in the interests of another endows the "life" sacrificed with a significance it could not have possessed had the instinct of self-preservation prevailed.

Dr. Hertz is, of course, right that it would be an impossibility for all men to attempt to go through life loving their neighbors *more* than themselves. *As thyself* is the only rule for society. But the rare individual, who in a moment of tremendous crisis, can rise to the heights of giving his life for his friend—like the Sidney Carton of fiction and the Captain Oates of fact, is a saint and would be recognized as such by Judaism. Jewish history has not lacked such "Fools of God."

Notes

1. John, 15, 13.
2. *Essays, Letters, Memoirs—Ahad Ha'am,* translated by Leon Simon, East and West Library, Oxford, 1946, p. 128 f.
3. *Baba Mezia* 62a, *Sifra,* ed. Weiss, *Behar* VI, p. 109 c.
4. The *Sifra* has the reading "in the desert" but in *Baba Mezia,* the reading is "on the way," cf. Bacher: *Die Agada der Tannaiten,* Pt. I, Chapter 4. 6.
5. Lev. 25, 26.
6. Lauterbach, *Rabbinic Essays,* Hebrew Union College Publications, Cincinnati, Ohio, 1951, p. 539, roundly disposes of the view that Ben Petura is Jesus.

7. Judges 5, 18.
8. See Judges 5, 15-17 and 23.
9. Gen. 16, 14-16.
10. Gen. 19.
11. Gen. 12, 10-20; 20, 1-18; 6-11.
12. *Sotah* 10b.
13. See Gen. 38, 25.
14. Ex. 2, 11-15.
15. Ex. 2, 17-19.
16. Ex. 32, 32.
17. Num. 16, 2-20.
18. Judges 16, 28-30.
19. I Sam. 17.
20. Lev. 18, 5.
21. *Yoma* 85b and freq.
22. *Sanh.* 74a.
23. *Sanh.* loc. cit.
24. *Yad, Hil. Yesode Ha Torah,* 5,1 and 4.
25. Tos. *Avodah Zara* 27b, s.v. *Yachol.*
26. See *Yore Deah,* 157, 1.
27. *Keseph Mishneh* loc. cit.
28. *Sanh.* 75a.
29. *Sanh.* ibid.
30. *Pesachim* 25b.
31. *Pesachim* ad loc.
32. This *motif* appears in the well-known Talmudic anecdote (*Pesachim* 50a) of the Rabbi who was transported in a trance to the next world, where he observed a "topsy-turvy world," the insignificant on earth of great significance there, and the significant on earth, of no significance there.
33. *Mishpat Kohen,* Jer., 1937, No. 143.
34. *Terumot* 8, 12.
35. *Keseph Mishneh* to *Yad Hil. Yesode Ha-Torah,* 5, 5.
36. *Terumot* 8, 12 and *Tos. Ter.* 7, 23.
37. II Sam. 20.
38. For the question of the Jewish attitude towards saving the mother giving birth, at the expense of her child, see my article in the London *Jewish Chronicle:* "Mother or Baby?", Nov. 16, 1951.
39. *Pesachim* 50a, *Taanit* 18b.
40. *Mishpat Kohen* l.c.
41. *Mishpat Kohen* l.c.
42. *Baba Mezia* 62a.
43. Lev. 15, 16.
44. Deut. 15, 16.
45. See *Tos.Kiddushin,* 20a, s.v. *kol.*
46. Comment to *Baba Mezia,* 62a.

ISSUES

Political Ethics

The decade of the sixties was a traumatic period for all Americans. This was especially true of the Jews, who had been raised to see America as the Golden Land, defender of Jews and of the downtrodden the world over. The reality of Vietnam was difficult to behold. Similarly, the Black struggle for civil rights forced many Jews to question America's moral posture at home. It is hardly surprising, therefore, that recent years have seen an outpouring of Jewish debate on questions of political ethics.

The essays presented here deal with the related issues of pacifism, conscientious objection, resistance to immoral authority, and civil disobedience. They all accept the general Jewish teaching that where the words of the Master (God) conflict with those of the disciple (any human agency), the former take precedence over the latter. This unanimity of principle aside, these essays demonstrate wide differences in their specific views.

Three of the essays—those by Gendler, Lamm and Greenberg—also share a common methodology. They are basically halakhic studies, seeking to determine what the core texts and major authorities of Judaism have taught with respect to the questions they raise. Gendler takes this methodology further than the other two, citing medieval authorities in some detail. All three of the authors seek to extrapolate "the Jewish position" from the halakhic sources they cite. Milton Konvitz, however, seeks to derive the Jewish teaching on civil disobedience from Biblical and historical materials, putting relatively little emphasis on the *halakhah*. This is a non-traditionalist approach to the materials, rather typical of Reform Jewish writings on ethical matters.

Everett Gendler examines the attitude of the Jewish tradition towards war and concludes, unhappily it seems, that the tradition cannot honestly be characterized as pacifist. Those pacifists who ground their resistance to war in the teachings of Judaism would argue

187

that Gendler has given up the case too easily, ignoring the pacifist implications of messianism. Gendler does, however, make a case for selective conscientious objection, a case which is obliquely criticized by Maurice Lamm. While Gendler tries to show how far towards pacifism the Jewish tradition has gone, Lamm, looking at the question from a politically more conservative position, tries to show how far away from pacifism the tradition has stayed.

Moshe Greenberg examines the so-called Nuremberg defense ("I was only following orders") from the perspective of Judaism. He concludes, on the basis of a close study of key rabbinic passages, that a person faced with an illegal order must refuse to obey it. Even compliance in the face of the threat of death is condemned, although it is not legally actionable.

Milton Konvitz examines a number of instances of what might be called civil disobedience from the Jewish past. He then seeks to derive a Jewish approach to civil disobedience from their common features. Konvitz also finds in the rabbinic ordinance that one must die rather than commit idolatry, murder, or grave sexual immorality, a precursor to the modern doctrine of civil disobedience.

11.
War and the
Jewish Tradition

EVERETT E. GENDLER

At the outset, two source-problems of some seriousness confront any Jewish approach to the issue of "just war" doctrine, individual conscience, and selective conscientious objection.

The first of these Professor Julius Kravetz has called an "embarrassment of poverty."[1] For reasons easily enough understood, there is no great corpus of biblical and rabbinic legislation dealing directly with these issues. Augustine and Aquinas may have fancied that their findings about just and unjust wars would have application to the body politic of Christendom, represented by the Christian kings. The rabbinic fathers had no such hopes that Roman Emperors would seek their religious findings, nor could Maimonides and other Jewish medieval scholars expect their halachic deliverances to be heeded by regnant powers. Naturally, then, there was no felt urgency to formulate anything so directive of the use of power as a fully elaborated "just war" doctrine, and the elements we do have are somewhat incomplete and unsystematic. As for the biblical material, it too is somewhat limited in extent, and its *locus classicus* in Deuteronomy places it, documentarily at least, well after the period of the Conquest of the Land. Nevertheless, as I will indicate, there are quite valuable elements in both the biblical and rabbinic material, however limited in quantity and comprehensiveness this material may be.

The second problem is the application of such source-material as we

Reprinted by permission of the Bobbs–Merrill Company, Inc. from *A Conflict of Loyalties,* edited by James Finn. Copyright © 1968 by Western Publishing Co.

have to present circumstances. The social, political, religious, and human context of the material differs considerably both from our present self-understanding and our present situations, and these differences must be kept clearly in mind. Even within the same historical and social setting, the application of rules to cases is often difficult, as the workings of any legal system indicate. When there are additional differences the difficulties are compounded.

These two source-problems do not, of course, dictate that the grave issues confronting us should be avoided, nor do they render the source-material inapplicable. They do, however, urge upon us a constant appreciation of the difficulty and subtlety of the task, an appreciation which, combined with the felt sense of the present urgency of the issue, may yield certain findings which are both fair to the sources and relevant to our own times.

One last introductory caution. The following material, while hopefully an accurate presentation of some major teachings of the Jewish tradition in these areas, does not pretend to be comprehensive. A comprehensive treatment would necessarily extend far beyond the limits of an essay, developing many points that are only alluded to here. (References to fuller treatments of some of the relevant issues will be found in the footnotes.)

1. Biblical Material

Most discussions of the biblical material focus on the specific regulations of Deuteronomy 20, and these will be considered. However, without some preliminary indication of the variety of communal contexts within which armies were mobilized in biblical times, there is great danger that invalid analogies will be drawn with our own times. To reduce this danger, a brief summary of some parts of Roland de Vaux's fine survey of Israelite Military Institutions will be helpful.[2]

Recruitment of fighting men. Details of the nomadic period are scanty, but it seems reasonable to assume that "there is no distinction between the army and the people." By the period of the Judges, however, there is more information, some of it of particular relevance for us. Most significant are the following findings:

a. During this period individual tribes and families decided within their own intimate groupings whether or not to respond to the general call to arms. "During the period of the Judges, the response to these appeals depended on each group, which made its own decision. The Song of Deborah twice insists on this freedom to fight or not to fight (*Jg*. 5:2 and 9), and expresses nothing stronger than reproach or regret about the tribes which chose to stand aside (*Jg*. 5:15—17)."

b. "The units of the army were based on those of society. The unit was the clan (*mishpahah*) . . ."

c. The voluntarism extended to individuals within the clan and tribal groupings. "Gideon's action against the Midianites is even more typical; of the 32,000 men who answered his call, he sent home all who had no heart to fight, and only 10,000 remained; of these, he chose 300. . ."

d. "From time to time, two enemy forces would agree to settle the issue by single combat."

e. ". . .it must not be forgotten, even now, that the warriors of Israel were upheld by their firm belief that Yahweh fought with them and that He could grant them victory whatever the odds against them (*I Sam*. 14:6, 17:47)."

This period of small group autonomy and individual voluntarism was succeeded by a period of professional armies with mercenaries and chariotry, "the work of the first kings of Israel," and still later (and at times simultaneously) by conscript labor forces and conscript armies as well.

These latter developments were ambivalently regarded within the biblical literature. On the one hand there is a stream of thought distinctly favorable to the monarchy (*I Sam*. 9 and 11, praise of the Davidic dynasty, etc.). On the other hand, there is a strong current severely critical of the monarchy and its implications for the life of the people.

"Then all the elders of Israel gathered together and came to Samuel at Ramah, and they said to him,
  'Consider, you have become old and your sons do not follow in your footsteps. Now set up for us a king to judge us like all the nations.'
  But the thing was evil in the sight of Samuel, when they said,
  'Give us a king to judge us.'
  Nevertheless Samuel prayed earnestly unto the Lord, and the Lord said to Samuel,
  'Listen to the voice of the people according to all that they say to you; for they have not rejected you, but they have rejected Me from being king over them. Like all the deeds which they have done to Me from the day I brought

them up from Egypt even to this day, inasmuch as they have forsaken Me and served other gods, so they are also doing to you. Now therefore listen to their utterance, except that you shall certainly warn them, and show them the procedure of the king who shall reign over them'

Then Samuel told all the words of the Lord to the people who were asking of him a king; and he said,

'This will be the procedure of the king who shall reign over you; he will take your sons and appoint them for himself for his chariots and for his horsemen; and they shall run before his chariots; and he will appoint for himself commanders of thousands and commanders of hundreds, and some to do his plowing and to reap his harvests and make his implements of war and the equipment of his chariots. He will take your daughters for perfumers, for cooks, and for bakers. He will take the best of your fields and your vineyards and your olive orchards, and give them to his servants. He will take the tenth of your grain crops and of your vineyards and give it to his eunuchs and to his servants. He will take your male and female slaves, and the best of your cattle and your asses, and make use of them for his work. He will take a tenth of your flocks; and you yourselves will become his slaves. Then you will cry out on that day because of your king whom you will have chosen for yourselves; but the Lord will not answer you on that day.' "—*I Sam.* 8:4–18.

The legislation restricting the king in Deuteronomy 17:14–20, and passages from Hosea (7:3–7, 8:4, 13:9–11) reveal the continuation of suspicion and hostility toward the king as divine surrogate and usurper. In this latter respect, the attitude toward the census of the people for military purposes is especially significant.

'Now the Lord was again angered against Israel, and He incited David against them, saying,

'Go number Israel and Judah!'

So the king said to Joab and the commanders of the army which was with him,

'Go about now throughout all the tribes of Israel, from Dan even to Beer-sheba, and take a census of the people that I may know the number of the people.'

Joab said to the king,

'May the Lord your God add to the people a hundred times as many as they are, while the eyes of my lord the king look on! But why does my lord the king take delight in this thing?'

But the word of the king prevailed over Joab and the commanders of the army. Therefore Joab and the commanders of the army went out from the king's presence to take the census of the people of Israel. They crossed the Jordan and started from Aroer, and from the city that is in the midst of the torrent valley, toward Gad and on to Jazer. Then they came to Gilead and to the land of the Hittites, to Kadesh; and they came to Dan, and from Dan they went around to Sidon, and came to the fortress of Tyre and all the cities of the Hivvites, and of the Canaanites; and they went forth to the Negeb of Judah at Beersheba. When they had gone about through the whole land they came to Jerusalem at the end of the nine months and twenty days; and Joab gave the number of the census of the people to the king, and Israel consisted of eight hundred thousand able-bodied men who drew sword, and the men of Judah were five hundred thousand.

But David's conscience smote him after he had numbered the people. Then David said to the Lord,

'I have sinned exceedingly in what I have done. But now, O Lord, take away, I pray thee, the iniquity of thy servant, for I have done very foolishly.' "—*II Sam.* 24:1-10.

In the words of de Vaux: "Thus the tradition of a people under arms persisted, but the mass response to a call from a leader inspired by God had given place to mobilization organized by the royal administration. The first indication of this development can be seen as early as David's reign: his census had a military purpose and was equivalent to drawing up a register for conscription, but this step was condemned as an abandonment of the rules of a holy war, and a profanation (cf. verses 3 and 10)."

Varieties of Biblical Wars. Scholarly classifications of biblical wars tend to coincide. Thus Kaufmann distinguishes three main types: Wars of Conquest, Wars of Liberation, and Wars of Empire, with one intermediate type, Wars of Tribute.[3] De Vaux's division into wars of conquest, defensive wars, and wars of expansion, is essentially the same. The basic biblical legislative differentiation is, however, confined to the distinction between wars with "towns that lie very far from you" and wars with "towns that belong to nations hereabout."

"When you invest a city, you must offer it terms of peace. If it agrees to make peace with you, and surrenders to you, then all the people to be found in it shall become forced laborers for you, and serve you. But if it will not make peace with you, but wages war with you, you are to besiege it, and when the Lord your God delivers it up to you, you must put every male in it to the sword; but the women and children and livestock and everything that is in the city, that is, all its spoil, you may take as your booty, and yourselves use the spoil of your enemies which the Lord your God gives you. So shall you treat all the cities that are very far away from you, that do not belong to the cities of the nations here. However, in the cities of the peoples here, which the

Lord your God is giving you as a heritage, you must not spare a living soul; but you must be sure to exterminate them. Hittites, Amorites, Canaanites, Perizzites, Hivvites, and Jebusites, as the Lord your God commanded you, so that they may not teach you to imitate all the abominable practices that they have carried on for their gods, and so sin against the Lord your God."
—*Deut.* 20:10–18.

The primary characteristic of wars of conquest, the *herem,* "the anathema carried out on the vanquished enemy and his goods," was understood to be by the express command of God, applied only to the "seven nations" inhabiting the promised land (cf. *Dt.* 7:2), and characterized these wars only and no others. "The characteristic quality of the wars of conquest is that they are exclusively Canaanite . . . Ammon, Moab, Edom, and Aram, whose lands were never promised to Israel, are excluded from these wars."[4] From the Biblical text itself it is clear that the *herem,* the total destruction of persons and goods, is limited in application to a single category of conflict: the wars of conquest of the promised land. Any additional instances, such as the total destruction of the Amalekites, were exceptions and understood to be only at the direct instigation of God, not by inferential human discretion.

There is one other characteristic, common to all the varieties of biblical wars, which requires some clarification: the holy or sacred character of the wars. De Vaux uses the term "holy war," a term which appears to suggest what we might designate an ideological conflict, but de Vaux is emphatic in rejecting such an identification. To attempt to spread one's faith by force of arms was utterly foreign to Israel, and until the time of the Maccabees the concept of a war of religion had not appeared. "Israel did not fight for its faith, but for its existence." War was indeed "a sacred action, with its own particular ideology and rites," but so were many other actions and activities, and the religious character of biblical war was quite distinct from those distortions which we designate medieval religious or modern ideological "crusades." De Vaux summarizes the meaning of this in the following words: "This is the principal fact: it was Yahweh who fought for Israel, not Israel which fought for its God. The holy war, in Israel, was not a war of religion."

The sacred character of biblical war was reflected in such acts as sacrifices prior to marching to battle (*I Sam.* 7:9; 13:9, 12), the consultation with Yahweh by means of the Urim and Tumim (*I Sam.* 23:9 f.; 30:7 f.), requirements of ritual cleanliness for combatants (*Jos.* 3:4) and for the camp (*Dt.* 23:10–15), and the frequent presence of the Ark (*Num.* 10:35–36).

Most important for our considerations, however, are the implications for the combatants of the sacred character of biblical war. "Faith was an indispensable condition: they had to have faith and to be without fear (*Jos.* 8:1; 10:8, 25). Those who were afraid did not have the necessary religious dispositions and were to be sent away (*Jg.* 7:3; cf. *Dt.* 20:8, where the dismissal of such men is explained by a psychological reason, which was not the original reason for the custom)."

With the establishment of the monarchy ". . . this strictly sacred character of war disappeared with the advent of the monarchy and the establishment of a professional army. It is no longer Yahweh who marches ahead of His people to fight the Wars of Yahweh, but the king who leads his people out and fights its wars (*I Sam 18:20*). The combatants are no longer warriors who volunteer to fight, but professionals in the pay of the king, or conscripts recruited by his officials."

De Vaux traces this "profanation" of war as it became the state's concern; adduces prophetic retentions of the original idea which serve as the bases for criticism of the later secular wars of the Jewish state; and analyzes the reappearance of certain elements of the holy war in the Maccabees (which do not, however, make theirs a holy war in the older sense, but rather a "war of religion": "The Maccabees and their men are not inspired by God. God did not order the war and He does not intervene directly in it"). He makes very clear, in short, the nontransferable nature of the "holy war" and so enables us to guard against that fearful tendency to identify our own impulses and ideologies with the sacred as such.

Specific Biblical Regulations. The major remaining, though sketchy, biblical regulations concerning the waging of war find their classic formulation in Deuteronomy 20.

"When you go out to battle against your enemies, and see horses, and chariots, forces greater than your own, you must not be afraid of them; for the Lord your God who brought you up from the land of Egypt is on your side. When you are on the eve of a battle, a priest must come up and speak to the people. He shall say to them, 'Listen, O Israel; today you are on the eve of a battle against your enemies; do not be faint-hearted, nor afraid, nor alarmed, nor stand in dread of them; for the Lord your God is going with you, to fight for you against your enemies and give you the victory.' Then the officers shall say to the people, 'Whoever has built a new house, but has not dedicated it, may leave and return home lest he die in the battle, and another dedicate it. Whoever has planted a vineyard, but has not had the use of it, may leave and return home, lest he die in the battle, and another get the use of it. Whoever has betrothed a wife, but has not married her, may leave and return home, lest he die in the battle and another marry her.' The officers shall say further to the people, 'Whoever is afraid and faint-hearted must leave and return home, so that his fellows may not become faint-hearted like him.' As soon as the officers have finished addressing the people, the army commanders shall place themselves at the head of the people."—20:1–9

(Verses 10–18 cited above)

"When you have to besiege a city a long time in your war on it in order to capture it, you must not destroy its trees by taking an ax to them, because you can eat their fruit; you must not cut them down; for are trees in the field men to be besieged by you? It is only trees which you know are not fruit trees that you may destroy and cut down for the construction of siegeworks against the city that is waging war with you, until it is razed." — 20:19–20

Of these provisions, those respecting the morale functions of the priest and the officers can be well understood in the light of de Vaux's discussion of the role of faith in the rallying of men to combat. One also notes the necessity of individual consent, as it were (verse 8), a provision highly significant for our own considerations.

In the case of siege warfare outside the promised land, peace terms must first be offered, and if the population accepts, it may be subjected to forced labor but to nothing else (verses 10–11, cited above). If it refuses, the possibilities are specified in verses 12–15, including the execution of the males and the appropriation of the remaining persons and property.

The *herem* provisions of verses 16–18 have already been discussed above, leaving two final elements for comment: rules of exemptions (verses 5–7) and limitations on destruction (verses 19–20). In both cases, the penetrating comments of Johannes Pedersen are especially illuminating.[5]

With respect to personal exemptions or deferments, Pedersen suggests that the following profound human consideration is at work: ". . .the army should only admit to its ranks men who can be entirely merged in the whole and act as part of it. In the military laws of Deuteronomy we find the following passage (verses 5–7). In these three laws we find the same considerate spirit which prevails in many of the laws of Deuteronomy and which is generally characterised by the honourable name 'humane.' A close inspection will show, however, that the laws are not considering casual instances, but something greater and more profound. In all three cases a man has started a new, important undertaking without having finished it yet. In such a case something has been created, which is greater than the man himself, a new totality has come into existence. To make a breach in this prematurely, that is to say, before it has attained maturity or has been finished, involves a serious risk of sin. This risk must be avoided for the sake of the cause itself, and the man who came to the army after committing such a breach might mean a danger much more than a help in the psychic whole constituted by the army." (pp. 9–10).

As for the law requiring that the enemy's trees be spared to some extent: "Here there is a demand for the moderation characteristic of the old time. Life is to be respected, it must not be entirely destroyed, . . . Reduction is allowed, but not extermination." (23, 24.)

Or in the beautiful summary of this spirit by Isaiah:

". . .the Lord who created the heavens
(He is God!),
Who formed the earth and made it
(He established it),
He did not create it a wasteland
He formed it to be inhabited!" (45:18.)

2. Rabbinic Material

As I have noted, one does not find ready-at-hand a fully developed rabbinic formulation of a "just war" doctrine, and the problem of application is further increased by the fact that much of the legislation presupposes the existence of a divinely established state in the Holy Land. Further, since such a state was regarded as divinely ordained, it is especially perilous to extrapolate from permissions granted it to any other situation.

Neither does one find a systematic elaboration of the individual moral considerations considered appropriate for determining individual participation or non-participation in any given conflict. Yet there is, scattered throughout the classical rabbinic writings, some significant amount of teaching relating to these questions, material which, with due caution, is quite relevant. Much of it is biblically based, though it often goes beyond the biblical texts, sometimes expanding, sometimes modifying, sometimes applying them. I will attempt to show that some selections from these teachings are pertinent to the specific issues confronting us.

The traditional rabbinic classification of wars distinguishes three types: *milhemet hovah* (obligatory), *milhemet mitzvah* (mandatory), and *milhemet reshut* (discretionary) (*Talmud Sotah*, 44b). For almost all practical purposes, however, the first two categories are one, leaving in effect the distinction between mandatory and discretionary wars (*mitzvah* and *reshut*).

Which specific wars fall into these categories? Although there are some points at issue, it is widely agreed among rabbinic authorities that mandatory wars obtained in only two or possibly three instances: (a) Joshua's war of conquest against the seven Canaanite nations (directly commanded by God); (b) the campaign against Amalek (directly commanded by God); (c) a war of clear and immediate defense against an attack already launched (included by Maimonides but not classical-rabbinic).[6]

Instances of discretionary wars (*reshut*) include the following: (a) expanding the boundaries (perhaps to strengthen one's strategic position); (b) increasing one's power or prestige.[7] In the opinion of all, such wars anticipatory of future power-political problems are at best discretionary (*reshut*), even in the case of the divinely ordained state, and thus subject to the checks and limitations to be indicated below.

Especially significant with respect to classification is one particular case, that of "preventive" or "pre-emptive" attack. In the classic statement of the issue in the *Talmud*, Raba, discussing a difference of opinion between the Rabbis and R. Judah, says the following:

"The wars waged by Joshua to conquer Canaan were mandatory (*mitzvah*) in the opinion of all; the wars waged by the House of David for territorial expansion were discretionary (*reshut*) in the opinion of all; where they differ is with regard to wars against heathens so that these should not march against them. One calls them mandatory (*mitzvah*) and the other discretionary (*reshut*) . . ." (*Sotah* 44b).

Or, in the wording of the *Talmud Jerushalmi*:

"Rabbi Judah designated discretionary (*reshut*) a war in which we attacked them, and obligatory (*hovah*) a war in which they attacked us."

In short, the majority opinion of Talmudic thinking is that a war "preemptive of future danger. . .is at best a *milhemet reshut.*"[8]

In evaluating these classifications it is well to keep in mind that they are largely theoretical findings after the fact, and further that subsequent authoritative opinions tend to reduce severely the range of "discretion" in the case of *milhemet reshut.* Thus Maimonides forbids the waging of war against any nation before peace offers are made to it, and insists that even in the case of a supposed *milhemet mitzvah* (mandatory war), "if the inhabitants make peace, accept the seven Noahide commandments, and submit to certain conditions of taxation and service, one may not kill a single person."[9]

There is also evident among Jewish authorities a strong tendency to emphasize limitations on the so-called "discretionary" wars. Thus Rabbi David S. Shapiro, in a learned and well-documented essay, states the following:

> "The category of *milhemet reshut* includes wars against the avowed enemies of Israel, nations that flagrantly violate the Seven Commandments and recognize no international obligations. This kind of war may be declared only after the sanhedrin of seventy-one, the highest tribunal in Israel, the king of Israel, and the high-priest through the Urim and Tumim have given their approval. Its purpose may not be conquest, plunder, or destruction. It may be waged only for the protection of Israel and for the sanctification of the name of God, that is the imposition of the Seven Commandments.
>
> No war may be waged against a nation that has not attacked Israel, or that lives up to the fundamental of the Universal Religion. Even Edom, Ammon, and Moab, who had throughout their history displayed hostility to Israel, were not be attacked, not to speak of those nations who were not bellicose. It would seem that the *milhemet reshut* was limited by the ideal boundaries of the Holy Land."[10]

And the eminent Israeli halachist, Rabbi Shelomo Yosef Zevin, suggests that "in fact a war of attack, though designated a *milhemet reshut* (discretionary war), is forbidden to the nations of the world."[11]

With this caution in mind, it will now be of value to consider briefly the traditional significance of these distinctions among wars. In the three cases of *milhemet mitzvah,* it is the rabbinic view that such wars may be initiated by the king without his consulting the Court of Seventy-One, that the claim of conscription applies to all, even those specifically exempted by the provisions in Deuteronomy 20:8 and 24:5, and that all may be coerced to participate. It is interesting (and ironic) that

Maimonides takes those critical threats in I Samuel, cited above, and reads them as sanctions for such acts by the ruling power!

On the other hand, in instances of discretionary wars *(reshut)* it is rabbinic opinion that the king may not involve the people without the sanction of the Court of Seventy-One and the sanction of the Urim and Tumim (oracles) consulted by the high priest, and that the various exemptions do indeed apply. Thus while reducing in some respects the application of biblical exemptions, the rabbinic authorities in other respects extend them. Relying on Deuteronomy 24:5,

> "When a man is newly married, he is not to go out with the army, nor be counted with it for any duty; he is to be free at home for one year, to enjoy himself with his wife whom he has married,"

the rabbis apply it as follows:

> "The following do not move from their place (to join the army and then claim exemption): He who built a new house and dedicated it, planted a vineyard and used its fruit, married his betrothed, or took home his brother's childless widow . . . These do not even supply water and food or repair the roads (for the army)." *(Mishnah Sotah* 8:4.)

The exemption in such cases is thus total.

We further note in passing that the provision of *rakh levav* ("tender of heart") in all opinions applies to all cases of discretionary war, a fact of some import since no war today can be regarded as either *hovah* or *mitzvah*.[12]

Other elements of rabbinic teachings are relevant to our current considerations; for example, attempts to limit destruction of resources during war. Among the provisions from the classical rabbinic tradition attempting to limit the destructive consequences of war, the following are clearly relevant to our own age:

> 1. "It is forbidden to cut down fruit-bearing trees outside a (besieged) city, nor may a water channel be deflected from them so that they wither, as it is said: 'Thou shalt not destroy the trees thereof' (Deut. 20:19). Whoever cuts down a fruit-bearing tree is flogged. This penalty is imposed not only for cutting it down during a siege; whenever a fruit-yielding tree is cut down with destructive intent, flogging is incurred. It may be cut down, however, if it causes damage to other trees or to a field belonging to another man or if its value for other purposes is greater (than that of the fruit it produces). The law

forbids only wanton destruction." (Maimonides *Code*, "Laws of Kings and Wars," Ch. 6, Law 8.)

2. "Not only one who cuts down (fruit-producing) trees, but also one who smashes household goods, tears clothes, demolishes a building, stops up a spring, or destroys articles of food with destructive intent, transgresses the command 'Thou shalt not destroy.' He is not flogged, but is administered a disciplinary beating imposed by the Rabbis." (*Ibid.*, Law 10.)

3. "It was after these things and this loyalty, that Sennacherib, king of Assyria, came and invaded Judah, and besieged the fortified cities and expected to take them. When Hezekiah saw that Sennacherib had come determined to attack Jerusalem, he decided in council with his princes and his leading men to stop the water of the fountains that were outside the city, and they helped him. Indeed a great crowd of people collected and stopped up all the fountains and the torrent that coursed through the midst of the land, saying,

'Why should the kings of Assyria come and find abundant water?' "
— *II* 32:1-4.

"It was Hezekiah who stopped the upper springs of Gihon and directed the waters straight down on the west side of the city of David." — *II* 32:30.

"Our Rabbis taught: Six things King Hezekiah did; in three they (the Sages) agreed with him, and in three they did not agree with him . . . and he closed the waters of Upper Gihon, and they did not agree with him . . . ."
— *Pesahim* 56a

Other teachings are directly applicable to traditional attempts to limit injury of persons during war. The rabbinic tendency to modify the biblical meaning of certain texts toward what we might designate "humane ends" was noted above with Maimonides' insistence that even the "seven nations" were first to be offered peace rather than *herem*, and that such acceptance meant that "not one person was then to be slain." The attempt to prevent unnecessary injuries and deaths during conflict, especially among noncombatants, is expressed in a number of rabbinic rulings:

1. "When siege is laid to a city for the purpose of capture, it may not be surrounded on all four sides but only on three in order to give an opportunity for escape to those who would flee to save their lives, as it is said: 'And they warred against Midian, as the Lord commanded Moses' (*Num.* 31:7). It has been learned by tradition that that was the instruction given to Moses." (Maimonides, *op. cit.*, Ch. 6, Law 7.)

2. (During their festivals) One should not sell them (gentiles) bears, lions, or anything which may injure the many. (*Mishnah Avodah Zarah* 1:7.)

"The reason is because they may injure the many." (*Talmud Avodah Zarah* 16 a,b.)

Maimonides spells out more fully the implications of this dictum:

3. "It is forbidden to sell to idolators any weapons of war. Neither may one sharpen their weapons nor make available to them knives, chains, barbed chains, bears, lions, or anything which might cause widespread injury. One may sell to them shields or shutters which are purely defensive." (Maimonides *Code*, "Laws of Murder and Defense," Ch. 12, Law 12.)

One notices, incidentally, that the nature of the weapons themselves, and *not* the purported intentions of their users, determines the prohibitions!

In further treating this provision, Maimonides extends the principle to include indirect supplying of such material, and makes clear that the prohibition applies to Jewish brigands as well:

4. "That which is prohibited for sale to idolators is also prohibited for sale to Jews who are suspected of then selling such material to idolators. Likewise, it is forbidden to sell such weapons to Jewish brigands *(listim.)*" (Maimonides *Code*, "Law of Idolatry," Ch. 9, Law 8.)

Zevin, relying on Maimonides, states the following principle as well:

5. "In all cases of *milhemet reshut* (discretionary war), it is forbidden to kill women and children." (Zevin, *op. cit.*, p.44.)

There is no developed rabbinic doctrine on the scale or dimensions of any given conflict, although some of the previously indicated limitations suggest that in practice any war had to be rigorously bounded. Two further remarks on this specific question should be cited, however:

1. "R. Eleazar said: Every war which is waged with more than sixty thousand men is waged in disorder (*milhemet irbuviah*, a chaotic war)." (*Song of Songs Rabbah*, IV, 4.)

2. "Samuel said: A government which kills up to one out of six (by going to war) is not punished. . ." (*Talmud Shevuoth* 35b.)

implying, of course, that beyond this such a government is liable to punishment. From Rashi's comment, this would seem to apply to those conscripted by the king, and would refer to the casualty rate among the soldiers themselves. From the current text reading, however, it would appear to apply to the nations attacked. In either case, however, it clearly excludes a war of "attrition" or a war of mutual extirpation.

Rabbi Immanuel Jakobovits, addressing himself to the issue in modern terms, states emphatically:

> A major source in the *Torah* for the law of self-defense is the provision exonerating from guilt a potential victim of robbery with possible violence if in self-defense he struck down and, if necessary, even killed the attacker *before he committed any crime* (Ex. 22:1). Hence, in the words of the rabbis, 'if a man comes to slay you, forestall by slaying him!' (*Rashi; Sanhedrin* 72a). Now this law confers the right of self-defense only if the victim will thereby *forestall* the anticipated attack and save his own life at the expense of the aggressor's. But the defender would certainly not be entitled to frustrate the attack if this could be done only at the cost of both lives; for instance, by blowing up the house in which he and the robber encounter each other. Presumably the victim would then have to submit to the robbery and even to death by violence at the hands of the attacker rather than take 'preventive' action which would be sure to cause two deaths.
>
> In view of this vital limitation of the law of self-defense, it would appear that a defensive war likely to endanger the survival of the attacking and the defending nations alike, if not indeed of the entire human race, can never be justified. *On the assumption, then, that the choice posed by a threatened nuclear attack would be either complete mutual destruction or surrender,* only the second alternative may be morally vindicated."[13]

Besides such regulations dealing with the body politic and its policies, there are a number of rabbinic teachings which deal with considerations of conscience for the individual facing a situation of war. Most significant is the fact that in these life-and-death confrontations, restraint, limitations, and scruples are explicitly affirmed as appropriate. This is so in both individual and collective confrontations.

1. "It has been taught by Rabbi Jonathan ben Saul: If one was pursuing his fellow to slay him, and the pursued could have saved himself by maiming a limb of the pursuer, but instead killed his pursuer, the pursued is subject to execution on that account." (*Talmud Sanhedrin* 74a.)

2. Especially revealing are the classical rabbinic comments on the anticipation of war between Jacab and Esau, deriving from the following verse in Genesis (32:8):

" 'Then Jacob was greatly afraid and was distressed.' R. Judah b. R. Ilai said: Are not fear and distress identical? The meaning, however, is that 'he was afraid' lest he should be slain, 'and was distressed' lest he should slay. For Jacob thought: If he prevails against me, will he not slay me; while if I am stronger than he, will I not slay him? That is the meaning of 'he was afraid' — lest he should be slain; 'and was distressed' — lest he should slay." (*Genesis Rabbah* 76:2.)

Another rabbinic comment ascribes to Jacob the following sentiment: "If he overpowers me, that is bad, and if I overpower him, that is bad!"[14]

3. There are two classical statements, referring to the same verse in *Genesis*, which affirm explicitly that murder (*shefichut damim*) is a category applicable to armed conflict:

" 'And Jacob was greatly afraid and was distressed.' One might think that Jacob was literally afraid of Esau, fearing that he might not be able to defeat him; but this is not the case. Why, then, was Jacob afraid of Esau? Because Jacob took seriously the prohibition against murder (*shefichut damim*). And so Jacob reasoned as follows: If I succeed and kill him, behold, I have transgressed the commandment 'thou shalt not murder.' And if he kills me, woe is my lot! Hence it is written: 'And Jacob was greatly afraid and was distressed.' "[15]

Even more remarkable is the comment of Rabbi Shabetai Bass, compiler of *Sifte Hahamim*, the classic subcommentary on the commentary of Rashi. Bass takes explicit note of the Talmudic permission to defend oneself, yet suggests that murder is still an issue, even in a situation of armed combat!

". . .Yet one might argue that Jacob surely should have had no qualms about killing Esau, for it states explicitly, 'If one come to slay thee, forestall it by slaying him' (*Talmud Sanhedrin* 72a; *Berachot* 58a and 62b.) Nonetheless, Jacob did indeed have qualms, fearing that in the fray he might kill some of Esau's men, who were not intent on killing Jacob (for only Esau had this intention) but merely fighting against Jacob's men. And even though Esau's men were pursuing Jacob's men, and every person has the right to save the life of the pursued at the cost of the life of the pursuer, nonetheless that provision applies which states: 'if the pursued could have been saved by maiming a limb of the pursuer, but instead the rescuer killed the pursuer, the rescuer is liable to capital punishment on that account.' Hence Jacob rightly feared lest, in the confusion of battle, he kill some of Esau's men outright when he might instead have restrained them by merely inflicting injury upon their limbs."[16]

Thus, Bass, whose subcommentary is a summary of "the best work of his fifteen predecessors who had commented on Rashi,"[17] relays the opinion that even in an actual combat situation, the principle does obtain that the least possible and least injurious force should be applied, even to combatatants!

4. Rabbinic comments on Abram's participation in the War of the Kings (Genesis 14) sustain the validity of this concern.

"After these things the word of the Lord came unto Abram in a vision, saying: 'Fear not, Abram. . .' (Genesis 15:1). This relates to the verses from Proverbs: 'Fortunate is the man who fears perpetually; But he who hardens his conscience shall fall into evil' (Prov. 28:14); and 'A wise man is fearful and turns away from evil, but a fool is overbearing and careless' (14:16). Who is the wise and fortunate man alluded to? Abraham. And of whom was he afraid? Of Shem, for he killed in battle Chedarlaomer, King of Elam, and his three sons, descendants of Shem. . . . Thus Abram was afraid, saying: 'I have killed the sons of a righteous man, and now he will curse me and I shall die. . . .' " (Midrash Tanhuma on Lech L'cha, 19, ed. Buber.)

Even more telling is the further speculation in Midrash Tanhuma:

"Still another reason for Abraham's fear after killing the kings in battle was his sudden realization: 'Perhaps I violated the Divine commandment that the Holy One, Blessed be He, commanded all men, "Thou shalt not shed human blood" (Gen. 9:6). Yet how many people I killed in battle!' " (—Ibid.)

For this reason too the Midrash imagines Abram needing divine reassurance.

Among other explanations of the grounds for Abram's fear, R. Levi suggests the following:

"Abraham was filled with misgiving, thinking to himself, Maybe there was a righteous or God-fearing man among those troops which I slew. . . ." (Midrash Rabbah on Genesis, 44:4.)

There are, of course, other explanations advanced which take Abram's fear in the most self-concerned sense; he feared for his life when the avengers of the dead would set out for him. Yet the interjection of scruples about killing in the midst of conflict is highly significant for our considerations, and that Abram needed direct divine reassurance indicates that the bloodshed consequent upon warfare was not to be lightly regarded.

5. The provision in Deuteronomy 20:8, which provides exemption from combat for one who is "fearful and/or tender-hearted," has received comment from the rabbinic tradition also:

> "R. Akiba says: 'Fearful and tender-hearted' is to be understood literally, viz., He is unable to stand in the battle-ranks and see a drawn sword. R. Jose the Galilean says: 'Fearful and faint-hearted' alludes to one who is afraid because of the transgressions he had committed. . ." (*Sotah* 44a.)

Lest Rabbi Akiba's interpretation be understood in purely "medical or psychological" terms, the *Tosefta* cites Akiba's position in these words:

> "Why are both terms, 'fearful' and 'tender-hearted,' specified? To indicate that even the most physically fit and courageous, if he be a *rachman* (compassionate, gentle), should be exempted. . ."

There are, further, teachings which concern obedience to established authority.

1. The respect which Judaism accords the law is well-known, and this respect extends to the civil laws of the secular state. Frequently cited is the rabbinic dictum: *dina d'malchuta dina*, "the law of the government is the law."

Not so often cited, however, are the precise conditions in which this dictum is asserted. The four Talmudic instances concern: the validation of a deed of sale, the method for acquisition of real property, tax collectors exceeding their authority, and extortioners, official oppressors, or tax-farmers behaving illegally.

All four cases involve monetary matters or matters of civil procedures, not matters of life and death. Furthermore, in the two cases where officials exceed their rightful authority, the dictum does *not* determine the issue, but rather tax-refusal/resistance/evasion is countenanced! (Cf. *Talmud Gittin* 10b–11a, *Baba Batra* 54b, *Baba Kama* 113a, *Nedarim* 27b–28a.)

2. In the *Talmud* a discussion is recorded between Resh Lakish and R. Johanan concerning the respect which should be shown a king. At issue is a legend that Moses struck Pharaoh in contempt and anger just before stalking out. While one of the rabbis is of the opinion that no matter

what the ruler's nature, respect must be accorded him because of his office, the other maintains that a ruler's wickedness should call forth contemptuous behavior in his presence! Thus, it is not at all certain that the man in office is to be accorded the respect due the office if he, in that office, violates the dignity of the office itself.

3. There is on record a specific case in which constituted authority commands an act contrary to the most basic moral teaching of Judaism. In such a case, the *Talmud* and later rabbinic tradition are at one in counseling refusal no matter what the personal consequence.

> "In every other law of the *Torah*, if a man is commanded, 'Transgress and suffer not death,' he may transgress and not suffer death, excepting idolatry, incest, and shedding blood . . . Murder may not be practiced to save one's life . . . Even as one who came before Raba and said to him, 'The governor of my town has ordered me, "Go, and kill so and so; if not, I will slay thee.' " Raba answered him, 'Let him rather slay you than that you should commit murder, who knows that your blood is redder? Perhaps his blood is redder.' " (*Talmud Sanhedrin* 74a.)

4. Many instances could be cited of disobedience to established authority, whether Jewish or non-Jewish, where such authority violated the basic moral and religious convictions of Judaism. Abraham, Moses, Elijah, Jeremiah, Shimon bar Yochai, Jochanan ben Zakkai, etc., are the heroes of numerous tales and legends lauding their refusals to obey illicit authority and unjust laws.

It should be mentioned, finally, that a well-established principle of Talmudic law is: "There is no agent for a sinful act." This is held to mean that a responsible adult cannot evade the legal consequences of the act committed by pleading that he was "merely following orders."

More precisely, in the opinion of the *Talmud* he is guilty of following the wrong orders: "If there is a conflict between the words of the Master (God) and the words of the student (man), whose are to be obeyed?" (*Talmud Baba Metzia* 10b; *Kiddushin* 42b, 43a.)

3. Coda

The foregoing selections should already have suggested some direct implications, both negative and positive, for our own situation. It is clear that the biblical period prior to the establishment of the monarchy was characterized by intimate family and tribal groupings, considerable local autonomy, and a high degree of voluntarism with respect to recruitment of fighting men. Professional armies and conscription of individuals by the central monarchy seemed to some of the prophets a serious violation of divine intent. The first biblical record of monarchical conscription receives unqualified condemnation.

It should be evident from these facts that any attempt to validate a centralized and bureaucratized system of mass conscription on the basis of early biblical practice and later prophetic evaluation is a serious misreading of the meaning of that tradition.[18] Inferences from an intimate community to a mass society are extremely dubious, to say the least.

It is further evident from the biblical material that there were distinctions among categories of wars; that "ideological wars" have no biblical basis; that individual willingness to participate in war was an indispensable condition; that a premature breach in a man's involvement in life was explicitly prohibited; and finally, except for the limited specific cases of the wars of conquest (from which no analogies to modern times can be drawn in any respect), a war which destroys the bases of human existence, i.e., a war of scorched earth or extermination, is strictly prohibited.

One further detail should be made explicit. There were two occasions on which exemptions were granted: *before* conscription (*Dt.* 24:5) and *after* entering the ranks (*Dt.* 20:5-8). This option did not apply once a force went off to battle, but it did apply during what we might call the training period, when the implications of war became evident to the person. It is, in fact, precisely to such a situation that the provision of *Rach-levav* (tender of heart) applies.

The rabbinic material, though not a complete statement of a "permissable war" doctrine, evidently supplies significant criteria for determining whether or not one should participate in a given conflict. It is further evident that individual scruples were regarded as appropriate to war situations, that obedience to established authority is *not* sufficient justification for participation, and that individual responsibility for actions could not be evaded by appeal to superior human authority.

It seems evident from the foregoing that Judaism cannot be characterized, in the strict sense of the term, as a "pacifist" tradition. It seems equally evident that Judaism does not regard every war as permissible, nor does it regard every means of prosecuting war as permissible. It is further evident that while Judaism is highly respectful of duly constituted authority, this does not absolve the individual from the duty of making responsible moral decisions. Neither these moral decisions nor their bases are delegated to human authority in any unchallengeable way.

If the above be an accurate rendering of an essential part of the Jewish tradition, it would appear that "selective" conscientious objection on moral grounds is a fundamental teaching of Judaism and a fundamental demand of its adherents.

Notes

1. Julius Kravetz: "Some Cautionary Remarks," in *CCAR Journal*, Vol. XV, No. 1, January 1968, pp 78–79 (Central Conference of American Rabbis).

2. Roland de Vaux: *Ancient Israel: Its Life and Institutions* (New York: McGraw-Hill Book Company, 1961). Especially pp. 213–267.

3. Yehezkel Kaufmann: "Traditions Concerning Early Israelite History in Canaan," pp. 304–309, in *Scripta Hierosolymitana*, Volume VIII. Jerusalem, 1961.

4. *Ibid.*, p. 304.

5. Johannes Pedersen: *Israel: Its Life and Culture*, Vol. III–IV (Oxford University Press, London, 1959).

6. Cf. Maimonides *Code*, "Laws Concerning Kings and Wars," Ch. 5, Law 1.

7. *Ibid.*

8. Cf. the sensitive article by Prof. Irving Greenberg of Yeshiva University on "Judaism and the Dilemmas of War," in *Judaism and World Peace: Focus Viet Nam* (Synagogue Council of America, New York, N.Y.).

9. Maimonides, *op.cit.*, Ch. 6, Law 1.

10. David S. Shapiro: "The Jewish Attitude Towards War and Peace," in Leo Jung, ed., *Israel of Tomorrow* (N.Y., 1946), p. 237.

11. Rabbi Shelomo Yosef Zevin: *L'or Hahalacha* (Tel Aviv, 5717), p. 17.

12. Such a statement may appear doubtful today given the strong feelings concerning the value, perhaps even the sanctity, of the reestablished State of Israel. Without entering into the question of any of the specific wars involving the modern State of Israel, it is surely clear that in the strict sense of the terms they cannot be regarded as anything more than *reshut*. As recently as 1946, before the establishment of the State of Israel, Rabbi Shapiro could plainly state: "Since the destruction of its state, Israel can no longer wage wars, for its war-declaring agencies are no longer in operation. All attempts at armed reconquest of the Holy Land are expressly forbidden. God has imposed an oath upon Israel to that effect. The Land of Israel will be restored to its people in God's own good time." *(op. cit., ibid.)* It must also be remembered that so inspired a teacher as Jeremiah raised serious questions about particular wars involving the ancient Jewish State, that very State established by Divine edict according to the Biblical tradition. To insist that all wars today are at most *reshut* is

simply to insist that every single one must be subject to serious moral evaluation, and that no claims of sanctity can serve to exempt any conflict whatsoever from this moral judgement.

13. In *Tradition: A Journal of Orthodox Jewish Thought*, Vol. 4. No. 2, Spring, 1962, p. 202. Cf. also the paper by Morris Laub: "Maimonides on War and Peace (with Special Application to Vietnam)." Available from the American Jewish Congress, 15 East 84 Street, New York, N.Y. 10028.

14. Lekach Tov, cited in *Torah Shlemah* (ed. M. Kasher), Vol. 6, page 1266, footnote 49.

15. Schechter Genizah Manuscript of an early edition of Midrash Tanhuma, cited in *Torah Shlemah, ibid.*

16. Sifte Hahamim on *Gen.* 32:8.

17. Louis Ginzberg in *The Jewish Encyclopedia* (New York, 1904), Vol. 2, p. 584.

18. Cf. the outrage expressed by Rabbi Aaron Samuel Tamaret as early as 1905 at the violation of individual existence by modern collective nationalist demands (in *Judaism*, Vol. 12, No. 1, Winter, 1963, esp. pp. 42–46).

12

Rabbinic Reflections on Defying Illegal Orders: Amasa, Abner, and Joab

MOSHE GREENBERG

It has always been recognized that the Israelite king of biblical times was not accorded unlimited power. The base subterfuges used by David to do away with Uriah and by Ahab to do away with Naboth are oblique tributes to the subjection of Israel's kings to custom and law. The strong censure that Nathan and Elijah directed at these kings, the rebukes that kings generally received for their misdeeds from the mouths of prophets show a common acknowledgement of royal accountability to a higher law. The idea was legally formulated in Deut. 17:14-20—the only ordinance concerning kings in the Torah—where the king is bound by various strictures and admonished to be humble and Godfearing, and to keep the Torah all his life.

Nevertheless, the powers of the king were broad and only vaguely delimited. Samuel's catalogue of despotic privileges (I. Sam. 8:11-18), Saul's whimsical massacre of the priests of Nob, and the free hand kings had in exterminating rivals and their families illustrate the lack of effective checks against arbitrary exercise of royal authority. While the laws of the Torah define insubordination to parents and to the high court (Deut: 17:8-13; 21:18-21) their predominantly premonarchic orientation excludes treatment either of the rights of the king or their limitations. For the conception of treason we are dependent on occasional notices in the

Reprinted from *Judaism*, Vol. 19, no. 1. Copyright © 1970 by the American Jewish Congress.

historical books; of justified defiance of royal authority we scarcely have a clue.[1]

This lack was partly made up by the Talmudists, whose elaboration of biblical law and ethics included such topics, even though they were no longer practical issues. Their views on the limitations of royal authority were not set forth in legal exegesis, since no relevant biblical laws exist. Instead, incidents in the books of Samuel and Kings were used as points of departure. The army chiefs Abner, Amasa, and Joab, endowed with the requisite authority to make their words and deeds legally significant,[2] became representative of opposed courses of action in the face of a conflict between the king's orders and higher law. Although the treatment is far from systematic, the scattered rabbinic observations reflect a coherent underlying doctrine, which eventually found statutory expression in Maimondes' Code (see below).

The legal-constitutional principle in the rabbinic discussion facilitates comparing it with other systems and applying it to other situations. Royal authority to coerce obedience on pain of death (as opposed to royal election) is not regarded as divinely ordained, nor are its opponents divinely appointed prophets, as in the Bible. On the contrary, the royal authority is derived from the people, and the opponents of the king are courageous, morally sensitive men who take their stand on a constitutional ground.

The basic text relates an episode in Solomon's trial of Joab for treason. The entire passage is a typical rhetorical exercise, in which arguments are put forward for and against historical figures. But these arguments are not improvised just for the occasion; they recur in other contexts, as we shall see, and thus have a claim to be taken seriously.

It is significant, at the outset, that the summary execution described in I Kings 2:31ff. is here preceded by a trial; even in the case of treason the king must act through the proper judicial procedure.[2a] Joab is required to answer the charge that he slew Abner and Amasa unlawfully (cf. I Kings 2:5). He defends himself successfully in the case of Abner: Abner had needlessly killed Joab's brother, Asael, so Joab was only doing his duty as a redeemer of blood.

> Then Solomon said to him, "What warrant had you to kill Amasa?" He replied, "Amasa defied the king, as the record shows:
>
> > The King said to Amasa, "Go call up the men of Judah for me in three

days, and be here yourself." Amasa went to call up the Judahites, but he delayed beyond the time that the king had set for him (II Sam. 20:4f.).

Solomon retorted, "Amasa construed *buts* and *onlys* in the law. He found the Israelites engaged in studying a tractate and reasoned thus: It is written,

Whoever defies your order and disobeys your command, whatever it may be, shall be put to death (Josh. 1:18).

Can this apply even if it conflicts with a matter of the Torah? The end of the verse indicates that it does not:

Only be sure and resolute.   (Sanhedrin 49a)

This elliptical repartee needs explanation. The king's right to execute defiant subjects arises out of the people's solemn asseveration to Joshua that anyone who disobeyed him would be put to death. It was conferred by the people upon their leader, and is not a divinely ordained rule of the Torah.[3] The conferral was made in a war camp and was particularly necessary for military discipline. General Joab understandably took the language of the conferral literally: any infringement whatever of the king's order was a capital offense. Thus he justified slaying Amasa for having transgressed the king's deadline. Such rigor accords with Joab's character and devotion to David. External warrants can also be adduced for Joab's severity. Amasa had been the commander of the rebel forces of Absalom, and had yet to prove his loyalty to David. Moreover, David himself had stressed the importance of speed in nipping Sheba's new revolt in the bud (II Sam. 20:6). Amasa's delay was therefore suspicious, and in the circumstances, downright injurious to the king. There was some color to Joab's judgment that Amasa was in defiance of the king.

But Solomon rejects Joab's argument and exculpates Amasa, citing with approval his reason for the delay. When Amasa undertook to mobilize the people, he found them busy in the study of the tractate (the reference is to the semi-annual *kalla* sessions, in which a pre-announced tractate was publicly taught for a month to thousands of students). Should he interrupt the session—an implementation of God's command to study and teach the Torah—for the sake of meeting the king's deadline? He reasoned his way out of the dilemma thus: The people (in Josh. 1:18) could not have meant to confer upon their leader authority higher than God's. A formal indication that they did not is the *only*-clause that they appended to their conferral, "only be sure and resolute". "*Onlys* and *buts* are restrictive," runs the hermeneutical rule used by Amasa; they limit the application of the law to which they are attached. The nature of the limitation here was doubtless suggested by an identical *only* clause a few verses earlier (vs. 7), in which God admonishes Joshua, "Only be sure and resolute in carefully observing all of the Torah that My servant Moses commanded. . ." The people's exhortation echoed God's admonition, thereby implying that the authority they granted their leader was subject to God's Torah.

Amasa then went on to decide that public study of the Torah was a matter that superseded royal authority. For this further step he adduced no scriptural authority; it appears as his own, innovative decision. By such bold reasoning Amasa felt authorized to delay the mobilization briefly to allow the study session to run its course (we are evidently to understand that it was nearing its end anyway).

Joab was thus wrong in regarding Amasa as a rebel and killing him. Yet the trial goes on and a new charge is brought against him—of being himself a rebel (cf. 1 Kings 2:28)—and of that he is apparently convicted. One must conclude that although he was morally guilty of Amasa's death, he was not legally culpable. This distinction will be enlarged upon later.

The model for defying illegal orders is found by the Rabbis in I Sam. 22. Suspecting the priests of Nob of having conspired with outlawed David, Saul commanded his men to

> Go round and put the priests of the Lord to death, for they too are David's partisans. But the king's servants were unwilling to lift their hand to harm the priests of the Lord (vs. 17)

The Palestinian Talmud asks:

> Who were those servants? R. Samuel son of R. Isaac said: they were Abner and Amasa. They replied to Saul, "Do we owe you anything beyond this belt and mantle (insignia of office)? Here, take them back (Sanhedrin 29a).

They would rather resign the high position held by them than accede to the king's demand.[4] As we shall see, the Babylonian Talmud grounds their definance on their "construing *buts* and *onlys*." In the event it proved inadequate to prevent execution of the king's orders; he found another instrument to carry out his will. This raised the question as to whether Abner and Amasa had really done all they could to stave off the massacre. There is one opinion that they did not.

> R. Judah said in the name of Rab: Why did Abner meet an untimely death? Because he might have made a stand against Saul but did not. R. Isaac said: He did make a stand but was overruled (Sanhedrin 20a).

Both Rabbis agree that by merely refusing to carry out an illegal order Abner did not discharge his full moral responsibility. It is not enough to dissociate oneself from wrongdoing—even at the price of demotion;[5] one must actively oppose it, even if one is eventually overruled. Not to do so is a moral dereliction, guilty in the sight of God.

> R. Zera once said to R. Simon, "You must censure the Exilarch's court." He replied, "They won't listen to me." R. Zera retorted, "You must censure them all the same," and that accords with R. Aha's homily:
>
> The only time God ever reversed himself with regard to a benign decision was when he said to his scribe,
>
> > Go through the city, through Jerusalem, and put a mark upon the foreheads of the men who sigh and groan over all the abominations that are committed in it" (Ezek. 9:4).
>
> The Holy One said to Gabriel: "Go mark the foreheads of the righteous with an X of ink so that the angels of death do not harm them, and the foreheads of the wicked with an X of blood so that the angels of death do harm them."[6] Hearing that, Justice spoke up and said, "Lord of the Universe, what's the difference between them?" God answered, "Why, these are wholly righteous and those wholly wicked." She replied, "Lord of Universe, they could have protested but did not." Said He, "But I know that even if they had protested no one would have listened to them." Said she, "Lord of the Universe, you knew it but did they?" Now God had at first said, "Pass through the city and smite it . . . but touch no one who bears a mark" (Ezek. 9:5f). But then we read, "and begin with my sanctuary (miqdaši)". R. Joseph taught, "Read it 'begin with my holy ones' (mequaddašay)—those who kept my Torah from A to Z" (Shabbat 55a).

The first to be punished in an evil society, says the homily (with typical hyperbole), are those who could have taken a stand against the evil but did not—regardless of the fact that they kept themselves apart from it.[7]

The example of insensitivity to the demands of the higher law is

Joab—who received David's letter ordering him to contrive the death of Uriah in battle and complied with it unhesitatingly.[7a] An unfavorable comparison of Joab with Abner and Amasa occurs in a rabbinic comment on Solomon's condemnation of Joab,

> Now the Lord has brought his bloodguilt down upon his head, for having struck down two men more righteous and better than he [Abner and Amasa] (I Kings 2:32).
> Better—in that they construed buts and onlys, while he did not. More righteous—in that they received their command by mouth yet defied it, while his came by letter and he obeyed it (Sanhedrin 49a).

The two men were better than Joab because they showed awareness of the moral problem posed by the king's illegal order, and a capacity to authorize refusal to obey it. As Maharsha suggests, their goodness saved the goodness of the law. Had the king's right been absolutized (as Joab was inclined to do), it would have been destructive of the value-context that law aims to preserve. Only by making the larger context determine the construction of particular laws can the Torah be kept from dissolving in a welter of incoherent rulings, adding up to no intelligible pattern of goodness.

The righteousness of Abner and Amasa consisted in their readiness to act on their interpretation, novel and risky as it was. And they acted in the most difficult of situations—confronting the king in person and having received the order from his mouth. Thus they were superior in theory and more righteous in practice than Joab.

The rabbis' disapproval of Joab is so obvious that the question must now be posed, how is it that they failed to reprobate Joab's compliance with David's criminal order concerning Uriah in their story of Joab's trial? Did they clear him of culpability in the matter? The issue is raised in connection with the law of agency.

> If a man says to his agent, "Go kill so-and-so," and he does it, the agent is culpable and the principal is exempt. Shammai the elder said in the name of the prophet Haggai: the principal is culpable, as it says, "And him (Uriah) you (David) killed by the sword of the Ammonites" (II Sam 12:9; David the principal is blamed for the murder, not Joab the agent) (Quiddušin 43a).

The rule is that "there is no agency for wrongdoing": an agent who commits a wrong cannot defend himself on the ground that he was merely executing orders; his moral autonomy is not cancelled by his agency and he remains responsible for his acts. The rule is eminently just; "when a master's orders conflict with a servant's (sc., God's with man's), whose should be obeyed?" (Quiddušin 42b). Hence an agent-killer is regarded as autonomous and culpable for his crime. Yet the prophet blames David for Uriah's death, not Joab; whence Shammai inferred a contrary ruling: in a murder by proxy, the principal is culpable.[7b]

But Shammai's inference is problematic. Murder by proxy under orders of a king is too special a case to serve as a basis for a general rule.

> Even though it is always the case that "there is no agency for wrongdoing," and the principal is exempt and the agent culpable, the case of Uriah is different; the text calls David the killer. The reason is, that since he was a king and nobody disobeyed him he is the killer. Similarly with Saul, who ordered the massacre of the Nob priests—it is as though he killed them (I Sam. 22:21). Now it is true that in such a situation one should not execute the king's orders [reference is made to construing *buts* and *onlys*] . . . but since not everyone is aware of this or knows how to construe *buts* and *onlys*, punishment falls on the king (Radaq at II Sam. 12:9).

The king's right to obedience on pain of death was an established, notorious right, which the people were conditioned to respect. Knowledge of its limits and discernment to know when its limit were transgressed could not be presupposed in everyone. The right was recorded in writing; the limitation was a bold construction of morally sensitive men. A good soldier like Joab could very well have been ignorant of his obligation to refuse an illegal order; or, having heard of the notion, might have (mistakenly) argued that it was dangerous policy to adopt. He might be condemned as morally obtuse; he might be held guilty in the eyes of God. He cannot be held legally culpable for a wrong committed under royal orders.[8]

Amasa and Abner had to depend on their insight to set limits to the king's authority; later ages did not. For what was earlier the property only of those who knew how to construe *buts* and *onlys* became the property of all Jews who could read the law. The great Code of Maimonides, aimed at the common man, incorporated the limitation of royal power in a statute and published it to the world.

> Whoever disregards a royal order because he is busy with God's commandments—even the slightest commandment—is exempt (from blame of

defying the king). If the master's orders conflict with the servant's, the master's take precedence. And it goes without saying, that if a king ordered violation of God's commandments, he is not to be obeyed (Laws of Kings, 3:9).

This spare statement of the principle leaves unsaid what the subject *is* to do with that illegal order, or what penalty he incurs if he obeys it. Joab's compliance went unpunished because he was excusably ignorant or mistaken. Now that the obligation to disobey has been published, everyone is on notice that an illgeal order of the king is to be defied. He who receives such an order now is therefore on a different footing from Joab; he is in one respect like Abner and Amasa who knew that a royal order could be illegal and must then be defied. But if he is an ordinary Jew he suffers a crucial disadvantage: the lack of that learning and insight that those ancient worthies had (by rabbinic convention), and that authorized them to decide rightly when to defy the king. He is, to be sure, competent enough to decide that to massacre a townful of priests is a crime, but he may puzzle over the postponement of a mobilization order for the sake of finishing a public lecture series on Torah. He will want to take advice from an authority before deciding on action—and exposing himself to risk of death for defying a legal order of the king.[8a]

But if, when all is done, he finds himself with an order he knows to be illegal, what is his duty? On the basis of the Talmudic material here assembled we can sum it up in three propositions:

1. He must refuse to carry out the order even if it means a fall in rank and status;

2. He must actively oppose the order and try to prevent its execution; otherwise he will be guilty before God.[9]

3. If he voluntarily obeys the order, he is not only guilty before God, but legally culpable as well. He cannot exempt himself on the ground of being merely the king's agent, for there is no agency for wrongdoing—and, unlike Joab, he can no longer plead ignorance of the limitations on royal authority.

Notes

1. See I. Benzinger, in *Encyclopaedia Biblica* (ed. Cheyne and Black), Vol. II, art. "Government," sec. 22–23, col. 1909–10; T. H. Robinson, *A History of Israel*, Vol I, pp. 225, 228ff.; S. W. Baron, *A Social and Religious History of the Jews* I/1, pp. 91–93; D. J. Silver, "Monarchy," in D.J. Silver, ed., *In Time of Harvest: Essays in Honor of Abba Hillel Silver* . . . (New York, 1963), 421–432; G. Fohrer, "Der Vertrag zwischen König und Volk in Israel," *Zeitschrift fur die altestamentliche Wissenschaft* 71 (1950), 1–22 (studies such passages as II Sam. 3:21; 5:3; II Kings 11:17). On the concept of treason, cf. M. Greenberg, in *Interpreters Dictionary of the Bible*, art. "Crimes and Punishments," p. 740b.

2. Abner and Amasa were "lions in the Torah" (Pal. Tal. Peah 16a); Joab was the president of the Sanhedrin (Pesikta Rabbati 11 [ed. Friedman, 43b]); cf. Louis Ginzberg, *Legends of the Jews* VI, p. 240[91], 258[76]

2a. Tosafot to Sanhedrin 36a (s.v., Rabba bar bar Ḥanna) resolves conflicting views on the subject thus: Treason cases must be heard by the Sanhedrin, but some of its rigid procedural requirements may be relaxed. See further, Zevi Hirsch Chajes, *"Din Melek Be yisra'el,"* in *Kol Sifre Mahraz Chajes* I, 43–49. I am indebted to Sid Leiman of Yale University for calling my attention to this interesting study.

3. The Meiri in his commentary (*Bet Habbe ḥira*, ed. Sofer, p. 204) says expressly that the king's authority to put rebels to death is not derived from the Torah (*'en be din tora ken*). Chajes develops the theory that the royal prerogatives flow from a contract (*ke tav hitqaśśe rut*) between the people and the king: the people surrender some of their rights in property and life to a single leader who will lead them in battle and provide for the general welfare (pp. 46–47). Cf. Fohrer's article (fn. 1), pp. 17ff.

4. Ginzberg, *Legends* VI, p. 240[92].

5. Assuming, for the sake of a systematic presentation, that R. Judah (Rab) held the view of R. Samuel son of R. Isaac that Abner had at least refused to carry out Saul's order, with an offer of resignation.

6. On these two X's (originally one an X cancelling debts—a mark of freedom, the order a Greek *theta* (*θ*) for *thanatos* "death" —a sign of death), see S. Lieberman, *Greek in Jewish Palestine*, pp. 185–191.

7. The complexity of the injunction to protest wrongs actively is only suggested by the Tosafot *ad loc.*, who absolve one from the duty when it is certain to be futile; and cf. Yebamot 65b "Just as one is enjoined to speak out when he will be listened to, so he is enjoined not to speak out when he will not be listened to." *Sefer Hahinuk*, sec. 218 (ed. Chavel) offers a convenient summary of the injunction with some indications of its limits.

7a. Though, for practical reasons, and in order to conceal the plot, he did not execute the king's orders literally; cf. U. Simon, "The Poor Man's Ewe-Lamb," *Biblica* 148 (1967), 216f.; M. Perry and M. Sternberg, "The King Through Ironic Eyes: The Narrator's Devices in the Biblical Story of David and Bathsheba . . .," *Hasifrut* I (Tel-Aviv University, 1968), 278f.

7b. That Shammai's ruling reflects a patrician viewpoint is plausibly argued by L. Finkelstein, *The Pharisees* (Philadelphia, 1962), p. 285.

8. Compare the formulation of the U.S. Dept. of the Army, Field Manual: the Law of Land Warfare 182, which admonishes military courts "to take into consideration the fact that obedience to lawful orders is the duty of every member of the armed forces; that the latter cannot be expected, in conditions of war discipline, to weigh scrupulously the legal

merits of the orders received . . ." The American Law Institute's Model Penal Code (from which the above is cited, p. 41) has the following to say on military orders (Section 2.10, p. 41): "It is an affirmative defense that the actor, in engaging in the conduct charged to constitute an offense, does no more than execute an order of his superior in the armed services which he does not know to be unlawful." I owe this to Stephen R. Goldstein of the U. of P. Law School.

8a. The complexity of this question is suggested by the juxtaposition in Maimonides, Code, Kings 3.8, 10; 5.3 of extraordinary rights (e.g., capital punishment for crimes evidenced only circumstantially; right of expropriating to build the king's highway) alongside prohibitions against unlawful actions (e.g., confiscation without compensation). Chajes looks to the principle of the general welfare for an explanation of the apparent inconsistency: the people have relinquished their rights to the king for the common good; but where a royal act violates Torah-given rights for the private good of the king only, it falls outside the contract with the king and is illegal. Regrettably, Chajes did not inquire at all into the right of the people to defy an illegal royal command.

9. These two propositions assume that the king will not unlawfully coerce his subject to execute his illegal order on pain of death. If he does apply such duress, the compliance of the subject cannot be legally culpable. See Maimonides, Code, $Y^{e}sode$ Ha-Tora 5.4 and Encyclopedia Talmudit, s.v., 'ones.

13.

After the War— Another Look at Pacifism and Selective Conscientious Objection (SCO)

MAURICE LAMM

The slowing of the revolutionary tempo allows us a moment of respite in which to reexamine the great issues of war and peace from a Jewish vantage point, and, especially, the question of pacifism and selective conscientious objection. Such a discussion must now also reckon with the recent 8 to 1 Supreme Court decision that the SCO can have no legal standing in American society.

The problem is acute at the present time because of the possibility, however remote we believe it to be, that Jewish youth may have to face this conceptual crisis in terms of the Middle East rather than the Far East, with the battlefield at the Suez rather than in Laos.

We have debated long and hard the question of the Jewish attitude toward absolute pacifism, the moral rejection of the validity of any and all wars. The Jewish Peace Fellowship has made a convincing case for, and has significantly inclined Jewish public opinion toward, a more ready acceptance of pacifist doctrine. Some scholars have made serious attempts to prove that, essentially, the Jewish tradition espouses pacifism, the exceptional case being when God Himself commands war.

Reprinted from *Judaism*, Vol. 10, no. 4. Copyright © 1971 by the American Jewish Congress.

Others, such as Jacob Agus and Abraham Cronbach, have asserted that the Jewish tradition offers no decisive stand either for or against pacifism. Cronbach goes so far as to say that a Jewish pacifist quotes Jewish Scriptures and a Christian pacifist quotes Christian Scriptures and that neither tradition influences the conception. Still other pacifists, such as Everett Gendler, are begrudgingly constrained to admit that pacifism is "not characteristic" of Judaism.

The further question of selective pacifism is much stickier. Yet almost all rabbinic groups that have addressed themselves to it, and almost all statements made by Jewish organizations, have taken the quite liberal view that supports selective pacifism.

Unfortunately, as Fr. Courtney Murray notes about the general tenor of the debate on the subject in the American public, in order to arrive at a proper perspective we must separate the specific question of the justice of the Vietnam War from the general one of pacifism and selective pacifism. Almost all those concerned with the morality of war and with the position of pacifism have stated their views in regard to this one Vietnamese can of worms, and one doubts whether these expositions of Jewish tradition would have arrived at the same conclusion had the discussion taken place during World War II.

I propose to discuss pacifism and SCO without any specific reference to Indo-China, as though the Vietnam war were over and done with. My critique will consider the two issues as such, and especially test the claims of their advocates that these doctrines genuinely reflect the Jewish tradition. I shall attempt to show that while the Jew has a passion for peace, the mainstream of his religious and philosophic tradition does not lead him, inevitably, to embrace pacifism.

Citing Sources Does Not Prove The Case

Jewish pacifists rely on a number of quotations from Scriptures in order to support their view. To Isaiah and Zechariah they add Jeremiah, who urged, "Bring your necks under the yoke of the King of Babylon and serve him and live." Support for their view is also derived from the patriarch Isaac's non-resistance to the perpetual Philistine vandalism. (Genesis 26:18-22). A remarkable passage is quoted from Josephus who said that the Jewish statesman, Agrippa, pleaded with his countrymen for non-resistance to the Romans, and, in a speech, said, "Nothing so much damps the force of strokes as bearing them with patience; and the quietness of those who are injured diverts the injurious persons from afflicting" (*Jewish Wars II* 16–351). Many quotations can be cited from Talmudic literature which reflect a spirit of non-violence. For example, "Be of the persecuted rather than the persecutors" (*B.K.* 93A). "Who is the hero of heroes? He who transmuteth a foe into a friend." (*Avot De Rabbi Nathan* 23).

Clearly, however, the citation of verses is inconclusive. For every illustration of an Isaac's non-resistance to vandalism by the Philistines, there are five examples of resistance to violence, such as Abram's war with the kings. For every verse supporting pacifism there are five supporting war when a just peace cannot be achieved. God is called *Shalom,* "Peace"; He is also called *Ish Milhamah,* "A man of war." The Psalms (33:16) say, "A mighty man is not delivered by great strength;" while Deuteronomy (13:6) says, "Thou shalt forcibly remove evil from the midst of thee." Although Isaiah and Micah pleaded that swords be beaten into plowshares and spears into pruning hooks, Joel, in bitter irony, cautioned the nations to transform plowshares into swords and pruning hooks into spears.

In addition, there is a "sense of the Bible" that can be derived from the spirit and the style of the whole Biblical and rabbinic literature. If an ideal such as pacifism were a divine imperative, a fundamental Jewish ethic, one would not need a verse here or there, an incident in Genesis, a quotation from *Avot,* in order to substantiate it. There would be an unmistakable literary and historical pattern. Instead, the pronouncements, even if they are pacifistic in nature, are without pathos and passion. One looks in vain, in the few declarations of *pacifism,* for the same intensity that we find uttered in the cause of *peace (shalom),* which appears some 220 times in Scripture alone, and in almost every major prayer.

The prophets preach peace, but denounce those who cry "'peace' when there is no peace." The greatest desire for peace cannot, by itself, avert war. "The watchman," Ezekiel cries, "who sees the sword come, and blows not the horn so that the people may be forewarned for battle, and someone thereby dies in the vain hope for peace; his blood will I require at the watchman's hand" (33:6). Leading Jewish thinkers have recognized that no definitive Jewish stand can be derived from explicit statements in the Bible.

It is my conviction that the Jewish tradition rejects pacifism, the comprehensive objection to *all* wars, not only because there is no specific

Biblical authority, but because the very concept contradicts, and even betrays, the Jewish spirit. I maintain this point of view for three basic reasons:

A Good Idea Is Not An Idol

First, pacifism *absolutizes* the concept of peace. In Judaism no value is considered absolute. Only God is absolute—He is Almighty and All-Wise and the Creator of all. Everything else in the world is relative to the absolute that we call God. When we transform a relative into an absolute, we create an idol. When the ancients worshipped the stars rather than the Creator of the stars, or the Nile River rather than Him who made the river flow, they made a relative object into an absolute. They were worshipping an idol.

Idols, obviously, are not only the fetishes that were worshipped by the primitives. Even concepts and values, when they are transformed from the relative to the absolute, become idols.

Generally, from the primitive totem to the latest concept, the items that are absolutized and made into idols, are, for the most part, not evil things but good ones. Thus, we find in the Midrash that the elders of Rome placed the question before the rabbis: "Why, if God detests idols, does He not destroy them?" Their response was that the idols which the ancients worshipped were mountains and trees and stars and rivers. Should God destroy the good simply because it is worshipped? If He does so, would He not have to destroy the world?

It is clear that even the highest of values are not absolute. For example, life is a primary value. Yet who doubts that a loving mother standing by her sick and dying child would not wish that she, rather than her child, would be dying? A mother is willing to sacrifice her life for an ideal higher even than the value of life itself. Freedom, too, is a value, but not an absolute. A part of it must be surrendered in order to achieve social cohesiveness. If people were free to do everything they wished, they would have no orderly society—only anarchy. Even truth, which surely ranks high in any hierarchy of values, must sometimes be modified into the "white lie" even if only for the sake of frictionless social intercourse. Interestingly, Rabbi Menahem Mendel of Kotzk interpreted the verse "Take heed . . . lest you make a graven image, even the likeness of anything which the Lord thy God hath commanded thee" (Deuteronomy 4:23), to imply "do not make an image, an idol, out of any *miẓvah* which God commanded you." No *miẓvah* should be considered absolute unto itself, but relative to the God who commanded it.

Not only do absolutized good concepts become idols, they can become positively demonic. Thus, a good such as order when it is absolutized, becomes tyranny; liberty can become licentiousness; loyalty can degenerate into collaboration with tyranny; parental respect can be transformed into ancestor worship; science can become a goal and not an instrument, a deity that commands unmercifully instead of a tool; justice unmodified by compassion can become a destroyer of God's house; love, absolutized, can become a destroyer of God's world. The crusader of medieval Europe and the Grand Inquisitor of Spain killed people for the sake of love of God. Thus, we may understand why the Talmud always bracketed idolatry with immorality and bloodshed.

Pacifism is the idolizing of peace. If nothing is worth fighting for, if everything must be subordinated to peace, then peace is an absolute, an idol. If a man says: "I will sue for peace regardless of the circumstances," and thereby increases the possibility of losing justice and freedom which took thousands of years of history to produce and refine; if a man is willing to sacrifice religion and equality and liberty and homeland for the sake of physical survival; then he has made of peace an unsatiable, satanic idol.

This idol is a moral outrage, also, because it can induce people to consider only one thing worthwhile—physical survival. And if that is the goal on the international scene, what havoc will be wrought within our own society when our children grow up with the concept that physical survival, peace, is the only value worth living for?

Pacifism, therefore, is an idea that flies in the face of the Jewish spirit. Strange as it may appear, to a people whose life and literature are saturated with the passionate pursuit of peace, pacifism is something of a moral aberration.

The World Is Far From Perfect

Second, in addition to the theological error of absolutizing a single value, the pacifist also misreads political reality. In urging pacifism, he is advocating a purely ideal possibility as a practical course of action; trying to apply an absolute ethic to a complex political reality; foisting an uncompromising value on a world whose very existence is dependent upon social and political compromise. In this sense, the pacifist is a perfectionist who either does not see, or does not wish to see, the imperfect world as it really is.

Now, the pacifist is correct when he affirms the world *ought* to be pacific; that war is horror. But he cannot assume that the world therefore is ready for pacifism or that it can become pacific merely by wishing it so. He betrays a naive faith in the automatic upward progress of society which, especially in the past fifty years, has not made notable moral progress. He believes in the presently-achievable perfectibility of man—which is a beautiful hope—but hardly a reality. The world is a world of struggle, more specifically, of power struggle. We live in a coercive society where people function, not necessarily because they *want* to do good, but because they *have* to do good. People require police. Governments require the use of force. Human aggression will not disappear for the wanting of it to disappear. This is reality—unfortunate but true.

The pacifist believes that pacifism is in the national interest; that by espousing a pacifistic tactic, the nation can overcome all military threats to it. But that is hardly realistic. Is it believable that Communist Russia would respond to pacifism with peaceful non-aggression? That Red China would honor total disarmament by reciprocal disarmament? Or that Germany or Japan (now silently rearming) or even Israel, will abandon the interests of their own national security to the good will of their enemies?

This defect in the pacifist's analysis is not only an intellectual error—it may bear tragic moral consequences. In essence, it is a species of moral irresponsibility to "cop out" on the complex realities of this world, a fleeing from combat in order to preach in the mountain caves behind the rear lines. Pacifism cannot combat power by preachment, and religion becomes irrelevant when all it has to say to those who are in power is that they should not use their power. Professor C.E.M. Joad, chairman of the National Peace Council of England before the Second World War, noted that all the homilies and preachments of non-violence to the contemporary world were like the "squeak of a mouse in a den of lions." They cannot be seriously entertained by those who are responsible for lives and those who are held accountable for the security of the nation.

To embrace pacifism in a world of power-brokers and power-wielders and power-movements positively serves to encourage the divorce of ethics from politics and to induce an irresponsible relationship of morality to the world-at-large. Preaching peace when there is no peace is to invite disaster from warring nations.

Indeed, it may be that the failure to use adequate power energetically lies at the origin of many great wars of modern times. Confronting totalitarian regimes with pacifism may have caused far greater evil than the proper use of force against them. One can readily adduce as proof the fiasco at Munich before the Second World War, and the terrible recent defeats of the Hungarian and Czechoslovakian people's revolution against tyranny when the enemy simply overran the country and dug his spiked boot into the throat that innocently cried for freedom. Would it not be morally irresponsible for a man who witnesses another man beating a child to death to try to reason with words, in obvious futility, rather than act with force? In reflecting on Saul's sparing the King of the Amalekites, the Rabbis of the Midrash say: "One who makes himself overly compassionate toward the cruel will end being cruel to the compassionate." (Kohelet Rabbah)

The pacifist will counter with the declaration that, far from "copping out," he is "throwing himself into the breech" between warring nations. But how realistic is that, in terms of a positive effect upon either side? It points to great courage but, at the same time, to an abdication of moral responsibility. This is not to say that we should hold no ideas of perfection in religion and morality. There is a relevance of the "impossible" ethic ideal in that it shows us in which direction to strive and what ideals to hope for in our *ultimate* quests, and it raises our standard of morality ever higher in pursuit of those perfect goals. But to expect to apply perfection directly to a world of imperfection is to be unreal and, in effect, irresponsible.

The Roots of Pacifism in the Soil of Perfectionism

Judaism, unlike Buddhism and fundamentalist Christianity, would not counsel the application of perfectionism to this imperfect world and so it cannot accept pacifism as a way of life. One simply cannot equate the ethic of the Gospel with the ethic of the Bible without emphasizing the subsequent development of Judaism in Rabbinic literature, which dominated Jewish life at the very time that the Gospels were being written. While the Christian ethic was simple and direct, and addressed itself primarily to individuals, the Jewish ethic, from Bible through Talmud and Codes and Responsa, was wholly intertwined with the Jewish people's politics. The nationhood of Israel is integral to the religion of Israel. There is a specific area considered The Holy Land. Sin and punishment concern not only God and individuals, but God and the nation and the soil. While individuals may have been chosen by God, it was primarily the nation that was covenanted by Him. In a situation where the national entity is as real as the individual, politics and morals cannot be separated. Moral realism is built into the fabric of Judaism. There is no "religious" enemy in Israel but, being a national entity, there is a "political" enemy. Simply, if there exists a Jewish nation, there exist other legitimate nations outside its borders, that are either in conflict or in cooperative arrangement with the Jewish nation. Viewing other competing nations as legitimate heirs to their own soil brought tolerance home to the Jews. The prophets of Israel dealt not only with orphans and widows but with the morality and wisdom of treaties and alliances, of boundary agreements and trade agreements. Because Israel is a nation, it had to implement an ethic dealing with aggregates of peoples and international understanding. Because it was a nation, it dealt with competing claims of aggregates within the nation. In its concern with the society of people and the relationship of groups to one another, Judaism was, from the beginning, forced to deal not only with abstract ideals, with faith in God and obedience to Him, but with problems of competition between store owners, with management and ownership and labor, with people's bread and air and light, with conflicting interests among communal institutions, with possessions and with pollution. Its ethics had to bring heaven down to earth and to make it work here. Adjacent to the area of the altar in the Temple was the court and, also, the throne. There was no division between Caesar and God which enabled one to conduct himself according to an arbitrary standard of morality in the service of Caesar but with a strict perfectionist morality in the service of God.

In Judaism, then, ethics had to be operative for the collectivity as well as for the individual. No perfectionist demands could legitimately be made on the nation.

Judaism Is For People, Not For Saints

Jewish law *(halakhah)*, is not an abstract discipline for religious *saints*, but an ethical *modus operandi* for religious *people*. Thus, in the Jewish tradition, unlike the Christian tradition, it was not expected that man would actually love a neighbor who might be hateful to him. Nahmanides, in analyzing the syntax of the Hebrew phrase "love thy neighbor," notes that love has no direct object, only an indirect one. Thus, the verse reads, not "love thy neighbor's personality," but "act with love *toward* thy neighbor." All that we can hope for is that the man can *act* lovingly *toward* his neighbor. Love was taken to mean "speak favorably of your neighbor" and "protect the interest of your neighbor." Indeed, Hillel interpreted this negatively: "What is hateful to you, do not do unto your neighbor," so that it should be more pragmatic than perfectionist. In Hillel's dictum, what is remarkable is not merely that it is phrased in the negative, which renders the love concept workable, but that the word *love* is now transformed into *do*. It is an ethic of action, a pragmatic ethic, and not a perfectionist one.

Judaism could never adopt a perfectionist ethic. Its ethic had to guide men in their day-to-day activities. It had to be brought to earth, it could not stay in heaven. In this scheme there could be no "cop-out" on reality. While it revered perfect ideals as goals for which to strive, it insisted that its principles be actionable.

Counter-Power

Third, Judaism did not sidestep evil, and never preached pacifistic meekness as a strategy for combating power. Its ethic could be best described, not as "sweetness and light," but by the phrase which the Bible uses to describe Samson's finding honey in the carcass of the lion he slew, "sweetness and *strength*." It developed an ethic which is a sophisticated blend of power and mercy, of gut and heart, and, with it, directly confronted the social and political problems of the day. This muscular morality commanded, not submission to evil, not capitulation to the arrogant enemy, not "love" in the face of imminent invasion—but the combat of evil, often with violent means—when every other peaceful strategy had been exhausted.

Not only did the Torah not subscribe to the Gospel's counsel, "resist not evil," it admonished "and thou shalt eradicate the evil from your midst." Indeed, this admonition appears not once, but four times in the Book of Deuteronomy. Further, it was not sufficient merely to *love good*, one was commanded to *hate evil* — not the evil doer but evil, itself. Amos (5:15) commands: "Hate evil! Love the good! And establish justice in the gate!" One is not permitted the moral luxury of declaring oneself a pacifist in the face of terrible evil. One of the cardinal principles of the Jewish social ethic is: "Thou shalt not stand idly by the blood of thy fellow man." Martin Buber observes: "Power abdicates only under stress of counter-power." It is the "counter-power" that Judaism demands of its adherents rather than isolationism and submission.

This muscular morality of Judaism, in contrast to that of other major religious moralities, can be traced in the striking differences of the very first moral-reflex responses of the founders of the major Western world religions. They are initial reactions, yet they all characterize their subsequent growth. These distinctions are perceptively detected by Professor Yehuda Bergmann:

Buddha was born and educated in the wealth and splendor of his father's mansion. When he went out into the city he saw three men—one poor, one sick and one dead one being buried. He concluded that life was filled with pain and, thereupon, he fled his father's house and the city of men and became a recluse. He denied the validity of reality and concluded that "good" could be achieved only be inner personal contemplation.

Jesus went out into the society of man and everywhere he turned he saw sin, deprivation, immorality, and the oppression of the Roman tyranny. He concluded that the "end of days" had come and that only in the Kingdom of Heaven, but not in life on earth, could man find salvation. Society was doomed, but the individual could save himself by the miraculous grace of proper belief.

Mohammed, in the arid desert, heard the voice of God call to him that man's evil actions ascended before Him. Thereupon the prophet announced that Judgment Day was near, that the world would be destroyed, that there was no hope for man and that only in the belief in Allah and in the offering of one's own life for Him would man be able to earn a berth in the glorious world to come.

Moses left the palace of Pharoah and went out into the world where he saw the pain and the agony of his people's slave labor. He did not hide from society. He announced no miraculous personal salvation by virtue of man's faith. He physically jumped into the ugly fray to end injustice. Thereafter he began his lengthy preparation to break the bonds of men, to free the masses of Jews—in this world, in his time—in a flurry of action which was to make justice and righteousness operative in the world of men.

This actionism of Moses characterizes the attitude of the Jew toward international relations. As the Israelites set out from Egypt to conquer the Promised Land, the Bible commanded the conquest of the Canaanites so that "they not teach you to do after their abominations." The same purpose is expressed differently in Deuteronomy 9:5 "Not for *thy* righteousness or for the uprightness of *thy* heart dost thou go in to possess their land, but for the wickedness of these nations the Lord thy God doth drive them out before thee." Later, the Israelites were commanded to "blot out the memory of Amalek," not only to take revenge for blood-thirsty aggression, but because Amalek was the symbol of international malice and mercilessness and moral baseness. In order to build the ideal society the Jew needed not only positive ideals but also a sensitive awareness of treachery and a dedicated intent to combat the terrors of evil. This commandment was considered not only a war among human beings, but "a war between *God* and Amalek from generation to generation." Maimonides explains it as punishment for the violation of divinely established universal statutes: "In the same way as one individual is punished in order that others shall hear it and be afraid and not accustom themselves to practice mischief" (*Guide* 3:41).

It was obligatory for the nation not only to improve *itself*, it was fundamental to its moral life to try to improve the *world*. The pages of Jewish history are not bloodstained with wars for the propagation of the faith, as it had no concept of "religious" enemies, but Judaism did emphasize the basic idea that the unpunished international lawlessness of a nation, and its reliance solely on the rule of force, jeopardizes the security of the whole human family. A treacherous nation, like Amalek, impervious to moral condemnation and oblivious of international law, was a threat to just living. The very survival of the Jewish people and their way of life was dependent, therefore, on the eradication of the Amalekites.

Power, Like Energy, is Fundamental and Neutral

Further, Judaism, unlike early Christianity, recognized the presence and influence of power in society, both in the structure of government and in interpersonal relationships. Far from denying the existence of power, it confirmed it as being natural. The rabbis of the Talmud (Hagigah 12a) note that *gevurah*, power, was one of the ten media with which the world was created and continues to be created. They comment wryly on the use of power in international relations when they muse (*Kiddushin* 49b): "Of the total power that descended to the world, the Persians (the contemporary enemy) took off 90% and 10% was distributed to the remainder of the world!" They confirm, to a large extent, the view of Bertrand Russell that "In the same sense in which energy is the fundamental concept in physics," power is fundamental to the development of men's affairs. While the rabbis recognized the pervasiveness of power as a social phenomenon, they did not attribute it to instinctive unruliness or some combative antisocial quality in human nature. Rather, they implied, it is neutral but necessary in each society so that the society be not merely an aggregate or rabble, but that men be organized and institutionalized for greater effectiveness and helpfulness.

Acknowledging that power is a necessary characteristic of every organized society, Judaism set about to limit it and to refine it. It took its cue from one of the attributes of God: the *gevurah*, with which He created the world, but which was effective only as He elected to limit it, so that there be, not endless creation, but, rather, a finite world and finite men. God gave us power and, by example, He taught that we have to practice restraint on that power. Society has power. Institutions have power. But there must be a check and a balance and a counter-power that says to that original power, "Enough!"

As Judaism attempted to *control* power it also attempted to *refine* it—to use it for proper purposes and to insure that it went hand-in-hand with social utility. The Talmud tells of a strange conversation between Alexander the Great and the "Elders of the South;" "Alexander said: What should a man do in order to be liked by his fellows? They said: Let him hate kingship and rule. He said: My thought is better than your thought. I say let him love kingship and rule and do good to mankind." The fact that the Talmud incorporates this statement indicates their high estimate of Alexander's thought.

Inasmuch as Judaism saw society as an intricate web of power relationships—competing claims, conflicting interests, business and social competition—it had to provide a "counter-power" for every demonstration of power, a check and balance of opposing forces. It is precisely this dialectic of power which formed the grand covenant of society. Counter-power is the charter for man living in peace with his neighbor. It is the basis for the rabbinic statement that we should "Seek the welfare of the city, for if not for it each man would swallow his neighbor alive!" Coercive society, wielding the proper use of force, enables men to live in peace. Since power could never be rendered completely innocuous, it had to be recognized and controlled and refined. It is for the recognition of counter-power that, in Judaism, unlike in Christianity and Buddhism, civil law is an integral part of the religion, and that religion is not only an elaborate statement of love; there is a jurisprudence in Judaism and not only a preachment.

Judaism also diffused power through society. No one man, not even a king selected by a prophet and approved by the people, had "safe" enough hands in which to vest limitless power. In like fashion, a man who proclaimed himself a prophet was not always accepted. His credentials had to be examined, and if they were found wanting, he was to be declared a "false" prophet. The priest, even the High Priest, was not without necessary recourse to the people, and even his ability to serve in the Temple was not always guaranteed, but dependent upon his religious and moral qualifications that were to be determined by *others*. Even the Elder, who in some societies was to be totally and absolutely revered, was considered *zaken mamre*, a rebellious Elder, if he repudiated the law of Moses as authoritatively expounded by his peers.

Similarly, Judaism limited the power of the rich and distributed some of that power to the poor. It protected the employer, but even more was it sensitive to the lack of protection of the employee, and safeguarded his interests. It could not do away with slavery simply by fiat, and it therefore severely limited the dynastic control of the master, Judaism protected parents from children, but it also gave children power —vested in the hands of the court—against parents who might be vindictive and who would bring their own children to trial as juvenile delinquents. So it limited and checked and balanced the power of the public sector by the private sector, and vice versa. It protected the stranger from the citizen and, also, the citizen from the sometimes harsh demands of strangers. It set aright the competing claims of men by counter-power properly utilized, rather than by preaching not to use power.

Weakness as Prelude to Disaster

Not only is counter-power considered positively necessary, but its negative aspect, the lack of power or the pacifist decision not to use power, is an invitation to potential diaster.

First, the sense of weakness has a debilitating effect upon those who propose it, even for idealistic purposes. Eric Hoffer, with the sharp insight of a layman philosopher, writes that "it has been often said that power corrupts, but it is perhaps equally important to realize that weakness, too, corrupts. Power corrupts the few, while weakness corrupts the many. Hatred, malice, rudeness, intolerance and suspicion are the fruits of weakness. The resentment of the weak does not spring from any injustice done to them, but from the sense of their inadequacy and impotence. They hate, not wickedness, but weakness." Who can deny that the laborer, before the development of union power, considered himself, not merely preyed upon, but inadequate and impotent—that he hated himself as much as he hated his employers? The powerlessness of the weak, even though it be for idealistic purposes, leads eventually to violence. One need only observe the legitimate protests of society's weakest components in the past few years to trace the movement from peaceful urging to passive resistance to incendiary confrontation. Thus, the Blacks, the Puerto Ricans and other minorities, the poor and the students, have all successively moved from the passive to the active, from the position of relative weakness to the position of wielding power—even though not the power of might or of wealth or of position, but the power of disruption to society. Power comes not only from shooting the pistol; it can come as well from loading the pistol and aiming at a target without ever shooting at all. Rendering people powerless is not love of man which we celebrate and seek so desperately. Love needs power if it is to be institutionalized and made operative in society. Powerlessness may play into the hands of those who are less than ethical and moral. It is instructive to note Maimonides' statement regarding "Love thy neighbor as thyself." He says, "Everything that you want others to do unto you, do unto your brother in Torah and Commandments." Dr. Simon Federbusch explains the phrase, "Your brother in Torah and Commandments," to mean that, apparently, Maimonides' intention was to say that it is impossible to apply the love principle to a murderer to the extent that society should absolutely acquit him, as it is used in fact, to mitigate the form of capital punishment. The very execution of punishment, the flexing of society's power, is, in a larger sense, an act of altruistic love—for others. If the murderer were not to be punished, would the love principle not serve to protect the guilty instead of the innocent? Society cannot exist under a system of simplistic and untutored pacifism.

Third, weakness can invite disaster because it is, tactically, a blunder. If this country were to broadcast the fact that, on principle, it will not go to war under any circumstances and that, in the final analysis, it would have to settle for the best arrangement obtainable through negotiation, it would invite the enemy simply to wait until our inevitable collapse. Unless the opponent somehow becomes willing to negotiate in love and with the sweet reasonableness (which we have learned not to expect from opponents) what we would be saying is that we consider war the greatest evil and we are willing to surrender if we cannot get our way. Judaism recognized that the intelligent, restrained and moral use of counter-power is the only method by which we can neutralize evil. It affirmed that evil must be fought and not submitted to in every circumstance.

A Choice of War Requires a "Community Conscience"

While Judaism rejected pacifism, it opted, on the national level, for selective pacifism. It developed, therefore, a Just War criterion for judging the legitimacy of wars undertaken by the Jewish government. In pronouncing against certain "types" of war, it demonstrated selective conscientious objection.

Without filling in the entire spectrum of possible conflicts, Judaism divided wars largely into two categories: "Mandatory Wars," *Milhemet Mizvah*, and "Permitted Wars," *Milhemet Reshut* (wars for which one needed *reshut*, permission). "Mandatory War," other than Joshua's war and the battle with Amalek, refers only to strictly-defined defensive wars, fought under a moral imperative. It is a defense of one's land, one's family. Such a war is a moral reflex, calling forth a unanimous and instinctive response. It requires no convening of judges, leaves no options

to the people. There are no draft exemptions whatever for all males between ages 20 to 60, including students, cowards and the physically defective. "Permitted War," today, refers to only one type—the preventive
war which reaches out to a known enemy who is judged to be preparing
for a future attack, who has the men and weapons and motivation to in-
vade. This war is initiated to enable a first strike, in the enemy's cities
and amidst his civilian population. Such a war is "permitted" because it
is not a clearly-defined, morally-instinctive response, and, therefore,
requires (even according to R. Judah who quarrels with the more conservative Sages) not only the declaration of the Chief Executive, but the
authorization of the Sanhedrin. The decision involves choosing among a
hierarchy of values, the assessment of the possibilities of defeat, a
strategic evaluation of military and political alternatives and a determination of the immediacy of the enemy's threat. There undoubtedly
was included a judgment of the moral criteria involved in the just
war—determining the possibility of victory and the proportionality of
the means, as Jeremiah and Rabbi Johanan ben Zakkai have done in different circumstances. Even after the 71 most highly revered and wisest
people in the country have pronounced on the morality of the war, the
King is still discouraged from unnecessary adventures by the exemption
of thousands of the youngest and most capable men from the
draft—people involved in almost any major personal transaction,
whether in property or family.

The single most crucial difference between the two categories is this
requirement of authorization by the Sanhedrin, an aggregate of Judges
with the best brains and the most heightened moral awareness in the
nation. The Sanhedrin was representative of the people, as the King was
not. In fact, as noted by R. Meir Simha Cohen of Dvinsk, in his *Meshekh
Hokhmah*, a consensus of the nation, itself, could substitute for the formal Sanhedrin: *zib'bur b'Erez Yisroel yesh lahem din bet din ha-gadol.*
Whether it was a clear mandate of the national consensus or the formal
approval of the Sanhedrin, the "Community Conscience," no war, except one of defense, could be declared simply by the Chief Executive.
Milhemet Reshut required the validation of this "Community Conscience"— the physical embodiment of what Socrates called "the conscience of the laws."

This selective pacifism is a characteristic response of Jewish law to the
harsh realities of this world. It is a pragmatic pacifism which determines

each situation over against the eternal values. It avoids the pitfalls of absolutism and perfectionism and applies, positively, the Jewish quality of counter-power. Even more, opting for selective pacifism requires a more sophisticated level of moral discrimination as it seeks to balance values and choose among the competing claims of the soul. It requires a heightened awareness of the political as well as the military dilemmas in the context of moral values.

But there is a sleeper in this affirmation of Jewish selective conscientious objection. It is true only on a *national* level, not on a *personal* one. Determination of the justice of a war was never left to individual decision. That burden devolved upon the state and, other than strictly for defense, war could not be embarked upon without the prior legitimization of the moral conscience of the *community*, the Sanhedrin.

Those who maintain that Judaism espoused *personal* selective conscientious objection as a legitimate draft deferment have based their argument on a 9-word addendum of the Tosefta to Rabbi Akiba's explanation of the meaning of one category of exemption, the *yarei verakh ha-levav*, "the fearful and the faint-hearted" (*Sotah* 44a). "Rabbi Akiba says: 'fearful and faint-hearted' is to be understood *literally*, viz., he is unable to stand in the battle ranks and see a drawn sword." Adds the Tosefta: "Even the most powerful, and the mightiest of the mighty—if he is a compassionate soul, he must return from the ranks." With the best of intentions and with the greatest desire to transform the Biblical phrase into relevant, liberal, modern terminology, the Tosefta's "compassionate soul" who must return from the war is not a conscientious objector. First, the Tosefta's addendum itself must accord with Akiba's principle that the phrase be taken literally, viz. "faint-hearted." This "compassionate soul" has a psychological revulsion from bloody combat, but hardly relates to the tough-minded conscience and its religious or humanistic base. Indeed, how would one interpret the Biblical prescription, immediately following, that the anointed priest preach to the soldiers, *Al yarekh levavkhem*, "do not be faint-hearted." Surely he did not warn, "Do not be compassionate!" Further, if we here refer to a conscientious objector, why is he not included among those who never leave for the war, instead of with those who must go to war but are now entitled to return. Obviously his faint-heartedness is an intuitive reaction, not a considered and deliberate moral judgment. Finally, the Halakhah placed no additional burden of proof on the "compassionate." On the contrary, it exempted this category from the requirement made of all others who claim exemption and return from the camps—that they bring testimony (else, as Naḥmanides says, hordes of soldiers would invent similar situations and deprive Israel of ever being able to wage war). Only the faint-hearted, according to Rabbi Akiba, need bring no evidence—"His evidence is with him at all times!"

Most important, however, for the assertion that there is no *personal* C.O., is that it is highly unlikely that after the Sanhedrin had rendered a moral decision affirming the right to war, the individual could place himself above them, in a position of greater insight or greater authority, and declare that, for himself, the war was immoral.

After the war, far from the blood and bullets of the battlefield, it must be affirmed that Judaism rejected total pacifism, but that it believed strongly in pragmatic pacifism as a higher and morally more noteworthy religious position. Nonetheless, this selective pacifism is only a public, national decision, and not a personal one. The public was not permitted to embark on mortal combat without the prior authorization of the Sanhedrin, functioning as the community conscience. That having once been declared, however, it was expected that all individuals would subscribe to the decision. In an American culture and a Protestant ethic which places a premium on the individual conscience these words may register as anachronistic. But that is how I read my Judaism.

14

Conscience and Civil Disobedience in the Jewish Tradition

MILTON R. KONVITZ

In the first chapter of Exodus it is related that the new ruler of Egypt, alarmed by the increase in the number of Israelites, spoke to the Hebrew midwives and directed them to kill all male infants born to Hebrew women. "But the midwives feared God," the Bible goes on to relate, "and did not as the king of Egypt commanded them, but saved the men-children alive" (1:15—17). Thereupon the king issued a new decree, directed not to the midwives but to the people generally, who were ordered to kill all newborn Hebrew males by throwing them into the river Nile (1:22).

These events, which may have happened some thirty-four hundred years ago, relate to what may well be the first recorded instance in history of what is today called non-violent civil disobedience. From the Biblical text it is not clear that the midwives were themselves Hebrews; for they acted as they did not because they were Hebrews but because they "feared God." The text twice mentions the fact that they "feared God"—or, as we say today, that they listened to the voice of conscience rather than to the law of the state or the voice of the king.

In the First Book of Samuel there is another clear and dramatic instance of non-violent civil disobedience. It is related that when King Saul learned that a certain priest had given David food and other assistance,

Reprinted by permission of The Viking Press from *Judaism and Human Rights*, edited by Milton R. Konvitz. Copyright © 1972 by the B'nai B'rith Commission on Adult Jewish Education.

he ordered the priest to appear before him and decreed his death and the death of all his kin. The crucial words of the Biblical text are as follows: "And the king said to the guard who stood about him, 'Turn and kill the priests of the Lord; because their hand also is with David, and they knew that he fled, and did not disclose it to me.' But the servants of the king would not put forth their hand to fall upon the priests of the Lord" (I Samuel 22:17). This may be the first recorded instance of non-violent civil disobedience by military men in refusing to obey superior orders. It is not clear why the men of the guard refused to lay hands on the priests and their families—because the victims belonged to the priestly class, or because they were civilians; whatever the reason, their action was a clear case of civil disobedience.

In the Book of Daniel we find the first instance of what became a pattern in Jewish life and history: the worship of God without regard to the fact that such worship had been prohibited at the price of one's life. The book relates (chapter 6) that Darius the king had appointed Daniel chief of his officers. The officers then conspired to bring about the fall of Daniel, and to this end they contrived an ingenious trap. They induced Darius to issue a decree that for thirty days no man was to offer petition to any man or god except to the king, on pain of death in the lion's den. Daniel, however, went on to pray to God three times daily, with the window of his chamber open toward Jerusalem. His enemies came upon Daniel when he was thus petitioning God rather than Darius, and then naturally went with their report to the king. After trying to find a way out, the king felt compelled to order his law to be enforced, and Daniel was put into the den of lions. The following morning, however, the king found Daniel unharmed, saved by an angel.

The case of Daniel, it should be noted, differs from our two previous instances. In the cases of the Egyptian midwives and Saul's guards, there was simply a refusal to commit an act which was deeply felt to be inconceivable by the persons ordered to perform it. In the case of Daniel, however, there was a positive act: he did not merely *refuse* to perform an act; he *performed* an act in violation of a law. Furthermore, while the first two cases involved the moral conscience—orders to commit murder—the case of Daniel was an act in the realm of religious worship. While these differences are significant, the concept of non-violent civil disobedience is broad enough to accommodate these as well as additional types of conduct.

The four Books of Maccabees in the Apocrypha offer numerous instances of civil disobedience during the period of the Hellenization of Judea, when the Second Temple was defiled and was dedicated to Zeus Olympius. Some Jews assisted in the work of Hellenization and even in the persecution of fellow Jews who tried to obstruct the process. The Syrian overlords forbade the Jews to offer sacrifices and to observe the Sabbath and festivals. They were compelled to make and to worship idols, to sacrifice swine, and to leave their sons uncircumcised. Disobedience meant death. But I Maccabees records (chapter 1) that "many in Israel were firmly resolved in their hearts not to eat unclean food. They preferred to die rather than be defiled by food and break the holy covenant, and they did die." When the king's officers came to Modin to enforce the decrees against religious observances, Mattathias answered them with these resounding words: "Yet will I, my sons and brothers, walk in the covenant of our fathers. . . . We will not listen to the decrees of the king by going astray from our worship, either to the right or to the left." And then he issued his call: "Let everyone who is zealous for the Law, and would maintain the covenant, follow me" (I Maccabees 2).

The second Book of Maccabees records many dramatic instances of martyrdom when Jews resorted to civil disobedience: women hurled from the city wall with their infants held to their breasts because they had violated the law prohibiting circumcision; men who had secretly observed the Sabbath in caves burned alive. Special mention may be made of Eleazar, one of the foremost scribes, whom the authorities tried to compel to eat swine's flesh which apparently had been used in a forbidden sacrifice. The officers tried to induce him to bring his own meat but pretend that he was eating meat of the sacrifice as ordered by the king. But he refused, saying that if he were to comply, the young would say that old Eleazar had been converted to heathenism and would thus be led astray by his example. He died on the rack (cf. IV Maccabees 5).

The second and fourth Books of Maccabees relate the story of the martyrdom of a mother and seven brothers who refused to eat forbidden food associated with idolatrous sacrifices. The position of non-violent civil disobedience is stated without ambiguity by them as they cry out to the king's officers: "It is certain that we are ready to die rather than transgress the laws of our fathers" (II Maccabees 7:2). The seven brothers, called Maccabees by the Church, became models for Christian martyrs;

and though the Rabbis rejected the Books of the Apocrypha from the canon of Sacred Scriptures, they too made a great deal of their story.

What may be the first recorded instance of *mass* non-violent civil disobedience is found in Josephus' *Antiquities of the Jews* (Book 18, chapter 8).[1] The incident he relates took place in the reign of Emperor Caligula (37-41) and revolved around the latter's decision to place his statue in the Temple in Jerusalem. Petronius, the emperor's agent, was given a large army but was instructed to try, in the first instance, to persuade the Jews to permit the installation of the statue peacefully. If, however, they refused, then Petronius was to install the statue by force. Petronius got ready an army of Romans and auxiliaries to carry out this mission and in due course arrived at Acre (referred to as Ptolemais). What happened after that is graphically reported by Josephus:

> But there came ten thousands of the Jews to Petronius at Ptolemais to offer their petitions to him that he would not compel them to violate the law of their forefathers. "But if," they said, "you are wholly resolved to bring the statue and install it, then you must first kill us, and then do what you have resolved on. For while we are alive we cannot permit such things as are forbidden by our law and by the determination of our forefathers that such prohibitions are examples of virtue."
>
> Petronius, however, was angry at them, and said: ". . . Caesar has sent me. I am compelled to observe his decrees. . . ." Then the Jews replied: "Since, therefore, you are so disposed, O Petronius, that you will not disobey Caesar's orders, neither will we transgress the commands of our law. . . ."
>
> When Petronius saw by their words that their determination was hard to be removed, and that . . . he would not be able to be obedient to Caligula in the dedication of his statue, and that there must be a great deal of bloodshed, he took his friends and servants and hastened to Tiberias, to see how the Jews there felt about the affair; but many ten thousands of Jews met Petronius again when he came to Tiberias. . . .
>
> Then Petronius came to them (at Tiberias): "Will you then make war with Caesar, regardless of his great preparations for war and your own weakness?" They replied: "We will not by any means make war with Caesar, but we will die before we see our laws transgressed." Then they threw themselves down on their faces and stretched out their throats and said that they were ready to be slain. And this they did for forty days, neglecting to till their soil, though this was the season which called for sowing. Thus they continued firm in their resolution and proposed to themselves to die willingly rather than see the statue dedicated.
>
> When matters were in this state . . . Petronius determined to listen to the petitioners in this matter. He called the Jews together in Tiberias, who came many ten thousands in number. . . . Said Petronius: "I do not think it just to

have such a regard to my own safety and honor as to refuse to sacrifice them for your preservation, who are so many in number and who endeavor to preserve the regard that is due to your law. . . . I will, therefore, send to Caligula and let him know your resolutions, and I will assist your cause as far as I am able, so that you may not suffer on account of your honest designs, and may God assist you . . . But if Caligula should be angry and turn the violence of his rage on me, I would rather undergo that danger and affliction on my body or soul than see so many of you perish. . . ."

When Petronius had said this and had dismissed the assembly of Jews, he asked the principal men among them to look after their fields, to speak kindly to the people and to encourage them to have hope. . . . He then wrote to Caligula . . . to entreat him not to drive so many ten thousands of these men to distraction; that if he were to slay these men, he would be publicly cursed for all future ages.

Recording the same incidents, Philo reports the Jewish plea to Petronius in essentially the same words as Josephus. The core of the plea, according to Philo, was as follows:

We are evacuating our cities, withdrawing from our houses and lands; . . . We should think ourselves gainers thereby, not givers. One thing only we ask in return for all, that no violent changes should be made in this temple. . . . But if we cannot persuade you, we give up ourselves for destruction that we may not live to see a calamity worse than death. We hear that forces of cavalry and infantry have been prepared against us if we oppose the installation [of the image of Caesar]. No one is so mad as to oppose a master when he is a slave. We [therefore] gladly put our throats at your disposal.[2]

With the instances before us—from the Hebrew Scriptures, the Apocrypha, and Josephus—it is now possible to state the essential elements for a case of civil disobedience:

1. There was a law or an official decree.

2. Those whose obedience was commanded considered the law to be unconscionable.

3. They refused to obey.[3]

4. They resorted to non-violent resistance.

5. They stood ready to put their lives on the line; they showed a readiness to suffer for their conscience.

6. The incident in Josephus discloses an additional element—i.e., civil disobedience, in which the above five elements are manifested, seeks to convert the opponent, to achieve reconciliation by the assertion of the force of truth and love in the place of fear, hate, and falsehood.

The texts cited above do not formulate a principle of civil disobedience in abstract terms. The ancient Hebraic mind did not tend to conceptualize but moved instead in an existential way, within a specific configuration of facts and forces. It did not become engaged in philosophic analysis beyond the small range disclosed by the Wisdom Literature. But with our hindsight it is not difficult to see the modern philosophy of civil disobedience prefigured in the cited incidents. Neither Thoreau nor Gandhi nor Martin Luther King detracted from or added to the elements of civil disobedience as formulated above. Each of them, because of his own situation, tended, however, to emphasize one element or another. Thoreau stressed the duty of conscience to assert itself against the evil law or state action. Gandhi emphasized the need of resistance to be non-violent and to seek by that means and the practice of humility to penetrate to the heart of the enemy, to transform him into friend. Dr. King put first the need to be non-violent and the readiness to submit to penalty for willful breach of the law. What element is singled out for stress at any one time is decided not abstractly but by the circumstances of time, place, and people.

In the light of some of the events in the late 1960s—demonstrations by black students, by opponents of the Vietnam war on college campuses, by welfare recipients and others making demands of government officials—perhaps the element in non-violent civil disobedience that most needs emphasizing, apart from the stress on non-violence, is the willingness to submit oneself to the penalty of the law that has been broken. Such submission is important for several reasons.

First, it clearly marks off the civil disobedient from the ordinary criminal who tries to suppress evidence of his action and escape punishment. It also marks him off from the person who seeks to *evade* a law which he considers unconscionable by flight to another jurisdiction—e.g., the thousands of American draftees who have gone to Sweden or Canada because of their opposition to the Vietnam war, but who feared that they could not prove their conscientious objection to the satisfaction of the Selective Service authorities or the courts. This is not the place to consider the moral arguments for or against *evasion* of a law considered unconscionable; all that is meant is that there are significant differences between civil disobedience and evasion.

We should also note that readiness to submit to legal punishment does not preclude a willingness to appeal one's conviction through a hierarchy of courts. This was the practice of Martin Luther King, and at times he succeeded in persuading the Supreme Court that the law under which he or demonstrators associated with him were convicted was in fact unconstitutional. A willing submission to the penalty implies a valid judgment of conviction under a law sustained by the Constitution.

Second, the posture of readiness to suffer the punishment prescribed by the law demonstrates the seriousness with which the defendant considers the law that he has knowingly violated and the response of his conscience to its demands; for in effect the defendant says he would rather lose his liberty, or even his life, than obey the law which is against his conscience. In the words of the second Book of Maccabees, he says: "It is certain that I am ready to die rather than transgress the law of my conscience." To break the law and to fail or refuse to submit to its sanction may lead to the inference that the defendant wants to have the best of both worlds: to break the law for the sake of his conscience, but at the same time to treat the law as if it were a mere scrap of paper and not a test of his conscience.

By willingly submitting to the law's penalty the defendant shows himself—as well as the community—that he has faced his conscience squarely. A member of society accepts or tolerates the burden of countless laws which he does not approve or like. He makes no claim that he has the power to veto or nullify laws which he, for one reason or another, dislikes. By resorting to civil disobedience and submitting to the sanction of the breached law, the defendant shows that he has deliberated; that he has weighed and measured; that he is not acting on a mere impulse or whim; that he has made a decision that is of supreme importance to himself.

Third, by showing his willingness to accept the punishment, the defendant declares or affirms his membership in the community and his respect for the rule of the law. This will mark him off from the radical revolutionary and the anarchist, who may wish to subvert the whole social order. This was the position taken by Gandhi and King, both of whom could have looked to Socrates as the classical model of this argument. When Socrates was in prison awaiting execution, his friends urged him to make the escape which they had arranged. But Socrates spurned the suggestion. He himself, he argued, would *do* no wrong; but it was not against his conscience *to suffer* a wrong. It was his duty, he said, willingly to accept the punishment even if the verdict of guilty was an injustice. For he was not, Socrates in effect said, an anarchist. He profoundly respected the legal order. It had its imperfections—witness the unjust judgment against him; but it is a citizen's duty to respect the legal order as such, for without it life as a human being would be impossible. Who, he asked in the *Crito*, would care for a city without laws? Goodness and integrity, institutions and laws, he said, are the most precious possessions of mankind.

This must, indeed, be the position if civil disobedience is to be differentiated from the acts of the anarchist and social revolutionary, who wish to subvert the entire legal and social order. He who resorts to civil disobedience "obeys the laws of the state to which he belongs, not out of the fear of the sanctions, but because he considers them to be good for the welfare of society," wrote Gandhi. "But there come occasions, generally rare, when he considers certain laws to be so unjust as to render obedience to them a dishonor. He then openly and civilly breaks them and quietly suffers the penalty for their breach."[4]

In the same spirit of submission to the rule of law Martin Luther King wrote from his Birmingham cell: "I submit that an individual who breaks a law that conscience tells him is unjust, and willingly accepts the penalty by staying in jail . . . is in reality expressing the very highest respect for law."

Finally, breaking the immoral law openly and standing ready to pay the price demanded by the very law that was broken will, it is hoped, have the effect of opening the eyes of others to the way the law in question offends the conscience. This happened, according to Josephus, when the Roman general saw the anguish and suffering of the Jews, and their fixed determination to face torture and death rather than permit the perversion of their religion. This is the appeal that non-violent civil disobedience is supposed to make to the instincts of truth, justice, and peace as it pushes out ignorance, prejudice, and hate.

Leaving out for the moment the incident from the Book of Daniel, the Biblical instances of civil disobedience already cited—the Egyptian midwives and the case of Saul and his guards—involved orders to commit murder. The cases cited from the Books of the Maccabees and from Josephus involved orders to commit the sin of idolatry. Now a man of conscience may readily agree that he would prefer martyrdom rather than commit murder or practice idolatry. But what of laws or decrees that call for acts not so heinous as murder or idolatry but that are nonetheless against the conscience? In the course of the war that Hadrian waged to destroy Judaism and the Jewish nation, countless Jews stood ready for martyrdom. But the Rabbis saw that indiscriminate martyrdom might itself be a peril to Jewish survival. With this consideration before them, they decreed that the duty to prefer martyrdom be restricted to three transgressions: murder, idolatry, and incest (or adultery or gross unchastity). The Rabbis attached this legal principle to Leviticus 18:5: "And you shall guard My statutes and My ordinances, by doing which a man shall live." They concluded from this passage that the Torah was given to enhance life rather than to induce death. The emphasis of the Torah is on holy living and not on holy dying. The Rabbis also pointed to the fact that the passage stated that the statutes and ordinances are such that by observing them "a man" shall live—not an Israelite, but a man. With these two highly significant interpretations in mind, the Rabbis felt that martyrdom had to be limited to instances that involved laws transgressing the most basic principles of what came later to be called natural law or the laws of nature. (There can hardly be any question about murder and incest falling into this category.[5] Idolatry was so closely associated with grossly immoral practices that it could rank with the transgressions of the basic precepts of natural law, and that association was made and stressed by the prophets of the Bible and the Rabbis of the Talmud.)

The *locus classicus* of the legal formulation of the principle concerning martyrdom is in the Babylonian Talmud:

> For every law of the Torah the rule is that a man may transgress the commandment rather than suffer death—excepting idolatry, incest and murder. . . . Murder may not be commited (even) to save one's life. . . . For example, someone came to Raba and told him: "The general of my town has ordered me to go and kill a named person, and if not, the general will kill me." Raba said to him: "Let the general kill you rather than that you should commit murder. Who knows that your blood is redder? Maybe his blood is redder!" (*Sanhedrin* 74a).

In the face, then, of laws or orders that command idolatry, incest, or murder, the above-stated halakhic (legal, jurisprudential) principle calls for the duty of civil disobedience, even at the cost of one's life.[6]

What of the incident from the Book of Daniel? As the story is related, Daniel was not called on to perform any act at all. If he had not petitioned (prayed) at all for thirty days, he would have complied with the king's decree. Why, then, did he resort to civil disobedience? Was his conduct consistent with the halakhic principle later formulated by the Rabbis?

It seems that the incident may be interpreted consistently with the above principle. The Persians believed that their king was a god; accordingly, they set a trap for Daniel, for they suspected that he would refuse to pray to the king as one prays to God. Had Daniel failed to offer prayers to anyone for thirty days, his enemies could have used this as evidence of a rejection by him of a belief in the king as a divinity. From this point of view, the story in its essentials is not significantly different from the story in Josephus of Caligula's desire to have his statue installed in the Temple on Mount Moriah. By praying to God while looking out the window that faced toward Jerusalem, Daniel acted out his rejection of Persian idolatry. Accordingly, the story of Daniel is not only an instance of civil disobedience, but is also an instance of the later legal formulation of the duty of civil disobedience to avoid the commission of idolatry, incest, or murder.

Going beyond the three-fold principle of the duty of civil disobedience, Halakhah formulated a duty of civil disobedience that is operative even when the act that is commanded falls short of constituting idolatry. This second principle applies only in times of persecution, when the government seems determined to destroy Judaism. In such circumstances, when one is ordered to violate a commandment in public (i.e., in the presence of ten adult Jews), he must refuse to comply with the order, even at the cost of his life. This is the principle of *Kiddush ha-Shem* (sanctification of the Name). To violate a commandment under these circumstances would be a desecration of the Name (*Ḥillul ha-Shem*). The principle applies, under these circumstances, even if the religious commandment is a relatively minor one—even if it involves merely the deviation from an established custom in Jewry. In such a case, the principle that applies is the same as that when idolatry is commanded: "Let yourself be killed but do not transgress the law of the Torah."

While the threefold principle involving the duty of civil disobedience applies to any man, for it is based on the demands of natural law, the second principle, limited to the persecution of Judaism, applies only to Jews. While the cases of Eleazar and of the mother and the seven brothers, as related in Maccabees, could be interpreted as involving the ban on idolatry, they could also be interpreted, more simply perhaps, as falling under the second principle. For the Jews were ordered to violate a dietary ban in a time of religious persecution, and under circumstances which would have given their compliance publicity within the Jewish community. Their death was therefore a martyrdom, a *Kiddush ha-Shem*.

The second principle may at times appear to run counter to the thinking of the Rabbis when they decided to limit the duty of civil disobedience to idolatry, incest, and murder. For was not the time of Emperor Hadrian a time of religious persecution? If in such a time the second principle is also operative, may not its operation itself be a threat to Jewish existence and survival? The contradiction was probably resolved by Jewish community leaders *ad hoc* in the light of the facts and circumstances as they were known and interpreted at the time. It may thus be that the nature of the Hadrianic persecution, and the character and temper of the people, made the threefold principle necessary, and that it was sufficient to meet the danger. Other persecutions, like that described in II Maccabees, called for the additional principle of *Kiddush ha-Shem*.

The relations between law and conscience—conscience in which civil disobedience is rooted—in classical Jewish thought are extremely subtle and complex.[7] In the present discussion we shall limit our exploration to three aspects:

1. Conscience, as a specific concept of value, does not appear in the Hebrew Scriptures. It is, however, clearly implied. The story of Cain and Abel would have no point unless conscience were assumed; for there had been no supernatural revelation of a law against murder before one brother killed the other, nor was there at that time an enacted criminal code. The same may be said of the judgment on Sodom and the other cities of the plain; and so, too, of Noah and the judgment on his generation; and so, too, of the judgments on Egypt and on the people of Canaan. Much of the Bible, including many passages of the prophets, assumes that there are laws written on the tablets of the heart (Proverbs 7:3), that there is a law in the heart (Deuteronomy 30:14).[8]

The words of Jeremiah (31:32), "I will put my law in their inward parts, and in their hearts will I write it," were not only a promise but also a statement of basic belief as to the nature of man. Without this belief in a law written by God on the tablets of the heart of every man, God could not be the judge of all the universe, of all peoples and nations. Without this belief, God would be only the tribal God of Israel, and He could not have been their judge before the revelation of the Ten Commandments at Sinai; without this belief, the commandments not to kill, not to commit adultery, or not to commit theft would have binding force only on Israel. Indeed, it may be argued that the conception of man made in the image of God means primarily that man is made with a moral conscience—and with the freedom to act against it. It is this that the Bible means when it states that the Egyptian midwives "feared God"; that Amalek, when he acted cruelly, showed that "he feared not God" (Deuteronomy 25:18); that Abraham pretended to be the brother of Sarah because when they came to Gerar he thought, "Surely the fear of God is not in this place; and they will slay me for my wife's sake" (Genesis 20:11).

Indeed, in Biblical contemplation, there may be said to be a special category of sin which is an act committed "against the Lord," that is, a sin which implies the denial of the existence of God, or atheism. This applies to a wrong done to another person secretly, under circumstances where there are no witnesses—no witnesses but God. In Leviticus this type of sin is referred to as follows: "If any one sin, and commit a trespass against the Lord, and deal falsely with his neighbor in a matter of deposit, or of pledge, or of robbery or have oppressed his neighbor; or have found that which was lost, and deal falsely therein, and swear to a lie; in any of all these that a man does, sinning therein . . ." (Leviticus 5:21,22). Rabbi Akiba attached great significance to the phrase "against the Lord," for, he believed, it points up the fact that the guilty man denies that God was a witness to the deposit or the other acts, and thus impliedly he denies God's existence or presence. This, in my view, gives the phrase in Leviticus the same meaning as the phrase "feared God," and is a meaning based on what we generally speak of as conscience.

It was with such views in mind, and especially the story of Noah and the flood, that the Rabbis of the Talmud formulated what they called "the seven commandments given to the descendants of Noah" (Sanhedrin 56a). These commandments prohibit idolatry, murder, theft, incest, blasphemy, and the eating of flesh taken from living animals, and require the establishment of courts of justice.[9] How were these seven commandments "given" and to whom? They were "given" on the "tablets of the heart," and to every man everywhere, since Noah was a kind of second Adam. These commandments spell out, therefore, a natural law, a law binding on the conscience of every man, and from which no man, nation, or generation can claim exemption.

2. This principle of a law of nature, elaborated into the seven commandments given to the descendants of Noah, is obviously the source from which Jewish tradition selected the threefold principle of civil disobedience: that a man must choose to die, if necessary, rather than obey a law or decree that he commit murder, incest, or idolatry.

One significant aspect is that the duty of civil disobedience is not extended to all of the seven commandments but only to those three. Thus, if the order is to commit theft, for example, on the pain of death, the person should commit the theft.[10]

Suppose that the sanction for a refusal to commit theft, however, is imprisonment, not death. May a person, then, resort to civil disobedience and choose to go to prison rather than commit the wrong? The principle is silent as to such cases. The principle only states explicitly that one must choose to suffer a wrong rather than commit it when the wrong to be committed is idolatry, incest, or murder. And the principle implies only that when the wrong to be suffered is death as a penalty, one must commit the wrong ordered—except idolatry, incest, or murder—and avoid death. A great deal is, therefore, left open—when the wrongs commanded are other than the three cardinal ones, or when the penalty threatened for disobedience is something other than death.

3. Finally, our discussion should have demonstrated the distinctly halakhic approach to the problem of conscience versus law that is an expression of the genius of classical, normative Judaism. The legal order provides a constitutional or higher law by which a man is commanded to disobey certain orders, even when they are made by the king or other high officers of the state. Halakhic normative Judaism thus speaks not of a right but of a *duty*, a *legal* duty, of civil disobedience. Thus, while it recognizes conscience, or "the fear of God," or the laws written on the tablets of the heart, it converts morality into law by demanding that, given proper circumstances, the higher law become the living law—a living law that contradicts, and even nullifies, the enacted law—or what wrongly pretends to be the law.

The dialectic of the conceptual relations between the demands of conscience (or of the inner or natural law) and those of enacted law or orders of the state is probably impossible to express with any precision, or in terms of logical consistency. The ancient Jewish authorities were wise not to make the attempt but instead resorted to existential terms by conjuring up the case of the governor of the town ordering X to go and kill Y. What did Raba say to X? "Let the governor slay you rather than that you should commit murder. Who knows that your blood is redder? Perhaps Y's blood is redder than yours." Thus, as is often the case in Hebraic-rabbinic thought, an example symbolizes a principle,[11] the commentary becomes the text—as if there were a fear of making the word into a thing, of accepting the notion that in the beginning was the Logos, the word. For the ultimate sanctity is life, God's creation, and not what is said about it in some abstract formula. Yet life, sacred as it is, is given and sustained for certain ends. If these ends are threatened—by coerced idolatry, immorality, or "the shedding of blood"—life becomes worthless and must well be given up. Yet the ends are such only because they enhance life. It is "holy living" and not "holy dying" that is sought and hoped for and cherished.

But the values for which life itself must, if the tragic need arises, be sacrificed, are very few. This perhaps explains the silence of the Talmud regarding the 960 men, women, and children who defended Masada, the fortress on the Dead Sea, in the course of the Judean revolt against Rome. Especially repulsive to the Rabbis must have been the agreement among the members of the garrison's council, as their final act of defiance, to kill the members of their own families and to put one another to death. As against the nationalist Zealots, the Rabbis stressed the need to save the lives of Jews from fruitless martyrdom; the value of non-violent, non-military action; and, of supreme importance to them, the winning of the right to continue to study and to teach Torah without distraction or fear.[12]

In the light of the Talmudic principles of non-violent civil disobedience, the attitude of the Rabbis to Masada and its defenders, led by Eleazar ben Yair, is entirely understandable. To them, what was indispensable for life was not political independence but the independence of their religious life and the values it contained and sustained (which included, of course, as a minimum, life in conformity with the natural law as formulated in the seven commandments to the descendants of Noah—a natural law which, it could have been reasonably assumed, the Roman overlords would respect and observe).

The unsympathetic critic may say that we have constructed a rather heavy and imposing superstructure on a meager foundation of small incidents, like that of the Egyptian midwives and Saul's bodyguards. Until our own tumultuous days, one would not have thought of such incidents as implying and foreshadowing a principle so momentous for the human spirit as that of civil disobedience. But often it takes many centuries and a great deal of history to disclose the existence of an ideal, theory, or principle. In the Preface to his *Poems* (edition of 1853), Matthew Arnold glibly wrote: "An action like the action of the *Antigone* of Sophocles, which turns upon the conflict between the heroine's duty to her brother's corpse and that to the laws of her country, is no longer one in which it is possible that we should feel a deep interest." One may be sure that when read in 1853 this judgment seemed to be eminently to the point. But would Arnold have made this statement in 1953 after the Nürnberg Tribunal judgments, after the other many war-crime trials, after the Eichmann Trial? Would he have made this statement in the light of Gandhi's non-violent struggle to end untouchability in India? Would he have made this judgment in the 1960's in the light of the lunch-counter sit-ins led by Martin Luther King?

Great actions, whether those of a bereaved young girl, midwives, or young soldiers engaged to protect their king, have a way of surviving the ravages of time, and demonstrate, when the moment is appropriate, their relevance and significance for that which is "permanent in the human soul." That demonstration can be made by Antigone or Socrates, by Thomas More or Bronson Alcott or Thoreau, by Gandhi or Martin Luther King, or by thousands of nameless Jews who were not afraid of a Roman general, nor of the Roman emperor who sent him, nor of death, but who did have the "fear of God"—a "fear" that gives boundless courage to a spirit that suddenly discovers itself as boundless. These men and women found it easy to act but impossible or difficult to give a rational account of their actions. But this is natural, for conscience demands that the act be justified before God and not necessarily before men; God knows the heart and its inner thoughts and secrets.

And God does not demand great sacrifice when the occasion is not one of transcendent importance; God makes demands only when man is called upon to perpetrate murder or commit immorality or idolatry. Only then does the law of God demand violation of the law of man at the cost of one's life. Civil disobedience is not offered as an everyday method for meeting unwelcome situations, for the amelioration of which society and individuals must find other methods and agencies.

Beyond this, however, Jewish tradition and Halakhah place the highest value on martyrdom that is the price paid for defiance of a tyrant whose policy it is to destroy the Jewish religion. In the solemn service of

Yom Kippur, a prominent place is given to a recital of the heroism and martyrdom of the ten great scholars who, during the Hadrianic persecutions, steadfastly refused to accept the prohibitions on observances and the ban on study of Torah. At the risk of their lives they acted in defiance of imperial edicts and gladly suffered torture and death in order to sanctify the Name of their God *(Kiddush ha-Shem)*. Within the Jewish tradition of non-violent civil disobediance, these ten martyrs have played a role in the education of the Jewish conscience that is at least comparable to that of Socrates in Western society; as witnesses to the force of the moral and religious conscience and its imperious claims to obedience—claims more pressing than those of any state or emperor.

Notes

1. But see Haim Cohn, *The Trial and Death of Jesus* (New York, 1971), p. 341, note 23.
2. Philo, *De Legatione ad Gaium*, vol. 10 of *Philosophical Works*, Loeb Classical Library (Cambridge, Mass.: Harvard University Press, 1929-62), pp. 232 ff.
3. It may be noted that while the Egyptian midwives refused to assist in the proposed genocide of the Israelites, they did not openly avow their intent knowingly to violate the king's decree. They resorted to a subterfuge by claiming that the Hebrew women did not really require the services of midwives (Exodus 1:19).
4. Mohandas K. Gandhi, *Non-Violent Resistance*, ed. Bharatan Kumarappa (New York: Schocken Books, 1961), p. 7.
5. Compare the Oedipus cycle in Greek drama for a similar feeling of revulsion against an incestuous act.
6. In post-Talmudic Judaism, authorities did not all agree that Halakhah imposed an absolute duty freely to choose martyrdom under the circumstances in view of the great degree of duress. They also stressed the question whether the cardinal sin was required to be committed publicly or secretly. The post-Talmudic discussions are not considered in this essay. See Samuel Belkin, *In His Image* (New York: Abelard-Schuman, 1960), 210-211; David Daube, *Collaboration With Tyranny in Rabbinic Law* (New York: Oxford University Press, 1965), especially pp. 26-27, 31, 35-36, 40, 83; Henri Clavier, *The Duty and the Right of Resistance* (Strasbourg and Oxford, 1956); and Samuel G. Broude, "Civil Disobedience and the Jewish Tradition," in *Judaism and Ethics*, ed. Daniel J. Silver (New York: Ktav, 1970).
7. See Milton R. Konvitz, "Law and Morals: In the Hebrew Scriptures, Plato, and Aristotle," in L. Finkelstein, ed., *Social Responsibility in an Age of Revolution* (New York: Jewish Theological Seminary, 1971).
8. Cf. Romans 2:14-15.
9. Cf. Jubilees 7:22; Acts 15:20,29.
10. See Maimonides, *Hilkhot Yesodei Ha-Torah*, 5, 4. Cf. Belkin, *op. cit.*, pp. 102, 132.
11. Cf. Daube, *op. cit.*, 99-100.
12. Cf. Bernard Heller, "Masada and the Talmud," *Tradition*, vol. 31 (Winter 1968).

Medical Ethics

Moral questions relating to medical problems have been at the forefront of ethical discussion in recent years. Although this discussion has been stimulated by recent advances in medical technology, many of the problems involved are perennial. This is certainly the case with abortion. Although discussions of abortion can be found in all historical strata of halakhic literature, the practice itself was very rare among Jews until recently. The pressure of contemporary events has forced Jewish thinkers to confront the question of abortion in great detail and it has received wide attention.

Three discussions on abortion are presented here. Two are by traditional thinkers, one Orthodox and one Conservative. They are both included, not because their conclusions are so different, but because they exemplify two different methodologies in recent Jewish ethics. Rosner and Klein both agree that the weight of the Jewish tradition militates against a liberal, abortion-on-demand position. They further agree that the tradition takes a generally conservative view on the conditions justifying therapeutic abortion. In building his case, however, Rosner appeals only to the halakhah and follows a strict method of citing cases and precedents to arrive at his conclusions. He presents an halakhic position, pure and simple.

Klein, on the other hand, seeks out what might be called the "cardinal principles" of the halakhah, the spirit of the law which he derives from its letter. He presents a conclusion based, not so much on halakhah per se, as on the "religious tradition" of Judaism. He also makes explicit appeal to non-halakhic issues, arguing for example that "at the present time, when life has lost so much of its sanctity, we dare not add measures that will increase disregard for life." These two essays generally exemplify the differing approaches of Orthodox and Conservative interpreters of Judaism to the analysis of ethical problems.

It should not be inferred from the fact that both Rosner and Klein defend relatively conservative positions that all interpreters of the Jewish tradition speak with one voice on the issue of abortion. Some spokesmen, Reform theologians prominent among them, advocate positions much more liberal than those presented by Rosner and Klein. Such, for example, is the case with Balfour Brickner's testimony before a U. S. Senate sub-committee considering an anti-abortion amendment.

The two other essays in the section take what Seymour Siegel calls the Jewish tradition's "bias towards life" and in that light analyze the problems of fetal research and euthanasia. Siegel presents a non-halakhic interpretation of this "bias towards life" and is led to recommend very conservative criteria to guide fetal experimentation. David Bleich's discussion of the tragic case of Karen Ann Quinlan demonstrates the same conservative bias with respect to questions of life and death. In the present essay, he seeks to articulate the general attitudes towards life, death and mastery of one's body which are embodied in the halakhah.

15

The Jewish Attitude Toward Abortion

FRED ROSNER

The question of intentional abortion is not raised directly in the Bible. We deduce the status of the fetus from the following relevant passages.

An unborn fetus in Jewish law is not considered a person (Hebrew: *nefesh*, meaning soul) until it has been born. The fetus is regarded as a part of the mother's body and not a separate being until it begins to egress from the womb during parturition. In fact, until forty days after conception, the fertilized egg is considered as "mere fluid." These facts form the basis for the present day Jewish legal views on abortion. Biblical, Talmudic and Rabbinic support for these statements will now be presented.

In Exodus (21:22-23) we find the following: "When men fight and one of them pushes a pregnant woman and a miscarriage results, but no other misfortune ensues, the one responsible shall be fined as the woman's husband may exact from him, the payment to be based on judges' reckoning. But if other misfortune ensues, the penalty shall be life for life. . . ."

Rashi quotes the *Mechilta* which interprets "no other misfortune" to mean no fatal injury to the woman following her miscarriage. In that case, the attacker pays only compensation for the loss of the fetus. Most other Jewish Bible commentators including Ramban, Ibn Ezra, Malbim, Torah Temimah, Hirsch, and Hertz agree with Rashi's interpretation. We thus see that when the mother is unharmed following trauma to her abdomen and only the fetus is aborted, our major, if not only, concern is

Reprinted by permission of the author from *Tradition*, Vol. 10, no. 2. Copyright © 1968 by the Rabbinical Council of America.

to have the one responsible pay damages to the husband since the fetus is his property. No prohibition is evident from this Scriptural passage against destroying the unborn child.

Based upon this Biblical statement Maimonides in his code asserts as follows: "If one assaults a woman, even unintentionally, and her child is born prematurely, he must pay the value of the child to the husband and the compensation for injury and pain to the woman." [1] Maimonides continues with statements regarding how these compensations are computed. A similar declaration is found in Karo's *Shulhan Arukh*.[2] No concern is expressed by either Maimonides or Karo regarding the status of the miscarried fetus. It is part of the mother and belongs jointly to her and her husband and thus damages must be paid for its premature death. However, the one who was responsible is not culpable for murder since the unborn fetus is not considered a person.

Murder in Jewish law is based upon Exodus 21:12 where it is written: "He that smiteth a man so that he dieth shall surely be put to death." The word "man" is interpreted by the Sages to mean a man but not a fetus.[3] Thus, the destruction of an unborn fetus is not considered murder.

Another pertinent Scriptural passage is Leviticus 24:17 where it states: "And he that smiteth any person mortally shall surely be put to death." However, an unborn fetus is not considered a person or *nefesh* and, therefore, its destruction does not incur the death penalty.

Turning to Talmudic sources, the *Mishnah* in *Tractate Oholoth* 7:6 asserts the following: "If a woman is having difficulty in giving birth (and her life is in danger), one cuts up the fetus within her womb and extracts it limb by limb, because her life takes precedence over that of the fetus. But if the greater part was already born, one may not touch it, for one may not set aside one person's life for that of another."

Tosafot Yom Tov, in his commentary on this *Mishnah*, explains that the fetus is not considered a *nefesh* until it has egressed into the air of the world and, therefore, one is permitted to destroy it to save the mother's life. Similar reasoning is found in Rashi's commentary on the Talmudic discussion of this *Mishnah* where Rashi states that as long as the child did not come out into the world, it is not called a living being *i.e. nefesh*.[4] Once the head of the child has come out, the child may not be harmed because it is considered as fully born, and one life may not be taken to save another.

The *Mishnah* in *Tractate Arachin* 1:4 states: "If a pregnant woman is taken out to be executed, one does not wait for her to give birth; but if her pains of parturition had already begun, (literally: she had already sat on the birth stool), one waits for her until she gives birth. . . ." One may conclude from this *Mishnah* that one does not delay the execution of the mother in order to save the life of the fetus because we wish to avoid causing grief to the mother.

The Talmud explains[5] that the embryo is part of the mother's body and has no identity of its own since it is dependent for its life upon the body of the woman. However, as soon as it starts to move from the womb, it is considered an autonomous being *(nefesh)* and thus unaffected by the mother's state. This concept of the embryo being considered part of the mother and not a separate being recurs throughout the Talmud[6] and Rabbinic writings.[7] The Talmud continues[5]: "Rab Judah said in the name of Samuel: If a (pregnant) woman is about to be executed, one strikes her against her womb so that the child may die first, to avoid her being disgraced." Rashi explains that if the child escaped death and came forth after the mother's execution, it would cause vaginal bleeding and disgrace the executed mother. Thus we have evidence that an unborn fetus does not have the status of a living being and destroying it to save the mother embarrassment is permissible if it is going to die anyway.

A very difficult and bizarre *Tosefot* states that "it is permissible to kill an unborn fetus."[8] Some authorities[9] consider these words of *Tosefot* verbatim whereas others are of the opinion that *Tosefot* should not be interpreted literally.[10] Yet others state that these words of *Tosefot* are erroneous.[11]

Prior to forty days after conception, a fertilized egg is considered nothing more than "mere fluid"[12] and one "need not take into consideration the possibility of a valid childbirth."[13] However, after 40 days have elapsed, fashioning or formation of the fetus is deemed to have occurred. Laws of ritual uncleanliness must be observed for abortuses older than 40 days.[14] This period of uncleanliness is similar to that prescribed following the birth of a child and is not the same as that for a menstruant woman. Furthermore, a woman who aborts after the 40th day following conception is required to bring an offering just as if she had given birth to a live child.[15] These laws of ritual impurity and offerings apply even where the abortus "resembles cattle, a wild beast or a bird" or a "shapeless piece of flesh." These facts imply that the unborn fetus, although not considered a living person *(nefesh)*, still has some status. Nowhere, however, does it state that killing this fetus by premature artifical termination of pregnancy is prohibited.

Based upon these Talmudic sources as well as the Scriptural passages cited earlier, one may again ask why do most Rabbinic authorities prohibit abortion, except in certain situations, as a serious moral offense even though it is not considered murder? Distinguished Jewish physicians of ancient and more recent times also admonished against abortion. Denunciations of the practice of abortion are recorded in the medical oaths and prayers of Asaf Judaeus[16] in the seventh century, Amatus Lusitanus[17] in the sixteenth century and Jacob Zahalon[18] in the seventeenth century. What are the objections to abortion in the opinion of these Jewish physicians in view of the fact that an unborn fetus does not have the status of a person (nefesh) by Jewish law? If abortion is not considered murder, on what legal basis is it prohibited?

This question will be answered by establishing the time that a fetus becomes equal to an adult human being. We have referred to the Mishnah in Tractate Oholoth 7:6 upon which the Jewish legal attitudes toward therapeutic abortion is based. The Mishnah states in part that if the "greater part was already born, one may not touch it, for one may not set aside one person's life for that of another." Thus the act of birth changes the status of the fetus from a non-person to a person (nefesh). Killing the newborn after this point is infanticide. Many Talmudic sources[19] and commentators on the Talmud[20] substitute the word "head" for "greater part" in the above Mishnah. Others[21] maintain the "greater part" verbatim. Maimonides[22] and Karo[23] also consider the extrusion of the head to indicate birth. They both further state that by Rabbinic decree, even if only one limb of the fetus was extruded and then retracted, childbirth is considered to have occurred.[24]

Not only is the precise time of the birth of paramount importance in adjucating whether aborting the fetus is permissible to save the mother's life, but the viability of the fetus must also be taken into account. The newborn child is not considered fully viable until it has survived thirty days following birth as it is stated in the Talmud[25]: "Rabban Simeon ben Gamliel said: Any human being who lives thirty days is not a nephel (abortus) because it is stated (Num 18:16): 'And those that are to be redeemed of them from a month old shalt thou redeem,' since prior to 30 days it is not certain that he will survive." Further support for the necessity of a 30 day post partum viability period for adjucating various Jewish legal matters pertaining to the newborn comes from Maimonides who asserts[26]: "Whether one kills an adult or a day-old child, a male or a female, he must be put to death if he kills deliberately. . . provided that the child is born after a full-term pregnancy. But, if it is born before the end of nine months, it is regarded as an abortion until it has lived for 30 days, and if one kills it during these 30 days, one is not put to death on its account."

Thus, although the newborn infant reaches the status of a person or *nefesh* which it didn't have prior to birth, it still does not enjoy all the legal rights of an adult until it has survived for 30 days *post partum*. One is not liable for the death penalty if one kills such a child until it has established its viability but it is certainly prohibited because "one may not set aside one person's life for that of another."[27]

The permissibility to kill the unborn fetus to save the mother's life rests upon the fact that such an embryo is not considered a person *(nefesh)* until it is born. Maimonides[28] and Karo[29] present a second reason for allowing abortion or embryotomy prior to birth where the mother's life is endangered and that is the argument of "pursuit" whereby the fetus is "pursuing" the mother. The argument of pursuit is based upon two passages in the Pentateuch:

(1) Deut. 25:11-12. "When men strive together one with another, and the wife of one draws near to save her husband from the hand of the one that smiteth him, and she puts her hand and taketh hold of his genitals, then you shall cut off her hand, your eye shalt have no pity."
(2) Leviticus 19:16. "Thou shalt not stand idly by the blood of thy neighbor."

In the former case, the woman is pursuing the man by maiming him and she should be stopped. The latter case is interpreted by Rashi and most other commentators to mean that one should not stand idly by without attempting to rescue one's fellow man whose life is threatened by robbers, drowning or wild beasts. Based upon these Biblical passages, the *Mishnah* states[30]: "These may be delivered at the cost of their lives he that pursues after his fellow man to kill him. . . ." The *Talmud*[31] follows with a lengthy discussion asserting that it is one's duty to disable or even take the life of the assailant to protect the life of one's fellow man.

This discussion prompted Maimonides to state: ". . . Consequently, the Sages have ruled that if a pregnant woman is having difficulty in giving birth, the child inside her may be excised, either by drugs or manually (i.e. surgery) because it is regarded as pursuing her in order to kill her. But, if its head has been born, it must not be touched for one may not set aside one human life for that of another, and this happening is the course of nature" (i.e. an act of God, that is, the mother is pursued by Heaven, not the fetus). An identical statement is found in Karo's Code.

Many Rabbinic authorities[32] pose the following question to Maimonides: How can the argument of pursuit be invoked here since, if it were applicable, then killing the fetus even after the head or greater part is born should be permissible? *Tifereth Israel*[33] states that the argument of pursuit is totally inappropriate because the child endangering the mother's life is an act of God. The child does not intend to kill the mother. It is a case of Heavenly pursuit. This concept of Heavenly pursuit is discussed in the *Talmud* and mentioned by both Maimonides and Karo. Jakobovits[34] amplifies the problem. He states that a contradictory ruling seems to be emerging. On the one hand, we invoke the argument of pursuit to allow therapeutic abortion and on the other hand, the validity of this argument is dismissed because nature and not the child pursues the mother.

The problem is resolved by several Rabbis whose separate Responsa state that the non-person status of the fetus prior to birth is not sufficient to warrant the embryo's destruction since this would still constitute a serious moral offense, even if it is not a penal crime. Thus one must invoke the additional argument of pursuit. After the baby's head has emerged, however, the fetus attains the status of a *nefesh*, even prior to proved 30 days *post partum* viability, and the "weak" argument of pursuit no longer justifies killing the child even if the mother's life is threatened since it is a case of Heavenly pursuit. However, even after egress of the head, if *both* lives are threatened one may kill the fetus to save the mother. The reason is that the mother's life is a certainty without the fetal threat whereas the viability of the fetus is in doubt until 30 days have elapsed following birth. This viewpoint is also subscribed to by Rabbi Moses Schick[35] and Rabbi David Hoffman.[36] Others[37] dispute this ruling.

We now return to the original question. If the unborn child is not considered a *nefesh*, why should its destruction not be allowed under all circumstances? Why is only a threat to the mother's life or health an acceptable reason for therapeutic abortion?

One answer is given by Rabbi Ya'ir Bacharach who, contrary to the *Mishnah* in Tractate *Arachin* 1:4, states that one waits for a condemned pregnant woman to give birth because a potential human being can arise from each drop of human seed (sperm). Interference with this pregnancy would constitute expulsion of semen for naught, an act akin to coitus interruptus as practiced originally by Er and Onan[38] and strictly prohibited by Jewish law. This reason for prohibiting therapeutic abortion upon demand is also subscribed to by others.[39]

A second reason for not allowing abortion without specific indication is that the unborn fetus, although not a person, does have some status. This is evident from the laws regarding ritual impurity and offerings that a woman who aborts after 40 days of conception must adhere to. These requirements are similar to those prescribed following the live birth of a child. Thus the fetus may be considered as a "partial person."[40]

A third reason for prohibiting abortion on demand is that one is not permitted to wound oneself[41] and thus a woman undergoing vaginal abortion by manipulative means is considered as intentionally wounding herself. At least two Rabbinic authorities adhere to this viewpoint.[42]

A fourth reason for prohibiting abortion without maternal danger is asserted by at least one Rabbi[43] who states that the operative intervention entails danger. One is prohibited by Jewish law from placing oneself in danger based upon Deuteronomy 4:15: "Take ye therefore good heed unto yourselves. . ."

Another reason for prohibiting thereapeutic abortion in cases where no threat to the mother exists is stated by the present Chief Rabbi of Israel, Isser Yehuda Unterman. He states that one may desecrate the Sabbath to save the life or preserve the health of an unborn fetus in order that the child may observe many Sabbaths later.[44] As a result, destroying the fetus, although not legally murder, is nevertheless forbidden because of an appurtenance to murder. Rabbi Bacharach, who permits abortion prior to 40 days of pregnancy because the fetus has no status at all but is considered mere fluid, is taken to task by Rabbi Unterman who states that even prior to 40 days there is an appurtenance to murder.

Another argument of Rabbi Unterman is that a fetus, even less than 40 days after conception, is considered a potential (literally: questionable) human being which, by nature alone, without interference, will become an actual human being. Thus a potential person (sofek nefesh) has enough status to prohibit its own destruction.

A final argument of Rabbi Unterman comes from the interpretation of R. Ishmael for the Scriptural verse[45]:" Whoso sheddeth man's blood, by man shall his blood be shed, for in the image of God did He make man." This can be translated "whoso sheddeth the blood of man in man, his blood shall be shed. . . ." The "man in man" is interpreted to mean a fetus.[46] This Noachidic prohibition of killing a fetus applies also to

Israelities even though the Jewish legal consequences might differ.

A final reason for prohibiting abortion on demand in Jewish law is suggested by the present Chief Rabbi of the British Commonwealth, Immanuel Jakobovits[47] and Belgian Rabbi Moshe Yonah Zweig, among others. They point to the *Mishnah* in *Tractate Oholoth* 7:6 which permits abortion prior to birth of the child only when the mother's life is endangered. The implication is that when the mother's life is not at stake, it would be prohibited to kill the unborn fetus.

Summary of Rabbinic Opinion Regarding Therapeutic Abortion

A small minority of Rabbinic Responsa are of the opinion that prior to forty days after conception, the fetus has no status at all and is not a *nefesh* and abortion at this stage might be permissible for the slightest reason. According to these few Rabbis, such a reason might be the fear that a deformed child may be born, due to exposure of the mother early in pregnancy to German measles or a teratogenic drug such as thalidomide or possibly even for socio-economic reasons or family planning. Such rulings are vigorously denounced by others who prohibit therapeutic abortion both in the case where the mother was exposed to German measles[48] or where the mother ingested thalidomide early in pregnancy.[49] Most Rabbinic authorities permit therapeutic abortion where the health or life of the mother is threatened. Some are more stringent and require the mother's life to be in danger, however remote such danger,[50] whereas other authorities permit abortion for a threat to the mother's health.[51] Such dangers to maternal health may include deafness,[52] cancer, pain or psychiatric disease.[53] Psychiatric indication for abortion would be acceptable only if some grave danger to the mother is in fact anticipated to result from her fears or nervous condition, as certified by competent medical opinion, and only on the basis of previous experiences of mental strain by the mother.[54]

Some authorities extend the permissibility to perform therapeutic abortion to any maternal need.[55] This would include cases of incest or rape[56] where shame or embarrassment to the mother in the continuance of the pregnancy are considered threats to the mother's health. This, however, is a minority viewpoint. Only a very small group of Rabbinic Responsa regard the possibility of a deformed child being born to prey so much on the mother's mind as to constitute impairment of her health.

This "maternal" indication is not acceptable to most Rabbinic opinions. If the mother becomes pregnant while nursing a child and the pregnancy changes her milk so that the suckling's life is endangered, then considerable Rabbinic opinion would permit abortion in this case.[57]

Malformed Babies and Monster Births

The Talmud[58] contains the following quotation: "In the case of a birth given to a creature which possesses a double back or a double spine, Rab said: If it was a woman (who miscarried), it is not regarded as an offspring. . . .", that is, the laws concerning a birth are not observed. However, this creature, once it has been born, has the status of a person and killing it would be considered infanticide which is prohibited.

The thirteenth century *Sefer Chasidim*[59] describes the case of a child born with teeth and a tail. It was said that the end will be that people will eat him, therefore it is better to kill him. The reply by the author was that one should remove the teeth in the front and tail from below so that the infant will be like a human body and he will not be able to do any harm. Thus we see that the killing of monster births is prohibited.

An early Rabbinic responsum relating to a malformed child is that of Rabbi Eleazar Fleckeles in the nineteenth century.[60] His ruling is that once a child is born of a human mother and survives, it is a living human being in all respects and may not be destroyed. Starving it to death is considered homicide.

The problem of malformed babies usually born without one or more limbs or with seal-like limbs to mothers who ingested the teratogenic drug thalidomide early in pregnancy is discussed by two recent Rabbinic responsa. Rabbi Moshe Yonah Halevi Zweig of Antwerp, Belgium, writing in a Hebrew periodical,[32] condemns the killing of the thalidomide deformed baby which resulted in the famous Liège, Belgium trial involving parents, relatives and a physician charged with the murder of this drug-damaged child.[61] Rabbi Zweig's lengthy dissertation, however, deals primarily with abortion (i.e. antenatal) and not infanticide (i.e. postnatal).

Rabbi Immanuel Jakobovits, writing in a London journal,[62] concludes as follows: a physically or mentally abnormal child has the same claim to life as a normal child because it is considered a person (*nefesh*). Furthermore, while only the killing of a born and viable child constitutes murder in Jewish law, the destruction of the fetus, too, is a moral offense and cannot be justified except out of consideration for the mother's life or health. Consequently, the fear that a child may or will be deformed is not in itself a legitimate indication for its abortion, particularly since there is usually a chance that the child might turn out to be quite normal. Killing a cripple is similarly prohibited.

Once a malformed child has been born, one cannot use the argument of euthanasia or mercy killing to sanction its destruction. This act is positively prohibited by Jewish law as nothing less than murder (infanticide). The Jewish attitude toward euthanasia in general is discussed at length elsewhere.[63]

Conclusion

Prior to forty days following conception, the fertilized egg is considered by some Rabbinic authorities as nothing more than "mere fluid." From forty days until birth, the fetus is not considered a living person (nefesh) but is regarded as part of the mother's flesh and aborting it might not be legally considered murder. However, the destruction of an unborn fetus without sufficiently strong indication is still condemned for a variety of reasons. Abortion is permitted by most Rabbinic authorities where a medical or psychiatric threat to the mother's life exists. Many authorities permit abortion not only if her life is in danger but even if her health may deteriorate by continuation of the pregnancy. A small minority of Rabbinic opinion allow therapeutic abortion for reasons such as incest, rape and fear that a malformed child may be born. Justification for this position rests on the grounds of concern for the mother, i.e. that such a birth would adversely affect her mental or physical health by causing her anguish, shame or embarrassment. This latter viewpoint is not subscribed to by most Rabbinic authorities, however.

After the head or greater part of the body of the infant is born, only a threat to both lives would allow sacrifice of the child to save the mother because the mother's life is a certainty without the fetal threat, whereas the fetus has not proved its viability until thirty days post partum have elapsed. After thirty days of life, every human being, whether deformed, crippled or otherwise deficient has rights equal to every other adult human being.

Since many important legal and moral considerations which cannot be spelled out in the presentation of general principles may weigh upon the verdict in any given case, it seems advisable to submit every individual case to Rabbinic judgment in the light of the prevailing medical and other circumstances.

Notes

1. Code of Maimonides (*Mishneh Torah*). "Laws of Wounding and Damaging," (*Hilchoth Chovel Umazik*), Chapter 4, Paragraph 1.

2. *Shulchan Arukh, Choshen Mishpat,* Chapter 423, par. 1.

3. *Tractate Sanhedrin* 84b.

4. *Tractate Sanhedrin* 72b.

5. *Tractate Arachin* 7a.

6. *Tractates Chulliń* 58a, *Gittin* 23b, *Nazir* 51a, *Baba Kamma* 88b, *Temura* 31a.

7. *Responsa Maharit:* Section 1, no. 97 and no. 99; *Responsa Chavat Ya'ir,* no. 31; *Responsa Noda Biyehuda: Choshen Mishpat,* no. 59; *Chidushei Ramban on Niddah* 44b; *Peri Megadim: Orach Chayim* 328:7:1; *Me'iri on Sanhedrin* 72b; *Ha-Eshkol:* "Laws of Circumcision," no. 36; *Responsa Torat Chesed: Even Ha'ezer,* no. 42:32; *Responsa She'elath Ya'avetz,* Vol. 1, no. 43; *Responsa Beth Shlomoh: Choshen Mishpat,* no. 132; *Responsa Tzitz Eliezer,* Vol. 9, no. 51:3 and numerous others.

8. *Tractate Niddah* 44b.

9. *Responsa Tzitz Eliezer,* Vol. 9, no. 51:3 by Rabbi Eliezer Waldenberg, present Chief Justice of the Rabbinic High Court in Jerusalem; *Responsa Chavath Ya'ir.* no. 31 by Rabbi Ya'ir Bacharach (1639-1702).

10. Unterman, I. Y., *Be'inyan Peekuach Nefesh Shel Ubar* (Regarding danger to life of the fetus). NOAM (Jerusalem), Vol. 6; 1-11, 1963; *Responsa She'elat Yaavetz,* Vol. 1, no. 43 by Rabbi Jacob Emden.

11. *Responsa Bet Yitzchak, Yoreh Deah,* Part 2, no. 162.

12. *Tractates Yevamot* 69b; *Niddah* 30b; *Mishnah Keritoth* 1.

13. *Mishnah Niddah* 3:7.

14. *Mishnah Niddah* 3:2-6.

15. *Mishnah Keritoth* 1:3-6.

16. Rosner, F. and Muntner, S., "The Oath of Asaph," *Annals Int. Med.,* 63 (2): 317-320 (August 1965).

17. Friedenwald, H., "The Oath of Amatus," in *The Jews and Medicine* (Baltimore: Johns Hopkins Press, 1944), pp. 368-370.

18. Savitz, H., "Jacob Zahalon and his book, 'The Treasure of Life'." *New England J. of Med.,* 213: 167-176 (1935); Simon, I., "La Prière des Médecins, 'Tephilat Harofim', de Jacob Zahalon, Médicin et Rabbin en Italie (1630-1693)," *Rev. Hist. Med. Hebr.,* 8:38-51, (1955); Friedenwald, H., "The Physician's Prayer of Jacob Zahalon of Rome," in *The Jews and Medicine* (Baltimore: John Hopkins Press, 1944), pp. 273-279.

19. *Mishnah Niddah* 3:5; *Tractates Sanhedrin* 72b; *Niddah* 29a; *Tosefta Yevamot* 9:9.

20. Commentaries of *Bartinoro* (Rabbi Obadiah ben Abraham of Bertinoro, Italy, 15th Century); *Rosh* (Asher ben Yechiel, 1250-1327) and *Rishon Letzion* (Rabbi Isaiah Berlin of Breslau) on the *Mishnah* in *Oholoth* 7:2; and the commentaries of *Rashi* on *Tractate Sanhedrin* 72b and *Tosefot* on *Tractate Sanhedrin* 59a.

21. Jerusalem or Palestinian Talmud, *Tractates Shabbat* 14:4 and *Avodah Zarah* 2:2.

22. *Mishneh Torah, Hilchoth Essurey Biyah*, Chapter 10, Par. 3.

23. *Shulchan Arukh, Choshen Mishpat*, Chapter 425, Par. 2.

24. *Shulchan Arukh, Yoreh Deah*, Chapter 194, Par. 10 and ref. 49.

25. *Tractate Shabbat* 135b.

26. *Mishneh Torah, Hilchoth Rotzeach Ushemirath Hanefesh*, Chapter 2, Par. 6.

27. *Mishnah Oholot* 7:3.

28. *Mishneh Torah, ibid.*, Chapter 1, Par. 9.

29. *Shulchan Arukh, Choshen Mishpat*, Chapter 425, Par. 2.

30. *Sanhedrin* 87.

31. *Sanhedrin* 72b and 73a.

32. Zweig, M. Y. H., *Al Hapalah Melachutit* (Regarding Therapeutic Abortion), NOAM (Jerusalem), Vol. 7: 36-56, (1964); *Commentary on Tosefot Rabbi Akiba Eger* (1761-1837) on the *Mishnah Oholot* 7:6; *Responsa Noda Biyehudah* Part 2, *Choshen Mishpat* no. 59 by Rabbi Ezekiel Landau (1737-1793) and ref. 36.

33. Commentary of Rabbi Israel Lipschutz (1782-1860) on the *Mishnah Oholoth* 7:6.

34. Jakobovits, I., "Abortion and Embryotomy" in *Jewish Medical Ethics* (New York: Bloch Publishing Co., 1959), pp. 170-191.

35. *Responsa Maharam Schik, Yoreh Deah* no. 155.

36. *Responsa Melamed Leho'il, Yoreh Deah* No. 69.

37. Rabbi Chayim Sofer in his *Responsa Machanay Chayim, Choshen Mishpat* no. 50; Rabbi Mayir Ashkenazi Eisenstadt in his *Responsa Panim Me'iroth*. Part 3, no. 8.

38. Genesis 38:9.

39. *Responsa Ateret Chachamin, Ehven Ha'ezer* no. 1; *Responsa She'elat Yaavetz*, Vol. 1, no. 43 by Rabbi Jacob Emden.

40. *Responsa Tzofnat Paneach*, Vol. l, no. 49.

41. *Bava Kamma* 91b; *Mishneh Torah, Hilkot Chovel U'mazik*, Chapter 5, Par. 1.

42. *Responsa Marahit*, Vol. l, no. 99 by Rabbi Joseph Trani; M. Y. H. See ref. 59.

43. *Responsa Beth Shlomoh, Choshen Mishpat* no. 132.

44. *Ramban on Niddah* 44b.

45. Genesis 9:6.

46. *Sanhedrin* 57b.

47. Jakobovits, I., "Jewish Views on Abortion," in *Abortion and the Law*, edited by D. T. Smith, pp. 124-143; Jakobovits. I., "Artificial Insemination, Birth Control and Abortion," *Hebrew Med. J. (Harofe Haivri)*, Vol. 2, pp. 183-169, Eng. ed. and pp. 114-129, Hebrew ed.; Jakobovits, I., *Jewish Law Faces Modern Problems* (New York: Yeshiva University Studies in Torah Judaism Series, 1965), pp.74-79.

48. Unterman, I. Y., *Be'inyan Peekuach Nefesh Shel Ubar*, NOAM, Vol. 6, pp. 1-11, 1963.

49. Jakobovits, I., "Deformed Babies and Thalidomide Babies," in *Journal of a Rabbi* (New York: Living Books, 1966), pp. 262-266.

50. *Responsa Aryeh Debey Eelaye: Yoreh Deah* No. 19; *Responsa Peri Hasadeh*, Vol. 4, no. 50; *Responsa Bet Shlomoh: Choshen Mishpat* no. 132; *Responsa Binyan David* No. 47; *Responsa Levushei Mordechai: Choshen Mishpat* no. 39; *Responsa Ko'ach Schor* no. 21; *Responsa Tzur Yaakov* no. 141; *Responsa Avnei Tzedek: Choshen Mishpat* no. 19.

51. *Responsa Rav Pa'alim*, Vol. 1, *Even Ha'ezer* no. 4; *Sdei Chemed Pe'at Hasadeh*, Vol. 1, no. 52.

52. *Responsa Mishpetei Uziel*, Part 3, no. 46, 47 by Rabbi Z. Uziel, late Chief Rabbi of the Sephardic Community in Israel.

53. *Responsa Peri Ha'aretz, Yoreh Deah* no. 21 by Rabbi Israel Meir Mizrachi; *Responsa Netzer Mata'ai*, Part 1, no. 8 by Rabbi Nathan Zvi Friedman.

54. Jakobovits, I., *Personal Communications*, May 24, 1968.

55. *Responsa Torat Chesed: Even Ha'ezer* no. 42:32; *Responsa Tzitz Eliezer*, Vol. 9, no. 51:3.

56. *Responsa She'elat Yaavetz*, Vol. 1, no.43.

57. *Responsa Chayim Ve shalom*, Vol. 1, no. 40; *Responsa Bet Yehuda: Even Ha'ezer* no. 14; *Responsa She'eilot Yitzchak* no. 69; *Responsa Tzitz Eliezer*, Vol. 9, no. 51:3.

58. *Tractate Bekhorot* 43b.

59. Authored by Rabbi Judah ben Samuel the Pious. Reprinted in Buenos Aires in 1952, no. 186, p. 568.

60. *Responsa Teshuva Me'Ahavah*, Part 1, no. 53.

61. Colebrook, L., "The Liège Trial and the Problem of Voluntary Euthanasia," *Lancet* 2:1225, (1962).

62. *The Jewish Review* (London), November 14, 1962.

63. Rosner, F., "Jewish Attitude Toward Euthanasia," *New York State J. of Medicine*, 67 (18): 2499-2506 (Sept. 15, 1967).

16.

Abortion and Jewish Tradition

ISAAC KLEIN

While the problem of abortion is an old one, it has become particularly pressing today because of many new social, scientific and religious developments. Attention is focused on the problem currently because of the pressures which come from many quarters to change the existing laws, and the proposed legislation to liberalize them.

Because the question of abortion is not new, various religious traditions have crystalized definite attitudes and views on the problems that it poses. Underlying the Jewish view of abortion is the general attitude toward life as expressed in the religious tradition of the Jewish people. This attitude is expressed in two biblical verses: "See, I have set before thee this day life and good, death and evil" (Deuteronomy 10:15); and "Ye shall therefore keep My statutes and My judgments which if a man shall do, he shall live by them" (Leviticus 18:15).

In these two verses life is equated with the good, and the observance of the commandments with the enhancement of life. This identification has been a cardinal principle in Judaism. The Rabbis repeatedly emphasized that the words "he shall live by them" mean that God's commandments are to be a means for the furtherance of life and not for its destruction. Therefore, with the exception of three prohibitions, all commandments of the Torah are to be kept in abeyance whenever their performance endangers life. The exceptions are idolatry, murder and adultery.

The Bible does not speak about abortion but does refer to the status of a foetus in the following passage: "If men strive and hurt a woman with child so that her fruit depart from her, and yet no mischief follow, he shall surely be punished according as the woman's husband will lay upon him; and he shall pay as the judge determines. And if any mischief follow, then thou shalt give life for life" (Exodus 21:22-23).

The mischief refers to the death of the woman. It is only when the mother dies from the injury that capital punishment is inflicted. The death of the unborn is punishable by fine only, because the unborn child is not accounted as a living person.

Philo and Josephus also dealt with abortion, but their statements are confused and inconsistent. Furthermore, these have not been in the mainstream of Jewish tradition and have not influenced its development. (See I. Jakobovits, *Jewish Medical Ethics*, p. 179f.)

We must therefore go to the Talmud and its commentators for guidance.

The classical source for the Jewish attitude to abortion is found in the Mishnah, a code of laws that dates back to the second century and forms the basis of the Talmud. It states: "A woman who is having difficulty in giving birth, it is permitted to cut up the child inside her womb and take it out limb by limb because her life takes precedence. However, if the greater part of the child has come out it must not be touched, because one life must not be taken to save another" *(Ohalot 7:6)*.

The statement of the Mishnah is repeated in the Tosefta, a contemporary Rabbinic work, with slight variations (Tosefta *Yebamot* 9:9).

The Talmud comments on the Mishnah in this fashion: "Once the child's head has come forth (while the Mishnah requires extrusion of the greater part of the child, the Tosefta speaks about the extrusion of the head) it may not be harmed, because one life may not be taken to save another. But why so? Is he not a pursuer with intent to kill? There it is different, for she is pursued by heaven" *(Sanhedrin 72b)*.

This passage explains the distinction between the case where the mother's life takes precedence, and where it does not. Rashi, the pre-eminent commentator on the Bible and the Talmud, explains the talmudic passage as follows: "As long as the child did not come out into the world it is not called a living being and it is therefore permissible to take its life in order to save the life of its mother. Once the head of the child has come out, the child may not be harmed because it is considered as fully born, and one life may not be taken to save another."

Rashi's view that the embryo is not considered a living being, and thus taking its life cannot be called murder, is supported by the biblical law concerning harm done to a pregnant woman, quoted above. In that case, too, the unborn child is not considered a living being.

In his code, Maimonides explains the Mishnah's position in terms of the child, in this case, endangering the life of the mother and thus being subject to the law of the "pursuer". He states: "This is moreover a negative commandment, that we have no pity on the life of a pursuer. Consequently, the sages have ruled that if a woman with child is having difficulty in giving birth, the child inside her may be taken out either by drugs or by surgery, because it is regarded as one pursuing her and trying to kill her. But once its head has appeared, it must not be touched, for we may not set aside one human life to save another" (Laws of the Murderer 1:9).

This difference in interpretation of the Mishnah may lead to a difference in legal decisions. According to Maimonides we would permit abortion only where there is clear danger to the life of the mother. According to Rashi other reasons besides a threat to the life of the mother might be considered adequate to permit an abortion.

The contemporary discussion of the problem seems to revolve around the question of whether the foetus is considered a living being, and would reflect Rashi's view of the question. However, the opinion of Maimonides is also relevant because much of the discussion on abortion today also hinges on the welfare of the mother and the family.

These are the main halachic sources for the problem of abortion. We shall now bring one relevant statement from aggadic sources. The Talmud reports the following conversation between Rabbi Judah the Prince and Antoninus the Roman Emperor (Sanhedrin 91b).

Antoninus said to Rabbi (Judah): "When is the soul given unto man, at the time that the embryo is formed, or at the time of conception?"

He replied, "At the time the embryo is formed."

The Emperor objected: "Is it possible for a piece of meat to stay for three days without salt and not putrify? It must thus be at conception."

Said Rabbi (Judah): "This thing Antoninus taught me and scripture supports him, as it is said (Job 10:12), 'and Thy visitation has preserved my spirit'."

If this discussion sounds naive and irrelevant, let me remind you that this controversy still goes on today. Only the terminology has changed. It was also a point of argument among the Greek philosophers. According to Aristotle the rational soul is infused the fortieth day after conception in the case of a male, and the eightieth day in the case of a female. According to the Platonic tradition the soul entered at conception. The Stoics believed that the soul entered at birth.

Roman jurists followed the Stoics and maintained that abortion was not murder. According to common law as well, taking a life is punishable only after complete extrusion of the child from the body of the mother.

The difference of attitude among the various religious traditions regarding abortion reflects this difference between Plato, Aristotle and the Stoics.

Surprisingly, medical science considers the foetus a living thing from the moment the ovum is fertilized (Joseph B. Lee, *Obstetrics*, fourth edition, p. 274).

Actually, being a living thing and being a separate entity are not the same thing. Even if we say that the foetus is a living thing we can maintain that it is *pars viscera matrum* or, as the Talmud expresses it, the foetus is accounted as the loin of its mother. When abortion is therapeutic, therefore, there can be no objection to it because it is like any surgery where we sacrifice a part for the whole.

Threat to Life

This is the attitude the Rabbis have taken. Abortion is not murder under any circumstance. Since it is the destruction of potential life, it is not permitted unless it is therapeutic.

The problem now is to define therapeutic. We shall cite a number of practical cases that came before the Rabbis during the past few centuries. Their answers will give us guidance to a definition of therapeutic.

The example cited in the Mishnah would indicate that permission for abortion is limited to instances where there is a direct threat to the mother's life. Examples in later literature reflect a wider area of concern.

Rabbi Yair Hayyim Bachrach (1639-1702), the author of a collection of responsa entitled *Havoth Yair*, reports this strange case in one of his responsa. A married woman committed adultery and became pregnant. She then had pangs of remorse, wanted to do penance, and asked whether she could swallow a drug in order to get rid of the "evil fruit" in her womb. In his answer Rabbi Bachrach makes it clear immediately that the question of the permissibility of abortion has nothing to do with the legitimacy of the child to be born. The only question involved is whether abortion is considered as taking a life or not. He distinguishes the various stages in the development of the foetus, i.e., forty days after conception, three months after conception. Rabbi Bachrach then concludes that *theoretically* abortion might be permitted during the early stages of the pregnancy, but we do not do so because of the custom adopted by both the Jewish and the general community.

Rabbi Meir Eisenstadt (1670-1744), in his collection of responsa entitled *Panim Me-iroth*, raises the following question: A woman had difficulty in giving birth, and the child came out feet first. Is it permitted to cut up the child, limb by limb, in order to save the mother?

This seems to be the very case stated in the Mishnah. The difficulty arises when we read how this case is restated in Maimonides. Whereas the Mishnah mentions that if the greater part of the child has come out we do not take the life of the child to save the mother, Maimonides, following the text of the Tosefta, says that if the head of the child or the majority thereof came out first it is considered as born and we do not take its life in order to save the mother.

The commentators tried to resolve this contradiction by saying that birth is constituted by the extrusion of the head or the majority thereof, or in the case where the head came out last, the extrusion of the majority of the body.

Rabbi Eisenstadt then asks if it is still forbidden to take the life of the child when, should we let nature take its course at this stage, death would result to both the mother and the child. He leaves the question unanswered. A later authority is very explicit and answers that in this case, too, we take the child in order to save the mother.

Rabbi Eliezer Deutsch (1850-1916), the author of a collection of responsa entitled *Peri Hasadeh* treats the following problem: A woman who had been pregnant a few weeks began to spit blood. Expert physicians said she must drink a drug in order to bring about a miscarriage. Should she wait, it would become necessary to remove the child by cutting it up, endangering the life of the mother. Is it permissible to induce the miscarriage by means of the drug?

Rabbi Deutsch answers that in such a case it is certainly permissible to do so. He also draws a distinction between the various stages in the development of the foetus, between the use of drugs and the use of surgery, and between another person inducing abortion or the woman inducing it herself. He concludes that abortion is permitted in this case for three reasons: 1) Until three months after conception there is not even a foetus. 2) No overt act is involved in this abortion. 3) The woman herself is doing it and it is thus an act of self-preservation. Current halakhic literature is replete with similar questions. Rabbi B. H. Uziel, the late Chief Rabbi of the Sephardic community of Israel, and Rabbi I. J. Unterman, the present Chief Rabbi of the Ashkenazic community of Israel, are among those who have dealt with the question.

Rabbi Uziel treated the case of a pregnant woman who was threatened with deafness if she were to go through with the pregnancy. He decided that since the foetus is not an independent life *(nefesh)* but only a part of the mother, there is no sin in destroying it for the sake of the mother (B. H. Uziel, *Mishpetei Uziel III*, Sec. 46,47).

Rabbi Unterman dealt with the question of abortion in a case where the expectant mother contracted German measles, and it was feared that the child might be born with serious physical and mental abnormalities *(Noam, Vol. 6, 5723)*. Rabbi Unterman is unalterably opposed to any abortion except in a case, like that mentioned in the Mishnah, where the child poses a direct threat to the mother's life.

Two other contemporary responsa shed light on the problem of abortion. Rabbi Isaac Oelbaum, formerly of Czechoslovakia and now residing in Toronto, Canada, treats one case. A woman has a sickly child who, according to the doctors, will not live unless it is breast-fed by the mother. The mother is now four weeks pregnant and feels that there has been a change in her milk. Can she destroy the unborn child, the doctors asked, by an injection, in order to save the child that she is nursing?

The author first discusses the reliability of doctors in these things (they sometimes exaggerate and are overcautious), and whether the question could be solved by substituting a proper formula for bottle feeding. He concludes that if there is expert evidence that danger may result from a continuing pregnancy, abortion is permitted *(She'eilot Yitzhak, Sec. 69)*.

In this responsum a new issue is introduced. Until now we have spoken of danger to the mother. In this case there is no danger to the mother, but to another child.

The other responsum is by Rabbi Gedaliah Felder, also of Toronto. The case concerns a pregnant woman who is afflicted with cancer of the lungs. The doctors say that if a premature birth is not induced, the cancer will spread faster and hasten her death. May one permit an abortion where the mother is saved only temporarily? *(Kol Torah, Heshvan 5719)*.

The main factor in determining the permissibility of abortion in this case is the claim that allowing the pregnancy to take its natural course will constitute a threat to the mother. The classic case of the Mishnah would indicate that abortion is permissible only when it is a direct threat to the *life* of the mother. The later responsa widen the meaning of the word "threat" to include a threat to the *health* of the mother.

Threats to Mental Health

Another consideration in questions of abortion involves psychological factors. All the cases mentioned thus far speak in physical terms. However, a very large number of the cases that involve abortion have to do with mental anguish, and threats to the mental health of the mother or the child. The concept of mental anguish is not new; it is just that we know more about its deleterious consequences today. Attacks of hysteria and suicidal tendencies are as much of a threat to the life of a mother as the physical ailments mentioned in earlier cases.

One responsum going back to the seventeenth century deals with this problem. Rabbi Israel Meir Mizrahi permitted abortion when it was feared that the mother would otherwise suffer an attack of hysteria (*Peri Ha-aretz Yoreh Deah*, Sec. 21; see also I. J. Unterman, *Ha-Torah V' Ha-Medinah*, pp. 25, 29).

Contemporary authorities have dealt with cases that involved thalidomide babies, victims of rape, and mothers of large families where another child would harm the ability to care for the existing children.

With a few notable exceptions, Jewish authorities agree that, once conceived, a child has a right to live even if there is a chance for it to be born malformed or in poor health. We introduce, however, the question of what this does to the mother in terms of mental anguish, psychological disturbances, attacks of hysteria and suicidal tendencies. Examples of such results are abundant (I. Jakobovits, *The Jewish Review*, London, Nov. 14, 1962).

Guidelines

From the foregoing we would reach the following conclusions, suggested by the weight of opinion as well as by present sociological and medical factors.

There is a distinction between the early and the later stages of pregnancy.

In the later stages we would permit abortion only when the birth of the foetus would be a direct threat to the *life* of the mother. This threat should be interpreted to include cases where continuation of the pregnancy would have such a debilitating effect, psychological or otherwise, on the mother as to constitute a hazard to her life, however remote such danger may be.

In the earlier stages we would allow therapeutic abortions whenever there is any threat to the *health* of the mother, directly or indirectly, physically or psychologically. Since such an interpretation is very flexible and therefore subject to abuse, the facts have to be established by reliable medical evidence.

We would therefore permit abortion in the case of thalidomide babies, cases of rape and the like, not because such a foetus has no right to life but because it constitutes a threat to the health of the mother. This is an area of controversy. Many authorities would disagree and limit abortion to cases where the threat to the life of the mother is direct.

We would not permit abortions that are prompted merely by the desire of the mother not to have another child.

Those who advocate permitting all abortions and leaving the decision completely to the mother, have taken this stand as an answer to the widespread practice of illegal abortions which often result in the sickness and death of the mother, and also to the problem of the population explosion.

While we recognize the gravity of these problems, we are of the opinion that there are other and equally effective methods of dealing with them which do not bear the moral stigma of abortion. At the present time, when life has lost so much of its sanctity, we dare not add measures that will increase disregard for life. A prominent obstetrician of Buffalo called my attention to this passage in a medical textbook of over thirty years ago:

> There is abundant evidence that the frequency of criminal induction of abortion is increasing at an alarming rate, although accurate statistics cannot be obtained. Numerous reasons may be advanced for this deplorable situation, the most probable being: 1) Twentieth century standards of living have made children an economic liability for a large percentage of the population. This may be contrasted with more primitive rural conditions where a large family was considered an economic asset. 2) As a by-product of

the woman's freedom movement, a very large number of women have come to believe that pregnancy should be regulated by their personal desires. 3) The present-day lack of religious feeling and the wide teaching that pregnancy may be controlled have contributed to a lowering of moral standards among women, with a resulting increase in the number of undesired pregnancies.

(Carl Henry Davis, *Gynecology and Obstetrics*, ch. X, p. 1.)

Thirty years is a comparatively short time in the history of man. The period of the last thirty years, however, has been the most momentous in the annals of man. It has witnessed World War II, the rise of many new nations, the awakening of Africa, the re-awakening of Asia, the birth of the nuclear age, the advent of the space age, and the imminence of the population explosion. And yet in the case of abortion, the above analysis is still relevant, and the situation described has been aggravated rather than changed. Giving a *carte-blanche* to all abortions would spell moral defeatism, that buys time at the sacrifice of moral values. When proposing legislation we must balance one against the other. We therefore favor only therapeutic abortion, liberally interpreted, and believe that that is the view of the religious tradition of Judaism.

Judaism and Abortion

BALFOUR BRICKNER

I am delighted and somewhat saddened to be here; delighted, by the opportunity to make known to this august subcommittee the views of Reform Judaism on the subject of abortion, but saddened by the need to do so. One would have hoped that fourteen months after the U.S. Supreme Court's historic decision of January 22nd, 1973 in the case of Jane Roe vs. Henry Wade, it would no longer be necessary to justify whether there should be available to women in this country the freedom to choose whether or not to have an abortion, especially during the early weeks of pregnancy. I am saddened that again one has to defend against those who, by constitutional amendment, would seek to overturn the judicial decision of the highest court of our land in a matter which, in our judgment, ought to remain a matter of individual conscience. I do not question the right of any individual or group to seek such a reversal, that is indeed inherent in our democratic style, but it does sadden me to realize that once again the forums of government are burdened with a matter which competing religious groups have turned into an ugly, emotionally charged confrontation.

Unhappily, I find myself concurring with those reflective judges, scholars and commentators who have perceived and deplored the fact that historically it is religious beliefs that underlie the retention of abortion laws denying those with differing beliefs, religious or otherwise, the right to that act. It is probably quite correct to suggest as some have that opposition, can be traced to organized, militant religious groups. The American Law Institute was undoubtedly correct when they determined

Reprinted by permission of the author from his testimony before Senator Birch Bayh's Subcommittee on Constitutional Amendments, March 7, 1974. (Balfour Brickner's testimony was criticized by J. David Bleich in *Sh'ma* [5/85 — January 10, 1975]. The same issue carries Brickner's rejoinder.)

that objections to abortion reform are not primarily grounded on legal considerations but rather on some religious beliefs which deem abortion sinful. If it is true, that religious views play an inordinately important role in determining our value judgments on the subject of abortion — then how much the more should the view of Oliver Wendell Holmes be heeded when he said that "moral predilections must not be allowed to influence our minds in settling legal distinctions." (Oliver Wendell Holmes, *The Common Law*). The coercive powers of the state must not be employed in the service of sectarian moral views. To do otherwise would be to violate the establishment clause of the first amendment: "Congress shall make no law respecting an establishment of religion . . ." The presentation of that right of individual conscience was essentially what the Supreme Court sought to support in its historic decision. Just as the state must never say, (and has not said) that a person *not* wishing an abortion *must* have one, so too the state must never be allowed so to legislate as to prevent a woman wishing an abortion from having one. *The right of individual conscience must be maintained.*

That right is now being challenged again. There are those who maintain that a fetus is a full human being from the moment of conception. S.J. resolution 119 (Senator Buckley's proposed resolution) makes that equation when it suggests that the word "person" as used in the Fifth and Fourteenth articles of Amendment to the Constitution be construed as "human being" and applied also to the unborn in every stage of their biological development. S.J. resolution 130 (Senator Helm's proposal) in essence makes the same equation. Were either of these resolutions to become law it would follow that anyone electing to have an abortion would be guilty of murder, i.e. taking a human life. The thrust of these resolutions is clearly to make abortion illegal and therefore impossible, frustrating the effect of last year's Supreme Court decision. We in Reform Judaism must therefore oppose these amendments and any similar efforts and we do so on the basis of our understanding of our tradition of Jewish law.

Judaism does not believe that the word "person" connotes a full human being. It does not equate abortion with murder. To the contrary, in Judaism, a fetus is not considered a full human and for this reason has no "juridical personality" of its own. Jewish law is quite clear in its statement that an embryo is not reckoned a viable living thing (in Hebrew, a *bar kayyama*) until thirty days after its birth. One is not obliged to observe the Laws of mourning for an expelled fetus. As a matter of fact, the laws of mourning, etc. are not applicable for a child who does not survive until his thirtieth day.

In Judaism the fetus in the womb is not a person (*lav nefesh hu*) until it is born. (Rashi, Yad Ramah, and Me'iri, all to Sanhedrin 72b). According to Jewish law, a child is considered a "person" only when it is "come into the world." Thus, there is no capital liability for foeticide. By this reckoning, abortion cannot be considered murder. The basis for this decision is scriptural. The Biblical text states:

> "if men strive, and wound a pregnant woman so that her fruit be expelled, but no harm befall her, then shall he be fined as her husband shall assess, and the matter placed before the judges. But if harm befall her, then thou shalt give life for life." (Exodus 21:22)

Talmudic commentators made the teaching of this biblical passage quite explicit. They said that only monetary compensation is exacted of him who causes a woman to miscarry. No prohibition is evident from this scriptural passage against destroying the unborn child. Clearly, and here the major rabbinic commentators on the Bible agree, the one who was responsible is not culpable for murder, *since the unborn fetus is not considered a person*. This concept is reiterated in many different instances and in many different places in rabbinic writing. The classic source for this Jewish attitude towards the status of a fetus and thus towards abortion may be found in the Mishnah, a preliminary code of Jewish law that dates back to the second century of the common era and forms the basis of the Talmud, the most definitive statement of Jewish law available in our tradition. Here it states: "A woman who is having difficulty in giving birth, it is permitted to cut up the child inside her womb and take it out limb by limb because her life takes precedent. However, if the greater part of the child has come out, it must not be touched, because one life must not be taken to save another." (Mishnah Ohalot 7.6) Rashi, the preeminent commentator on the Bible and the Talmud, explains the talmudic passage as follows: "As long as the child did not come out into the world, it is not called a living being and it is therefore permissible to take its life in order to save the life of its mother. Once the head of the child has come out, the child may not be harmed because it is considered as fully born, and one life may not be taken to save another."

There are, to be sure, laws relating to fetuses more than forty days old. Laws of ritual uncleanliness must be observed for abortuses older than forty days (see the Mishnah Niddah 3.5) suggesting that the unborn fetus though not considered a living person (*nefesh*) still has some status. However, nowhere does it state that killing this fetus by premature artifical termination of pregnancy is prohibited.

Thus, it is clear that Jewish law does not consider abortion murder. Moreover, it totally disagrees with those who consider a fetus "a person," certainly not a human being. In this, Jewish law agrees with the majority opinion of those on the Supreme Court who in their January 22nd, 1973 decisions stated:

> "The Constitution does not define 'person' in so many words. The use of the word is such that it has application only *postnatally.*"

> "The unborn have never been recognized in the law as persons in the whole sense."

Despite this plethora of evidence from Judaism recognizing the legality of abortion, Orthodox Jewish authorities have taken and continue to hold a negative view towards abortion. Indeed, most Orthodox rabbis prohibit this act, except in such special instances as when a woman is impregnated through rape or incest or when it is clear that continuation of the pregnancy to birth would constitute a clear danger to the life and/or health of the mother.

The reasons traditional Judaism generally prohibits abortion despite the rabbinic literature permitting abortion are complex and diverse. Some Orthodox rabbis are more lenient in this than are others. Conservative and Reform Judaism drawing from this long tradition take a more liberal stance. While Jewish law teaches a reverent and responsible attitude to the question of abortion, reasons affecting basic life and health may sanction or even require abortion.

One final word. My religious tradition is one which has revered and sanctified human life for nearly four thousand years. During the time when "religious men" were marching heedlessly across the face of the world in wanton destruction of the family of man, in the name of Christ or Allah, we, the Jewish people, were teaching our children that the home was a *mikdash m'at*, a miniature sanctuary where parents and children ministered in the house as priests before an altar of God. We have always sought to preserve a sensitive regard for the sanctity of human life. It is precisely because of this regard for that sanctity that we see as most desirable the right of any couple to be free to produce only that number of children whom they felt they could feed and clothe and educate properly: only that number to whom they could devote themselves as real parents, as creative partners with God. It is precisely this traditional Jewish respect for the sanctity of human life that moves us now to support that legislation which would help all women to be free to choose when and under what circumstances they would elect to bring life into the world. It is that regard for the sanctity for human life which prompts us to support legislation enabling women to be free from the whims of biological roulette and free mostly from the oppressive crushing weight of anachronistic ideologies and theologies which, for reasons that escape my ken, continue to insist that in a world already groaning to death with overpopulation, with hate and with poverty, that there is still some noble merit or purpose to indiscriminate reproduction.

I am well aware that the issue of abortion is one that is emotionally charged. I am well aware there are some citizens of this country who hold deep religious convictions which cause them to consider abortion as morally wrong. I do not quarrel with that conviction or with those who hold it. I strongly support their right to hold to that view. But, I cannot believe that the state has the right to foist through legislation the religious conviction of any one group upon all the citizens of the country. There is nothing in the existing legislation which makes abortion mandatory. Thus, those whose religious convictions cause them to oppose abortion, remain free to refrain from practicing it *if they so choose*. On the other hand, not to have the option of abortion would be to deny full protection under the law to those whose religious conviction does in certain circumstances recognize abortion. It would discriminate against large segments of our population and foster illegality and the continuation of deception. Therefore, I as a religious Jew of the Reform Jewish persuasion, urge that Senate resolutions 119 and 130 and all similar legislation be defeated and that the principles enunciated by the Supreme Court in its historic decisions of January 22nd, 1973, be reaffirmed and upheld.

18

Fetal Experimentation

A Bias for Life

SEYMOUR SIEGEL

My topic this afternoon* is not abortion, but a whole host of ethical and moral questions which have come to the fore because of the legalization of abortion in this country and in other countries.

I would like to say in passing that although I agree with most of what Rabbi [David M.] Feldman said, and that it is obvious that from the Jewish point of view some kinds of abortions are legitimate under certain circumstances, I believe that part of being a liberal is to recognize the possibility that other points of view may be as legitimate as my own. I think that it behooves us to recognize that just as there are many people in the United States and other countries who believe that abortion is no different from pulling a tooth, there are also great numbers of people in this country who out of sincere and dedicated religious, metaphysical and other commitments believe that abortion is murder, literal murder. They also have the right to propagandize for their point of view; if we thought something was murder, we too would propagandize against it, regardless of the fact that we might be in a minority. It is therefore wrong, in my judgment, to call those people "sinister forces," "foolish forces," "unfair forces." They are exercising not only a constitutional right but also a human right to prohibit something they believe no one should do—to murder someone else.

---

*This paper was first presented at the Conference on Biomedical Ethics, sponsored by The Rabbinical Assembly and the Jewish Theological Seminary of America, March 18, 1975.

I have to say this in light of the fact that I agree with Rabbi Feldman that feticide is not homicide according to Jewish law. According to the Talmud, only the Jews are not subject to prosecution for feticide; non-Jews are. You can interpret that to mean that they are subject to punishment even though they are not murderers, because of stronger and more stringent applications. But that we will discuss later on.

Fetal Research

Because of the large numbers of fetuses which are now available in medical centers around this country, and because of induced abortions, biomedical thinkers and practitioners are facing a new problem—fetal research.

This question involves three different types of research. The first type would be an experiment performed on a woman and fetus while the fetus is being carried by the woman in anticipation of abortion. To illustrate, let me cite a quotation from a medical journal: "To evaluate the fetal hazard of accidental administration of live rubella vaccine during pregnancy, the vaccine was given to 35 women certified for legal abortion. The gestational age at the time of vaccination counted from the first day of the last menstrual period ranged from between 49 and 107 days, and the interval between vaccination and abortion, 11 and 30 days. Various specimens, including the products of conceptions, were tested for rubella virus independently in three collaborating laboratories. Rubella virus was recovered from the placenta in 6 cases and from the fetus in one. The results indicated a hazard of placental and fetal invasion by the vaccine virus, and emphasized the need to observe precautions when post-pubertal female patients are vaccinated."

As I understand this type of experimentation, it is done mostly in testing drugs to see whether a drug which is administered to a woman carrying the child crosses the placenta into the fetus itself, and thereby see in future cases what kind of drugs can be prescribed. When the abortion is carried out and the fetus is removed, then the testing is carried on to see whether these drugs have entered into the life system of the fetus. That would be the first kind of experiment.

The second type of experiments, which may include some pre-abortion preparatory procedures, are those which are carried on at the time of abortion—that is, while the fetus has not yet been removed. Certain experiments are done on the fetus at the point immediately preceding its removal from the woman's system.

The third type of abortion experimentation is done on the fetus after it has been removed from the womb and is still living—that is, while it still shows life signs of heartbeat or brain activity or sometimes even some respiratory activity.

These last types of experiments are divided into two further categories: those experiments performed on the previable fetus somewhere before twenty weeks of gestation, and those performed on the viable fetus—the fetus that might survive. Most problems involve the previable fetus after it has been removed from the womb.

Guidelines

These questions arise because of the vast numbers of abortions being done in the United States. There are more abortions taking place in New York State than there are live births, and these aborted fetuses are available for experimentation. As a result of the agitation of various groups, the National Institutes of Health published various guidelines in 1973 and 1974 about fetal experimentation. The last legislation, in 1973, declared a moratorium on fetal research, which was then to be financed by the Health, Education and Welfare Department. This meant that no fetal research could be done for four months until a National Commission would present its findings to the Secretary of HEW, who would then decide what guidelines, if any, should be set regarding fetal research.

The Commission appointed eight ethicists, as they are now called, to advise them on the ethical dimensions of this question, and it was my honor to be one of the eight, one of two Jews. I would now like to read you a short recommendation and report which I submitted to this Commission in Washington.

Experimentation on Fetuses which are Judged to be Nonviable

The most general principle which should inform our decisions in these crucial matters is a bias for life. This bias is the foundation of the Judeo-

Christian world view as well as the motivating force behind medical research and practice. It flows, for most people, from a theistic belief, but it has been and can be affirmed by those whose views of reality do not include the existence of God.[1] The bias for life requires that all individuals—especially those involved in the healing arts—should direct their efforts toward sustaining life where it exists; that procedures which terminate life or harm it are unethical; and that where there is a doubt, the benefit of that doubt should always be on the side of life.

Another implication of this bias is that any individual life which claims our efforts and attention at the present moment takes precedence over life that might come afterwards. In certain situations individuals are called upon to sacrifice their lives or their comfort for future generations. This is part of our character as members of the human race tied to those who came before us and to those who will come after. However, the burden of proof is always on those who wish to subordinate the interests of the individual before us for the sake of those who will come later. Experiments for the "good of medicine" or for the sake of the "progress of knowledge" are not automatically justified if they cause harm to people now so that someone in the future might benefit. What comes in the future is what the talmudic literature calls "the secrets of the Almighty." Although we are not absolved of our responsibility to the future, we have a greater responsibility to those who are now in our care. These reflections do not, of course, preclude the scientist's search; they are only intended to make him or her more cautious.

The bias of life is exercised whatever the status of the life before us. The fact that the life will certainly be terminated, that it is flawed or doomed, does not preclude activating the bias. This idea is expressed in the 1973 U.S. Guidelines published by the Department of Health, Education and Welfare: "Respect for the dignity of human life must not be compromised whatever the age, circumstance, *life expectation of the individual*" [emphasis mine].

Not even the most expert scientific intelligence can predict the future with certainty. This is especially true of medical science, which is full of cases where certain treatments were administered to human subjects with the expectation that these procedures would be positive in their effect, only to have them turn out harmful. Therefore, the decision to permit experimentation on human subjects must be made with the utmost caution. If some of the experiments involve the mother as well as the fetus, it is not impossible to imagine that these very procedures could change the mother's organism so as to preclude further births, or have other adverse effects.

In speaking of the future results of experimentation we should not overlook the social consequences of policies in the area. Already the public is beginning to believe that physicians are not merely the saviors of human life but also its destroyers. While this allegation is, of course, unfair, it is still important to keep the social effects in mind when setting guidelines in this very sensitive field. This century has seen the consequences of the breach of the notion of life's sanctity. The Nazi horrors began with the legitimation of the destruction of "useless" life and concluded with the most horrible phenomenon of this or any other century. The ethicist Leroy Walters has stated: "An unexamined premise of both the British and the American policy statements on fetal experimentation is that the consequences of such research will be *medical* and that they will be *good* . . . It is equally plausible to argue that serious social consequences will follow such experimentation and that these consequences will be mixed, at best."[2]

The Status of the Fetus

The central issue is the status of the fetus.[3] That a fetus does not seem to be identical with an infant is the view of many religious and ethical traditions, including the rabbinic one: the fetus has no independent life system and is literally tied to the mother; it has not developed the social and personal qualities generally assumed to be part of a full human being. Common sense also supports those who wish to distinguish ontologically and ethically between a born infant and a fetus. Before viability, then, feticide is not the same as *homicide*.[4]

But this does not mean that from an ethical standpoint there is no difference between a fetus and a mother's tooth or fingernail—to be disposed of as the mother wishes. It is indeed part of the mother's body, but a unique part. It is the only part that will leave the mother's body in order to take on independent existence as a human being. This special status gives the fetus certain rights that other organs of the mother do not have. Western religious thought has therefore "ascribed a high value to prenatal human life."[5] Nor should we forget that even thinking of the fetus as merely a limb of the mother does not absolve society of its responsibility for what the mother does with her limbs. No civilized community allows individuals to capriciously cut off limbs from their own bodies, even if they wish to do so. Of course, limbs can be amputated for the sake of the whole individual. But this must be justified by the "interests" of the individual. These "interests" must stand the test of common sense as well as medical opinion.

What then is the status of the fetus, if it is not either a whole individual or mere tissue? The answer must be that the status of the fetus is that of "potential human life." Both Aristotle and Thomas Aquinas and many medieval thinkers saw human life as a process developing from step to step. In the case of the ancients it was from vegetative to animal to rational levels. However, it is clear that successive stages of human ontogeny contain within themselves the future stages,[6] that is to say all "higher" stages are present *in potentia* in the "lower" ones.

The character of the fetus as "potentially human" raises it above the level of "mere tissue." It evokes within us a sense of responsibility for its welfare as well as for the welfare of the mother. And yet because it is not fully human, the fetus has fewer rights than it would have if it were fully born. When the fetus threatens the mother's life or the lives of its potential siblings, the mother then has a right to protect herself against the fetus. That is why most religious traditions permit abortion under some circumstances. When one harms the fetus, however, "potential life is being thwarted."[7]

The Rights of the Fetus

Because the fetus has potential human qualities, it therefore has rights. These rights are encapsulated in the claim it has on us that it benefit from our bias toward life, the bias which makes us responsible to guard and preserve life where it exists. The responsibility to preserve the life of the fetus is not an *absolute* responsibility; in most civilized societies war is legitimate even though it means the inevitable loss of life. But war is used to serve a larger and more comprehensive goal of society—its self-protection. In the same way the fetus' right to our concern for its life is mitigated when it threatens someone else's life or health—its mother's or its prospective siblings'. But when there is no threat, the fetus' potential humanity and its present life signs entitle it to benefit from the ethical imperative to protect and revere life. Those who do interfere with its life system—physicians, experimenters, or others—are ethically permitted to do so only to help the fetus sustain that life system. It must be stressed that this consideration involves all fetuses, whether viable or not. To declare that a fetus or abortus is not viable is never the same as declaring that a living previable fetus or abortus has died.[8]

Not every kind of experimentation is prohibited. Experiments, even when non-therapeutic, could be carried on if they pose no discernible threat to either the mother or the fetus. Though the fetus can hardly give consent to such experiments, its guardians can give consent. Andre Helleghers has described many important experiments that can be carried on within these guidelines, especially those related to amniocentesis.[9]

It would be most unfortunate if the respect for the life of the fetus were related to the fact that it is soon to be aborted. Both the British and the American guidelines[10] insist that a fetus *in utero* not be the subject of procedures which can cause it harm, even when it is destined to oblivion through abortion. Paul Ramsey warns against skewing the medical ethical issue involved here by the abortion issue.[11] It is possible to be against fetal research *in utero* even while approving of abortion. The analogy has been drawn to a condemned prisoner who is facing execution or someone who is *in extremis:* medical ethical practice condemns experiments on such individuals, even if they will redound to the benefits of scientific progress, unless such experiments or procedures are designed to help the patient in some way. "Still I suggest that someone who believes that it would be wrong to do non-therapeutic research on children, on the unconscious or the dying patient, or on the condemned, may have settled negatively the question of the morality of fetal research."[12]

The Fetus in Utero

The interventions that would be sanctioned when the fetus is *in utero* are those which help the mother, are harmless to the fetus, or are designed to help the fetus in its own life system. The latter are permissible even if they have a negative outcome, for it is ethical to undertake procedures which have a good chance of success even when some risk is involved. The view expressed here reflects the prevailing opinion that "no procedures be carried out during pregnancy with the deliberate intent of ascertaining the harm they might do to the fetus" (Peel Commission). Furthermore, it has been pointed out that permission to initiate procedures which will harm the fetus, even when there is an announced intention of abortion, make it impossible for the parent to change his or her mind about the fate of the fetus. That the opportunity to reverse the decision about abortion should remain open to the last possible moment is a convincing argument, to my mind.

The assertion that there might be a different ethical consideration for experiments carried out in the course of the abortion does not merit approval. The circumstances of life do not mitigate the right to benefit from our bias for life. To cite the analogy used above: even when the rope is around the neck of the condemned prisoner, he cannot be used for any procedure except that which is designed to bring him confort or well-being.

The Fetus Ex Utero

The living fetus *ex utero*, even when not viable, would seem to have more rights than the fetus *in utero*. When the fetus has been severed from its mother's body, it can no longer pose a threat to her. There is no question of the woman doing with her body as she wishes, or the right of privacy, or the consideration of the mother's health. It would seem, therefore, that the fetus' right to enjoy our bias for life would be enhanced when it passes out of the mother's uterus. Life is valuable wherever it exists, and therefore evokes our responsibility. The fact that the abortus is sure to die—it is, after all, nonviable—does not mean that our concern for the life is diminished. That it will never be a real child does not make it right to consider it "nothing more than a piece of tissue."

We should understand "live" to include the presence of a heartbeat or any other discernible sign of life. The Louisiana statute on the subject reads: "A human being is live born, or there is a live birth, whenever there is the complete expulsion or extraction from the mother of a human embryo or fetus, irrespective of the duration of the pregnancy, which after such separation breathes or shows any other evidence of life such as beating of the heart, pulsation of the umbilical cord or movement of voluntary muscles, whether or not the umbilical cord has been cut or the placenta is attached."[13]

The prohibition against experimental procedures on live abortuses should be operative against both the artifical prolongation of life systems such as heartbeats for the purpose of observation, or against the stopping of any of the life signs. Any procedure which breaches the dignity of the abortus, such as prolongation of life systems or destruction of existing life systems, should not be permitted, in keeping with the guidelines suggested by both the Peel Commission and the regulations proposed by the Department of Health, Education and Welfare.

Fetal Death

The question of when an abortus can be presumed dead is central to our consideration. There are those who believe that the only meaningful distinction is viability or nonviability. For the reasons cited above, this approach is against the ethical canons of medicine, which do not allow the life prospects of the subject to affect its right to be treated with dignity and concern. While the dividing line between viability and nonviability is crucial, the dividing line between life and death is even more crucial. It is life—real and potential—that has an ethical claim upon us.

The best approach to this problem is the one suggested by Professor Paul Ramsey: "The difference between life and death of a human fetus abortus should be determined substantially in the same way physicians use in making other pronouncements of death."[14] He quotes Doctor Bernard Nathanson, who gave the only intellectually coherent reply that can be given to the question put to us by the Commission:

> The Harvard Criteria for the pronouncement of death assert that if the subject is unresponsive to external stimuli (e.g. pain), if the deep reflexes are absent, if there are no spontaneous movements or respiratory effort, if the electroencephalogram reveals no activity of the brain, one may conclude that the patient is dead. If any or all of these criteria are absent—and the fetus does respond to pain, makes respiratory efforts, moves spontaneously and has electroencephalographic activity—life must be present.

These signs of life do not make the abortus a viable infant, but they do make it possible for the abortus to merit the fruits of our bias for life.

It is interesting that the proposed DHEW guidelines do not present criteria for fetal death. The Peel Commission defines death as "the state in which the fetus shows none of the signs of life and is incapable of being made to function as a self-sustaining whole." These criteria have been criticized by Leroy Walters as too vague.[15] The last criterion, for example, ("being made to function as a self-sustaining whole") might determine that infants are dead. The idea of "signs of life" without designating what these "signs" are is also too vague. Leroy Walters writes: "As a general formal requirement for defining fetal death, I would suggest that any criteria developed for determining death in human adults should be applied, insofar as it is technically feasible, to the fetus. This requirement of simple biological consistency would rule out in advance the special pleading contained in hypothetical claims that the fetus is dead because it is about to die or that the fetus was never really alive."[16]

Consent

The concept of informed consent is essential in formulating guidelines for experiments on human subjects. In the case of fetuses, this concept has doubtful application. The fetus obviously cannot give consent. The consent of the parents is made questionable by the fact that they have decided to terminate their relationship to the fetus by agreeing to an abortion. The concept of consent is related to the concept of responsibility: those who give consent must in some way be prepared to assume the consequences of their decision. Since in the case of abortuses and fetuses this does not really apply, it would therefore seem appropriate that a special board give the requisite consent for the experiments that are legitimated. This board would closely scrutinize the proposed procedure and determine that there is no real risk in carrying it out, that all precautions have been taken, and that there be separation between physician doing the abortion and the researcher.

Proposed Guidelines

In light of the above it is recommended that:

1. Research and experimentation on fetuses be limited to procedures which will not be harmful, or which have as their aim the enhancement of the life system of the subjects.

2. No procedures be permitted which are likely to harm the fetus, even when the decision to abort has already been made, and even when the abortion procedure has been initiated or is in progress.

3. When the fetus is *ex utero* and alive, no procedures should be permitted which do not have as their primary aim the enhancement of the life systems of the fetus, unless such procedures present no risk to the subject. This prohibition would also apply to the artifical sustaining of life systems for the sole reason of experimentation.

4. Criteria for determining death in the fetus be the same as the criteria applied to viable fetuses and other human individuals.

Notes

1. The literature on the subject is enormous. For a summary of the views of Jewish tradition see Jacob B. Agus, *The Vision and the Way, an interpretation of Jewish ethics* (New York: Frederic Ungar Publishing Co., 1966) and the bibliography cited there. It would, of course, be a mistake to believe that this principle is so obvious as to be banal: we have seen in our century whole societies based on opposite suppositions such as "to kill is good."

2. Leroy Walters, "Ethical Issues in Experimentation on the Human Fetus," *Journal of Religious Ethics* 2/1, 1974, p. 42.

3. For an interesting summary of the issues involved in the status of the fetus see the work cited above by Leroy Walters; H. Tristam Englehardt, Jr., "The Ontology of Abortion," *Ethics*, v. 84, no. 3, April 1974, p. 217 ff.; Gary L. Reback, "Fetal Experimentation: Moral, Legal, and Medical Implications," *Stanford Law Review*, May 1974. For the Jewish views on the matter see David M. Feldman, *Birth Control in Jewish Law* (New York: New York University Press, 1968); Immanuel Jakobovits, *Jewish Medical Ethics* (New York: Bloch, 1959); and V. Aptowitzer, "Observations on the Criminal Law of the Jews," *Jewish Quarterly Review*, Philadelphia, 1924, p. 111 ff.

4. See especially the book by Feldman, *op. cit.*, and the discussion from a philosophical point of view by Englehardt, *op. cit.*

5. Walters, *op. cit.*, p. 48 and the literature cited there. Walters believes that the religious opposition to abortion is based on theories of ensoulment. Though this is certainly a factor, it would seem that the intuitive feeling of dealing with a potential human being led to the religious attitude toward abortion.

6. Englehardt, *op. cit.*, while citing and generally approving the Aristotelian and Thomistic approach, draws the conclusion that it is not ontologically correct to say that the *future* effect is present in the present. He believes that each step is independent and ontologically self-contained. Thus the fetus is really like a vegetable until it develops the quality of movement; then it is an animal until it shows signs of rationality. This argument is not convincing to me. Potentiality has an ontological status—that is, what I am to

become is present in what I am, for the simple reason that I cannot become what I will become unless I am what I am now. Therefore, there is an organic relationship between what I am now and what I will be later.

7. Feldman, *op. cit.*, p. 268 ff.

8. See Paul Ramsey, *The Ethics of Fetal Research* (New Haven and London: Yale University Press, 1975). The new work will be a standard one in the field of fetal research.

9. Statement by Andre E. Helleghers, M.D., before Senate Health Subcommittee, Senator Edward M. Kennedy, Chairman, July 19, 1974.

10. These guidelines were formulated after the Supreme Court decision on abortion.

11. Ramsey, *op. cit.*

12. Ramsey, *op. cit.*, p. 30.

13. Cited in Reback, *op. cit.*, p. 1199.

14. Paul Ramsey, statement submitted to National Commission for the Protection of Human Subjects, p. 2 ff.

15. Walters, *op. cit.*

16. *Ibid.*

19.

Karen Ann Quinlan:
A Torah Perspective

J. DAVID BLEICH

Karen Ann Quinlan's tragic life—and protracted death—have not been in vain. Unconscious though she may be, she has served as the fulcrum of a recurring moral dilemma. Euthanasia, usually passive, but at times active, has been and continues to be practiced with a high degree of frequency, albeit clandestinely. The physicians at St. Claire's Hospital are to be commended for not opting for the path of least resistance and for their tenacity in scrupulously discharging the moral and professional duties with which they are charged. The controversy surrounding the care of Karen Quinlan has called attention to and sharpened the question which will be posed over and over again: Who is the arbiter of life and death, man or God?

The Quinlan case, particularly as tried in the press, presented three critical issues. The first: whether or not Karen should be pronounced dead, was a specious question from the start. It quickly became evident that Karen Quinlan is alive even according to the most liberal definitions of death. The second question was that of vicarious consent: May parents authorize withdrawal of treatment? From the legal perspective, proxy consent remains a clouded area; from the perspective of Jewish law parents have no standing whatsoever in this matter. The obligations which exist with regard to treatment of the sick are autonomous in nature and are not at all contingent upon the desire of parents, or for that matter, of the patient. Judge Muir's statement, ". . .the only cases where a parent has standing to pursue a constitutional right on behalf of an infant are those involving continuing life styles," is quite consistent with Jewish ethics. The third question is by far the most crucial: Does anyone have the right to choose death over life? Since the New Jersey Supreme Court had already ruled in a unanimous opinion that no one has a "right" to die, Judge Muir's decision was a foregone conclusion. His decision was but a procedural prologue to a re-examination of this fundamental question by the New Jersey appeals court and perhaps ultimately by the federal courts as well. It is this issue which will be debated in the months—and perhaps years—to come.

There was a time, not too long ago, when man could do but little when afflicted by serious illness and found himself powerless before the ravages of nature. Man could only proclaim with resignation: "The Lord hath given; the Lord hath taken; let the name of the Lord be blessed." In our day, many feel that since scientists and physicians have succeeded in prolonging life through the application of human intellect and technology it is therefore fitting and proper that members of the scientific community be the arbiters of whether the quality of such life is worth preserving. The argument acquires a measure of cogency when the decision to terminate life is reached for a purportedly higher purpose, such as transplantation of an organ from a moribund individual to a patient with greater chances for recovery. The new dictum appears to be: "Science hath given; science hath taken; let the cause of science be blessed."

The same argument is also heard in instances in which there is simply scant hope that the patient will recover. Man, it is argued, should not become the victim of his own technology. Man should not be forced to cling to life simply because he has the technical ability to do so. Nature should be permitted to take its course.

Man is instinctively repulsed by the prospect of becoming the agent responsible for the death of his fellow. This repugnance is keenly felt regardless of the patient's condition and of whether the contemplated act of euthanasia is active or passive. The reconciliation of termination of the life of a fellow human being with one's instinctive moral feelings is indeed a formidable challenge.

The widespread press coverage of the Quinlan case highlighted a most curious aspect of contemporary thought processes. Now that a decision has been handed down and the case is being appealed before the Supreme Court of the State of New Jersey, every informed person recognizes that the issue being adjudicated is that of "refusal of treatment", that is, does a person—or his proxy—have a right to demand that he be permitted to die or does the state have an overriding, compelling interest in the preservation of the life of each of its citizens. Yet, when the case first received publicity in the media, it was presented in an entirely different guise. It was then presented as a "definition of death" case. We were urged, both on editorial pages and in what passed for straightforward news reports, to accept "brain death" as the scientifically precise criterion of cessation of life. This tactic was abandoned only when it became patently obvious that Karen Quinlan must be considered to be alive even if the newly-advocated definitions of death were to be accepted.

Why the confusion? Psychologically, it is not at all difficult to understand what has transpired. No one really wants to sanction murder. Homicide is abhorrent; man is endowed with a moral consciousness which recoils with shock at the very idea of taking the life of a fellow human being. No one wants to let another human being die. Man has a deeply-ingrained sense of responsibility for his fellow; man *does* perceive himself as his brother's keeper. Confronted with the tremendous emotional and financial toll exacted by the protracted care of a comatose patient, man finds himself impaled upon the horns of a dilemma. Moral sanction for abandoning the patient eludes him, yet the burden of sustaining life seems intolerable. The resolution of the problem is to pass between the horns of the dilemma by means of a lexicographical sleight-of-hand. If the patient may somehow be pronounced "dead" the problem is dispelled. Treatment may then be suspended without doing violence to ethical sensitivities.

This exercise in semantics can be, and has been, extended to resolve other bioethical problems. If one wishes to avoid the moral onus of snuffing out a human life when performing an abortion it is logically imperative that the fetus be denied status as a person. The transition from one position to the next is clearly delineated in a letter to the editor which appeared in *The New York Times* on March 6, 1972. The author, Cyril C. Means Jr., Professor of Constitutional Law at New York Law School, writes: "An adult heart donor, suffering from irreversible brain damage, is also a living human 'being,' but he is no longer a human 'person.' That is why his life may be ended by the excision of his heart for the benefit of another, the donee, who is still a human person. If there can be human 'beings' who are nonpersons at one end of the life span, why not also at the other end?" Once one moral concept is abrogated by the process of "redefinition" does any norm remain sacrosanct?

Another case in point is the problem of defective newborns. Babies born with severe congenital abnormalities or suffering from serious mental retardation are bound to be a burden to their parents, their siblings, and society. What can be done? Killing them is unthinkable. Abandoning the baby to custodial care in public institutions merely shifts the financial burden from parents to society at large and carries in its wake feelings of guilt to boot. Moreover, the extensive care and treatment which such infants require does create a genuine strain upon already limited and inadequate health care resources. Resolution: Let us redefine birth. Birth shall no longer be regarded as taking place at the moment of parturition but as occurring seventy-two hours after emergence of the infant from the birth canal. Since the baby is not yet born, in the event that it is found to be physically or mentally defective it could be destroyed with impunity up to the moment of "birth." This proposal was made, in all earnestness, by Dr. James Watson, co-discoverer of the double-helix in DNA. Situation ethicist Joseph Fletcher counsels that such infants should not be considered human children but should rather be viewed as "reproductive failures." And so the game continues.

"Compulsory Death"

Quite apart from theological considerations, definitions of death which, in reality, are value judgments in disguise are fraught with danger. Who is to decide at which stage of physical or mental deterioration life is no longer worthwhile? It is but a short step from the notion of "brain death" to the formulation of a definition of death centering around "social death," that is, an individual's capacity to serve as a useful member of society. It is entirely conceivable that eventually the concept of death will be broadened to include a person who consumes more of society's resources than he produces. Such a person is not productive and, from a *societal* perspective, his life appears to be hardly worth preserving. Fears such as these should not be dismissed as absurd. England's eminent biologist and Nobel Prize laureate, Dr. Francis Crick, has already advanced beyond this point in advocating compulsory death for all at the age of eighty as part of a "new ethical system based on modern science."

Human civilization has in the past witnessed attempts to make the right to life subservient to other values. Exposure of the aged to the elements was practiced by primitive societies; infanticide was not at all uncommon in 18th-century England; the Nazis broadened their infamous "final solution" to encompass the mentally ill and feebleminded. Each policy was undertaken in the name of enhancing the quality and dignity of human life. This is a road which men have trodden in the past. The achievement was never dignity, but ignominy.

It is quite true that man has the power to prolong life far beyond the point at which it ceases to be either productive or pleasurable. Not infrequently, the patient, if capable of expressing his desires and allowed to follow his own inclinations, would opt for termination of a life which has become a burden both to others and to himself. Judaism, however, teaches that man does not enjoy the right of self-determination with regard to questions of life and death. Generations ago our Sages wrote, "Against your will you live; against your will you die." While conventionally understood as underscoring the irony that a baby wishes to be born no more than an adult wishes to die, these words today take on new meaning. They may be taken quite literally as an eloquent summary of the Jewish view with regard to both euthanasia and the withholding of life-sustaining treatment. Judaism has always taught that life, no less than death, is involuntary. Only the Creator who bestows the gift of life may relieve man of that life even when it has become a burden rather than a blessing.

In the Jewish tradition the value with which human life is regarded is maximized far beyond the value placed upon human life either in the Christian tradition or in Anglo-Saxon common law. In Jewish law and moral teaching life is a supreme value and its preservation takes precedence over virtually all other considerations. Human life is not regarded as a good to be preserved as a condition of other values, but as an absolute basic and precious good in its own stead. Even life accompanied by suffering is regarded as being preferable to death. (See Sotah 20a).

Man does not possess absolute title to his life or his body. He is charged with preserving, dignifying, and hallowing that life. He is obliged to seek food and sustenance in order to safeguard the life he has been granted; when falling victim to illness or disease he is obliged to seek a cure in order to sustain life. The category of pikuach nefesh (preservation of life) extends to human life of every description and classification including the feeble-minded, the mentally deranged and yes, even a person in a so-called vegetative state. *Shabbat* laws and the like are suspended on behalf of such persons even though there may be no chance for them ever to serve either God or fellow man. The *mitzvah* of saving a life is neither enhanced nor diminished by virtue of the quality of the life preserved.

Distinctions between natural and artificial means, between ordinary and extraordinary procedures, and between non-heroic and heroic measures recur within the Catholic tradition, but no precisely parallel categories exist within Jewish law. Judaism knows no such distinctions and indeed the very vocabulary employed in drawing such distinctions is foreign to rabbinic literature. Rambam in his *Commentary on the Mishnah, Pesachim* 4:9, draws a cogent parallel between food and medication. God created food and water; we are obliged to use them in staving off hunger and thirst. God created drugs and medicaments and endowed man with the intelligence necessary to discover their medicinal properties; we are obliged to use them in warding off illness and disease. Similarly, God provided the materials and the technology which make possible catheters, intravenous infusions, and respirators; we are obligated to use them in order to prolong life.

Judaism does recognize situations in which certain forms of medical intervention are not mandatory. This is so not because such procedures involve expense, inconvenience, or hardship, but because they are not part of an accepted therapeutic protocol. The obligation to heal is limited to the use of a *refuah bedukah,* drugs and procedures of demonstrated efficacy. (See R. Ya'akov Emden, *Mor u-Ketziah* 338). Man must use the full range of benefits made available by science; but he is not obliged to experiment with untried and unproven measures. Nor is he obliged to avail himself of therapeutic measures which are in themselves hazardous in the hope of effecting a complete cure. Even *Chayyei sha'ah,* a short, transitory period of existence, is of such inestimable value that man is not obliged to gamble with precious moments of life, even in the hope of achieving health and longevity.

The physician's duty does *not* end when he is incapable of restoring the lost health of his patient. The obligation, "and you shall restore it to him" (Deuteronomy 22:2) refers, in its medical context, not simply to the restoration of health but to the restoration of even a single moment of life. Again, *Shabbat* and other laws are suspended even when it is known with certainty that human medicine offers no hope of a cure or restoration to health. Ritual obligations and restrictions are suspended as long as there is the possibility that life may be prolonged even for a matter of moments.

The sole exception to these principles which *halacha* recognizes is the case of a *goses*, a moribund patient actually in the midst of death throes.[1] The physiological criteria indicative of such a condition must be spelled out with care. (See Rema, *Even Ha-Ezer* 121:7 and *Choshen Mishpat* 221:2). It is surely clear that a patient whose life may be prolonged for weeks and even months is not yet moribund; the death process has not yet started to commence and hence the patient is not a *goses*. The halachic provisions governing care of a *goses* may most emphatically not be applied to all who are terminally ill.

The aggressiveness with which Judaism teaches that life must be preserved is not at all incompatible with the awareness that the human condition is such that there are circumstances in which man would prefer death to life. The Gemara, *Kesubos* 104a, reports that Rabbi Judah the Prince, redactor of the Mishnah, was afflicted by what appears to have been an incurable and debilitating intestinal disorder. He had a female servant who is depicted in rabbinic writings as a woman of exemplary piety and moral character. This woman is reported to have prayed for his death. On the basis of this narrative, the thirteenth-century authority, Rabbenu Nissim of Gerondi, in his commentary to *Nedarim* 40a, states that it is permissible, and even praiseworthy, to pray for the death of a patient who is gravely ill and in extreme pain.

Although man must persist in his efforts to prolong life he may, nevertheless, express human needs and concerns through the medium of prayer. There is no contradiction whatsoever between acting upon an existing obligation and pleading to be relieved of further responsibility. Man may beseech God to relieve him from divinely imposed obligations when they appear to exceed human endurance. But the ultimate decision is God's and God's alone. There are times when God's answer to prayer is in the negative. But this, too, is an answer.

In the *Republic* (I, 340) Plato observes that a physician, at the time that he errs in treating a patient, is not worthy of his title. When the physician's knowledge fails him, he ceases to be a practitioner of the healing arts. Our teachers went one step further: They taught that a physician who declines to make use of his skills is not a physician; they admonished that a physician who gives up his patient as hopeless is not a physician. *"And he shall surely heal*—From here it is derived that the physician is granted permission to heal" (*Baba Kamma* 85a). The Chassidic Seer, the *Chozeh* of Lublin, added a pithy comment: "The Torah gives permission to heal. It does not give the physician dispensation to refrain from healing because in his opinion the patient's condition is hopeless."

This lesson is the moral of a story told of the 19th-century Polish scholar, popularly known as Reb Eisel Charif. The venerable Rabbi was afflicted with a severe illness and was attended by an eminent specialist. As the disease progressed beyond hope of cure, the physician informed the Rabbi's family of the gravity of the situation. He also informed them that he therefore felt justified in withdrawing from the case. The doctor's grave prognosis notwithstanding, Reb Eisel Charif recovered completely. Some time later, the physician chanced to come upon the Rabbi in the street. The doctor stopped in his tracks in astonishment and exclaimed, "Rabbi, have you come back from the other world?" The Rabbi responded, "You are indeed correct, I *have* returned from the other world. Moreover, I did you a great favor while I was there. An angel ushered me in to a large chamber. At the far end of the room was a door and lined up in front of the door were a large number of well-dressed, dignified and intelligent-looking men. These men were proceeding through the doorway in a single file. I asked the angel who these men were and where the door led. He informed me that the door was the entrance to the netherworld and that the men passing through those portals were those of whom the *Mishnah* says, 'The best of physicians merits *Gehinnom*.' Much to my surprise, I noticed that you too were standing in the line about to proceed through the door. I immediately approached the angel and told him: 'Remove that man immediately! He is no doctor. He does not treat patients; he abandons them!' "

To depict any human condition as hopeless is to miss entirely the spiritual dimension of human existence. Dr. John Shepherd, a neurosurgeon at Nassau County Medical Center, claims the cure of at least two comatose patients whose vital signs were even more discouraging than those of Karen Quinlan—but that is not the point. Even were it true that medical diagnoses and prognoses are infallible, the decision to terminate treatment is not a medical decision; it is the determination of a moral question. That the physician possesses specialized knowledge and unique skills is unquestionable. However, his professional training guarantees neither heightened moral sensitivity nor enhanced acumen. He may quite legitimately draw medical conclusions with regard to anticipated effects of the application or withholding of various therapeutic procedures. But the decision to proceed or not to proceed is a moral, not a medical, decision. From the fact that a condition is medically hopeless it does not follow that the remaining span of life is devoid of meaning. "*Nistarim darkei Ha-Shem*"—"the ways of God are hidden." He has decreed that we must love, cherish and preserve life in all its phases and guises until the very onset of death. While even terminal life is undoubtedly endowed with other meaning and value as well, subservience to the divine decree and fulfillment of God's commandment is, in itself, a matter of highest meaning.

The sanctity of human life is not predicated upon hedonistic proclivity, pragmatic utility or even upon the potential for service to one's fellow man. The telos of human existence is service of God and the performance of His commandments. It is in this explanation of human existence that Me'iri (*Yoma 85a*) finds the rationale underlying the obligation to preserve the life of even the hopelessly ill. Me'iri observes that although the moribund patient may be incapable of any physical exertion he may be privileged to experience contrition and utilize the precious final moments of life for the achievement of true repentance.

One personal experience lives vividly in my mind. My family and I had travelled some distance to attend a family *simchah*. Arriving on *erev Shabbat* we were grieved to learn that an elderly relative had experienced renal failure and was in a critical condition. At the hospital I requested and was shown the patient's medical chart. It was readily apparent that the patient was not being treated aggressively and, indeed, none of several available forms of therapy had been instituted. I immediately telephoned the attending physician and demanded an explanation. In reply I was informed that the doctors were unanimous in their opinion that the patient was terminal though they could not predict how long she might survive in a comatose state. The doctor could see no point in prolonging life under such conditions. As a matter of *halacha* I had no choice but to insist upon the administration of therapeutically indicated medication. However, the decision, humanly speaking, was not an easy one. But then an incident occurred which put the entire matter into a different perspective.

Late *Shabbat* afternoon I returned from *Minchah* and, although the patient had been totally unresponsive for over thirty-six hours, I walked into the hospital room and said *"Gut Shabbos"* in a loud voice. I was greeted in response by the flickering of an eyelid and, in a weak but clear voice, the words *"Gut Shabbos"* in return. At that moment there flashed across my mind the comments of Rab Akiva Eger (*Orach Chayyim* 271:1) who declares that even the simple, standard *Shabbat* greeting expressed by one Jew to another constitutes a fulfillment of the *mitzvah:* "Remember the Sabbath day to keep it holy." At that moment I realized not only intellectually, but also emotionally, that every moment of life is of inestimable value. Here was a dramatic unfolding of the lesson that every moment of life carries with it the opportunity for the performance of yet one more *mitzvah.*

No scientist has ever determined the absolute (as distinct from recordable) threshold of psychic activity. No clinical experiment has ever been conducted to determine at what level of consciousness a comatose patient becomes incapable of remorse and repentance. But, even if possible, such an undertaking would be irrelevant. Me'iri's rationale adds a measure of understanding but does not establish the parameters of the halachic obligation. Halachic ramifications frequently remain operative even in situations in which the reasoning upon which they are grounded is not strictly applicable. *Halacha* acquires a sanctity, *sui generis,* of its own. Human life, regardless of its quality and, indeed, of its potential for even the most minimal fulfillment of *mitzvos,* is endowed with sanctity. (See *Bi'ur Halachah, Orach Chayyim* 329:4).

The coining of the phrase "death with dignity" by advocates of passive euthanasia was a stroke of genius. Opponents of such practices are immediately disarmed. Everyone respects "rights" and no one decries "dignity." Yet, while repeated use of a glib phrase by the press and media may influence attitudes, the coining of a cliché is not the same as making a case. Is sickness or frailty, however tragic, really an indignity? Is the struggle for life, in any form, an indignity? Is it not specious to insinuate that the attempt to sustain life is aught but the expression of the highest regard for the precious nature of the gift of life and of the *dignity* in which it is held?

There is a definite conflict between the ethical teachings of Judaism and the prevalent moral climate. Unfortunately, Jews are prone to celebrate Jewish thought when it coincides with what chances to be in vogue and to ignore it when it runs counter to ideas or practices heralded by the dominant culture. Judaism has something to say—and to teach—about all moral issues. Jewishness is more than a matter of ethnic identity and Judaism more than perfunctory performance of ritual. Jews who take their Jewishness seriously must necessarily search for the uniquely Jewish answers to the dilemmas of life and death which emerge from the Jewish tradition. Judaism teaches that man is denied the right to make judgments with regard to quality of life. Man is never called upon to determine whether life is worth living—that is a question over which God remains sole arbiter.

Notes

1. Some authorities, most notably *Bet Ya'akov*, no. 59, followed by *Iggrot Mosheh, Yoreh De'ah*, II, no. 174, maintain that it is forbidden to prolong the life of a *goses* by any means whatsoever. But the position is by no means universally accepted. *Shevut Ya'akov*, I, no. 13, cites *Yoma* 85a in demonstrating that *Shabbat* laws are superceded for the purpose of even marginal prolongation of life. *Shevut Ya'akov* declares that all accepted therapeutic remedies must be utilized in prolonging the life of a *goses* regardless of how brief a period of time he may be expected to survive. This authority evidently distinguishes between natural remedies of demonstrated efficacy involving readily recognizable causal relationships and non-scientific *segulot* of undemonstrable causal efficacy such as the placing of salt upon the tongue. The latter, according to this analysis, are not required in the case of a *goses* because they are not recognized medical procedures. The position of *Shevut Ya'akov* is also espoused by *Mishneh Berurah, Bi'ur Halachah* 329:4, and by the present head of the Jerusalem *Bet Din*, Rabbi Eliezer Waldenberg in his *Ramat Rachel*, no. 28.

While adjudication of this question is quite properly left to competent rabbinic decisors on a case-by-case basis, it is important to emphasize that withholding of treatment does not at all come into question unless the patient is actually in a state of *gesisah*. A detailed clinical profile of the halachic criteria which are indicative of this state is beyond the scope of these comments. It should, however, be stated that while the technical criteria must be carefully elucidated, it is clear that a *goses* is by definition a moribund person whose death is imminent. It seems incomprehensible to me that a patient whose physiological state permits survival for an indeterminate period of time and who has, in fact, survived for over fourteen months (at the time of this writing) can be considered a *goses*. It must be remembered that the quality of life which is preserved is not a determinant halachic factor. Sources for a definition of *gesisah* are to be found in *Shulchan Aruch, Yoreh De'ah* 339:2; *Rema, Even ha-Ezer* 121:7, and *Choshen Mishpat* 211:2 as well as *Rambam* and *Tosefot Yom Tov* in their respective commentaries on the *Mishnah, Arachin* 1:3 and in the comments of *Derishah, Tur Yoreh De'ah* 339.

Even in the case of a *goses*, the distinction between withholding treatment and an overt act designed to shorten life is a most crucial one. Note should be made of the suggestion that "pulling the plug" be considered a form of withholding of treatment. This thesis was advanced by Rabbi Baruch Rabinowitz of Holon in the Sivan 5731 issue of *Assia*, a publication of the Falk-Schlesinger Institute of Sha'arei Zedek Hospital. Whatever the cogency of the argument, the suggestion is one which has been considered and at present is rejected by the preponderant number of recognized halachic authorities who deem "pulling the plug" to be an act of overt intervention.

Capital Punishment

Analyses of criminal punishment and its justification—whether in terms of retribution, rehabilitation, or deterrence—are commonly encountered in contemporary ethical literature. There are almost no discussions of this subject in recent Jewish sources, however. It may be that this is due to the fact that Jewish criminal law has been basically inoperative for two millennia. But given the loud contemporary debate over capital punishment in particular, and the leading role which Jewish spokesmen have taken in that debate, it is indeed surprising that so little has been written on the subject from a Jewish perspective.

The two essays presented here illuminate different aspects of the traditional Jewish approach to capital punishment. Gerald Blidstein examines the dialectical analysis of capital punishment contained in Biblical and rabbinic sources, showing the presence of two tendencies, "one that regards the enforcing of retribution as most just and hence most merciful, and another, which finds mercy too divinely dynamic a quality to be forever denied and controlled by the demand for retribution." Blidstein also raises the issue of deterrence, showing that some Talmudic authorities viewed with alarm the attempts of their colleagues to render the death penalty practically unenforceable. Blidstein is concerned with the teachings of *halakhah,* but he goes beyond it in an attempt to discover the attitudes it expresses. Analyzing Biblical and Talmudic usage of the Hebrew words for "killing," Blidstein argues that, at a very basic level, Judaism refuses to distinguish between justified and unjustified bloodshed. It is this basic attitude which finds expression in the laws governing capital punishment.

It is with these laws themselves that Israel Kazis is concerned. He summarizes the procedural restrictions on trials involving the possibility of the death penalty. He shows how the Talmudic authorities rendered capital punishment unenforceable in practical terms, abolishing it in fact, if not in theory.

20.
Capital Punishment—
The Classic Jewish
Discussion

GERALD J. BLIDSTEIN

I

"Kill" and "murder" are words whose integrity is carefully guarded. "Kill" designates any taking of human life, while "murder" is reserved for unauthorized homicide, usually of a malicious nature. This fine distinction has become a vital one, serving in both legal and ethical Jewish thought.

Contemporary Jewish translators of the Bible have unanimously read the Sixth Commandment as a ban upon what we call murder: Old JPS gives, "Thou shalt not murder"; New JPS, "You shall not murder"; Buber-Rosenzweig, *"Morde nicht."* The Children of Israel were thus commanded at Sinai to desist from unauthorized killing, but they were not commanded regarding homicide of, say, a judicial or military nature.[1] The ideological conclusions to be drawn from this fact would tend to confirm Judaism as a realistic, hard-headed system, committed to a law of justice rather than a chaos of love. An obvious line is being drawn between a faith that reads, "You shall not murder," and one that naively and unrealistically demands, "You shall not kill."

This Jewish translation is also insisted upon by the 12th-century exegete, R. Samuel b. Meir (Rashbam), who states in his notes to *Exodus* 20:13 *"Rezichah* means 'unjustifiable killing' wherever it is used. . .but

Reprinted from *Judaism,* Vol. 14, no. 2. Copyright © 1965 by the American Jewish Congress.

harigah and *mitah* can be used for both unjustifiable [killing] . . .and justifiable. . .''[2] These definitions were denied, however, by Isaac Abarbanel, who finds in the Sixth Commandment a ban on killing *per se*, and in the word *rezichah* the equivalent of homicide. To illustrate such usage, he cites *Numbers* 35:27.[3] Actually, *Numbers* 35:30 makes the point even more dramatically:

27. ומצא אותו גאל הדם מחוץ לגבול עיר מקלטו ורצח[4] גאל הדם את הרוצח אין לו דם.

30. כל מכה־נפש לפי עדים ירצח[5] את הרוצח ועד אחד לא יענה בנפש למות.

Both verses certainly describe legal killings. In one, the blood-avenger takes advantage of the murderer's abandonment of the city of refuge to kill him. In the other, the murderer is killed after his guilt is established by witnesses.

Consider our three translations of these verses:

But if the manslayer shall at any time go beyond the border of his city of refuge, whither he fleeth; and the avenger of blood find him without the border of his city of refuge, and the avenger of blood slay [ve-razach] the manslayer, there shall be no bloodguiltiness for him . . .

Whoso killeth any person, the murderer shall be slain [yirzach et ha-rozeach] at the mouth of witnesses.

(Old JPS)

In the first passage, *razach* is consistently rendered "slay." In the second, the *rozeach* is branded a murderer, yet rather than being "murdered" himself (as a consistent translation of *yirzach* would require) he is "slain." Obviously, in English one cannot translate a judicial ("at the mouth of witnesses") killing "murder"—but the Hebrew text does not allow any such latitude.

The New JPS (of which I give the crucial phrases) goes the old version one better:

. . .and the blood-avenger kills the manslayer . . .

If anyone kills a person, the manslayer may be executed only on the evidence of witnesses;. . .

We have three persons in our drama, all described by some form of the root *r-z-ch-* and all, surprisingly, with different English names: the *manslayer*, the *killing* blood-avenger, and the executioner. Translation, then, reflects contemporary values; slayer, killer, and executioner are named with little regard for the Hebrew root but with much concern for the role (condemned or approved) each plays in our society.

Our third version, Buber-Rosenzweig, has the merit of consistency (of a rather didactic nature, one suspects):

> . . .*und der Bluteinloser mordet den Morder ab* . . .

> . . .*nach dem Mund von Zeugen soll man*[6] *den Morder abmorden*. . .[7]

Both Old and New JPS, by their discriminations, refuse to admit that the Bible makes no verbal distinction between a murderer and the approved surrogate of either family or society. Only Buber-Rosenzweig pursue an offending consistency with the vengeance of *had gadya: r-z-ch* is uniformly rendered "murder." But since, on the one hand, "murder" is to be defined by contemporary usage, and, on the other, the killing of the murderer is either commanded or regulated by Divine law, it can only be called killing. The conclusion will then have to be that *r-z-ch* must be rendered "kill" in all instances of its use.

One is, therefore, taken aback by the ingenious obscuring of Biblical thought in our contemporary translation, by the costuming of Biblical statement in diplomatic prose. There are, of course, instances where a translator must interpret an obscure text, but, on the other hand, a translator must always resist the impulse to manipulate the clear yet disconcerting phrase or sentence. This is especially so where preconceived moral judgments threaten to be imposed upon dissenting texts. Otherwise, the original statement becomes at best the victim of oversight; it is subdued by habit.

II

What of rabbinic usage? Does it make a hard and fast verbal distinction similar to that made between murder and kill? How does it deal with *razach*?

Exodus 21:14 states that a murderer is to be brought to justice even from the altar, which implies, if necessary, delaying the sacrificial service. The *Mekhilta* (ed. Horowitz-Rabin, p. 263) wishes to argue from this that executions could take place even on the Sabbath; it uses the term *rezichah*. One might object that the *rezichah* here spoken of is the case of murder committed by the accused,[8] rather than the execution administered by the court. The ensuing discussion in the *Mekhilta* (p. 264,1:1-4) specifically includes within the scope of the argument, however, all modes of execution, and hence all to be executed, not merely murderers. Still, the critical reader could justifiably bisect the two passages.[9]

The parallel passage in the Jerusalem Talmud (*Sanhedrin* 4:6;22b) places the matter beyond all doubt:

> Resh Lakish says: "Let them try him, convict him, and execute him on the Sabbath. For if the service, which overrides the Sabbath, is overridden by an execution (*rezichath-mitzvah*) . . .certainly the Sabbath, which is overridden by the service, should be overridden by execution (*rezichath-mitzvah*)."

The term *rezichath-mitzvah* could hardly refer to an act of murder; it must, then, denote an execution. *Mitzvah* is perhaps used in its usual sense of "commanded," as opposed to "permitted";[10] it may even emphasize that the only valid motive for the act is the fulfillment of the Divine command (see the discussion of R. Isaac b. Abdimi, *Yebamot* 39b). Whatever the correct explanation, one thing is clear: the Biblical meaning of *razach*—"to kill"—was perpetuated in Talmudic times.

A passage (seemingly from our *Mekhilta*) in the *She'iltot* (*Vayechi*, No. 34) is equally illuminating:

> The burial of a *met mitzvah* (neglected corpse) does not override the Sabbath, as it is stated: [*And if a man be put to death*]. . .*thou shalt surely bury him the same day* (*Deut.* 21:23),on the day on which you execute him (*rozcho*), do you bury him. . .

—and since no executions (*rezichot*) took place on the Sabbath, neither were such burials permitted. This passage is of the same fabric as the one previously discussed; in both, *rezichah* hardly means "murder."

Rezichah is used similarly in the *Midrash Hagadol*:[11]

> Most severe is the spilling of blood, which finds its atonement only in *rezichah*, as it is stated (*Num.* 35:33):. . .*and no expiation can be made for the land for the blood that is shed therein, but by the blood of him that shed it.*

This verse refers, of course, to the execution of the murderer. (A similar use of the term occurs in a medieval *midrash*.) [12] The citation of *Numbers* 35:33 is indeed relevant in our context. For the Bible pointedly indicates here the reciprocity[13] demanded by the execution of the killer —a reciprocity in harmony with the fact that Biblical language does not discriminate between executions and other killings.

The word is similarly understood by the *Zohar*. Noting the dual system of cantillation and pronunciation provided for the Ten Commandments, it comments that without the caesura thus created in v. 13 ". . .it would be illegal to kill anyone in the world, though he had violated the law of the Torah. . . ."[14] The verbal (as distinguished from the substantial) point implied here is that *razach* is best understood as "killing," rather than as "murder." So too Maimonides: "Anyone who kills a human being violates *lo tirzach* (*Hilchot Rozeach* 1:1)." And in the *Sefer Ha-mizvoth* (negative command 289):[15] "We are commanded not to kill one another, as it is stated, *lo tirzach*." The dialectic of Halachah can, of course, comprehend both a ban on killing and the duty to execute—much as it comprehends a ban on physical violence and a command to administer stripes.[16] Other resolutions of this problem could be suggested. But whatever the final nature of the dialectic, one thing is clear: Maimonides, both in the *Sefer Ha-Mizvoth* and in his *Code*, applies the Sixth Commandment to killing in general.[17]

We have thus seen that Biblical usage does not limit *rezichah* to murder, rather extending it to describe all killing, even to that which is Biblically ordained. We have also seen that subsequent Jewish usage never totally abandoned the Biblical insight that no word for the spilling of human blood could bear a less prohibitive denotation than any other.

The conclusion to be drawn from this usage is as concerned with the moral vision of the Hebrew language as it is with the proper rendering of the Sixth Commandment. For in the creation of certain words and meanings and the non-creation of others a basic and irretrievable moral step is taken. Some speak of the genius of the language. This is imprecise, for language itself is but the manifestation of a more significant and responsible entity.

Western thought distinguishes, at a basic and indelible level—at the level of the word—between homicide and murder. Jewish usage does not make this distinction. The verbal integrity of the spilling of human blood is never violated; homicide is not splintered into the justifiable and the criminal. Obviously, I do not speak here of Biblical law, which knows of authorized killings of war, self-defense, and execution. I speak of language, of the stuff in which law is articulated, from which it is nourished, and with which it (or any healthy human activity) is ultimately harmonized.

III

Is there a drive within Judaism that reflects the verbal scheme outlined above? Do we have here a linguistic quirk or rather the organic expression of a deeply rooted attitude? Let us examine the debate carried on in the study halls of Talmudic Palestine over the propriety and wisdom of capital punishment.

The famous clash of R. Akiba and R. Tarfon with R. Simeon ben Gamliel is provocative and ambiguous:

> R. Tarfon and R. Akiba say: "Were we in the Sanhedrin [during that period when it possessed capital jurisdiction], no man would ever have been killed."
> R. Simeon ben Gamliel says: "They, too, would multiply spillers of blood in Israel."[18]

It is clear the R. Tarfon and R. Akiba could not have expected mere sentiment to make the application of capital punishment impossible. They needed a device that would legally bind the Sanhedrin to their point of view; as the Talmud explains, such a device was to be found in an intense and meticulous questioning of witnesses (e.g., "Did the murderer kill a man about to die anyhow?" "Perhaps the murderer's dagger pierced the body at the very spot of the mortal weakness?"), a questioning designed to find the witness wanting. Yet while their strategy is clear enough, the motive of R. Akiba and R. Tarfon is not discussed. Why this radical and total disclaimer of a recognized judicial procedure?

Three possibilities suggest themselves. First, the very device sketched above may embody the germ of their opposition. R. Akiba and R. Tarfon feared human weakness, the inability of man ever to know an event in its accurate facticity. No witness can ever testify with an absolute knowledge, as their examination was designed to show. Execution then becomes no more than a judicial gamble—and the dice are always loaded when a man's life is the stake. The Sanhedrin, they held, must never arrogantly assume a certainty it cannot truly possess.

Yet this approach, though reasonable, is not totally satisfactory. In the Talmud the device of close interrogation answers the question, "What would they have done (to prevent execution)?" It is not adduced to explain the source of R. Akiba's and R. Tarfon's opposition to capital punishment. Furthermore, and most crucially, R. Simeon ben Gamliel's retort ("They, too, would multiply spillers of blood in Israel") is a *non sequitur*. For once the possible innocence of the man in the docket is admitted, one cannot have his head merely to insure public safety.

A second approach would be that R. Akiba and R. Tarfon agreed that human observation of events could be accurate enough to establish the guilt of an individual but that a society that practiced capital punishment was bound to err, that this license would, by the very frailty of human judgment, be abused, leading to the execution of an innocent. Yet, once again, R. Gamliel's reply is not to the point: can society purchase health at the price of innocent lives?

Perhaps, then, the opposition to capital punishment is rooted elsewhere; perhaps its source is not a fear of killing the innocent but a reluctance to kill the guilty. This reluctance to take the life of even a criminal could be translated into an effective legal restraint by the type of questioning outlined above—an interrogation on the unknowable. R. Gamliel's retort is now very much to the point: "You would not kill the guilty," he says, "because of your disdain to take the life of man; but you will in reality cause many more deaths than the one you now seek to avoid."

It were well to emphasize at this point the fact that this approach to capital cases was not a "mere theoretical" one.[19] True, both R. Tarfon and R. Akiba lived at a time when the Sanhedrin did not sit on such cases; hence their teachings had no immediate application. Yet they also lived at a time of intense political and military activity designed to regain for the Jews full autonomy, including, of course, the re-establishment of the Sanhedrin. The precise role played by R. Akiba in this struggle may be a matter of debate; but the existence of this struggle is a fact against which all utterances of the time must be measured. Hence, the teaching of these Tannaim cannot be relegated to the limbo of pure theory. It were also well to emphasize that R. Akiba hardly sanctifies human life beyond all other values. Did he not deliver up his own life for the love of God and His Torah? Naturally, he retained his objectivity in the construction of the Halachic scheme: while many sages understood the "death" decreed for the non-*Kohen* who performed the Temple service (*Num.* 18:7) as "heavenly (*biydei shamayim*)," R. Akiba maintained that capital punishment was intended.[20] Indeed, Jewish law abolished capital punishment in fact not by denying its conceptual moral validity but rather by allowing it *only* this conceptual validity.

This teaching of R. Akiba would be an accurate reflection of the categories of the Hebrew language. For when a language does not verbally distinguish between authorized and unauthorized killing, it implies one possibility of its people's morality. The point in time at which this morality becomes explicit, the moment at which linguistic insight crystallizes into legal fact, is irrelevant. We must see R. Akiba, then, as the final expositor of a muted tradition. Significantly, R. Akiba is identified as using the term *rezichah* for execution (*Mekhilta Ki Tissah,* p. 304, 1:13). Other teachings of this Tanna and his school fit into this same pattern. Thus, "R. Akiba says: 'Whoever spills blood destroys the image [of God].' "[21] This is the metaphysical fact of the matter, a fact unchanged by the motives behind the slaying. R. Meir (a student of R. Akiba) points out that the sight of an executed criminal hanging from a tree (*Deut.* 21:22-3) provokes the thought that the King [God, as it were] himself is hung.[22]

IV

It has long been a truism that Jewish law is so weighted as to make execution a virtual impossibility. Again, such an attitude was not "merely theoretical": the young R. Yochanan ben Zakkai attempted the actual disqualification of murder-witnesses by questioning them concerning the stems of the figs growing on the tree underneath which the crime was committed (*Sanhedrin* 41a). Such questioning (the Talmud [81b] tells us) had as its sole end the possibile evasion of the death penalty; it could not prove the innocence of the accused or free him. Similarly, Samuel regards the stringent requirements for proper *hatra'ah* (warning) of the murderer as relevant only to his execution but not to his imprisonment. These devices, then, were hurdles placed between the criminal and his execution.[23]

Yet R. Tarfon and R. Akiba go farther—if not in fact, then at least in formulation. Disdaining legal propriety, they bluntly do away with all pretense and announce their goal, a goal which legal ingenuity would then have to achieve. R. Jochanan had attempted the same result (see Rashi, 41a, *s.v. ke-hakiroth*)[24] but had not, to our knowledge, publicly acknowledged his aim. (R. Akiba similarly "teaches" a teleological orientation in *Shabbat* 64b.)

As we have seen, R. Tarfon and R. Akiba met with opposition. R. Gamliel was probably not alone in protesting this virtual abolition of the death penalty. His is merely the clearest voice. As we note some other expressions of opposition, we shall also see more fully the basis of the debate.

In *Midrash Tannaim* (p.115) we find the following comment to *Deuteronomy* 19:13:

> *Do not pity him*—this is an admonition not mercifully to spare the killer; we should not say, "The one has already been killed—of what use is the killing of the other?" Thus the execution will be neglected. Rather, he must be killed. Abba Hanon says in the name of R. Eliezer: "Wherever the Torah specifies an [apparently]*[25]* unjust punishment, it is written, *Do not pity.*"

Here we find R. Eliezer (an older contemporary of R. Tarfon) emphasizing the duty to execute; the passage as a whole rebukes those who would eliminate the death penalty as useless.

The corresponding comment in the *Sifre (Deut.* 18:7) is, despite its terseness, most instructive:

> Perhaps you will say, "Since the one has been killed, why should we incur the guilt of spilling the other's blood (*la-hov be-damo*)?"[26] Therefore the Torah says, *Do not pity him.*

Both passages deal with a man whose guilt is established beyond doubt. Nevertheless, there are those who protest his execution. In the *Midrash Tannaim* the uselessness of such execution is cited; the objecting voice in the *Sifre* would take the argument one step further—if such execution is useless, it is *co ipso* criminal, a "guilty spilling of blood." This is not merely circumstantial opposition to the death penalty; it cuts at the very root of the institution.[27] The guilt of the court, it contends, would be similar to that of the murderer: both would have spilled blood.

Yet the *Sifre* and *Midrash Tannaim* reject the suggestion that the death penalty is useless and immoral. Rather, it is both useful and moral; it functions as a deterrent (as R. Gamliel points out), and its morality is established by the fact that it is an ordinance of the Torah. To paraphrase, "The Judge of all the world has done justly"; is man to be more just than his Lord? In a similar vein, the Talmud tells that God rebukes him who mourns overmuch: "Do you love the departed more than I" (*Mo'ed Katan* 27b)? The correct response to such situations is not to be forged in human freedom. Man must abide not only by the pattern devised by God; he must also accept the evaluation and judgment implied by the set pattern.

This response is a natural one in a religious community; one expects to find it hurled as a general accusation at all departures from the popularly accepted norm. Furthermore, the accusation that man is arrogantly assuming Divine prerogative can, by slurring over man's dynamic responsibility of interpreting and implementing the Divine imperative, simplify the issue to a question of antinomianism.

One senses in the following Aggadah, too, an admonition to man to forego all reliance upon his own erratic judgment, especially in areas where he claims to be motivated by his moral or ethical sensibility:

> *Be not righteous overmuch (Eccles.* 7:16)—do not be more righteous than your Creator. This refers to Saul. . . who debated with his Creator and said, "God said, 'Go and smite Amalek.' If the men are guilty, the women and children are yet innocent; the oxen and donkeys are innocent too." A voice answered from heaven, "Be not more righteous than your Creator." . . .
>
> Resh Lakish said: "Whoever pities where he should be cruel will ultimately be cruel where he should pity. Whence do we learn that Saul was cruel instead of merciful? As it is stated: *And Nob, the city of the priests, smote he with the sword, both men and women, children and sucklings, and oxen and asses and sheep, with the edge of the sword (I Sam.* 22:19). Is Nob less than the seed of Amalek?"[28]

The problem with which the Aggadah grapples is clearly a crucial one— can man's moral insight, an insight implanted by God and further educated by Him, ever become self-reliant? Can man ever be master in his own house? In fact, any slackening of the rigor of the law is censured; again we hear that the universal terminus of such a course is moral bankruptcy. However generous the motive, the perversion of justice is evil, its motivation misguided. The Rabbis feared that true love of humanity could only be undermined by indiscriminate recourse to "mercy," which, as R. Gamliel pointed out, would deny to an innocent society the concern shown the criminal.

But thus stated, the problem is a simplistic, indeed meaningless, contrast in black and white—just as the situation selected by the Aggadist offers only the two opposed options of adherence to the command of God or total revolt against it. The Aggadah illustrates an instance where the answer had to be "No," for an absolutely unconditioned ethos is impossible. And so the Aggadist points out the incontrovertible: man never advances far beyond brutality; he is never educated out of cruelty. The tower, says Pascal, rises on an abyss.

Rabbi Jose b. Bon said: "They do not well who turn of God's *middoth* (attributes) into mercy, and also those who translate: 'My people Israel, just as I am merciful in heaven, so be you merciful on earth—*be it cow or ewe, you shall not kill it and its young both in one day* (Lev. 22:28).' "[29] The ban against killing both mother and young on the same day was apparently a favorite text of those who would sweep away law and enshrine mercy. R. Jose was contending with a spiritual temper that has always had its adherents and which read *Leviticus* 22:28 as a charge and a program. That the text was so used we see from the following:

> Bar Kappara said: "Doeg is called the Edomite because he forbade Saul to shed the blood *(dam)* of Agag. For Doeg said: 'It is written in the Torah, *Ye shall not kill it and its young both on the same day;* yet you are about to kill young and old, children and women in one day.' "[30]

Doeg (and those he represents) argue that the manifestation of God's mercies in certain rules should become the standard of all conduct. The Rabbis reject this as a superficial understanding of mercy.

V

Yet such statements always remained only one pole of the tension we have been examining; the act of mercy towards those held undeserving of it was practised and praised, for it was motivated by *imitatio Dei*. Thus we read[31] of R. Joshua b. Levi:

> In the neighborhood of R. Joshua b. Levi there lived a Sadducee [*min*] who used to trouble him greatly with [his interpretations of] texts. One day the Rabbi. . .thought. . ."I shall curse him." When the moment [propitious for cursing] arrived, R. Joshua was dozing. [On awakening] he said: "I see from

this that my intention was improper. For it is written *And His mercies are over all His works*, and it is further written, *Neither is it good for the righteous to punish."*

A Scripture-quoting heretic may not be a menace of the first rank. Yet R. Joshua's motive for abandoning the matter remains of interest. He does not withdraw because of the insignificance of the episode, nor because the heretic did not objectively deserve his curse. Rather, he takes his sleep as a sign that justice is to be subdued by mercy. For does not God extend His mercy even where He should visit justice upon the world? The righteous, then, must also stay their hand.

The Aggadah would praise even those reluctant to exact their due from the murderer: "The priests forgave [Saul, for his role in the slaughter at Nob], but the Gibeonites did not forgive him, and therefore God rejected them."[32] We have, then, come full circle: for some, the murder of the priests of Nob limns the irresponsibility and bankruptcy of Saul's earlier desire to save the Amalekite innocents, while for others it proves the opportunity for a merciful act of forgiveness to the guilty. We see, thus, that both legal and Aggadic discussions give witness to two tendencies, one that regards the enforcing of retribution as most just and hence most merciful, and another, which finds mercy too divinely dynamic a quality to be forever defined and controlled by the demand for retribution.

Both approaches, curiously enough, contend in the Midrashic interpretation of *Deuteronomy* 13:18: *And there shall cleave nought of the devoted thing to thy hand, that the Lord may turn from the fierceness of His anger, and show thee mercy, and have compassion upon thee, and multiply thee, as He hath sworn unto thy father:*

> *Show thee* [literally, "give" thee]: to your people is the quality of mercifulness given, and not to others, as we read, *And the Gibeonites were not of the children of Israel.*
>
> *Have compassion upon thee:* the punishing of the wicked is an act of mercy to the world.[33]

Notes

1. The Leeser translation (first published in 1855) does read, "Thou shalt not kill." Among the lexicographers, Gesenius' *Handwortebuch. . .über Das Alte Testament* (17th ed.) translates *r-z-ch "tödten, morden"* (earlier editions give only *tödten*). Ben-Yehudah allows that the word can mean either murder or kill but stipulates that it means murder in the Decalogue. Brown, *et al. (Lexicon of the O. T.)* takes the word to mean either "kill deliberately" or "murder."

2. R. Joseph Behor-Shor (12th cen.) adds to the explication of R. Samuel, "This is what is called 'murder' in the language of the land." See also n. 17 in D. Rosen's edition of *Rashbam;* both R. Samuel and R. Joseph were in polemic contact with Christians. R. Samuel further discusses *Deut.* 4:42 in the light of his distinction, but his remarks should not be applied to *Num.* 35:27, 30.

3. Warsaw, 1886, II, 38c. The editions of Abarbanel I was able to consult all cite a nonexistent verse. With the emendation of two letters, however, we have *Num.* 35:27.

4. The Talmudic discussion (*Makkoth* 12a) as to whether the blood-avenger's act of vengeance is required or optional in this context revolves around the conditionality of the sentence, not around the approval or disapproval expressed in *ve-razach.* The Torah itself, while allowing the slaying of the unintentional homicide before he reaches the City of Refuge or upon his leaving it (in this last case, one Tanna makes his slaying a *mitzvah:* see *Makkoth* 12a), and exonerating the blood-avenger ("there shall be no blood-guiltiness for him"), sees the accidental homicide as pitiably caught in the situation and in some way undeserving of the death he faces:". . .he shall flee to one of the cities and live. Lest the avenger of death pursue the manslayer. . .and kill him, whereas he is not deserving of death (so in Old JPS; New JPS gives, 'he was not guilty of a capital crime'; the crucial *mishpat* may also carry the connotation here of a normative judgment of some sort, rather than implying innocence—see *Ex.* 21:9). . .then shalt thou add three cities beside these three, that innocent blood be not shed" (*Deut.* 19:5, 6, 9, 10). The Torah paradoxically recognizes the legal right to kill a man in some sense undeserving of death, a right based upon the demands of "blood" and "earth." It was, perhaps, the unconditionality of this last statement ("innocent blood"), taken with a literal understanding of the introductory *vav* of v. 10, that led the Talmud (*Mo'ed Katan* 5a) to understand this verse as an admonition to the courts generally to maintain the safety of the roads.

5. The subject of *yirzach* is unclear and unexpressed (see n. 6). In pseudo-Jonathan either the blood-avenger or the court can function as subject. Y. Kaufmann (*Toledot,* II, p. 560; see also *I.C.C. ad loc.)* contends that the Torah knows of execution only at the hands of the blood-avenger supervised by the court. Apparently, then, the subject of *yirzach* would be the blood-avenger. The Talmud (*Sanhedrin* 45b) states that should no familial blood-avenger exist the court-appointed avenger functions both as prosecutor and as executioner; hence, every execution of a homicide could be seen, ideally, as the final working out of the process of blood-vengeance (see *Deut.* 19:12, *Ex.* 21:20 and *Mekhilta ad loc.*), and the subject of *yirzach* is in truth the avenger. Nahmanides, however (in his additional *'aseh* 13 to Maimonides' *Sefer Ha-Mitzvoth),* carefully avoids this approach, making both natural and appointed blood-avengers responsible only for the apprehension but not for the execution of the homicide where a court is capable of taking care of the latter. This places the execution of the murderer in a totally different judicial light.

6. In the use of the impersonal *soll man* Buber-Rosenzweig perhaps followed Luther's *soll man tödten*. In any case, it avoids assigning a subject to *yirẓach*.

7. This consistent translation preserves the power and intent of the original, in which the murderer is paid back in fitting verbal coin (as Rabbi M. Bernstein of Yeshiva pointed out to me)—a stylistic *middah k'neged middah*. Indeed, a *baraitha* quoted in the Jerusalem Talmud (*Sanhedrin* 7:3; 24b; *Mekhilta d'RSBI*, p. 169, l.19) would deduce from these words that a murderer should suffer the same death that he inflicted, were it not for verses to the contrary. (A vocalized fragment published by Prof. L. Ginzberg in *Yerushalmi Fragments from the Genizah*, p. 258, 1. 14, takes *y-r-ẓ-ch* as a *nif'al* form.) Such, in fact, was the demand of the *Book of Jubilees*, 4:31-33.

8. See *Mekhilta d'RSBI*, p. 171, l. 23. *Tosafot, Sanhedrin* 35b, *c.v. she-ne'emar* argue from the Biblical case. See, however, J. Levy, *Wortebuch über die Talmudim*, IV, 465.

9. Thus, *Mekhilta Vayakhel*, p. 347, 1:1ff. On the literary relationship of these sources, see Prof. A. Weiss, *Le-Heker Ha-Talmud*, pp. 425-9. R. Ishmael (*Mekhilta Ki Tissah*, p. 340. l.10) uses the expression, "*shefichuth damim* [spilling of blood], which pollutes the land and drives away the *shekhina* [after Num. 35:34]," to describe killing in self-defense. Though such killing is permitted and its legal status thus transmuted (see Rashi, *Yomah* 85a, *s.v. u-shefichuth*), there is a descriptive and Halachic level on which it remains "shedding of blood," with its usual adverse connotations. Interestingly enough, the Midrash takes note of the bloodshed in approved wars and condones it. Abraham, distraught over his role in the war of the kings ("perhaps I have violated the command of God,'He who sheds blood. . .' ") is reassured: "Fear not Abram, I shall reward you greatly, for you have rooted out the thorns, as it is stated, 'And the people shall be. . .as thorns cut down. . .' " (*Tanhuma*, ed. Buber I, p. 76; contrast the rebuke delivered to a self-justifying Jewish informer: "Let the owner of the vineyard [God] root out his thorns himself" [B. M. 83b]). David is similarly reassured: . . .When David heard that the blood on his hands prevented him from building the Temple [*I Chron*. 22:8] he feared he was unfit to build the Temple. R. Judah b. Illai said, "God said to him, 'Do not fear—by your life, all the blood you shed is as [permitted as] the blood of the gazelle and of the hart'. . ."(*Midrash T'hillim*, 62).

10. Maimonides (who uses the phrase *s'refath mitzvah* in his *Sefer Ha-Mitzvoth*, ed. R. Chayyim Heller, *shoresh* 14, p. 30a) apparently understands it in this sense. A parallel construction would be *milhemeth mitzvah* (*Sotah* 8:7). Note also the expression in *Midrash Shir Ha-Shirim* 4:10— ". . . for they [the Sanhedrin] order [*meẓavin*] stoning, strangulation, etc."

The precise relation of the words attributed to Resh Lakish with our *Mekhilta* is obscure. Certainly, the term *mitzvah* may be a later, explanatory addition—but then it may not. Such an addition would, however, be meaningless if *reẓichah* here meant murder. In the passage under discussion we have, then, either another version of our *Mekhilta* or an early Amoraic explanation of it.

11. *Midrash Hagadol, Exodus*, ed. Prof. M. Margulies, p. 428.

12. Quoted by Prof. S. Lieberman, *Hilchoth Ha-Yerushalmi La-Rambam*, p. 21, n. 24.

13. Maimonides, *Guide*, III, chap. 41; see also *Hovel U-Mazzik*, 1:3.

14. Vilna, 1894, II, 93b. See also *Meshekh Hokhma*, 70d.

15. *Sefer Ha-Mitzvoth*, ed. R. Chayyim Heller, p. 172, and see the editor's comments on p. 13. The peculiar placing of this command in the judicial section remains of interest.

16. See Rashi to *Deut*. 25:3; *Kethuboth* 33a (top), 32a; Rashi to *Yoma* 85a, *s.v. u-shefichuth*.

17. Maimonides' words in the *Code* bear a striking resemblance to the statement in *Midrash Tannaim* (*Deut.* 5:17), p. 23: "*lo tirẓach*—this is a ban on killing." But this segment of *M. T.* was collated from the *Midrash Ha-Gadol*, which is known to have incorporated Maimonidean material. Note also the unusual prooftext given in *M.T.*

18. *Makkoth* 7a.

19. See G. F. Moore, *Judaism*, II, pp. 186-8; Prof. L. Ginzberg, *On Jewish Law and Lore*, p.6.

20. *Sanhedrin* 81b, 84a.

21. *Tosefta Yebamoth*, 8:4. This same teaching is found in anonymous form as comment to "You shall not kill" (*Mekhilta Yithro*, p.233).

22. See A. J. Heschel, *Torah Min Ha-Shamayyim*, pp. 220-3. This last teaching of R. Meir is, of course, of a different order; it lives with the paradox of execution as a metaphysically destructive *desideratum*. Removal of the hung man at nightfall merely ends this tension.

23. *Hatra'ah* is apparently understood in this formal sense by the sages in their disagreement with R. Jose b. Yehudah, *Sanhedrin* 8b. Compare Maimonides, *Code. Hilchoth Eduth* 12:1.

In practice the Rabbinic authorities found the abolition of capital punishment inherent in Jewish law impossible to maintain (see S. Assaf, *Ha-Onshin Ahar Hatimath Ha-Talmud*). The large majority of medieval decisors balanced this abolition of capital and corporal punishment by citing the discretionary power granted, indeed imposed upon, the court to suspend all normal procedures and requirements should the general well-being of the community demand such action. Though some limited the scope of these powers (which are rooted in the *baraitha* cited in *Sanhedrin* 46a) in various ways, the majority read it as a *carte blanche* for effective government at all times and in all places (see *Tur* and *Bet Yossef, H. M.*, sec. 2, 425).

Yet if medieval practice is clear, Talmudic practice itself remains ambiguous. J. Mann's presentation of the evidence (*Ha-Zofe Le-Hochmath Yisrael*, X (1926), pp.202 ff.), though debatable at points (e.g., his rejection of Origen's testimony concerning the activities of the Palestinian Patriarch in the third century, and his interpretation of certain Talmudic practices), does lead one to conclude that the Babylonian Amoraim did not practice capital punishment. I would simply add to his discussion of *Sanhedrin* 27a-b that, while the court did in that case wish to inflict a punishment unknown to standard Jewish law, the witnesses were subject to Mishnaic requirements, and were ultimately disqualified by them. This practice would support the view of R. Jose (Jerusalem Talmud, *Hagigah* 2:2; 78a) that a court may only waive the requirement of *hatra'ah*, but may never act without competent witnesses (as the *P'nei Moshe* interprets the passage; here too we have a discrimination based on the obviously Pentateuchal requirement of witnesses and the formal nature of *hatra'ah* discussed above.) One also wonders whether the disagreement over King Solomon's right to try cases with neither warning nor witnesses (*Rosh Ha-Shanah* 21b denies him this right, while R. Yochanan [*Yalkut* to *Psalms*, 72] and other Palestinian Amoraim [*Midrash Shir Hashirim*, 1:10] grant it to him) is an Aggadic reflection of a contemporary problem. These last sources, in any case, present problems of internal analysis.

Even the medieval practice could be guided by Talmudic law. Thus we find R. Abraham b. Isaac of Narbonne (12th cen.) refusing—on various grounds of Talmudic law—to execute a murderer, though he does impose corporal punishment and financial liability upon the homicide (responsum published by S. Assaf, *Sifran Shel Rishonim*, pp.42-4).

Generally speaking, medieval practice also remained true to the theoretical structure of these discretionary powers, which stipulated that punishment be carried out for its salutary social effect rather than as a mode of dispensing justice to the body and soul of the criminal; see the responsum cited above, p. 43 (bottom) and that of R. Meir of Lublin (16th cen.) in the 1st or 2nd edition of his responsa (no. 138). This responsum was deleted in subsequent editions.

24. R. Yochanan's intentions in this matter are not yet clear. See Prof. A. Weiss, *Seder Ha-Diyyun*, p.207, n. 5. As *bedikoth* ("examinations") such questions could only serve to disqualify witnesses who contradicted each other in their answers, not witnesses ignorant of such information.

25. *Sic*. Rabbi David Hoffman.

26. The expression *la-hov* indicates a fear of actual guilt.

27. I am taking the view dismissed by the *Sifre* as representative of an existent tendency rather than as a rhetorical strawman, as we apparently find in *The Midrash on Psalms* (trans. Braude; to *Ps.* 56), I, p. 497. Yet even in this anonymous *midrash* the question presupposes a real problem; compare note 11 above.

28. *Kohelleth Rabbati* 7:33. This same *midrash* appears (in perhaps a more original form) with significant variations in *Yoma* 22b (and in R. Hananel) and *Midrash Zutah, Koheleth* (ed. Buber), p.138. The words here attributed to Resh Lakish are also found, with a slightly different twist to them, in the mouth of R. Joshua b. Levi (he and Resh Lakish share a nearly identical abbreviation of names) in *Yalkut* to *I Samuel*, sec. 121 (see also *Midrash Shmuel*, ed. Buber, p. 100. n, 8).

29. Jerusalem Talmud, *Berachoth*, 5:3; 9c.

30. *Midrash on Psalms* (to *Ps.* 52), I, p. 479; see II, p. 474, n. 11. See also *I Corinthians*, 9:8–10.

31. *Berachoth*, 7a.

32. *Shmoth Rabbah*, 30:12 (end). For the authors of the *midrash*, of course, Saul was not legally liable—there is no agency in criminal acts. In *Yebamoth* 79a the Gibeonites are criticized for not forgiving Saul, but no mention is made of the priests' contrasted behavior. Elsewhere (*Vayyikrah Rabbah*, 26:7) the ineradicability of Saul's murder of the priests is stressed, but here the king is arraigned before the heavenly court.

33. *Midrash Tannaim*, p. 69.

21

Judaism and
the Death Penalty

ISRAEL J. KAZIS

In order to understand the Jewish attitude toward capital punishment it is not sufficient to consult the Old Testament on this subject. It is necessary also to consult the Mishnah and the Gemara, which represent the codes of Jewish law compiled after the completion of the Bible. This is necessary because Jewish law was not static. It was dynamic and developmental, undergoing modifications through the centuries in terms of the requirements of different periods and places. This legal evolution had to proceed within a given framework; namely, that Biblical law, because it was divinely revealed, could not be abrogated. Consequently the Rabbis had to resort to legal techniques, which, while not abrogating the law technically, nevertheless made it practically unenforceable. The following two examples will illustrate this procedure:

The Prosbul. According to Biblical law all debts were canceled in the Sabbatical or seventh year (Deut. 15:1-3). Hillel, who lived during the first century, B.C.E., saw that this Biblical law worked a hardship on the commercial economy of his time. Those who had money refused to lend it to those who needed money because these loans would be forfeited in the Sabbatical year. Consequently, Hillel introduced an enactment whereby the creditor could turn over the promissory note to the court which in turn would collect the debts from the debtors. While this enactment did not technically abrogate the Biblical law, inasmuch as the creditor himself did not do the collecting of the debt, it did make the

---

Reprinted by permission of the Union of American Hebrew Congregations from *Man's Right to Life*, Ruth Leigh (Ed.). Copyright © 1959 by the Union of American Hebrew Congregations.

Biblical law unenforceable because, by this enactment, debts were not canceled in the seventh year. (See the *Jewish Encyclopedia*, Vol. 10, pp. 219-220)

The Law of Retaliation. The Bible provides for "an eye for an eye, a tooth for a tooth" (Lev. 24:20), etc. This law of retaliation was interpreted by the Rabbis in terms of monetary compensation for damages, and hence, physical retaliation was unenforceable.

Capital Punishment. The Bible prescribes capital punishment for fifteen different crimes (see the *Jewish Encyclopedia*, Vol. 3, pp. 554-558). However, an investigation of the many provisions and restrictions instituted by the Rabbis in the Mishnah and the Gemara in cases involving capital punishment will show that it became virtually impossible to enforce the death penalty.

Some of these provisions and regulations are:

1. Cases involving capital punishment had to be tried before a court of twenty-three qualified members.

2. Trustworthy testimony had to be presented by two qualified *eyewitnesses.* This requirement was most difficult to meet because the commission of such crimes is not usually attended by so much publicity.

3. Circumstantial evidence was not admitted. The Talmud gives the following example: "I saw a man chasing another into a ruin; I ran after him and saw a sword in his hand dripping with the other's blood and the murdered man in his death agony. I said to him, You villain! Who killed this man? Either I or you. But what can I do? Your life is not delivered into my hand, for the law says, at the mouth of two witnesses shall he that is to die be put to death." (Sanhedrin 37b)

4. The testimony of those related by blood or marriage is not admissible.

5. Men who were presumed to be lacking in compassion were not to be appointed to the court of twenty-three. In this regard the Talmud says: "We do not appoint to a Sanhedrin (court) an old man, a eunuch and a childless man." R. Judah adds, "One who is hard-hearted." (Sanhedrin 36b)

6. Witnesses were warned not to testify to anything that was based on their own inference, or that they know only second-hand.

7. Witnesses were interrogated separately about the exact time, place, and persons involved in the crime. If any material discrepancy was discovered in their testimony, the accused was acquitted.

8. Witnesses were asked whether they had warned the accused that he was about to commit a crime for which the penalty was death. Such warning was required.

9. The accused was presumed to be innocent until proven guilty and every reasonable effort was made in the cross-examination to bring out grounds for finding for the accused.

10. In order to prevent witnesses from conspiring to place the guilt on the accused, they were warned that if they testified falsely they would be liable to the same penalty which the accused would suffer if he were convicted on the basis of their testimony.

11. The contrast between procedures in civil cases and criminal cases as shown in the following provisions indicates the kind of restrictions that were imposed upon the deliberations of the court in cases involving criminal offenses.

A. In civil cases a majority of one was sufficient to find for the defendant or the plaintiff. In criminal cases a majority of one was sufficient to find for the accused, but a majority of two was needed to find against the accused.

B. In civil cases the judges could change their judgment in favor of either party. In criminal cases they could reverse their judgment in order to find *for* but not *against* the convict.

C. In civil cases all the judges could argue for either party. In criminal cases they could all argue to find *for* but not *against* the accused.

D. In civil cases a judge who argued against one party could later argue for the other, and vice versa. In criminal cases a judge who argued to convict could later argue to acquit but not vice versa.

E. In civil cases the opinions of the senior judges were expressed first. In criminal cases the opinions of the junior judges were expressed first to prevent them from being influenced by the opinion of their seniors. (For the procedure at the trial, see A. Cohen, *Everyman's Talmud*, N.Y., 1949, pp. 310ff.)

12. If the accused was found guilty and was being led to the place of execution, there still was a provision on his behalf. As he was led to the place of execution a herald preceded him, calling out his name, his crime, when and where it was committed, and the names of those upon the basis of whose testimony he was condemned. The herald proclaimed that anyone who possesses any evidence favorable to the condemned should hasten to produce it. Should such evidence be forthcoming or should the

condemned man declare that he can prove his innocence a stay of execution was granted. If the convict's testimony proved to be ineffective, he was still allowed to make another attempt at proving himself innocent, since two scholars walked along with him for the purpose of judging whether any further testimony that he might offer would justify a delay in execution.

13. If the accused was acquitted he could not be placed in jeopardy a second time regardless of what new evidence might be forthcoming.

It is quite clear that the many restrictions and provisions imposed by the Rabbis made it very difficult to inflict capital punishment. George Foot Moore, an eminent authority on Judaism, wrote in this connection: "It is clear that with such a procedure conviction in capital cases was next to impossible, and that this was the intention of the framers of the rules is equally plain." (See George Foot Moore, *Judaism*, Harvard University Press, 1927, Vol. II, p. 186.) The sentiment against capital punishment is expressed in the Mishnah in an opinion which maintains that a court which executes one man in seven years is a destructive one. R. Eleazar ben Azariah maintained that a court is destructive if it executes one man in seventy years. R. Tarfon and R. Akiba said, "If we had been in the Sanhedrin, no man would ever have been put to death." (Mishnah Makkot 1, 10)

From our discussion of the provisions and restrictions imposed by the Rabbis upon the procedure in the trial of capital cases, we believe that it is reasonable to maintain that they did not look with favor upon capital punishment.

Business Ethics

J ewish tradition has never recognized the distinctions usually drawn between civil, criminal, moral and ritual law. Cheating a customer, robbing a home, failing to honor one's parents and violating the Sabbath are all considered to be violations of halakhic norms. This may be one of the reasons why so little attention has been paid to the ethics of business within Jewish contexts: the issues were cut and dried, clearly defined matters of law. The law itself was detailed and explicit. The obligations arising out of commercial relationships are clearly spelled out in Talmud, codes and responsa.

The general attitude underlying these obligations is simply stated: all deception is forbidden and absolute honesty is demanded. The guidelines on the payment of income tax, presented below, show one of the ways in which this general attitude is translated into practical law. Leo Jung, in his essay, summarizes many of those *halakhot* and moral norms which are directly relevant to the subject of business ethics. At the same time he seeks to express the general attitude of the Tradition underlying the specific laws.

22.

The Ethics of Business

LEO JUNG

"You shall do no unrighteousness in judgment, in meteyard."[1]

This teaches that the judge who perverts justice is called by five (synonymous) names: unrighteous, hated, repulsive, accursed, abominable—also, evil, despiser, a breaker of the Covenant, an incenser, a rebel against God, for he pollutes the land, profanes the name of God, causes the *shekhinah* to depart, makes Israel fall by the sword and be exiled from their land. A judge who renders just judgment is a partner in His work of Creation.

Everyone who measures is called a judge; his decision has to do with the principles of right and wrong. Hence, the above applies to him who is abusive or fraudulent in weight, meteyard, or any other cognate commercial work.[2]

There is another kind of wrongdoing that is neither crude nor violent, but subtle—occasionally less subtle. It has to do with "respectable lawlessness," such as rigging of bids, monopolistic trickery, collusion between buyer and purchaser, or conspiracy between management and labor.

The *Talmud* says: "The first question a man is asked in the world to come is—'Hast thou been honorable in business?'"[3] Indeed, *Keddushah* (holiness) in business means honesty; on the baseball field, fair play; at home, decent relations between husband and wife, and mutual consideration between parents and children. This all-embracing character of *Keddushah* might be illustrated by the portion of the *Torah* called *Kedoshim* in Leviticus, chapters nineteen and twenty. Those chapters

---

Reprinted from *Between Man and Man,* by Leo Jung. Copyright © 1976 by the Board of Jewish Education Inc., New York, N. Y.

present a baffling, apparent jumble of laws of every type—partly ritual, partly agricultural, partly ethical. This summons to the whole of the Jewish Congregation, "Ye shall be holy because I, the Lord, am holy,"[4] is followed by the commandment to honor father and mother, to observe the Sabbath, not to turn to idols, to offer sacrifices in accordance with their respective regulations, to leave the corners of the field unharvested for the poor, not to steal, lie, or commit perjury, not to oppress a neighbor, not to curse the deaf nor put a stumbling block before the blind, not to go up and down as a talebearer, leading to, "Thou shalt love thy neighbor, he is as thyself,"[5] followed by the prohibition not to let the cattle gender with the diverse kind, not to lie carnally with a woman betrothed to another, to plant trees for food on entering the Holy Land, not to use enchantment, not to practice augury, not to make cuttings in the flesh of the dead, to keep the Sabbath, to honor the face of an old man, to love the stranger "as thyself," to do no unrighteousness in meteyard, weight, and measure, and ending with "and ye shall observe all My judgments and do them; I am the Lord."[6]

There is method to this apparent disorder, for Judaism views religion as coextensive with life. Indeed, it is not a set of principles, ideals, or hymns, which are proper only at certain appointed hours or seasons, on happy or mournful occasions, but at all other times are divorced from the temptations of the workaday world with its misery of moneymaking, and its hours of canned relaxation.

The *Torah* rather views religion as a challenge to the devotee to subject the whole of his life, in all of its manifestations, to the teachings of our faith. Religion must remain the upward and forward compelling influence from infancy to the last hour, the single white thread in all the grayness of man's walk on earth.

God is called holy, but "the holy God is sanctified through righteousness."[7] The major accent in Judaism is not so much on God's power, nor His uniqueness, nor on His absolute independence, but on His righteousness. He is the God of mercy who understands human frailty. He is the Judge before Whom no camouflage or specious pleading will avail. The laws He gave us are righteous because they flow from His nature. From it flows, as the perennial *Imitatio Dei*, the categorical imperative to live a righteous life. This command implies both means and ends. Right must remain the undeviating end of all life, but the means to that end must also be ever righteous. Unrighteous means would vitiate and destroy the righteous end. *Mitzvah ha'baah be'averah*[8] (the endeavor to achieve a justified end through unrighteous means), in Jewish law, is considered not a merit, but an offense, an *averah* (transgression of the Divine law).

This righteousness is based on the equality of the fellowman, the technical term for which is *re'a*, which includes both Jew and non-Jew. Even the Egyptian oppressor is called *re'a*.[9] The right which God demands of the Jew in intramural affairs is imperative also in one's dealing with non-Jews. It is mandatory, not only on the normal grounds of right, but especially to prevent *hillul hashem* (desecration of the name of God). Such desecration would result from any improper conduct of the Jew who is meant to testify for God in the concert of the nations.

Ona'ah means oppression, fraud, unfair dealing in business. It consists of financial damage inflicted upon a fellowman deliberately or through error. In any case, that damage must be repaired; the overcharge must be returned. If that *ona'ah* is committed deliberately, the offender becomes disqualified as a witness, his testimony would no more be admitted into Court. The Biblical passage reads: "You shall not oppress one another." "You shall not overreach one another, but you shall fear thy God, for I am the Eternal, your God."[10]

In antiquity, there were no prices, as today, standardized all over the country or the continent. Nevertheless, fair judgment would impose limitations of profit. The first consideration of Jewish law is control of weights and measures. The *Talmud*[11] mentions market commissioners whose task it was, periodically, to examine the weights and measures of the merchants. Violators of the mandate to keep weights uncorroded and undiminished would be very severely punished.[12]

There were two opinions in the *Talmud* regarding the tasks of these market commissioners. One held that all they had to do was to examine weights and measures without concern about high prices, the assumption being that anyone overcharging would gradually lose his customers and prove self-penalized. The other view held that protection of the customer implied the obligation to inspect both weights and measures, and prices. However, the latter would affect only people's basic needs—food and clothing. In case of overcharges for luxury articles no redress would be possible. As a rule, the maximum profit allowed was *pahut m'shittut* (just less than one-sixth). If the profit was one-sixth, the difference would have to be returned, but the purchase would be legitimate. If the profit was above one-sixth, the whole transaction would be invalid. The

Talmud mentions a number of other devices to prevent a sudden *hafka'at hasha'ar* manipulation of prices, arbitrary raising of prices.[13] If the merchant had by error sold the goods for a price one-sixth below its value, he could claim the difference. If it was more than one-sixth below the value, the transaction again would be *mikah ta'ut* (invalid).

One's responsibility legally depended upon the completion of a purchase ("signing on the dotted line," performing the statutory transfer of the article), but an oral undertaking was morally binding.

The *Talmud*[14] has a very telling illustration of the high standard taken for granted, especially by scholars. Rabbi Safra, a Babylonian scholar and merchant, famous for exceeding scrupulousness, is cited as an example of one "who speaketh truth in his heart",[15] who says what he truly means. He was once praying whilst a buyer offered him a price for some goods. Unwilling to interrupt his devotions, he would not answer. The buyer, mistaking his silence for unwillingness to accept the offer, increased the price. As Rabbi Safra concluded the prayer, he accepted the first offer, saying that he would have assented and that his silence was misunderstood.[16]

The Attitude of Rabbis Toward Monopolists

The father of Samuel, the famous head of the Babylonian Academy, took special care to prevent monopolistic tricks. He sold his plentiful harvest at low prices to prevent cornering of the market for higher profit. Rabbis were often called upon to give interpretations of the laws. Their decisions or enactments enjoyed absolute authority within the city, district, or province in which they were promulgated. This right was invoked particularly against monopolists and other abusers of the people's physical and spiritual needs.

One classic case is reported in the *Mishnah* of *Keritot*. Jewish women were required to offer two doves as a sacrifice after each confinement. They would normally do so when they came to the Holy City for a festival. But frequently, because of the distance or travel difficulties, they could not go to Jerusalem, where the sacrifices were given, for intervals of several years. When they did get there, they had to offer several pairs of doves, a pair for each confinement. The seasonal demand for doves was, therefore, high. At one time in Jerusalem, they cost two golden dinarim, many times more than the non-seasonal price. Rabbi Simeon ben Gamliel said: "By the Temple! I shall not sleep this night until they cost but one silver dinar (one twenty-fifth of a golden dinar)." He went to the house of study and taught: "If a woman suffered five miscarriages or five issues that were not in doubt, she need bring but one offering, and she may then be considered ritually clean; she is not obligated to offer the other offerings (usually due after each birth or miscarriage)." By the end of the same day, a pair of doves cost only one-quarter of a silver dinar each.

Samuel, a pupil of the great Rabbi Judah the Prince (the editor of the *Mishnah*), followed Rabbi Simeon and extended some of his interpretations. Samuel was one of the most brilliant personalities of Jewish History. He mastered Latin and Greek, medicine, astronomy, the lore of calendars, and above all, the whole field of Biblical and rabbinic literature. Fifteen hundred teachings are reported in his name. Countless students sat at his feet. He was called the "Judge of the Diaspora." Recognizing the evolutionary character of the law, through continued application of precedent or principle to new conditions, he made many brilliant and ingenious interpretations in order to further justice. He was a bold social reformer whose sympathies were with the common people. He understood not only their needs, but also their ways. From his father, Abba, who had sold his corn at harvest cheaply to prevent any rise in price, he had inherited a hatred for hoarders. Samuel warned against selfish disregard of the common good for one's own enrichment. "Let no man withdraw from the community," he said, "but let him identify the good with that of the common man." Samuel battled without compromise against every form of commercial oppression.

There have always been some persons who looked upon other people's ideals as a good source for their own profit. They appreciated the scruples of the religious, but only because they knew that these scruples would yield them additional income, fair or unfair.

One of Samuel's notable cases concerned these opportunists. The law of the *Torah* prohibits the use on Passover of every type of *hametz* (leavened food). With its emphasis on consistency, the *Torah* prohibits even the use of utensils which have absorbed leaven.

Rab, a famous colleague of Samuel's, had said: "(Earthenware) pots in which leaven is cooked, and which absorbed and retained some of it, must be broken on Passover."

The sellers of new pots saw a chance to enrich themselves during the Passover season when the demand for fresh pots would be great; the harassed housewife would have been forced to pay unreasonable prices. But Samuel told these merchants: "Unless you charge an equitable price for your pots, I shall decide in accordance with Rabbi Simeon who permits the use of such pots after Passover. Then people will not break their pots before Passover, as Rab suggested, and you will find yourselves abundantly overstocked." As Chief Justice and leading Rabbi of his day, Samuel had the power, in times of emergency, to ignore local law in order to uphold justice and fair prices. There was a buyer's market on the pot exchange that year and for a long time to come.

In 1648, thousands of Jews were in flight from the savage butchery of Chmielnicki, a Cossack headman who rebelled against the Polish overlords and revealed his "heroism" in unparalled sadistic orgies against defenseless Jews. It was a year fateful in the history of Europe. The Thirty Years' War was about to be concluded, and organized religions were to dedicate themselves no more to the indiscriminate slaughter of the various non-conformist denominations, but, it was hoped, to humane reconstruction.

In that year, Rabbi Menahem Mendel Krochmal was appointed Chief Rabbi of Moravia. A native of Cracow and a disciple of the great Rabbi Joel Serkes, he had held earlier positions in the country before accepting the post in Nikolsburg. In 1652 he presided at a synod at which the famed Three Hundred and Ten Statutes were enacted, among them that every community of tax-paying members is obliged to appoint a rabbi who should lecture on Talmudical subjects. Menahem Mendel was a renowned scholar whose collection of responsa, Tsemah Tsedek (The Branch of Righteousness), reveals great learning and incisive brilliance of mind; but his character was even greater than his learning.

Among the refugee scholars was one Sabbatai Cohen who had applied for the vacant position of local rabbi in Holleschau. The president of that community inquired of Menahem Mendel, his country's Chief Rabbi, as to the qualifications of Rabbi Sabbatai. By accident, the latter's teacher, a renowned halakhic authority, visited the Chief Rabbi at that moment, and when the latter showed him the note of inquiry, he said, with more enthusiasm than wisdom: "Rabbi Sabbatai is so excellent a disciple of mine that you would be justified in offering him your own position and accepting the Holleschau rabbinate for yourself."

The gentle Menahem Mendel conveyed this advice literally to the community. As a result, Rabbi Sabbatai Cohen received a unanimous call to the important position in Holleschau. But the same self-effacing Rabbi Menahem Mendel manifested no timidity when espousing the cause of the poor, nor did he hesitate to take drastic action on their behalf.

In the forty-fourth responsum of the *Tsemah Tsedek*, Menahem Mendel opposed a too literal interpretation of municipal statute and insisted that changes are lawful as long as the general spirit of the enactment is not violated. In such matters, "the criterion is the intent of the founding fathers, and not the wording of any particular authority." He also stressed the significance of service of Jewry to the whole country, as against narrow local interests, calling all selfish localism highly improper.

Menahem Mendel discusses this in the twenty-eighth chapter of *Tsemah Tsedek*. This chapter deals with the time-hallowed custom of the Jews to honor the *Pesach* festival by a special dish of fish.

The local fishmonger, well aware of the fact that Jews were anxious to buy fish for the Holy Day meal, even though the prices were high, decided to increase his profits. Community remonstrances with the profiteers proved unsuccessful and the question arose as to whether it would not be proper to make *hora'at sha'ah* (an emergency decision) on the principle of abiding vigilance to protect a basic matter. The court of justice and the executive of the community could avail themselves of such authority to protect decency, the needs of the poor, and the morality of the city. When all pleas to the profiteers proved unavailing, it was decided to break the iron ring of monopoly by declaring all fish prohibited for a period of two months (including the Passover season).

Another problem then arose: did the community have the right to use the device of prohibition, in view of the fact that it might interfere with proper observance and enjoyment of the holiday by the faithful?

Menahem Mendel endorsed the principle of the enactment. He declared the decision justified because his major concern was not so much with the rich who could buy the fish no matter how expensive, but with the poor who, because of the high prices, would be prevented from celebrating the holiday and relaxing for its duration from the burdens and tension of the workaday week.

Undoubtedly, this decree taught a powerful lesson to the fish interests and prevented them from ever again abusing the scruples of the faithful for the satisfaction of their greed.

The greatest twentieth-century teacher of Judaism was the universally revered Rabbi Israel Meir haKohen of Radin, the author of many books of moral instruction, most famous among them *Hafetz Hayyim* (Lover of Life). The last part of another book (The Love of Kindness) deals with labor law. This excerpt reveals the normal climate of Jewish social ethics: "If one plans to engage his fellowman in any kind of work for which he is to receive payment, let him arrange for a price or wage in advance. For otherwise he is most likely to become an oppressor by denying the wage demanded by the hired man, unless he chooses to be overgenerous with his money to escape all doubt of having wronged the worker. Most of us depend upon our fellowman to perform hundreds of actions for us, and it happens frequently that after such work is performed, disputes arise between employer and employee with regard to payment due. When they finally part with each other, each of them is convinced that the other had robbed him. Each is willing to engage in endless strife, but he does not forgive the wrong he feels to have been perpetrated against himself. In some cases, they protract their quarrel. As far as Jewish law is concerned, the place (local standard and custom), as well as the time when the work is being done, decides the proper payment. Even if he kept back only one penny of what is due to the worker, the employer on that account would be considered a robber 'withholding the hired man's wages.' Who is able to know exactly what the local standard or custom is, particularly with regard to any kind of work that he may impose upon the other? Of necessity, then, if he wishes to do what is right, he would be obliged to give the working man whatever he demands. And that, too, is very difficult. Hence, anyone who wishes to fulfill God's wish in this manner, to do what is proper, let him settle with him in advance what payment he should receive and thus obviate any doubt."

Rabbi Israel Meir haKohen eked out a very frugal living, travelling from place to place and selling his books among the Jews of Poland and Lithuania. One day he was left a little legacy by a relative, and the opportunity to remain in his native townlet seemed too good to resist.

He established himself in the grocery business. His assistant suffered from the Rabbi's exceeding scrupulousness and incessant worry about the perfect state of the scales, the absolute assurance of painstaking service to the customers, and the avoidance of any advertising—even by word of mouth—that might not be in complete agreement with the facts. Every customer had to be informed about the slightest imperfections of any commodity the store offered for sale, and the Rabbi, himself, would go out of his way to warn the would-be purchaser of possible flaws. To his amazement, Rabbi Israel Meir discovered that his business was prospering and he became conscience-stricken about the harm being done to his competitors. He felt sure that his reputation, rather than the quality of his goods, drew so many customers to his establishment. He felt that he had really become an unfair competitor. All his efforts to persuade purchasers to patronize his competitors proved a failure. Finally, Rabbi Israel Meir decided that "this oppression" must stop. He closed his shop.

Judaism pledges its adherents neither to socialism nor to capitalism. Socialism borrowed from Judaism its emphasis on responsibility for the fellowman's welfare, and for the creation of a society in which every human will receive essential protection and security. Capitalism borrowed from the Hebrew Bible the emphasis on a man's rights to the rewards of his honest labor, limited only by the common good. If any "ism" attaches to Judaism, it would be "Tsedekism," the rule of *tsedek*, which means righteousness, fair play, and human compassion. The same *tsedek* insists on full integrity in connection with commercial affairs—from weights and measures, to the limitation of profits, to the prevention of abuse in times of scarcity. But above the level of *tsedek* is that of *kiddush hashem* which warns each man that he must remain conscious of his obligation to do everything that will enhance reverence for God by man, to avoid any action that may reflect upon the Divine Lawgiver. Just as righteous conduct integrates the individual Jew in that historic task of his people, so does unrighteous conduct—especially in relation with non-Jews—make him a pariah. It is only by living these fundamentals of goodness, expressing them in private and business life, that all men can reach peace, security, and survival.

Fraud, say the Rabbis, is idolatry. No repentance will help the offender. Restitution is mandatory. The Day of Atonement, nay, even death itself, does not free one of the stain of wrongdoing. One must right the wrong, beg the pardon of the person defrauded, make private confession to God, and determine on honest dealing for the whole future.

There are two levels in Jewish teaching. One is legal; the other is moral. In Roman law, what mattered was conformity to the statute. In Jewish law what is enjoined is "going beyond the letter of the law," for the word *tsedek* is a homonym, meaning both righteousness and kindness. Therefore, our Code warns us not to take advantage of the protection that the law gives us, but to stay under the influence of morality and kindness that would grant relief and consideration.

The world firm of Beer, Sondheimer and Company is reported to owe its tremendous expansion to the following fact: On a Friday in 1870, just before the Franco-German War broke out, Mr. Beer left his office for the Sabbath rest. He had large holdings in copper and other metals necessary for the waging of war. The porter received a number of telegrams which he presented on Sunday morning to his employer. They came from the War Ministry and offered to buy all metals in the possession of Mr. Beer; each successive wire increased the price. When Mr. Beer, on Sunday, went through these messages, he informed the war department that he would have accepted the first offer and failed to answer it because it was the Sabbath. He was, therefore, prepared to let the government have all his merchandise at the rate originally suggested to him. The War Ministry was so impressed by this example of living Judaism that they made the firm its main supplier and thus established its global significance. But Mr. Beer, consciously or unconsciously, acted on a precedent reported in the *Talmud* about Rabbi Safra!

Abominations

The word *toevah* (abomination) in Jewish teaching is applied equally to heathen perversities, to any kind of hypocrisy, and above all, to fraud.

"There shall not be found among you anyone that maketh his son or his daughter pass through the fire, one that useth divination, a soothsayer, or an enchanter, or a sorcerer, or a charmer, or one that consulteth a ghost or a familiar spirit, or a necromancer. For whosoever doeth these things is an abomination unto the Lord; and because of these abominations the Lord, thy God is driving them out from before thee."[17]

"A woman shall not wear that which pertaineth unto a man, neither shall a man put on a woman's garment; for whosoever doeth these things is an abomination unto the Lord, thy God."[18]

"Thou shalt not have in thy bag diverse weights, a great and a small. Thou shalt not have in thy house diverse measures, a great and a small.

A perfect and just weight shalt thou have; that thy days may be long upon the land which the Lord thy God giveth thee. For all that do such things, even all that do unrighteously are an abomination unto the Lord thy God."[19]

The transgression of dietary laws is wrong. The violation of the Sabbath is much worse. But with genuine repentance, one may attain forgiveness both from fellowman and from God. Every sin against fellowman is also a sin against God who created him and made every human being brother to his neighbor. But there can be no *kapparah* ("re-at-one-ment") with God (or, in the interpretation of Rashi, "wiping away" the stain, the evil consequence upon personality of any wrong thought or action) unless one has righted every wrong. And one who has false weight could not possibly remember all the people to whom he has sold. When his conscience troubles him and he wishes to undo his wrong, the best available way for him would be to establish clearly what percentage in his gain was due to the profit from false weight, and then to apply the amount to such causes as may possibly reach a maximum number of those he defrauded. Support of cancer research or similar far-reaching methods of prolonging and enhancing life will reduce, though not abolish, the evil his fraud has perpetrated.

Morally, then, there is no difference between violence by fist and abuse by fraud. That is why, in Deuteronomy, chapter twenty-five, the prohibition and the execration of fraud is followed by reference to Amalek. "Remember what Amalek did unto thee by the way as ye came forth out of Egypt: how he met thee by the way and smote the hindmost of thee, all that were enfeebled in the rear, when thou wast faint and weary; and he feared not God. Therefore it shall be, when the Lord thy God hath given thee rest from all thine enemies round about, in the land which the Lord thy God giveth thee for an inheritance to possess it, that thou shalt blot out the remembrance of Amalek from under heaven; thou shalt not forget."[20]

Jews, throughout history, are to recall the abomination of the abuse of the weak or the ignorant. The law demands us "to wipe out" any conduct reminiscent of Amalek, the classical oppressor of the defenseless.

Most pregnant is the rabbinic interpretation of this sentence from Psalms: "I shall walk before the Lord in the lands of the living."[21] Rabbi Judah interprets the "lands of the living" as the market place.

Notes

1. Leviticus 19, 15.
2. *Midrash Rabba,* Ruth 1,2.
3. *Shabbat* 31b.
4. Leviticus 19, 12.
5. ibid. 18.
6. ibid. 19, 37.
7. Isaiah 5, 16.
8. *Succah* 31b.
9. Compare Exodus 11, 2 with Leviticus 19, 18.
10. Leviticus 25, 14, 17.
11. *Baba Bathra* 89a.
12. The technical word is "agardamin'" a corruption of "agoranomoi" (market commissioners). A literal translation of "agardamin" would be either "money's worth" or "bloodmoney"—a folkloristic change of the Greek term to indicate the swindler, to be sentenced by the court, or, as the expression of the angry purchaser—"bloodmoney".
13. *Baba Metzia* 60a.
14. *Makkot* 24a.
15. Psalms 5, 2.
16. *Baba Bathra* 88a, see Rashbah a.1. *Makkot* 24a.
17. Deuteronomy 18, 9-11.
18. Deuteronomy 22, 15.
19. Deuteronomy 25, 13-16.
20. Deuteronomy 25, 17-19.
21. Psalms 116, 9.

23.
Payment of Income Taxes: Halakhic Guidelines

EZRA BICK

The operative principle governing payment of taxes is the law quoted in the name of Shemuel (*Gittin* 10b, *Nedarim* 28a, *Baba Kama* 113a, *Baba Batra* 54b, 55a), "The law of the government is law." Although there is much controversy concerning the exact extent of the application of this principle, the Talmud explicitly applies it to taxation in tractates *Nedarim, Baba Kama* and *Baba Batra.* In *Nedarim* and *Baba Batra,* the context is whether collection of taxes is stealing; the answer being that it is lawful. In *Baba Kama,* the Talmud takes the next step and concludes that therefore deceiving the tax collector in any way is forbidden. Aside from the reason of *ḥillul hashem* — desecration of God's name (see *Kesef Mishneh, Hil. Gezeilah* 5, 11) — which is one of the most serious possible transgressions, the *Shulḥan Arukh* decides that nonpayment of taxes is stealing the government's money, (*Ḥoshen Mishpat* 369, 6). According to most authorities, the right of the government of any land to tax is of Torah authority and consequently, the transgression of stealing is from the Torah as well (see *Avnei Milu'im* 28,3; *Devar Avraham* 5. 1,1).

As is well known, the sin of stealing is considered by Jewish tradition to be a sign of acute moral corruption and is said to have been, by itself, a sufficient cause for the Flood (see Rashi to Genesis 6:11). It is therefore very important to define halakhic standards which apply to filling out a tax return in this country:

I. The first principle is that the return must be filled out honestly. All income must be recorded, whether it could be easily traced or not, and

Reprinted by permission of Yosher — A Jewish Ethics Committee. Copyright © 1976 by Yosher.

no deductions may be claimed which are not true. Violation of this principle involves either stealing, *ḥillul hashem*, or making a false statement. According to some opinions, this would be a false oath, in the full halakhic sense of that term.

II. The final arbiter of the applicability of a given clause of the tax return is the government through the agency of the IRS. If one feels that one is deserving of a certain deduction and the IRS disagrees, then their final opinion represents the law of the land, and must be accepted, subject only to the decision of the courts.

III. In cases where a deduction is valid, but proof is absent, it is permissible to take the deduction, in the expectation that there will not be an audit. If you do not have proof, you are still entitled to the deduction; you just cannot prove it.

IV. You may not deliberately exaggerate estimable deductions, even where the regulations allow you to estimate. The law obliges you to state the deduction as closely and honestly as you can.

V. It is understood that the following are not permissible:

a) deducting business expenses that have been reimbursed. Either the expense money should be declared as income and then deducted as an allowable expense, or neither should be done.

b) deducting charitable donations which have been recorded in your checkbook but were not actually made by you.

c) deducting tuition as charity. (The IRS has ruled a number of times that this is fraud.)

d) concealing facts, such as familial relationships, which, were they known, would adversely affect the return.

e) deducting as office expense a portion of household rent, when little or no work is actually done there.

f) in general, making any claim which one knows in advance would be disallowed, were all the facts known.

VI. In cases where a genuine doubt exists as to the applicability of a clause in the regulations, it is first of all one's obligation to verify that there is a genuine doubt, by seeking expert opinion. Wishful thinking, buttressed by some far-fetched reasoning, is not sufficient. In cases where the interpretation of the IRS is believed to be questionable, based on previous court rulings or in the absence of any court ruling, and where there is a well-founded, informed legal opinion that a court might rule against the IRS interpretation, one may take the deduction or exemption according to one's own interpretation and hope that there will not be an audit. It is the government's job to clarify the law according to the procedure of law, namely, through the courts. If you are not audited and your claim is not contested, then you may rely on your interpretation (under the talmudic principle of *kim li*).

VII. There is no *mitzvah* to overpay one's taxes; it is very conceivable that one is forbidden to do so. Hence, one should not hesitate to make use of loopholes, legal fictions, etc., so long as they are legal and no facts are being withheld. For instance, trips to Israel to attend a convention are partially deductible, even though the convention was just an excuse, so long as you really attended.

VIII. The *issur* (prohibition) of underpaying taxes is more severe than the *issur* of overpaying.

IX. A penalty imposed by law also comes under the category of a legal debt (Rambam, *Hil. Gezeilah* 5, 12).

X. Parsonage deductions can only be taken for expenses actually incurred, such as rent, utilities. It is not a blanket deduction.

XI. All income must be declared, as the IRS defines income, such as fees, tips, honoraria, etc. Read your return for elaboration of this *halakhah*.

XII. The same halakhic principles which apply to payment of taxes also cover the payment of customs duties and the bringing of articles into the country from overseas over the customs allowance. This is called smuggling and is, halakhically, stealing.

XIII. According to some, income taxes may be deducted before computing the 10% charity tithe that one is obligated to give to the poor and needy. Most other personal deductions are not deductible from this "Jewish tax." If you are unsure how to compute it, consult a Rabbi.

Sexual Ethics

Until very recently, moral discourse on the subject of relations between the sexes concentrated on questions like adultery, premarital sex, etc. Over the last few years, however, there has been a definite shift of concern, with the focus moving largely to discussions of sexual equality and sexual deviance.

Given the overwhelmingly male–oriented character of Western religious traditions, it is hardly surprising that so much of the discontent felt by contemporary women should focus on religion. Judaism bears its burden of responsibility with respect to sexual inequality and the issue has prompted lively discussion in the Jewish community. Rachel Adler's impassioned article argues that traditional Jewish attitudes and practices have stunted the development of women, forcing them to be only partial Jews. She demands change within the *halakhah*. Eliezer Berkovits, too, is seeking halakhic change. Arguing that the "ethos" of the *halakhah* is contradicted by certain religious practices, he urges that the latter be changed to make them consistent with the former. "The moral dignity of the Law itself," Berkovits says, "is at stake. The situation is ethically intolerable."

Adler and Berkovits both advocate change, but change within the *halakhah,* not outside of it. It is their position that the Jewish tradition, even construed in a conservative fashion, can and must change in order to give women a more meaningful role in Jewish life.

Norman Lamm confronts the problem of homosexuality from the perspective of a tradition which had always taught that such sexual deviance was an "abomination in the sight of the Lord." Lamm seeks to discover some way by which the homosexual can be accepted by the Jewish community. The definition of homosexuality as an illness makes it possible for him to deal compassionately with the homosexual, while withholding from him his approbation.

347

24

The Jew Who Wasn't There:

Halacha and the Jewish Woman

RACHEL ADLER

It is not unusual for committed Jewish women to be uneasy about their position as Jews. It was to cry down our doubts that rabbis developed their pre-packaged orations on the nobility of motherhood; the glory of childbirth; and modesty, the crown of Jewish womanhood. I have heard them all. I could not accept those answers for two reasons. First of all, the answers did not accept *me* as a person. They only set rigid stereotypes which defined me by limiting the directions in which I might grow. Second, the answers were not really honest ones. Traditional scholars agree that all philosophies of Judaism must begin with an examination of Jewish law, Halacha, since, in the Halacha are set down the ways in which we are expected to behave, and incontestably our most deeply engrained attitudes are those which we reinforce by habitual action.

Yet scholars do not discuss female status in terms of Halacha—at least not with females. Instead, they make lyrical exegeses on selected Midrashim and Agadot which, however complimentary they may be, do not really reflect the way in which men are expected to behave toward women by Jewish law. I think we are going to have to discuss it, if we are to build for ourselves a faith which is not based on ignorance and self-deception. That is why I would like to offer some hypotheses on the history and nature of the "woman problem" in Halacha.

Ultimately our problem stems from the fact that we are viewed in Jewish law and practice as peripheral Jews. The category in which we are

Reprinted from *Response*, no. 18, Summer, 1973. Copyright © 1973 by *Response*.

generally placed includes women, children, and Canaanite slaves. Members of this category are exempt from all positive commandments which occur within time limits.[1] These commandments would include hearing the shofar on Rosh HaShanah, eating in the Sukkah, praying with the lulav, praying the three daily services, wearing tallit and t'fillin, and saying Sh'ma.[2] In other words, members of this category have been "excused" from most of the positive symbols which, for the male Jew, hallow time, hallow his physical being, and inform both his myth and his philosophy.

Since most of the mitzvot not restricted by time are negative, and since women, children and slaves are responsible to fulfill all negative mitzvot, including the negative time-bound mitzvot, it follows that for members of this category, the characteristc posture of their Judaism is negation rather than affirmation.[3] They must not, for example, eat non-kosher food, violate the Shabbat, eat chametz on Pesach, fail to fast on fast days, steal, murder, or commit adultery. That women, children, and slaves have limited credibility in Jewish law is demonstrated by the fact that their testimony is inadmissible in a Jewish court.[4] The minyan—the basic unit of the Jewish community—excludes them, implying that the community is presumed to be the Jewish males to whom they are adjuncts. Torah study is incumbent upon them only insofar as it relates to "their" mitzvot. Whether women are even permitted to study further is debated.[5]

All of the individuals in this tri-partite category I have termed peripheral Jews. Children, if male, are full Jews *in potentio*. Male Canaanite slaves, if freed, become full Jews, responsible for all the mitzvot and able to count in a minyan.[6] Even as slaves, they have the b'rit mila, the covenant of circumcision, that central Jewish symbol, from which women are anatomically excluded. It is true that in Jewish law women are slightly more respected than slaves, but that advantage is outweighed by the fact that only women can never grow up, or be freed, or otherwise leave the category. The peripheral Jew is excused and sometimes barred from the acts and symbols which are the lifeblood of the believing community, but this compliance with the negative mitzvot is essential, since, while he cannot be permitted to participate fully in the life of the Jewish people, he cannot be permitted to undermine it either.

To be a peripheral Jew is to be educated and socialized toward a peripheral commitment. This, I think, is what happened to the Jewish woman. Her major mitzvot aid and reinforce the life-style of the community and the family, but they do not cultivate the relationship between the individual and God. A woman keeps kosher because both she and her family must have kosher food. She lights the Shabbat candles so that there will be light, and hence, peace, in the household. She goes to the mikva so that her husband can have intercourse with her and she bears children so that, through her, he can fulfill the exclusively male mitzvah of increasing and multiplying.[7]

Within these narrow confines, there have been great and virtuous women, but in several respects the tzidkaniot (saintly women) have been unlike the tzaddikim. Beruria, the scholarly wife of Rabbi Meir, the Talmudic sage, and a few exceptional women like her stepped outside the limits of the feminine role, but legend relates how Beruria came to a bad end, implying that her sin was the direct result of her "abnormal" scholarship.[8] There is no continuous tradition of learned women in Jewish history. Instead there are many tzidkaniot, some named, some unnamed, all of whom were pious and chaste, outstandingly charitable, and, in many cases, who supported their husbands. In contrast, there are innumerable accounts of tzaddikim, some rationalists, some mystics, some joyous, some ascetic, singers, dancers, poets, halachists, all bringing to God the service of a singular, inimitable self.

How is it that the tzaddikim seem so individualized and the tzidkaniot so generalized? I would advance two reasons. First of all, the mitzvot of the tzadeket are mainly directed toward serving others. She is a tzadeket to the extent that she sacrifices herself in order that others may actualize themselves spiritually. One has no sense of an attempt to cultivate a religious self built out of the raw materials of a unique personality. The model for the tzadeket is Rachel, the wife of Rabbi Akiva, who sold her hair and sent her husband away to study for twenty-four years, leaving herself beggared and without means of support; or the wife of Rabbi Menachem Mendel of Rymanov (her name incidentally, goes unremembered) who sold her share in the next world to buy her husband bread.

Frequently there is a kind of masochism manifest in the accounts of the acts of tzidkaniot. I recall the stories held up to me as models to emulate, of women who chopped holes in icy streams to perform their monthly immersions. A lady in the community I came from, who went into labor on Shabbat and walked to the hospital rather than ride in a taxi, was acting in accordance with this model. Implicit is the assumption that virtue is to be achieved by rejecting and punishing the hated body which men every morning thank God is not theirs.[9]

Second, as Hillel says, "an ignoramus cannot be a saint."[10] He may have the best of intentions, but he lacks the disciplined creativity, the sense of continuity with his people's history and thought, and the forms in which to give Jewish expression to his religious impulses. Since it was traditional to give women cursory religious educations, they were severely limited in their ways of expressing religious commitment. Teaching, the fundamental method of the Jewish people for transmitting religious insights, was closed to women—those who do not learn, do not teach.[11] Moreover, expressions of spiritual creativity by women seem to have been severely limited. Religious music written by women is virtually non-existent. There are no prayers written by women in the liturgy, although there were prayers written in Yiddish by women for women who were unable to pray in Hebrew.

It was, perhaps, most damaging that the woman's meager mitzvot are, for the most part, closely connected to some physical goal or object. A woman's whole life revolved around physical objects and physical experiences—cooking, cleaning, childbearing, meeting the physical needs of children. Without any independent spiritual life to counterbalance the materialism of her existence, the mind of the average woman was devoted to physical considerations; marriages, deaths, dinners, clothes and money. It was, thus, natural that Jewish men should have come to identify women with *gashmiut* (physicality) and men with *ruchniut* (spirituality).

The Talmudic sages viewed the female mind as frivolous and the female sexual appetite as insatiable.[12] Unless strictly guarded and given plenty of busywork, all women were potential adulteresses.[13] In the Jewish view, all physical objects and experiences are capable of being infused with spiritual purpose; yet it is equally true that the physical, unredeemed by the spiritual use, is a threat. It is therefore easy to see how women came to be regarded as semi-demonic in both Talmud and Kabbalah. Her sexuality presented a temptation, or perhaps a threat which came to be hedged ever more thickly by law and custom.[14] Conversing with women was likely to result in gossip or lewdness.[15] Women are classed as inadmissible witnesses in the same category with gamblers, pigeon-racers and other individuals of unsavory repute.[16]

Make no mistake; for centuries, the lot of the Jewish woman was infinitely better than that of her non-Jewish counterpart. She had rights which other women lacked until a century ago. A Jewish woman could not be married without her consent. Her ketubah (marriage document) was a legally binding contract which assured that her husband was responsible for her support (a necessity in a world in which it was difficult for a woman to support herself), and that if divorced, she was entitled to a monetary settlement. Her husband was not permitted to abstain from sex for long periods of time without regard to her needs and her feelings.[17] In its time, the Talmud's was a very progressive view. The last truly revolutionary ruling for women, however, was the Edict of Rabbenu Gershom forbidding polygamy to the Jews of the Western world. That was in 1000 C.E. The problem is that very little has been done since then to ameliorate the position of Jewish women in observant Jewish society.

All of this can quickly be rectified if one steps outside of Jewish tradition and Halacha. The problem is how to attain some justice and some growing room for the Jewish woman if one is committed to remaining *within* Halacha. Some of these problems are more easily solved than others. For example, there is ample precedent for decisions permitting women to study Talmud, and it should become the policy of Jewish day schools to teach their girls Talmud. It would not be difficult to find a basis for giving women aliyot to the Torah. Moreover, it is both feasible and desirable for the community to begin educating women to take on the positive time-bound mitzvot from which they are now excused; in which case, those mitzvot would eventually become incumbent upon women. The more difficult questions are those involving minyan and mechitza (segregation at prayers). There are problems concerning the right of women to be rabbis, witness in Jewish courts, judges and leaders of religious services. We need decisions on these problems which will permit Jewish women to develop roles and role models in which righteousness springs from self-actualization, in contrast to the masochistic, self-annihilating model of the post-Biblical tzadeket. The halachic scholars must examine our problem anew, right now, with open minds and with empathy. They must make it possible for women to claim their share in the Torah and begin to do the things a Jew was created to do. If necessary we must agitate until the scholars are willing to see us as Jewish souls in distress rather than as tools with which men do mitzvot. If they continue to turn a deaf ear to us, the most learned and halachically committed among us must make halachic decisions for the rest. That is a move to be saved for desperate straits, for even the most learned of us have been barred from acquiring the systematic halachic knowledge which a rabbi has. But, to paraphrase Hillel, in a place where there are no menschen, we may have to generate our own menschlichkeit. There is not time to waste. For too many centuries, the Jewish woman has been a golem, created by Jewish society. She cooked and bore and did her master's will, and when her tasks were done, the Divine Name was removed from her mouth. It is time for the golem to demand a soul.[18]

Postscript: The sort of *piskei halacha* requested in the text of this article are *genuine* decisions based on sources and understanding of the halachic process made by people who understand and observe the Torah. Rationalizations will not do. [R.A.]

Notes

1. Kiddushin 29a.
2. *ibid.*, but see also Mishna Sukkah 2:9 and Mishna Brachot 3:3.
3. Kiddushin 29a.
4. Sh'vuot 30a. See also Rosh HaShanah 22a.
5. Sotah 20a.
6. It must be admitted that Canaanite slaves were only to be freed if some overriding mitzvah would be accomplished thereby. The classic case in which Rabbi Eliezer frees his slave in order to complete a minyan is given in Gittin 38b.
7. Mikva is not itself a mitzvah. It is a prerequisite to a permitted activity, just as shechita is prerequisite to the permitted activity of eating meat. See *Sefer HaChinuch*, Mitzvah 175.
8. Avoda Zara 18b. See Rashi.
9. In the Traditional Prayerbook see the morning blessing, "Blessed are You, Lord our God, King of the universe, who has not created me a woman."
10. Avot 2:6.
11. Exactly this expression is used in Kiddushin 29b, where it is asserted that the mitzvah of teaching one's own offspring the Torah applies to men and not to women.
12. Kiddushin 80b contains the famous statement, "The rational faculty of women weighs lightly upon them." Interestingly enough, the Tosafot illustrate this with an ancient mysogynistic fabliau whose written source is the *Satyricon* of Petronius Arbiter. See also Sotah 20a.
13. Mishna Ketubot 5:5.

14. This is the context in which one may understand the statement of the *Kitzur Shulchan Aruch*, "A man should be careful not to walk between two women, two dogs, or two swine." Ganzfried, Rabbi Solomon, *Code of Jewish Law* I, trans. Hyman E. Goldin, 2nd ed., New York: 1961, p. 7.

15. Avot 1:5, See also the commentaries of Rashi, Rambam, and Rabbenu Yonah.

16. Rosh HaShanah 22a.

17. Mishna Ketubot 5:6.

18. There is a famous folk tale that the scholar Rabbi Loewe of Prague created a golem or robot, using the Kabbalah. The robot, formed from earth, came to life and worked as a servant when a tablet engraved with the Divine Name was placed in its mouth. When the tablet was removed, the golem reverted to mindless clay.

25

The Status of Woman
within Judaism

ELIEZER BERKOVITS

In recent times, Jewish communities the world over have been perturbed
by a number of problems of Jewish life which remain unresolved in accordance with the Torah. Is it really so that, because of the unfortunate
transformation of the Oral Torah into a stubborn text, nothing can be
done until we have succeeded in reversing the process from the text to the
living word? There are vast possibilities still present in the *halakhah* to
come to grips with problems arising from the contemporary situation.
Although the *halakhah*, contrary to its original essence and function, has
become solidified, it has not become petrified. Notwithstanding what has
been imposed upon it, due to the vicissitudes of the external history of
the Jewish people, it has still retained a high measure of its original
vitality. To this day, one may sense how the original life of the *halakhah*
tends to burst through the bonds of the written-down form of the Oral
Torah. Whether one is able to deal meaningfully with contemporary
problems halakhically is not just a matter of the extent of halakhic
scholarship. It is to a large extent dependent on the understanding of
what *halakhah* is about. One may be a great halakhic scholar and yet be
lacking completely an appreciation of the purpose and the functioning of
halakhah. Since *halakhah* deals with the concrete situation, it is essential
that the halakhist himself be personally involved in the life of the community within which the problems arise. There is no *halakhah* of the
ivory tower. The attitude to human needs is decisive. Without understanding, without sympathy and compassion, one cannot be an
authentic halakhist.

1

Unfortunately, very little is being done to cope with some of the most serious problems that afflict the Jewish people internally, which bodes ill for the future of Judaism. This is most disturbing in the ethical and moral realm. Our first concern in this regard is the status of woman within Judaism.

In the context of a religious civilization, the thought that the union between a man and a woman may be deserving of the company of the Divine Presence suggests a dignity granted to the woman which may hardly be surpassed. Nevertheless, it is extremely difficult to gain a clear view of how the woman was seen in Jewish tradition, how she was evaluated. There seems to be no consistent philosophy about her nature, no uniform designation of her function and place in society. Her position appears to differ on the different levels of experience and thought.

There are numerous statements in which the teachers in the Midrash and the Talmud expressed their opinions on the nature of women. Some of these are outright offensive, to which—we assume—no Jew can subscribe any longer; others are only a little less objectionable. For example, basing itself on the relevant Hebrew word of the biblical text, one homily comments:

Before God made woman out of the rib, He considered whether He should not make her from some other part of the body. The head? No! Not from the head, He said, for she would carry her head too high. Not from the eye that she should not desire to see everything. From the ear? Not from the ear either; she would be listening in to everything. From the mouth? She would become a chatter-box. Making her from the heart would make her an envious creature. He would not make her from the leg that she might not become a run-about, or from the hand, for she should want to touch everything. He made the woman from the rib, which is hidden in the body, that she might become retiring and modest. It did not help. All these characteristics are in her.[1]

As if this were not enough, others add that women are gluttonous, lazy, quarrelsome, and thievish.[2] They were believed to be addicted to witchcraft. Even the most kind and humane of teachers, Hillel, observed: The more wives, the more witchcraft.[3] Women were said to be weak-willed.[4] The woman was considered considerably more sensuous than man. It was maintained that a woman preferred one measure *(kab)* of life with sexual license to nine measures of it with the obligation of chastity.[5] We find also some appreciative statements. Women are merciful, more hospitable than men, more considerate of the needs of a stranger, and have greater understanding for them.[6] Yet, when Rab took leave of Rabbi Ḥiyya to go from the land of Israel to Babylon, Rabbi Ḥiyya blessed him with the words: May God protect you from what is worse than death. At first Rab did not understand. Could there be anything worse than death? He thought about it and found the verse in Ecclesiastes: ". . .and I find more bitter than death the woman. . ."[7] However, could indeed this be the final biblical word about women? Did not the author of *Proverbs*, who according to tradition is identical with that of *Ecclesiastes*, declare the very opposite when he said: "Whoso findeth a wife findeth a great good, and obtaineth favor of the Lord"?[8] How is the contradiction to be resolved? Simple. If she is good, there is no end to her goodness; if she is bad, there is no end to her wickedness.[9] Needless to say all these generalizations carry little convincing power. We shall yet discuss what we consider to be their significance.

It is surprising that such negative opinions could find their place beside most positive expressions of appreciation of the function of woman in the life of the people. The views of a number of rabbis in the Talmud may be condensed in the following comprehensive statement:

A man without a wife is not a complete human being; together they are Adam. A man without a wife dwells without joy, without blessing, without goodness, without atonement, without Torah, without peace; yes, without life.[10]

In the light of this, it is easily understandable that the rabbis should also have taught that a man should love his wife as himself and honor her more than himself.[11] Similarly, Rabbi Halbo taught that man should forever be caring about the respect with which he treats his wife, for blessing is found in the house only on account of her.[12] In the course of Jewish history, these appreciative views determined the quality of Jewish marriage and family life. In general, the wife was loved and respected to a greater degree than in any other culture and civilization. This was the source of the strength of the Jewish home in antiquity, through the Middle Ages, and right up to our own days, the source of its strength, joy and blessing. This view of the woman and her importance has guided Jewish family life as if the negative evaluation did not exist at all. It is rather mysterious how such contradictory outlooks could be part of the same tradition. Shall we perhaps say that there is no contradiction here? Different people thought about the same subject differently. After all, the same biblical phrase in the Hebrew original that, as we saw, was used in order to suggest that God was contemplating from which part of Adam's body to form Eve and thus became the basis of the rather objectionable description of the feminine characteristics, is in another place used to prove that God gave a greater measure of understanding and insight to the woman than to the man.[13]

It is difficult to accept such an explanation. The function of the woman has been established metaphysically in the Bible. Even if we should accept the biblical story at its face value, Eve was intended by God to be a helpmate to Adam. As such, it is hardly conceivable that those negative characteristics could be attached to her by nature. The biblical statement would then be the seed of any Jewish view of woman that in itself would bestow a certain dignity on her because of her place in the scheme of creation. One might say that her existential dignity received its metaphysical affirmation in the *Song of Songs*. Rabbi Akiba declared: All the songs (in the Bible) are holy; the *Song of Songs* is the holy of holies.[14] It is true that the love between Shulamit and the King was mystically interpreted as the love covenant between God and Israel, yet the very fact that the love relationship between a man and a woman could serve as a symbol for the purest and holiest of relationships within the reality of the Jewish experience elevates it to the rung of the holy of holies. The words "Love is strong as death,"[15] are illustrated in the Midrash as much by the love with which God loves Israel as with the love a husband loves his wife.[16]. The comparison does not mean that a sensuous element is being introduced into the God-Israel covenant, an idea which, as a result of questionable influences, abounds in certain forms of Jewish mysticism. On the contrary, the comparison is only possible because love between a man and a woman is the highest form of personalized relationship. This, however, should exclude those negative appreciations of female characteristics that we have quoted earlier from talmudic and midrashic sources. How is such a personalized relationship possible with one who is a gluttonous runabout, quarrelsome, thievish, and addicted to witchcraft? It would seem that there is a tension between teaching and certain forms of male experience.

2

Before suggesting a solution as to how the tension between teaching and experience might have come about, we shall have to consider another level on which the status of the woman finds its expression. From what has been shown thus far it should be obvious that it is always men who express views about women. While there are statements about how good a good wife is and how bad a bad one is, there is not a single saying recorded about how good a good husband is or how bad a bad husband may be. And even when statements are most appreciative of the women, they speak of her importance *for* man, as if the meaning of her existence were fully comprehended by what she represents as an adjunct to complete the life of a man. An opinion transmitted in the name of Rab, of whom we know that his marriage was not a very happy one, is characteristic. Regarding the importance of the man in the life of the woman he maintained: "A woman is a *golem* (an unfinished product). She will make a covenant only with one who makes her into a (completed) vessel."[17] At the root of it all is the idea that the manner in which the male and female principle complete each other in the world is determined by the aggressive or active nature of the male and the passive and receiving nature of the female.

This is mainly reflected in the legal status of the woman. Because of the legal form of the marriage contract she was originally greatly disadvantaged. While the husband could divorce her at will and against her will, she could not, and cannot to this day divorce her husband. The husband would inherit her property, but a widow does not inherit her husband's and has to be maintained by her children from the estate they inherit. The heirs of a man are his sons, not his daughters. The daughters have to be supported and must be provided with an appropriate dowry, but they do not inherit as equals with their brothers. Women are not admitted as witnesses or as judges. Similarly, their religious status is also severely limited. They are under no obligation to fulfill the highest commandment of Judaism, to study Torah. Since they are not obligated to study, they can have no obligation to teach. Therefore, while it is incumbent upon a father to teach his son Torah, the same duty does not apply to the mother. But not only was there no obligation for a woman to study Torah, the teaching of the written law to her was actually frowned upon, while the teaching of the oral tradition was forbidden.[18] Her place as a member of the religious community is strictly limited. While she is obligated to adhere to all the negative commandments, she is exempted from the duties to practice most of the positive commandments whose observance depends on a specific time of the day or the year. She does not have to put on *Tefilin* (phylacteries) or to wear *Zizit* on the corners of her clothes, she does not have to dwell in booths during the *Sukkot* festival, etc. She cannot be part of *Minyan*, a quorum of ten Jews required for a congregational religious service.

We may now be in a better position to understand how those negative opinions about female characteristics might have come about and might, notwithstanding their exaggerated generalization, often have been derived from experience. There is little doubt that notwithstanding these rather limiting rules and regulations, Judaism produced numberless *Zadkaniyot*, women who were pious, chaste, virtuous, and charitable often in a self-sacrificial sense and to an ideal degree. Yet we have to consider what must have been the effect of the position granted to the woman on the great majority of their sex. Since education was essentially Torah education, many women had no education at all. They were of course taught the duties appertaining to their responsibilities as wives and mothers, and also learned from the example of the living tradition that surrounded them. As compared to the education of the sons, many of the daughters of Israel must have been intellectually as well as emotionally stunted. They were largely excluded from and were often mere spectators of the drama of the creative forms of religious life. Their legal status, too, was often that of a passively receiving, protected member of society. It should not, then, be surprising if many of them were thievish, because they might have felt that they did not have the share in the family fortune that was due to them. That they were quarrelsome is quite believable; dissatisfied people often react to their surroundings in such a manner. With our better psychological insight, we may well understand that a deeply frustrated person may seek comfort in over-eating and become gluttonous. Some of the other negative charactertistics too, which were ascribed to women in talmudic times, are better understood as psychological reactions to their condition. We need not at all be convinced that the good woman, whose goodness was said to be limitless, was indeed potentially a better human being than the bad one, whose wickedness, it was maintained, was without end. Could it not have been that the good woman was meeker by nature and because of that readily accepted her status, whereas the bad woman was more vital, more energetic, with a stronger will of her own and because of that, much more frustrated. Her "wickedness" might have been her unconscious rebellion against her inability to make meaningful use of her natural gifts. Rabbi Eleazar, a talmudic teacher of the early part of the third century, has an interesting comment on the creation of woman, which has a bearing on this aspect of our discussion. We read in the Bible that God said, "It is not good that man should be alone; I will make him a help meet for him."[19] This rather awkward English phrase stems from the fact that an attempt is made to give as accurate a rendering of the idiosyncrasy of the Hebrew text as possible. A more literal translation of the second part of the sentence would read: I will make him a help meet *opposite* him. The phrase, "opposite him," is explained by Rabbi Eleazar to mean: If man deserves it, she will be a help meet *to* him; if not, she will be *"opposite* him," i.e. against him.[20] It may well have been the case that the numerous shrews about whom the talmudic records know were the kind of women that the society or some men deserved. All those sweeping generalizations about women may say very little about what women are, but rather about what they become in the circumstances in which they had to live.

3

In fact, talmudic tradition shows a great deal of compassionate awareness of the disadvantaged position of the woman. Rab, with whose opinions relating to women we are now somewhat familiar, urged husbands to be extremely careful not to hurt their wives by unkind words. For since a woman's tears run easily, the punishment is fast.[21] While a man had the right to divorce his wife, and legally it could be done for the least of reasons, yet, maintained Rabbi Eleazar, he who does it, causes the altar in the sanctuary to weep. He applies to the case the words of the prophet Malachi:

> And this further ye do:
> Ye cover the altar of the Lord with weeping, and with sighing,
> Insomuch that He regardeth not the offering anymore
> Neither receiveth it with good will at your hand.

Yet ye say: 'Wherefore?'
Because the Lord hath been witness
Between thee and the wife of thy youth,
Against whom thou hast dealt treacherously,
Though she is thy companion,
And the wife of thy covenant.[22]

Whereas Rabbi Eleazar states that the very altar of God weeps over the wrong done to a woman betrayed by an arbitrary divorce, the plain meaning seems rather to suggest that it is the women, in their misfortune, who surround the altar with weeping and sighing. Indeed, that is how Rabbi Haggee understood it and therefore applied the prophet's castigation to an event in the history of the Jewish people. According to him, the prophet, who lived during the period of the second Temple, was referring to the behavior of some Jews after they had returned from the Babylonian exile. During the long and arduous journey from Babylon to the land of Israel, the faces of their wives were blackened and parched by the sun, and they lost their attractiveness. At that, their husbands left them. The women came to the altar of God weeping. Said God: "How could I receive your temple offerings, when the misery of these women calls to Me from the same altar where you want to serve Me! You have robbed, you have violated, you have taken her beauty from her, and now you send her away. I am astounded."[23] This is a remarkable statement. God rejects their divine service, because of the injustice they have done to their wives. Yet what they did was perfectly legal. According to the marriage contract one may send one's wife away even because one has found a more attractive woman.[24] It is then the conscience of Judaism that finds fault with the moral quality of an action that is completely legal. Implied in the statement of Rabbi Haggee is a criticism of the form of that legality. Malachi's phrasing, that these men acted treacherously against their "companions" and "the wives of their covenants," is significant. Companionship is a fully personalized relationship, and it is because the union between a man and a woman is meant to be a covenant that it could have served as a symbol of God's covenant with Israel. It is then in the light of the covenant idea, identified as the fully realized personalization of the relationship, that the nature of the legality of the divorce becomes morally objectionable. One cannot live in an adequately realized convenanted relationship with God if one lives with one's wife in impersonality. Impersonality is injustice towards another human being, a crime; in the sight of God, sin.

The following moving story is told in the Talmud, illustrating the critical awareness with which Judaism viewed some of the practices which prevailed in the Jewish community in the talmudic period. It was customary for married students to leave their wives for long periods in order to go to distant schools to study Torah. In the Talmud, the question is discussed, if such a husband leaves his wife without her permission, how long would he be permitted to stay away from home: thirty days, or even two to three years? The codes disagree as to which opinion to follow. Nevertheless, it was said that even those who leave home for only thirty days without the consent of their wives were taking their lives into their hands. In support of the story it is told that one, Rabbi Rehumee, was wont to study Torah with Raba in Meḥoza. Normally, he would return home on the day before *Yom Kippur* (the Day of Atonement). Once, being deeply involved in his studies, he delayed returning. His wife was waiting anxiously, saying to herself: he is coming now, now he is coming! As he did not come a tear fell from her eyes. At that very moment her husband was on a roof; the roof collapsed under him and he died.[25] Needless to say, the death of her husband was not much help to the poor woman, yet the story shows an insight into the sacrificial service of these women. The severity of the punishment indicates that Rabbi Rehumee had no adequate appreciation of the loneliness of his wife. Though what he did was the accepted practice, there was something very wrong about it in the view of the Talmud itself, if an inadvertent delay could have brought death down on the man. Once again, we have an example of the moral conscience implying a rather severe criticism of a legally established form of married life.

It would seem that the conscience of Judaism was ill at ease with certain forms of the institutionalized order of the husband and wife relationship. This had its consequences for the legal status of the woman as well. Already in talmudic times certain aspects of the original marriage and divorce laws were modified in favor of the woman. In certain cases, for instance, when a condition developed after the marriage of a kind that the woman could not be expected to live with her husband, the authorities would compel the man to divorce his wife.[26] According to some authorities this meant that one could even use corporal punishment if he refused to do as he was ordered.[27] With what right one could do that presented a problem. According to the law, a divorce could only be effected by the husband himself and never against his will. Yet, these were situations when from the point of view of the conscience of the teachers of the Torah, one had to free the wife from the obligation of continuing the marriage. A solution was found by bringing pressure on the husband until he says, I am willing to divorce her. The legal validity of this formula has been well explained. It is important, however, to understand that the ethical conscience required and found a way to modify the application of the original law within the framework of the law. There are other similar cases where an even more drastic modification of law application was established within the confines of the law itself. In certain situations when problems arose, the rabbis hit upon much more elegant solutions. They formulated the phrasing of the declaration that is needed for the legal conclusion of the marriage in such a manner that they reserved to the recognized rabbinical authorities the right even to invalidate a marriage retroactively.[28]

Even more striking is the case of the *Moredet*, the "rebellious" wife, who refuses to continue to live with her husband. Basing himself on the Talmud, Maimonides formulates the law in this case as follows: "One (i.e. the court) asks her why she "rebels." If she says: "I dislike him and cannot willingly be intimate with him," one compels him (i.e. the husband) to divorce her immediately. For she is not like a prisoner that she should (be forced to) have intercourse with one whom she hates."[29] Maimonides' formulation reveals his psychological insight into what might be expected from the continuation of such a relationship. It starts out as incompatibility. The wife dislikes her husband. However, should she be compelled to continue the marital relationship with him, her dislike is bound to turn into hatred. Once again we have an example of how ethical considerations drastically limited the power of the husband to divorce his wife or to refuse to divorce her.

Similar considerations for the well-being of the woman brought about modifications in other areas of the law. We have discussed earlier the fact that in order to establish the death of a husband and thus free his widow to remarry, the legal requirement to establish a fact by two witnesses was dispensed with, and the testimony of a single witness was admitted as sufficient testimony. And whereas normally women could not qualify as witnesses, in this case the testimony of a woman was also accepted. Of course, very sound reasons were adduced in the Talmud for allowing this—and other changes—in the law. What matters is that in cases of conflicts between a moral principle that demanded the protection of the personal dignity and well-being of a woman, and the impersonal objectivity of the law, a specific law had to yield to the transcending ethos of the comprehensive concern of the Law. We might say that in all these cases the ultimate comprehensive concern of the Law in general was allowed to modify the form of the application of a specific law. Finally, toward the end of the tenth century, Rabbenu Gershom of Mayence imposed the Ḥerem (a form of excommunication) against divorcing a woman against her will.

4

There exists, then, a tension between the moral conscience of the tradition or, as we may also put it, between the ultimate ethos of the Law, and its institutionalization in specific laws. There can be little doubt that the tension is normally due to the fact that, inevitably, the actual institutionalization of the ethos is always time-conditioned; it cannot be achieved independently of the people whose adherence to it is demanded. This need not contradict the faith of a religious Jew who believes that the Torah as God's revelation has validity.

No less a halakhic authority than Maimonides expressed the same idea in his well-known interpretation of the biblical divine service by means of animal sacrifices. According to Maimonides, prayer, while not the highest form of divine service, is yet superior to that by animal sacrifices. Yet the sacrificial service was allowed, for, says Maimonides, human nature does not change suddenly. Since in biblical times animal sacrifices were the generally understood mode of serving a god, the Torah—in order, as it were, to wean the Jews from idolatry—tolerated sacrifices, but ordered the children of Israel to offer them to God and not to idols. At a certain juncture in the spiritual and social development of the Jewish people, this was the only way of teaching them how to serve the One God. To quote Maimonides' own words: ". . .God refrained from prescribing what the people by their natural disposition would be incapable of obeying, and gave the above mentioned commandments (i.e. regarding animal sacrifices) as a means of securing His chief objects, viz., to spread a knowledge of Him. . .and to cause them to reject idolatry." This educational method is ascribed to the "wisdom" of God. There was no other way of dealing with the problem, for while God may work miracles in the world, "the nature of man is never changed by God by way of miracles."[30]

Now theologians and religious thinkers may disagree with Maimonides' interpretation of the meaning of the sacrificial service in the Temple, but the principle of interpretation that he uses will still have his authority. For one who believes in the eternal validity of the Torah, the divinely revealed teaching, Maimonides' principle is vital to safeguard his faith. Is it not possible for a believing Jew to make peace with certain biblical laws without applying to them Maimonides' principle of interpretation? This is not the place to discuss the subject comprehensively, but let us consider one or two examples. Let us take the case of the Jewish slave. That a Jew should buy another Jew as a slave is an intolerable thought which is rejected by everything that the teaching of the Torah in its religious and ethical significance stands for, yet it was a fact accepted and incorporated in a law.[31] Obviously slavery was an institution that in biblical times, given human nature, social and economic conditions, could not have been abolished by any law. So the law limited the duration of the slavery. The slave had to be set free after six years of service. The Bible insists on calling the slave "thy brother," and prescribes how he is to be treated: "Thou shalt not rule over him with rigour; but shalt fear thy God."[32] The rabbis in the Talmud then went on to explain that the slave's standard of living had to be equal to that of the master. "Do not yourself eat fine bread and give him the coarse one. Do not you drink old wine and let him have only new wine. Sleep not on a soft bed, while he has to sleep on straw. So much so that people would say: 'He who buys himself a Jewish slave buys a master for himself.' "[33] The biblical law regarding a father selling his minor daughter (less than 12 years and a day old) to be a maid-servant is similar in essence.[34] It is inconceivable that today the most orthodox of orthodox Jews would allow such a practice. Even if the State of Israel were established in full conformity with Torah and Jewish law, it is inconceivable that both these laws should not be completely abolished and with the full approval of the orthodox rabbinate. Both cases are examples of time-conditioned practices, which could not be abolished by the law abruptly, but which were, however, legally limited, modified, humanized. They were absorbed by a net of laws and regulations that incorporated the thrust of the transcending ethos of the Torah, thus educating the people and guiding their moral development along lines which would lead to the complete abolition of the objectionable practices. What we learn from

Maimonides' principle of Torah interpretation[35] is that no matter what the meaning and the truth of the teaching may be *sub specie aeternitatis*, when the ethos of the teaching is incorporated in the legalized and institutionalized forms of social organization, one cannot disregard the capacities of human nature to understand and to implement the imperative of the teaching. This is the root cause of the tension that often prevails between the law and the transcending spirit that formulates the law, which has been responsible for the process within the *halakhah*.

Can there be any doubt that the status of the woman reflected in the Talmud was, to a large extent, influenced by the climate and the mores of a passing day? For instance, according to the Midrash, it is the "way" of the woman to stay in her house, whereas the "way" of a man is to go out into the market place and learn wisdom from other people.[36] This understanding of the "way" of the woman found its formulation in the code of Maimonides in the following manner:

". . .Every woman has the right to leave her house in order to visit her parents, pay condolence calls, to attend festive meals (on the occasion of weddings, etc.), rendering loving-kindness to her female friends or relatives so that they in turn would visit her, for she is not in a prison that she should not be able to go and to come. However, it is shameful for a woman to go out regularly, outside the house or into the streets. A husband should prevent his wife from doing this. He should not allow her to go out more than once or twice a month, according to need. For it is becoming for a woman to sit in the corner of her house, as it is written: All glorious is a king's daughter within the palace."[37] The biblical quotation may, of course, easily be interpreted differently and brought much nearer to its intended meaning. Yet this is how the verse was used in the Talmud and, in view of the mores of the times, with full justification. This has nothing to do with the intentional oppression of the woman. Considering the moral climate of the times, the daily life of the people in the streets and the market places, it might indeed have been in the best interest of the woman to stay indoors as much as possible. The reference to "a king's daughter" has to be taken seriously. In the consciousness of those days, the restriction on her movements did not contradict her dignity as a woman. On the contrary, it was understood as society's concern for the protection of her dignity as a princess. The duties of a wife toward her husband were formulated as follows:

"Every woman has to wash the face, hands, and feet of her husband, mix for him his cup of wine, prepare his bed, and stand and serve him, for instance, by handing him water, a dish, and clearing away from before him."[38]

Needless to say, the law as such is incompatible with the status that the woman had in the ethos of Judaism. In the actual practice of married life it could hardly have been reconciled with the injunction that one should honor one's wife more than oneself and love her as oneself. Surely, these "duties" were at cross purposes with the terms which the prophet Malachi uses for a married woman: a "companion," a "wife of the covenant." Once again, we have here an example of the tension between the more fundamental conscience of the Law and its formulation in a specific case in view of circumstance whose practical strength could not be ignored. From the point of view of the transcending conscience of the Law, the real significance of its formulation in this specific case found its expression not in what it imposed on the wife, but in that from which it liberated her. For this is how Maimonides, on the basis the talmudic determination, concludes the paragraph we have quoted: "However she does not have to stand and serve his father and his son." In the language of the time, the fact that she owed certain services only to her husband and not to any other member of his family meant that she was a wife and not a servant. In the circumstances of the times this was a great step forward. A law of this kind, joined to the moral admonition to honor her more than oneself and to love her like oneself, was in fact moving Jewish society towards the goal of the covenantal relationship between husband and wife.

What we have to see is the success of this method in bringing about the rich penetration of the Jewish marriage by the ethos of the covenantal personalization of the relationship between a man and a woman in the course of history. Indeed, through the ages the marital union in the Jewish home was sufficiently pure and consecrated to serve as the symbol of the covenant between God and Israel. There was no question at all of the woman not being granted the full dignity due to her as a person. The functions of husband and wife were different, the heavier burden did fall on the woman in the house, yet as to their equality in human dignity—in general—there could be no doubt. Normally, the ethical climate in the Jewish marriage was determined by the comprehensive ethos of Judaism, as if the legal disabilities of the wife did not exist.

5

What follows from all this for the contemporary situation? There can be little doubt in the mind of any thinking Jew that those time-conditioned elements that, in talmudic times and later still, influenced the formulation of the laws regarding the status of the woman, have been overcome to a very large extent by the Jewish people of today. And we are not thinking here of the majority of Jews who today may be considered secularists, but of the majority of religious Jews, who accept the Torah as divine revelation, who adhere to the laws of Judaism and strive toward the fullest realization of *halakhah* in their own lives as well as in that of the community. Who among religious Jews still adheres to the old law that, since "her house is not a prison," a wife should be permitted to leave it once or twice a month, according to need? Which Jewish husband still expects his wife to look upon him as if he were "a prince and a king,"[39] simply because he is her husband? In our understanding, a man who, independently of being a husband, indeed deserves to be respected like a "prince and a king," would neither demand of his wife such respect nor would he accept it from her. On the other hand, should he demand or even accept it, it would itself be proof that he was not worthy of it. Do religious Jews today allow their wives to serve them by washing their faces, hands, and legs, and fulfilling those other duties which are prescribed by the law? Apart from the respect due to our wives as human beings, our self-respect would not allow us to accept this kind of service from our wives, or even from any other human being. This is so not because we are modern Jews, not because this is the second half of the twentieth century. This is so because we are Jews. This has been so for many generations, on account of what Judaism has made of us. In my home in Rumania, we had a village girl working for us as a servant. In the morning, she would clean the shoes of the family, she would set the table and, of course, put a jug full of water on it. Occasionally, as would be the case with children, we would dirty our shoes during the day, but we were not permitted to ask the maid to clean them again for us. During the day, if we wanted clean shoes, we had to clean them ourselves. When during a meal the water bottle would be emptied, the maid might have been asked by the lady of the house to bring another jug of water to the table, but we children were not allowed to ask her to bring a glass of water especially for us. Our father explained: the maid has certain duties in this house, she works, and she is paid for her work. But she is not the personal servant of anyone in the house. Our father was not a modern Jew. His education was chiefly Bible, Talmud, and the codes of Jewish law. He was teaching his children what Judaism had taught him. Could it have been conceivable to him to pay any regard to those "duties" of a wife to her husband, with whose talmudic sources and codification he was well familiar?

The truth is, that in the Torah-educated Jewish conscience, the ethos of Judaism has overcome many of the time-conditioned elements that unavoidably found their way into the legal formulation of the Law in a distant past. Notwithstanding the biblical law of inheritance, today in orthodox Jewish families, wives do inherit their husband's property and daughters inherit together with sons. Of course, there are ways of justifying this within the *halakhah*. What is decisive is that these ways were found and a new practice has developed within the framework of the Law. We have heard that a woman cannot be admitted as a witness in court. Yet we also heard that in certain cases her testimony was accepted. Is this the ultimate limit of what is possible within the system of the *halakhah*? Of course, there was a reason for the exception; but have all the possible reasons been exhausted? A woman cannot be a judge, yet Deborah of biblical fame was a judge, indeed the supreme judge of her time. Again, there is an explanation for this exception,[40] but again one might ask, have all the explanations of what is possible within the Law already been given? One does not ask these questions because the Torah has become a burden and one wishes to break away from it; one asks because one believes in the eternal vitality of the divine revelation, because one is committed with one's whole existence to the proposition that the teaching is *Torat Ḥayim*, the way of life for the Jew.

We saw how within the *halakhah* itself there have been significant developments that would limit the power of the husband by compelling him, in certain cases, to divorce his wife by annulling the marriage retroactively, and recognizing the freedom of the wife to demand a dissolution of the marriage in certain circumstances. Yet we have to acknowledge that more has still to be done. The case of the *Agunah*, of the deserted wife or the wife whose husband has been missing for a long period of time, is still challenging the conscience of the Law for a solution. In our own days, with civil divorce, there are many cases when, after a marriage has been dissolved by the civil authorities, the husband, often out of spite, refuses to divorce his wife by the giving of a *Get* (a divorce document) as required by Jewish law. Many human tragedies result from the present situation.

In a halakhic work, published several years ago in Jerusalem, I have shown how these and other related problems may be solved and, thus, a great deal of human suffering avoided, within the rules of *halakhah*.[41] It is halakhically possible to introduce conditions into the *ketubah* (the marriage contract) that if certain eventualities should arise in the future, the marriage is to be annulled retroactively. Thus, for instance, in the case of soldiers missing in action, or in cases where civil divorce had taken place but the husband refuses to give a *get*, under appropriate safeguards the marriage would be annulled and the wife would be free to remarry. According to *halakhah*, annullment would have no detrimental effect on either the legal or moral status of the children.

Another problem that could easily be resolved is that of *Ḥalitzah*. According to biblical law, when a man dies without leaving any offspring behind, his brother must marry the widow and if he refuses, the ceremony of *Ḥalitzah* is to be performed. The widow is not free to remarry without first having been released by that ceremony. However, already in talmudic times, the levirate marriage was largely discontinued and replaced by *Ḥalitzah*. Needless to say, in the present social and moral climate, the institution of levirate marriage has lost its original meaning and purpose. On the other hand, that it has been in the main abandoned renders some aspects of the *Ḥalitzah* ceremony objectionable for the widow as well as for her brother-in-law. Understandably, in many cases, both parties are greatly embarrassed by it. In addition, all kinds of problems may arise as, for instance, when the whereabouts of the surviving brother cannot be ascertained. At times, the brother-in-law refuses to go through with the *Ḥalitzah* ceremony because he considers it demeaning. In other cases, worse still, he uses the need for his consent in order to blackmail the family of the widow. Every practising rabbi is familiar with the human agony arising from such situations, which befall especially Torah-observant women. I have proven conclusively that in the case of the husband's death, a childless marriage can be annulled retroactively by means of a *tenai* (condition) appropriately incorporated in the *ketubah*.

Unfortunately, the rabbinical establishment moves very slowly, if at all. At the time of this writing, two men are imprisoned in Israel. One, convicted as a rapist, has been condemned to a long prison term. He is married and the rabbinate, with the authority of the state, imposed an additional jail sentence on him until he divorces his wife. The other is a case of a Jew who, all through his married life, neglected his wife and family, never worked, and never accepted any kind of responsibility. He too was imprisoned and will have to stay there till he agrees to divorce his wife of his own free will. Both men are adamant in refusing to obey the demand of the rabbinate. It is difficult to understand how the Israeli rabbinate can remain insensitive to the indignity imposed upon the Torah itself by such degrading wrestlings with the inadequacies of human nature. In the meantime, of course, the misery of the wives deepens with every passing day. When these cases will be resolved, if they ever should be, other cases of a similar kind will follow and the indignity and the suffering will be repeated. Yet all this could be prevented by the introduction of an appropriate formula into the marriage contract, for which there is sufficient validation within the *halakhah.*

We are confronted with a challenge to the conscience of Judaism, with a very test of its humane quality. Apart from the happiness of numerous human beings, which alone should be a matter deserving the highest compassionate priority among the concerns of the rabbinate, the moral dignity of the Law itself is at stake. The situation is ethically intolerable.

The day will come when the problem of the *Agunah* and other similar problems will be solved, as they well may be, within the framework of the *halakhah.* More and more young couples who abide by the *halakhah* are now demanding that appropriate conditions be included in their *ketubah.* They do this as a requirement of their Jewish conscience, out of loving concern for each other, in order to avoid possible human misery in the future, and in order to protect the ethical dignity of their marriage. There is little doubt that as more and more Torah-observant young couples will realize that there are halakhically valid possibilities to eliminate those problems that have plagued us in the past, the pressure on the rabbinate will become strong enough to turn the halakhically possible into the humanly real.

In addition to the legal status of the woman, a new concern that agitates many of us today is the religious status of the woman in the daily life of the Jewish community. This is truly a contemporary problem, resulting from radically changed intellectual, social, and economic conditions. The concern deals with what should be the place of the contemporary Torah-observant woman, who adheres to the rules of the halakhah, in the religious life of the community. Many of these women are well educated at colleges and universities, and have a broad, and often highly specialized, secular education. Is it conceivable that they should continue to be excluded from any serious study of Torah and Talmud, and of the other disciplines in the study of Judaism, as they were in the past? What is bound to be the quality of Jewish life, in the homes and the communities, if intelligent, mentally alert women, otherwise fully involved in the moral, political, social and economic issues of the day should be—as a matter of religious principle—relegated to the status of the ignoramus within the realm where they ought to have their spiritual and religious roots, the realm of Judaism? Is the Jewish woman of today, who intellectually, socially, and, often professionally too, is indeed the equal of her husband, to remain only a passive participant in the daily religious life of the community, often only the spectator to Judaism which, apparently, is essentially a male concern and responsibility?

Once again, we have reached a juncture at which the comprehensive ethos of the Torah itself strains against its formulation in specific laws. It is, however, the very essence of the halakhah to be responsive to such a strain, and by its resolution to bring about an even richer realization of the Torah itself. Not only is the status of the woman at stake, but the status of Judaism itself. For if in its application it could not do full justice to the Jewish woman in her present state as she is longing for participation in the drama of Jewish realization in accordance with her capacity and spiritual need, its form of such application becomes itself highly questionable. Those who understand the true nature and function of halakhah, and are committed to halakhic Judaism, cannot accept such a suggestion. With unreserved openness and sensitivity to the genuineness of the problem, with faith in the vitality of the halakhah, with humility and yet with intellectual courage, the necessary halakhic work will be accomplished that will define the status of the woman anew, justly and meaningfully.

Notes

1. *Bereshit Rabbah* 18.
2. Ibid. 45.
3. *Mishnah Avot* 2, 8.
4. T.B. *Shabbat* 33b; *Kiddushin* 30b.
5. T.B. *Sotah* 20a.
6. Ibid. *Megillah* 14b; *Berakhot* 6b.
7. Ecclesiastes 7:26. For the talmudic reference see T.B. *Yevamot* 63b.
8. Proverbs 18:22.
9. *Midrash Soher Tov* 59.
10. Cf. T.B. *Yevamot* 63a; 62b; *Midrash Rabbah Kohelet* 9, 7.
11. T.B. *Yevamot* 62b.
12. T.B. *Baba Metzia* 59a.
13. T.B. *Niddah* 45b.
14. *Mishnah Yadayim* 3,5.
15. Song of Songs 8:6.
16. *Midrash Rabbah Shir HaShirim.*
17. T.B. *Sanhedrin* 22b.
18. See T.B. *Sotah* 20a, Maimonides, *Yad HaHazakah, Talmud Torah* 1,13; *Shulḥan Arukh, Yoreh De'ah* 246,6.
19. Genesis 2:18.
20. T.B. *Yevamot* 63a.
21. T.B. *Baba Metzia* 59a.
22. Malachi 2: 13-14; For Rabbi Eleazar see T.B. *Gittin* 90b. It is true that because of the biblical reference to "the wife of thy youth" he speaks only of a first divorce. Our concern is with the spirit of the statement, rather than its homiletical technicality.
23. *Midrash Rabbah, Bereshit,* 18,8.
24. Cf. the last *Mishnah* in *Gittin.*
25. T.B. *Ketubot* 62b.
26. Cf. e.g., T.B. *Ketubot* 77a.
27. See *Tosafot,* ibid. 70a. *Yotzee Veyitten ketubah.*
28. Cf., for instance, ibid. 3a.
29. *Yad HaHazakah, Hilkhot Ishut* 14,8.
30. Maimonides, *The Guide for the Perplexed,* III 32, translated by M. Friedlander.
31. Exodus 21: 1-6.
32. Leviticus 25: 39-43.
33. T.B. *Kiddushin* 22a.
34. Exodus 21: 7-11.
35. That it does have general validity and was not used by Maimonides exceptionally in the case of *Korbanot* (animal sacrifices) one can see by the fact that it is in essence the principle which guides his interpretaion of the reasons for the biblical commandments (*Ta'amei HaMitzvot*) practically in its entirety.
36. *Midrash Rabba, Bereshit* 18.
37. *Yad HaHazakah, Ishut,* 13,11; the biblical quotation is from Psalms 45:14.
38. Ibid. ch. 21,3.
39. Cf. Maimonides, *Yad HaHazakah, Hilkhot Ishut* 15,20.
40. See T.B. *Baba Kama* 14a, *Tosafot, Asher Tasim Lifnehem.*
41. C.F. my work *T'nai beNisu'in uveGet,* Mosad Harav Kook, Jerusalem, 1966.

26

Judaism and the Modern Attitude to Homosexuality

NORMAN LAMM

Popular wisdom has it that our society is wildly hedonistic, with the breakdown of family life, rampant immorality, and the world, led by the United States, in the throes of a sexual revolution. The impetus of this latest revolution is such that new ground is constantly being broken, while bold deviations barely noticed one year are glaringly more evident the year following and become the norm for the "younger generation" the year after that.

Some sex researchers accept this portrait of a steady deterioration in sex inhibitions and of increasing permissiveness. Opposed to them are the "debunkers" who hold that this view is mere fantasy and that, while there may have been a significant leap in verbal sophistication, there has probably been only a short hop in actual behavior. They point to statistics which confirm that now, as in Kinsey's day, there has been no reported increase in sexual frequencies along with the alleged de-inhibition to rhetoric and dress. The "sexual revolution" is, for them, largely a myth. Yet others maintain that there is in Western society a permanent revolution against moral standards, but that the form and style of the revolt keeps changing.

The determination of which view is correct will have to be left to the sociologists and statisticians—or, better, to historians of the future who will have the benefit of hindsight. But certain facts are quite clear. First, the complaint that moral restraints are crumbling has a two or three thousand year history in Jewish tradition and in the continuous history

Reprinted from *Encyclopaedia Judaica Yearbook 1974.* Copyright © 1974 by Keter Publishing House Jerusalem Ltd.

of Western civilization. Second, there has been a decided increase at least in the area of sexual attitudes, speech, and expectations, if not in practice. Third, such social and psychological phenomena must sooner or later beget changes in mores and conduct. And finally, it is indisputable that most current attitudes are profoundly at variance with the traditional Jewish views on sex and sex morality.

Of all the current sexual fashions, the one most notable for its militancy, and which most conspicuously requires illumination from the sources of Jewish tradition, is that of sexual deviancy. This refers primarily to homosexuality, male or female, along with a host of other phenomena such as transvestism and transsexualism. They all form part of the newly approved theory of the idiosyncratic character of sexuality. Homosexuals have demanded acceptance in society, and this demand has taken various forms—from a plea that they should not be liable to criminal prosecution, to a demand that they should not be subjected to social sanctions, and then to a strident assertion that they represent an "alternative life-style" no less legitimate than "straight" heterosexuality. The various forms of homosexual apologetics appear largely in contemporary literature and theater, as well as in the daily press. In the United States, "gay" activists have become increasingly and progressively more vocal and militant.

Legal Position

Homosexuals have, indeed, been suppressed by the law. For instance, the Emperor Valentinian, in 390 C.E., decreed that pederasty be punished by burning at the stake. The sixth-century Code of Justinian ordained that homosexuals be tortured, mutilated, paraded in public, and executed. A thousand years later, Gibbon said of the penalty the Code decreed that "pederasty became the crime of those to whom no crime could be imputed." In more modern times, however, the Napoleonic Code declared consensual homosexuality legal in France. A century ago, anti-homosexual laws were repealed in Belgium and Holland. In this century, Denmark, Sweden and Switzerland followed suit and, more recently, Czechoslovakia and England. The most severe laws in the West are found in the United States, where they come under the jurisdiction of the various states and are known by a variety of names, usually as "sodomy laws." Punishment may range from light fines to five or more years in prison (in some cases even life imprisonment), indeterminate detention in a mental hospital, and even to compulsory sterilization. Moreover, homosexuals are, in various states, barred from the licensed professions, from many professional societies, from teaching, and from the civil service—to mention only a few of the sanctions encountered by the known homosexual.

More recently, a new leniency has been developing in the United States and elsewhere with regard to homosexuals. Thus, in 1969, the National Institute of Mental Health issued a majority report advocating that adult consensual homosexuality be declared legal. The American Civil Liberties Union concurred. Earlier, Illinois had done so in 1962, and in 1971 the state of Connecticut revised its laws accordingly. Yet despite the increasing legal and social tolerance of deviance, basic feelings toward homosexuals have not really changed. The most obvious example is France, where although legal restraints were abandoned over 150 years ago, the homosexual of today continues to live in shame and secrecy.

Statistics

Statistically, the proportion of homosexuals in society does not seem to have changed much since Professor Kinsey's day (his book, *Sexual Behavior in the Human Male*, was published in 1948, and his volume on the human female in 1953). Kinsey's studies revealed that hard-core male homosexuals constituted about 4–6% of the population: 10% experienced "problem" behavior during a part of their lives. One man out of three indulges in some form of homosexual behavior from puberty until his early twenties. The dimensions of the problem become quite overwhelming when it is realized that, according to these figures, of 200 million people in the United States some ten million will become or are predominant or exclusive homosexuals, and over 25 million will have at least a few years of significant homosexual experience.

The New Permissiveness

The most dramatic change in our attitudes to homosexuality has taken place in the new mass adolescent subculture—the first such in history—where it is part of the whole new outlook on sexual restraints in general. It is here that the fashionable Sexual Left has had its greatest success on a wide scale, appealing especially to the rejection of Western traditions of sex roles and sex typing. A number of different streams feed into this ideological reservoir from which the new sympathy for homosexuality flows. Freud and his disciples began the modern protest against traditional restraints, and blamed the guilt that follows transgression for the neuroses that plague man. Many psychoanalysts began to overemphasize the importance of sexuality in human life, and this ultimately gave birth to a kind of sexual messianism. Thus, in our own day Wilhelm Reich identifies sexual energy as "vital energy *per se*" and, in conformity with his Marxist ideology, seeks to harmonize Marx and Freud. For Reich and his followers, the sexual revolution is a *machina ultima* for the whole Leninist liberation in all spheres of life and society. Rebellion against restrictive moral codes has become, for them, not merely a way to hedonism but a form of sexual mysticism: orgasm is seen not only as the pleasurable climactic release of internal sexual pressure, but as a means to individual creativity and insight as well as to the reconstruction and liberation of society. Finally, the emphasis on freedom and sexual autonomy derives from the Sartrean version of Kant's view of human autonomy.

It is in this atmosphere that pro-deviationist sentiments have proliferated, reaching into many strata of society. Significantly, religious groups have joined the sociologists and ideologists of deviance to affirm what has been called "man's birthright of unbounded ambisexuality." A number of Protestant churches in America, and an occasional Catholic clergyman, have pleaded for more sympathetic attitudes toward homosexuals. Following the new Christian permissiveness espoused in *Sex and Morality* (1966), the report of a working party of the British Council of Churches, a group of American Episcopalian clergymen in November 1967 concluded that homosexual acts ought not to be considered wrong *per se*. A homosexual relationship is, they implied, no different from a heterosexual marriage: but must be judged by one criterion—"whether it is intended to foster a permanent relation of love." Jewish apologists for deviationism have been prominent in the Gay Liberation movement and have not hesitated to advocate their position in American journals and in the press. Christian groups began to emerge which catered to a homosexual clientele, and Jews were not too far behind. This latest Jewish exemplification of the principle of *wie es sich christelt, so juedelt es sich* will be discussed at the end of this essay.

Homosexual militants are satisfied neither with a "mental health" approach nor with demanding civil rights. They are clear in insisting on society's recognition of sexual deviance as an "alternative life-style," morally legitimate and socially acceptable.

Such are the basic facts and theories of the current advocacy of sexual deviance. What is the classical Jewish attitude to sodomy, and what suggestions may be made to develop a Jewish approach to the complex problem of the homosexual in contemporary society?

Biblical View

The Bible prohibits homosexual intercourse and labels it an abomination: "Thou shalt not lie with a man as one lies with a woman: it is an abomination" (Lev. 18:22). Capital punishment is ordained for both transgressors in Lev. 20:13. In the first passage, sodomy is linked with buggery, and in the second with incest and buggery. (There is considerable terminological confusion with regard to these words. We shall here use "sodomy" as a synonym for homosexuality and "buggery" for sexual relations with animals.)

The city of Sodom had the questionable honor of lending its name to homosexuality because of the notorious attempt at homosexual rape, when the entire population—"both young and old, all the people from every quarter"—surrounded the home of Lot, the nephew of Abraham, and demanded that he surrender his guests to them "that we may know them" (Gen. 19:5). The decimation of the tribe of Benjamin resulted from the notorious incident, recorded in Judges 19, of a group of Benjamites in Gibeah who sought to commit homosexual rape.

Scholars have identified the *kadesh* proscribed by the Torah (Deut. 23:18) as a ritual male homosexual prostitute. This form of heathen cult penetrated Judea from the Canaanite surroundings in the period of the early monarchy. So Rehoboam, probably under the influence of his Ammonite mother, tolerated this cultic sodomy during his reign (I Kings 14:24). His grandson Asa tried to cleanse the Temple in Jerusalem of the practice (I Kings 15:12), as did his great-grandson Jehoshaphat. But it was not until the days of Josiah and the vigorous reforms he introduced that the *kadesh* was finally removed from the Temple and the land

(II Kings 23:7). The Talmud too (Sanh. 24b) holds that the *kadesh* was a homosexual functionary. (However, it is possible that the term also alludes to a heterosexual male prostitute. Thus, in II Kings 23:7, women are described as weaving garments for the idols in the *bate ha-kedeshim* [houses of the *kadesh*]: the presence of women may imply that the *kadesh* was not necessarily homosexual. The talmudic opinion identifying the *kadesh* as a homosexual prostitute may be only an *asmakhta*. Moreover, there are other opinions in talmudic literature as to the meaning of the verse: see Onkelos, Lev 23:18, and Naḥmanides and *Torah Temimah, ad loc.*)

Talmudic Approach

Rabbinic exegesis of the Bible finds several other homosexual references in the scriptural narratives. The generation of Noah was condemned to eradication by the Flood because they had sunk so low morally that, according to midrashic teaching, they wrote out formal marriage contracts for sodomy and buggery—a possible cryptic reference to such practices in the Rome of Nero and Hadrian (Lev. R. 18:13).

Of Ham, the son of Noah, we are told that "he saw the nakedness of his father" and told his two brothers (Gen. 9:22). Why should this act have warranted the harsh imprecation hurled at Ham by his father? The Rabbis offer two answers: one, that the text implied that Ham castrated Noah: second, that the biblical expression is an idiom for homosexual intercourse (see Rashi, *ad loc.*). On the scriptural story of Potiphar's purchase of Joseph as a slave (Gen. 39:1), the Talmud comments that he acquired him for homosexual purposes, but that a miracle occurred and God sent the angel Gabriel to castrate Potiphar (Sot. 13b).

Post-biblical literature records remarkably few incidents of homosexuality. Herod's son Alexander, according to Josephus (Wars, I, 24:7), had homosexual contact with a young eunuch. Very few reports of homosexuality have come to us from the talmudic era (TJ Sanh. 6:6, 23c: Jos. Ant., 15:25-30).

The incidence of sodomy among Jews is interestingly reflected in the *halakhah* on *mishkav zakhur* (the talmudic term for homosexuality: the Bible uses various terms—thus the same term in Num. 31:17 and 35 refers to heterosexual intercourse by a woman, whereas the expression for male homosexual intercourse in Lev. 18:22 and 20:13 is *mishkevei ishah*). The Mishnah teaches that R. Judah forbade two bachelors from sleeping under the same blanket, for fear that this would lead to homosexual temptation (Kid. 4:14). However, the Sages permitted it (*ibid.*) because homosexuality was so rare among Jews that such preventive legislation was considered unnecessary (Kid. 82a). This latter view is codified as *halakhah* by Maimonides (Yad, *Issurei Bi'ah* 22:2). Some 400 years later, R. Joseph Caro, who did not codify the law against sodomy proper, nevertheless cautioned against being alone with another male because of the lewdness prevalent "in our times" (*Even ha-Ezer* 24). About a hundred years later, R. Joel Sirkes reverted to the original ruling, and suspended the prohibition because such obscene acts were unheard of amongst Polish Jewry (*Bayit Ḥadash* to Tur, *Even ha-Ezer* 24). Indeed, a distinguished contemporary of R. Joseph Caro, R. Solomon Luria, went even further and declared homosexuality so very rare that, if one refrains from sharing a blanket with another male as a special act of piety, one is guilty of self-righteous pride or religious snobbism (for the above and additional authorities, see *Oẓar ha-Posekim*, IX, 236-238).

Responsa

As is to be expected, the responsa literature is also very scant in discussions of homosexuality. One of the few such responsa is by the late R. Abraham Isaac Ha-Kohen Kook, when he was still the rabbi of Jaffa. In 1912 he was asked about a ritual slaughterer who had come under suspicion of homosexuality. After weighing all aspects of the case, R. Kook dismissed the charges against the accused, considering them unsupported hearsay. Furthermore, he maintained the man might have repented and therefore could not be subject to sanctions at the present time.

The very scarcity of halakhic deliberations on homosexuality, and the quite explicit insistence of various halakhic authorities, provide sufficient evidence of the relative absence of this practice among Jews from ancient times down to the present. Indeed, Prof. Kinsey found that, while religion was usually an influence of secondary importance on the number of homosexual as well as heterosexual acts by males, Orthodox Jews proved an exception, homosexuality being phenomenally rare among them.

Jewish law treated the female homosexual more leniently than the male. It considered lesbianism as *issur*, an ordinary religious violation, rather than *arayot*, a specifically sexual infraction, regarded much more severely than *issur*. R. Huna held that lesbianism is the equivalent of harlotry and disqualified the woman from marrying a priest. The *halakhah* is, however, more lenient, and decides that while the act is prohibited, the lesbian is not punished and is permitted to marry a priest (Sifra 9:8: Shab. 65a: Yev. 76a). However, the transgression does warrant disciplinary flagellation (Maimonides, Yad, *Issurei Bi'ah* 21:8). The less punitive attitude of the *halakhah* to the female homosexual than to the male does not reflect any intrinsic judgment on one as opposed to the other, but is rather the result of a halakhic technicality: there is no explicit biblical proscription of lesbianism, and the act does not entail genital intercourse (Maimonides, *loc. cit.*).

The *halakhah* holds that the ban on homosexuality applies universally, to non-Jew as well as to Jew (Sanh. 58a: Maimonides, *Melakhim* 9:5, 6). It is one of the six instances of *arayot* (sexual transgressions) forbidden to the Noachide (Maimonides, *ibid*).

Most halakhic authorities—such as Rashba and Ritba—agree with Maimonides. A minority opinion holds that pederasty and buggery are "ordinary" prohibitions rather than *arayot*—specifically sexual infractions which demand that one submit to martyrdom rather than violate the law—but the Jerusalem Talmud supports the majority opinion. (See D. M. Krozer, *Devar Ha-Melekh*, I, 22, 23 (1962), who also suggests that Maimonides may support a distinction whereby the "male" or active homosexual partner is held in violation of *arayot*, whereas the passive or "female" partner transgresses *issur*, an ordinary prohibition.)

Reasons for Prohibition

Why does the Torah forbid homosexuality? Bearing in mind that reasons proferred for the various commandments are not to be accepted as determinative, but as human efforts to explain immutable divine law, the rabbis of the Talmud and later talmudists did offer a number of illuminating rationales for the law.

As stated, the Torah condemns homosexuality as *to'evah*, an abomination. The Talmud records the interpretation of Bar Kapparah who, in a play on words, defined *to'evah* as *to'eh attah bah.* "You are going astray because of it" (Ned. 51a). The exact meaning of this passage is unclear, and various explanations have been put forward.

The *Pesikta (Zutarta)* explains the statement of Bar Kapparah as referring to the impossibility of such a sexual act resulting in procreation. One of the major functions (if not the major purpose) of sexuality is reproduction, and this reason for man's sexual endowment is frustrated by *mishkav zakhur* (so too *Sefer ha-Hinnukh,* no. 209).

Another interpretation is that of the *Tosafot* and R. Asher ben Jehiel (in their commentaries to Ned. 51a) which applies the "going astray" or wandering to the homosexual's abandoning his wife. In other words, the abomination consists of the danger that a married man with homosexual tendencies may disrupt his family life in order to indulge his perversions. Saadiah Gaon holds the rational basis of most of the Bible's moral legislation to the preservation of the family structure (*Emunot ve-De'ot* 3:1: cf. Yoma. 9a). (This argument assumes contemporary cogency in the light of the avowed aim of some gay militants to destroy the family, which they consider an "oppressive institution.")

A third explanation is given by a modern scholar, Rabbi Baruch Ha-Levi Epstein (*Torah Temimah* to Lev. 18:22), who emphasizes the unnaturalness of the homosexual liaison: "You are going astray from the foundations of the creation." *Mishkav zakhur* defies the very structure of the anatomy of the sexes, which quite obviously was designed for heterosexual relationships.

It may be, however, that the very variety of interpretations of *to'evah* points to a far more fundamental meaning, namely, that an act characterized as an "abomination" is *prima facie* disgusting and cannot be further defined or explained. Certain acts are considered *to'evah* by the Torah, and there the matter rests. It is, as it were, a visceral reaction, an intuitive disqualification of the act, and we run the risk of distorting the biblical judgment if we rationalize it. *To'evah* constitutes a category of objectionableness *sui generis:* it is a primary phenomenon. (This lends additional force to Rabbi David Z. Hoffmann's contention that *to'evah* is used by the Torah to indicate the repulsiveness of a proscribed act, no matter how much it may be in vogue among advanced and sophisticated cultures: see his *Sefer Va-yikra,* II, p.54.)

Jewish Attitudes

It is on the basis of the above that an effort must be made to formulate a Jewish response to the problems of homosexuality in the conditions under which most Jews live today, namely, those of free and democratic societies and, with the exception of Israel, non-Jewish lands and traditions.

Four general approaches may be adopted:

1) REPRESSIVE. No leniency toward the homosexual, lest the moral fiber of the rest of society be weakened.

2) PRACTICAL. Dispense with imprisonment and all forms of social harassment, for eminently practical and prudent reasons.

3) PERMISSIVE. The same as the above, but for ideological reasons, viz., the acceptance of homosexuality as a legitimate alternative "life-style."

4) PSYCHOLOGICAL. Homosexuality, in at least some forms, should be recognized as a disease and this recognition must determine our attitude toward the homosexual.

Let us now consider each of these critically.

Repressive Attitude. Exponents of the most stringent approach hold that pederasts are the vanguard of moral malaise, especially in our society. For one thing, they are dangerous to children. According to a recent work, one third of the homosexuals in the study were seduced in their adolescence by adults. It is best for society that they be imprisoned, and if our present penal institutions are faulty, let them be improved. Homosexuals should certainly not be permitted to function as teachers, group leaders, rabbis, or in any other capacity where they might be models for, and come into close contact with, young people. Homosexuality must not be excused as a sickness. A sane society assumes that its members have free choice, and are therefore responsible for their conduct. Sex offenders, including homosexuals, according to another recent study, operate "at a primate level with the philosophy that necessity is the mother of improvisation." As Jews who believe that the Torah legislated certain moral laws for all mankind, it is incumbent upon us to encourage all societies, including non-Jewish ones, to implement the Noachide laws. And since, according to the *halakhah*, homosexuality is prohibited to Noachides as well as to Jews, we must seek to strengthen the moral quality of society by encouraging more restrictive laws against homosexuals. Moreover, if we are loyal to the teachings of Judaism, we cannot distinguish between "victimless" crimes and crimes of violence. Hence, if our concern for the moral life of the community impels us to speak out against murder, racial oppression, or robbery, we must do no less with regard to sodomy.

This argument is, however, weak on a number of grounds. Practically, it fails to take into cognizance the number of homosexuals of all categories, which, as we have pointed out, is vast. We cannot possibly imprison all offenders, and it is a manifest miscarriage of justice to vent our spleen only on the few unfortunates who are caught by the police. It is inconsistent, because there has been no comparable outcry for harsh sentencing of other transgressors of sexual morality, such as those who indulge in adultery or incest. To take consistency to its logical conclusion, this hard line on homosexuality should not stop with imprisonment but demand the death sentence, as is biblically prescribed. And why not the same death sentence for blasphemy, eating a limb torn from a live animal, idolatry, robbery—all of which are Noachide commandments? And why not capital punishment for Sabbath transgressors in the State of Israel? Why should the pederast be singled out for opprobrium and be made an object lesson while all others escape?

Those who might seriously consider such logically consistent, but socially destructive, strategies had best think back to the fate of that Dominican reformer, the monk Girolamo Savonarola, who in 15th-century Florence undertook a fanatical campaign against vice and all suspected of venal sin, with emphasis on pederasty. The society of that time and place, much like ours, could stand vast improvement. But too much medicine in too strong doses was the monk's prescription, whereupon the population rioted and the zealot was hanged.

Finally, there is indeed some halakhic warrant for distinguishing between violent and victimless (or consensual and non-consensual) crimes. Thus, the Talmud permits a passer-by to kill a man in pursuit of another man or of a woman when the pursuer is attempting homosexual or heterosexual rape, as the case may be, whereas this is not permitted in the case of a transgressor pursuing an animal to commit buggery or on his way to worship an idol or to violate the Sabbath, (Sanh. 8:7, and v. Rashi to Sanh. 73a, s.v. al ha-behemah).

Practical Attitude. The practical approach is completely pragmatic and attempts to steer clear of any ideology in its judgments and recommendations. It is, according to its advocates, eminently reasonable. Criminal laws requiring punishment for homosexuals are simply unenforceable in society at the present day. We have previously cited the statistics on the extremely high incidence of pederasty in our society. Kinsey once said of the many sexual acts outlawed by the various states, that, were they all enforced, some 95% of men in the United States would be in jail. Furthermore, the special prejudice of law enforcement authorities against homosexuals—rarely does one hear of police entrapment or of jail sentences for non-violent heterosexuals—breeds a grave injustice: namely, it is an invitation to blackmail. The law concerning sodomy has been called "the blackmailer's charter." It is universally agreed that prison does little to help the homosexual rid himself of his peculiarity. Certainly, the failure of rehabilitation ought to be of concern to civilized men. But even if it is not, and the crime be considered so serious that incarceration is deemed advisable even in the absence of any real chances of rehabilitation, the casual pederast almost always leaves prison as a confirmed criminal. He has been denied the company of women and forced into the society of those whose sexual expression is almost always channeled to pederasty. The casual pederast has become a habitual one: his homosexuality has now been ingrained in him. Is society any safer for having taken an errant man and, in the course of a few years, for having taught him to transform his deviancy into a hard and fast perversion, then turning him loose on the community? Finally, from a Jewish point of view, since it is obviously impossible for us to impose the death penalty for sodomy, we may as well act on purely practical grounds and do away with all legislation and punishment in this area of personal conduct.

This reasoning is tempting precisely because it focuses directly on the problem and is free of any ideological commitments. But the problem with it is that it is too smooth, too easy. By the same reasoning one might, in a *reductio ad absurdum* do away with all laws on income tax evasion, or forgive, and dispense with all punishment of Nazi murders. Furthermore, the last element leaves us with a novel view of the *halakhah*: if it cannot be implemented in its entirety, it ought to be abandoned completely. Surely the Noachide laws, perhaps above all others, place us under clear moral imperatives, over and above purely penological instructions? The very practicality of this position leaves it open to the charge of evading the very real moral issues, and for Jews the halakhic principles, entailed in any discussion of homosexuality.

Permissive Attitude. The ideological advocacy of a completely permissive attitude toward consensual homosexuality and the acceptance of its moral legitimacy is, of course, the "in" fashion in sophisticated liberal circles. Legally, it holds that deviancy is none of the law's business; the homosexuals' civil rights are as sacred as those of any other "minority group." From the psychological angle, sexuality must be emancipated from the fetters of guilt induced by religion and code-morality, and its idiosyncratic nature must be confirmed.

Gay Liberationists aver that the usual "straight" attitude toward homosexuality is based on three fallacies or myths: that homosexuality is an illness; that it is unnatural; and that it is immoral. They argue that it cannot be considered an illness, because so many people have been shown to practice it. It is not unnatural, because its alleged unnaturalness derives from the impossibility of sodomy leading to reproduction, whereas our overpopulated society no longer needs to breed workers, soldiers, farmers, or hunters. And it is not immoral, first, because morality is relative, and secondly, because moral behavior is that which is characterized by "selfless, loving concern."

Now, we are here concerned with the sexual problem as such, and not with homosexuality as a symbol of the whole contemporary ideological polemic against restraint and tradition. Homosexuality is too important—and too agonizing—a human problem to allow it to be exploited for political aims or entertainment or shock value.

The bland assumption that pederasty cannot be considered an illness because of the large number of people who have or express homosexual tendencies cannot stand up under criticism. No less an authority than Freud taught that a whole civilization can be neurotic. Erich Fromm appeals for the establishment of *The Sane Society*—because ours is not. If the majority of a nation are struck down by typhoid fever, does this condition, by so curious a calculus of semantics, become healthy? Whether or not homosexuality can be considered an illness is a serious question, and it does depend on one's definition of health and illness. But mere statistics are certainly not the *coup de grace* to the psychological argument, which will be discussed shortly.

The validation of gay life as "natural" on the basis of changing social and economic conditions is an act of verbal obfuscation. Even if we were to concur with the widely held feeling that the world's population is dangerously large, and that Zero Population Growth is now a desideratum, the anatomical fact remains unchanged: the generative organs are structured for generation. If the words "natural" and "unnatural" have any meaning at all, they must be rooted in the unchanging reality of man's sexual apparatus rather than in his ephemeral social configurations.

Militant feminists along with the gay activists react vigorously against the implication that natural structure implies the naturalness or unnaturalness of certain acts, but this very view has recently been confirmed by one of the most informed writers on the subject. "It is already pretty safe to infer from laboratory research and ethological parallels that male and female are wired in ways that relate to our traditional sex roles. . .Freud dramatically said that anatomy is destiny. Scientists who shudder at the dramatic, no matter how accurate, could rephrase this: anatomy is functional, body functions have profound psychological meanings to people, and anatomy and function are often socially elaborated" (Arno Karlen, *Sexuality and Homosexuality*, p. 501).

The moral issues lead us into the quagmire of perennial philosophical disquisitions of a fundamental nature. In a way, this facilitates the problem for one seeking a Jewish view. Judaism does not accept the kind of thoroughgoing relativism used to justify the gay life as merely an alternate life-style. And while the question of human autonomy is certainly worthy of consideration in the area of sexuality, one must beware of the consequences of taking the argument to its logical extreme. Judaism clearly cherishes holiness as a greater value than either freedom or health. Furthermore, if every individual's autonomy leads us to lend moral legitimacy to any form of sexual expression he may desire, we must be ready to pull the blanket of this moral validity over almost the whole catalogue of perversions described by Krafft-Ebing, and then, by the legerdemain of granting civil rights to the morally non-objectionable, permit the advocates of buggery, fetishism, or whatever to proselytize in public. In that case, why not in the school system? And if consent is obtained before the death of one partner, why not necrophilia or cannibalism? Surely, if we declare pederasty to be merely idiosyncratic and not an "abomination," what right have we to condemn sexually motivated cannibalism—merely because most people would react with revulsion and disgust?

"Loving, selfless concern" and "meaningful personal relationships"—the great slogans of the New Morality and the exponents of situation ethics—have become the litany of sodomy in our times. Simple logic should permit us to use the same criteria for excusing adultery or any other act heretofore held to be immoral; and indeed, that is just what has been done, and it has received the sanction not only of liberals and humanists, but of certain religionists as well. "Love," "fulfillment," "exploitative," "meaningful"—the list itself sounds like a lexicon of emotionally charged terms drawn at random from the disparate sources of both Christian and psychologically-oriented agnostic circles. Logically, we must ask the next question: what moral depravities can not be excused by the sole criterion of "warm, meaningful human relations" or "fulfillment," the newest semantic heirs to "love?"

Love, fulfillment, and happiness can also be attained in incestuous contacts—and certainly in polygamous relationships. Is there nothing at all left that is "sinful," "unnatural," or "immoral" if it is practiced "between two consenting adults?" For religious groups to aver that a homosexual relationship should be judged by the same criteria as a heterosexual one—i.e., "whether it is intended to foster a permanent relationship of love"—is to abandon the last claim of representing the "Judeo-Christian tradition."

I have elsewhere essayed a criticism of the situationalists, their use of the term "love," and their objections to traditional morality as exemplified by the *halakhah* as "mere legalism" (see my *Faith and Doubt*, chapter IX, p. 249 ff.). Situationalists, such as Joseph Fletcher, have especially attacked "pilpulistic Rabbis" for remaining entangled in the coils of statutory and legalistic hairsplitting. Among the other things this typically Christian polemic reveals is an ignorance of the nature of *halakhah* and its place in Judaism, which never held that the law was the totality of life, pleaded again and again for supererogatory conduct, recognized that individuals may be disadvantaged by the law, and which strove to rectify what could be rectified without abandoning the large majority to legal and moral chaos simply because of the discomfiture of the few.

Clearly, while Judaism needs no defense or apology in regard to its esteem for neighborly love and compassion for the individual sufferer, it cannot possibly abide a wholesale dismissal of its most basic moral principles on the grounds that those subject to its judgments find them repressive. All laws are repressive to some extent—they repress illegal activities—and all morality is concerned with changing man and improving him and his society. Homosexuality imposes on one an intolerable burden of differentness, of absurdity, and of loneliness, but the biblical commandment outlawing pederasty cannot be put aside solely on the basis of sympathy for the victim of these feelings. Morality, too, is an element which each of us, given his sensuality, his own idiosyncracies, and his immoral proclivities, must take into serious consideration before acting out his impulses.

Psychological Attitudes. Several years ago I recommended that Jews regard homosexual deviance as a pathology, thus reconciling the insights of Jewish tradition with the exigencies of contemporary life and scientific information, such as it is, on the nature of homosexuality (N. Lamm, in: *Jewish Life*, Jan-Feb. 1968). The remarks that follow are an expansion and modification of that position, together with some new data and notions.

The proposal that homosexuality be viewed as an illness will immediately be denied by three groups of people. Gay militants object to this view as an instance of heterosexual condescension. Evelyn Hooker and her group of psychologists maintain that homosexuals are no more pathological in their personality structures than heterosexuals. And psychiatrists Thomas Szasz in the U.S. and Ronald Laing in England reject all traditional ideas of mental sickness and health as tools of social repressiveness or, at best, narrow conventionalism. While granting that there are indeed unfortunate instances where the category of mental disease is exploited for social or political reasons, we part company with all three groups and assume that there are a significant number of pederasts and lesbians who, by the criteria accepted by most psychologists and psychiatrists, can indeed be termed pathological. Thus, for instance, Dr. Albert Ellis, an ardent advocate of the right to deviancy, denies there is such a thing as a well-adjusted homosexual. In an interview, he has stated that whereas he used to believe that most homosexuals were neurotic, he is now convinced that about 50% are borderline psychotics, that the usual fixed male homosexual is a severe phobic, and that lesbians are even more disturbed than male homosexuals (see Karlen, *op. cit.*, p. 223 ff.).

No single cause of homosexuality has been established. In all probability, it is based on a conglomeration of a number of factors. There is overwhelming evidence that the condition is developmental, not constitutional. Despite all efforts to discover something genetic in homosexuality, no proof has been adduced, and researchers incline more and more to reject the Freudian concept of fundamental human biological bisexuality and its corollary of homosexual latency. It is now widely believed that homosexuality is the result of a whole family constellation. The passive, dependent, phobic male homosexual is usually the product of an aggressive, covertly seductive mother who is overly rigid and puritanical with her son—thus forcing him into a bond where he is sexually aroused, yet forbidden to express himself in any heterosexual way—and of a father who is absent, remote, emotionally detached, or hostile (I. Bieber *et al, Homosexuality,* 1962).

Can the homosexual be cured? There is a tradition of therapeutic pessimism that goes back to Freud' but a number of psychoanalysts, including Freud's daughter Anna, have reported successes in treating homosexuals as any other phobics (in this case, fear of the female genitals). It is generally accepted that about a third of all homosexuals can be completely cured: behavioral therapists report an even larger number of cures.

Of course, one cannot say categorically that all homosexuals are sick—any more than one can casually define all thieves as kleptomaniacs. In order to develop a reasonable Jewish approach to the problem and to seek in the concept of illness some mitigating factor, it is necessary first to establish the main types of homosexuals. Dr. Judd Marmor speaks of four categories. "Genuine homosexuality" is based on strong preferential erotic feelings for members of the same sex. "Transitory homosexual behavior" occurs among adolescents who would prefer heterosexual experiences but are denied such opportunities because of social, cultural, or psychological reasons. "Situational homosexual exchanges" are characteristic of prisoners, soldiers, and others who are heterosexual but are denied access to women for long periods of time. "Transitory and opportunistic homosexuality" is that of delinquent young men who permit themselves to be used by pederasts in order to make money or win other favors, although their primary erotic interests are exclusively heterosexual. To these may be added, for purposes of our analysis, two other types. The first category, that of genuine homosexuals, may be said to comprehend two sub-categories: those who experience their condition as one of duress or uncontrollable passion which they would rid themselves of if they could, and those who transform their idiosyncracy into an ideology, i.e., the gay militants who assert the legitimacy and validity of homosexuality as an alternative way to heterosexuality. The sixth category is based on what Dr. Rollo May has called "the New Puritanism," the peculiarly modern notion that one must experience all sexual pleasures, whether or not one feels inclined to them, as if the failure to taste every cup passed at the sumptuous banquet of carnal life means that one has not truly lived. Thus, we have transitory homosexual behavior not of adolescents, but of *adults* who feel that they must "try everything" at least once or more than once in their lives.

A Possible Halakhic Solution

This rubric will now permit us to apply the notion of disease (and, from the halakhic point of view, of its opposite, moral culpability) to the various types of sodomy. Clearly, genuine homosexuality experienced under duress (Hebrew: *ones*) most obviously lends itself to being termed pathological, especially where dysfunction appears in other aspects of the personality. Opportunistic homosexuality, ideological homosexuality, and transitory adult homosexuality are at the other end of the spectrum, and appear most reprehensible. As for the intermediate categories, while they cannot be called illness, they do have a greater claim on our sympathy than the three types mentioned above.

In formulating the notion of homosexuality as a disease, we are not asserting the formal halakhic definition of mental illness as mental incompetence, as described in TB Hag. 3b, 4a, and elsewhere. Furthermore, the categorization of a prohibited sex act as *ones* (duress) because of uncontrolled passions is valid, in a technical halakhic sense, only for a married woman who was ravished and who, in the course of the act, became a willing participant. The *halakhah* decides with Rava, against the father of Samuel, that her consent is considered duress because of the passions aroused in her (Ket. 51b). However, this holds true only if the act was initially entered into under physical compulsion (*Kesef Mishneh* to Yad, Sanh. 20:3). Moreover, the claim of compulsion by one's erotic passions is not valid for a male, for any erection is considered a token of his willingness (Yev. 53b: Maimonides, Yad, Sanh. 20:3). In the case of a male who was forced to cohabit with a woman forbidden to him, some authorities consider him guilty and punishable, while others hold him guilty but not subject to punishment by the courts (Tos., Yev. 53b: Ḥinnukh, 556; *Kesef Mishneh, loc. cit.: Maggid Mishneh* to *Issurei Bi'ah*, 1:9). Where a male is sexually aroused in a permissible manner, as to begin coitus with his wife, and is then forced to conclude the act with another woman, most authorities exonerate him (Rabad and *Maggid Mishneh,* to *Issurei Bi'ah,* in *loc.*). If, now, the warped family background of the genuine homosexual is considered *ones,* the homosexual act may possibly lay claim to some mitigation by the *halakhah.* (However, see *Minḥat Ḥinnukh,* 556, end; and M. Feinstein, *Iggerot Mosheh* (1973) on YD, No. 59, who holds, in a different context, that any pleasure derived from a forbidden act performed under duress increases the level of prohibition. This was anticipated by R. Joseph Engel, *Atvan de-Oraita,* 24.) These latter sources indicate the difficulty of exonerating sexual transgressors because of psychopathological reasons under the technical rules of the *halakhah.*

However, in the absence of a Sanhedrin and since it is impossible to implement the whole halakhic penal system, including capital punishment, such strict applications are unnecessary. What we are attempting is to develop guidelines, based on the *halakhah,* which will allow contemporary Jews to orient themselves to the current problems of homosexuality in a manner articulating with the most fundamental insights of the *halakhah* in a general sense, and consistent with the broadest world-view that the halakhic commitment instills in its followers. Thus, the aggadic statement that "no man sins unless he is overcome by a spirit of madness" (Sot. 3a) is not an operative halakhic rule, but does offer guidance on public policy and individual pastoral compassion. So in the present case, the formal halakhic strictures do not in any case apply nowadays, and it is our contention that the aggadic principle must lead us to seek out the mitigating halakhic elements so as to guide us in our orientation to homosexuals who, by the standards of modern psychology, may be regarded as acting under compulsion.

To apply the *halakhah* strictly in this case is obviously impossible; to ignore it entirely is undesirable, and tantamount to regarding *halakhah* as a purely abstract, legalistic system which can safely be dismissed where its norms and prescriptions do not allow full formal implementation. Admittedly, the method is not rigorous, and leaves room for varying interpretations as well as exegetical abuse, but it is the best we can do.

Hence there are types of homosexuality that do not warrant any special considerateness, because the notion of *ones* or duress (i.e., disease) in no way applies. Where the category of mental illness does apply, the act itself remains *to'evah* (an abomination), but the fact of illness lays upon us the obligation of pastoral compassion, psychological understanding, and social sympathy. In this sense, homosexuality is no different from any other anti-social or anti-halakhic act, where it is legitimate to distinguish between the objective act itself, including its social and moral consequences, and the mentality and inner development of the person who perpetrates the act. For instance, if a man murders in a cold and calculating fashion for reasons of profit, the act is criminal and the transgressor is criminal. If, however, a psychotic murders, the transgressor is diseased rather than criminal, but the objective act itself remains a criminal one. The courts may therefore treat the perpetrator of the crime as they would a patient, with all the concomitant compassion and concern for therapy, without condoning the act as being morally neutral. To use halakhic terminology, the objective crime remains a *ma'aseh averah*, whereas the person who transgresses is considered innocent on the grounds of *ones*. In such cases, the transgressor is spared the full legal consequences of his culpable act, although the degree to which he may be held responsible varies from case to case.

An example of a criminal act that is treated with compassion by the *halakhah*, which in practice considers the act pathological rather than criminal, is suicide. Technically, the suicide or attempted suicide is in violation of the law. The *halakhah* denies to the suicide the honor of a eulogy, the rending of the garments by relatives or witnesses to the death, and (according to Maimonides) insists that the relatives are not to observe the usual mourning period for the suicide. Yet, in the course of time, the tendency has been to remove the stigma from the suicide on the basis of mental disease. Thus, halakhic scholars do not apply the technical category of intentional (*la-da'at*) suicide to one who did not clearly demonstrate, before performing the act, that he knew what he was doing and was of sound mind, to the extent that there was no hiatus between the act of self-destruction and actual death. If these conditions are not present, we assume that it was an insane act or that between the act and death he experienced pangs of contrition and is therefore repentant, hence excused before the law. There is even one opinion which exonerates the suicide unless he received adequate warning (*hatra'ah*) before performing the act, and responded in a manner indicating that he was fully aware of what he was doing and that he was lucid (J. M. Tykocinski, *Gesher ha-Hayyim*, I, ch. 25, and *Encyclopaedia Judaica*, 15: 490).

Admittedly, there are differences between the two cases: pederasty is clearly a severe violation of biblical law, whereas the stricture against suicide is derived exegetically from a verse in Genesis. Nevertheless, the principle operative in the one is applicable to the other: where one can attribute an act to mental illness, it is done out of simple humanitarian considerations.

The suicide analogy should not, of course, lead one to conclude that there are grounds for a blanket exculpation of homosexuality as mental illness. Not all forms of homosexuality can be so termed, as indicated above, and the act itself remains an "abomination." With few exceptions, most people do not ordinarily propose that suicide be considered an acceptable and legitimate alternative to the rigors of daily life. No sane and moral person sits passively and watches a fellow man attempt suicide because he "understands" him and because it has been decided that suicide is a "morally neutral" act. By the same token, in orienting ourselves to certain types of homosexuals as patients rather than criminals, we do not condone the act but attempt to help the homosexual. Under no circumstances can Judaism suffer homosexuality to become respectable. Were society to give its open or even tacit approval to homosexuality, it would invite more aggressiveness on the part of adult pederasts toward young people. Indeed, in the currently permissive atmosphere, the Jewish view would summon us to the semantic courage of referring to homosexuality not as "deviance," with the implication of moral neutrality and non-judgmental idiosyncracy, but as "perversion"—a less clinical and more old-fashioned word, perhaps, but one that is more in keeping with the biblical *to'evah*.

Yet, having passed this moral judgment, we cannot in the name of Judaism necessarily demand that we strive for the harshest possible punishment. Even where it was halakhically feasible to execute capital punishment, we have a tradition of leniency. Thus, R. Akiva and R. Tarfon declared that had they lived during the time of the Sanhedrin, they never would have executed a man. Although the *halakhah* does not decide in their favor (Mak. end of ch. I), it was rare indeed that the death penalty was actually imposed. Usually, the biblically mandated penalty was regarded as an index of the severity of the transgression, and the actual execution was avoided by strict insistence upon all technical requirements—such as *hatra'ah* (forewarning the potential criminal) and rigorous cross-examination of witnesses, etc. In the same spirit, we are not bound to press for the most punitive policy toward contemporary lawbreakers. We are required to lead them to rehabilitation (*teshuvah*). The *halakhah* sees no contradiction between condemning a man to death and exercising compassion, even love, toward him (Sanh. 52a). Even a man on the way to his execution was encouraged to repent (Sanh. 6:2). In the absence of a death penalty, the tradition of *teshuvah* and pastoral compassion to the sinner continues.

I do not find any warrant in the Jewish tradition for insisting on prison sentences for homosexuals. The singling-out of homosexuals as the victims of society's righteous indignation is patently unfair. In Western history, anti-homosexual crusades have too often been marked by cruelty, destruction, and bigotry. Imprisonment in modern times has proven to be extremely haphazard. The number of homosexuals unfortunate enough to be apprehended is infinitesimal as compared to the number of known homosexuals; estimates vary from one to 300,000 to one to 6,000,000! For homosexuals to be singled out for special punishment while all the rest of society indulges itself in every other form of sexual malfeasance (using the definitions of *halakhah*, not the New Morality) is a species of double-standard morality that the spirit of *halakhah* cannot abide. Thus, the Mishnah declares that the "scroll of the suspected adulteress" (*megillat sotah*)—whereby a wife suspected of adultery was forced to undergo the test of "bitter waters"—was cancelled when the Sages became aware of the ever-larger number of adulterers in general (Sot. 9:9). The Talmud bases this decision on an aversion to the double standard: if the husband is himself an adulterer, the "bitter waters" will have no effect on his wife, even though she too be guilty of the offense (Sot. 47b). By the same token, a society in which heterosexual immorality is not conspicuously absent has no moral right to sit in stern judgment and mete out harsh penalties to homosexuals.

Furthermore, sending a homosexual to prison is counterproductive if punishment is to contain any element of rehabilitation or *teshuvah*. It has rightly been compared to sending an alcoholic to a distillery. The Talmud records that the Sanhedrin was unwilling to apply the full force of the law where punishment had lost its quality of deterrence; thus, 40 (or four) years before the destruction of the Temple, the Sanhedrin voluntarily left the precincts of the Temple so as not to be able, technically, to impose the death sentence, because it had noticed the increasing rate of homicide (Sanh. 41a, and elsewhere).

There is nothing in the Jewish law's letter or spirit that should incline us toward advocacy of imprisonment for homosexuals. The *halakhah* did not, by and large, encourage the denial of freedom as a recommended form of punishment. Flogging is, from a certain perspective, far less cruel and far more enlightened. Since capital punishment is out of the question, and since incarceration is not an advisable substitute, we are left with one absolute minimum: strong disapproval of the proscribed act. But we are not bound to any specific penological instrument that has no basis in Jewish law or tradition.

How shall this disapproval be expressed? It has been suggested that, since homosexuality will never attain acceptance anyway, society can afford to be humane. As long as violence and the seduction of children are not involved, it would be best to abandon all laws on homosexuality and leave it to the inevitable social sanctions to control, informally, what can be controlled.

However, this approach is not consonant with Jewish tradition. The repeal of anti-homosexual laws implies the removal of the stigma from homosexuality, and this diminution of social censure weakens society in its training of the young toward acceptable patterns of conduct. The absence of adequate social reproach may well encourage the expression of homosexual tendencies by those in whom they might otherwise be suppressed. Law itself has an educative function, and the repeal of laws, no matter how justifiable such repeal may be from one point of view, does have the effect of signaling the acceptability of greater permissiveness.

Some New Proposals

Perhaps all that has been said above can best be expressed in the proposals that follow.

First, society and government must recognize the distinctions between the various categories enumerated earlier in this essay. It must offer its medical and psychological assistance to those whose homosexuality is an expression of pathology, who recognize it as such, and are willing to seek help. We must be no less generous to the homosexual than to the drug addict, to whom the government extends various forms of therapy upon request.

Second, jail sentences must be abolished for all homosexuals, save those who are guilty of violence, seduction of the young, or public solicitation.

Third, the laws must remain on the books, but by mutual consent of judiciary and police, be unenforced. This approximates to what lawyers call "the chilling effect," and is the nearest one can come to the category so well known in the *halakhah*, whereby strong disapproval is expressed by affirming a halakhic prohibition, yet no punishment is mandated. It is a category that bridges the gap between morality and law. In a society where homosexuality is so rampant, and where incarceration is so counterproductive, this hortatory approach may well be a way of formalizing society's revulsion while avoiding the pitfalls in our accepted penology.

For the Jewish community as such, the same principles, derived from the tradition, may serve as guidelines. Judaism allows for no compromise in its abhorrence of sodomy, but encourages both compassion and efforts at rehabilitation. Certainly, there must be no acceptance of separate Jewish homosexual societies, such as—or especially—synagogues set aside as homosexual congregations. The first such "gay synagogue," apparently, was the "Beth Chayim Chadashim" in Los Angeles. Spawned by that city's Metropolitan Community Church in March 1972, the founding group constituted itself as a Reform congregation with the help of the Pacific Southwest Council of the Union of American Hebrew Congregations some time in early 1973. Thereafter, similar groups surfaced in New York City and elsewhere. The original group meets on Friday evenings in the Leo Baeck Temple and is searching for a rabbi—who must himself be "gay". The membership sees itself as justified by "the Philosophy of Reform Judaism." The Temple president declared that God is "more concerned in our finding a sense of peace in which to make a better world, than He is in whom someone sleeps with" (cited in "Judaism and Homosexuality," *C.C.A.R. Journal*, Summer 1973, p. 38; five articles in this issue of the Reform group's rabbinic journal are devoted to the same theme, and most of them approve of the Gay Synagogue).

But such reasoning is specious, to say the least. Regular congregations and other Jewish groups should not hesitate to accord hospitality and membership, on an individual basis, to those "visible" homosexuals who qualify for the category of the ill. Homosexuals are no less in violation of Jewish norms than Sabbath desecrators or those who disregard the laws of *kashrut*. But to assent to the organization of separate "gay" groups under Jewish auspices makes no more sense, Jewishly, than to suffer the formation of synagogues that cater exclusively to idol worshipers, adulterers, gossipers, tax evaders, or Sabbath violators. Indeed, it makes less sense, because it provides, under religious auspices, a ready-made clientele from which the homosexual can more easily choose his partners.

In remaining true to the sources of Jewish tradition, Jews are commanded to avoid the madness that seizes society at various times and in many forms, while yet retaining a moral composure and psychological equilibrium sufficient to exercise that combination of discipline and charity that is the hallmark of Judaism.

The Holocaust

At first glance it might not seem wholly appropriate to include a discussion of the Nazi Holocaust in a text on Jewish ethics. The questions ultimately posed by the Holocaust are theological questions: it is the existence of God which is finally questioned, not only the goodness of God. Moreover, whatever ethical questions are raised by the Holocaust—questions of political obedience, of self-sacrifice, of martyrdom, etc.—could be discussed in other contexts.

To argue in this fashion, however, is to ignore the special character of the Holocaust and the impact it has had on Jewish thinking. Further, there were ethical questions raised by the Holocaust, the Jewish tradition was brought to bear on them, and they deserve separate treatment.

In the selections reproduced here, Irving Rosenbaum explains how it is that ethical questions were asked during the Holocaust and gives examples of some of them. Alexander Donat deals with the relative merits of resistance and martyrdom, or, put more correctly, the relative merits of spiritual and physical resistance. He argues passionately that martyrdom cannot be equated with submissiveness or cowardice, and that the Jews did resist the Nazis, both spiritually and physically. He also raises one of the central moral issues of the Holocaust: the silence of the "civilized" world.

27

Holocaust and Halakhah

IRVING J. ROSENBAUM

It has become almost an article of faith that the Holocaust was without precedent in Jewish experience. It was not! But the mistaken assumption that it was has not only spawned an entire literature of "Holocaust theology," but also has been responsible for an almost total unawareness of the role played by the Halakhah in the lives and deaths of the Holocaust's victims. It has been estimated that more than half of the millions of Jews caught up in the Holocaust observed the *mitzvot*, the commandments of the Torah, in their daily lives prior to the advent of the Nazis.[1] Did this commitment to the Halakhah, the "way" of Jewish religious law, crumble and disintegrate under the pressures of the "final solution"? Or did the Halakhah continue to bring not only some semblance of order, but of meaning, sanity, and even sanctity into their lives?

Precisely because the Holocaust was not without precedent, and because the Halakhah had confronted, dealt with, and transcended similar situations in the past, it was able to guide and sustain those who lived and died by it during the bitter and calamitous times of the German domination of Europe. While much of its technology was novel, the Holocaust simply duplicated on an extensive and enormous scale events which had occurred with melancholy regularity throughout Jewish history. The concept of the "final solution," it may be argued, differed in kind from earlier attempts at the destruction of Jews; but this could make little difference in the reaction of its victims, who were unaware of the comprehensive nature of the plan. Pillage, psychological degradation, exclusion from society, mass murder, mass graves, burning, torture, beatings, cremation, forced labor, imprisonment, death marches, infanticide, enforced prostitution, rape, and expulsion had all been experienced by Jewish communities in the past. Long, long before the Holocaust, the Halakhah had developed its theoretical "theology" and its practical course of action when confronted with such tragic events.

The Halakhah was, therefore, uniquely equipped to adjust to death and suffering as well as to life and joy. It would be blasphemous effrontery for anyone who did not himself experience the terrors and the madness of the Holocaust to speak rapturously of the supportive and sustaining power of the Halakhah during that insane and diabolical period. But the vivid and compelling testimony of survivors, the literary testaments of victims, even the eyewitness accounts of the SS and those in league with them, clearly indicate the significant and ennobling role of Jewish religious observance in the Holocaust kingdom. In the face of events which would make Job's trials seem trivial, Jews retained their confident belief in a just Creator, whose secret purposes they might not be able to fathom, but whose revealed and clear dictates in the Halakhah they were bound to observe.

But while the course of action prescribed by Jewish law under ordinary circumstances in normal times was clear to most observant Jews, even then, cases of an unusual or difficult nature required special rabbinic guidance. In such cases, especially when they had no obvious precedents or analogies in Talmudic or later Rabbinic literature, a *she'elah* (pl. *she'elot*)—a question—was directed to a rabbi whose halakhic competence was respected. His *teshuvah* (pl. *teshuvot*)—responsum—delineated the course of action he believed to be demanded by Jewish law.[2]

Thus, from the very beginning of the drastic changes in Jewish life instituted after the adoption of the Nuremberg Laws in Germany, *she'elot* began to proliferate. Incredible as it may seem, even in the death camps of Auschwitz and Dachau, and under the guns of the SS *Einzatzgruppen*[3] in the ghettos of Kovno and Warsaw, believing Jews inquired of their religious leaders as to what the Halakhah required of them.

The spectrum of their inquiries is as broad as the Halakhah itself. In this volume we shall examine a considerable number of these *she'elot u'teshuvot*, as well as the varying Holocaust matrices out of which they emerged. We shall also study anecdotal material concerning the tenacious adherence of observant Jews to halakhic norms under circumstances where no formal *she'elah* and *teshuvah* were possible—where the unspoken inquiry was directed to one's own tormented soul, and the response was received from the same source.

A study of this material cannot help but bring about not only an a-wareness of the all-embracing character of the Halakhah, which can speak to even the most bizarre and unimaginable aspects of the human condition, but also a recognition of the majesty of a system which elicited obedience in the fact of events which seemed to question the justice, if not the very existence, of its Author.

Perhaps the mind "set" out of which the she'elot of the Holocaust arose may be more clearly understood through the study of a moving episode described by Rabbi Zvi Hirsch Meisels in the foreword to his responsa volume, *Mekadeshei ha-Shem*.[4] Rabbi Meisels was the scion of a distinguished Hasidic and rabbinic family and was the *rav* of the city of Veitzen in Hungary. Before being transported to Auschwitz he had already achieved a considerable reputation as a halakhic scholar and was the author of a volume of responsa. After the liberation he was appointed chief rabbi of Bergen-Belsen and of the British sector, and was instrumental in clarifying the halakhic approaches permitting the remarriage of those whose spouses had been killed in the Holocaust.

He tells of the events which took place in Auschwitz on the eve of Rosh Hashanah in 1944. The Nazi commander of Auschwitz had determined to keep alive only those boys between the ages of fourteen and eighteen who were big enough and strong enough to work. The others would be sent to the crematorium. In the large "parade ground" behind the camp blocks some sixteen hundred boys who had hitherto managed to escape a *selektion* were assembled. The commander directed that a vertical post with a horizontal bar affixed at a predetermined height be planted in the ground. Each of the boys was forced to pass under the bar. Everyone whose head reached the horizontal bar was to be sent to a work detail. Those who were not tall enough were to be destroyed. Some youngsters, knowing what was intended, tried to stretch on their tiptoes to reach the bar and were bludgeoned to death on the spot. At the end of the *selektion*, the fourteen hundred boys who had not passed the "test" were imprisoned in a special cellblock under the guard of the Jewish *kapos*.[5] They were to receive no further food or drink, and it was understood that they would be sent to the crematorium the next night. Generally, the crematoria at Auschwitz were operated only during the night hours.

The next morning, the first day of Rosh Hashanah, fathers or other

relatives who had heard of the fate that awaited the children, tried to persuade the *kapos* to release them. The *kapos* replied that an exact count
had been taken of the boys, and they would have to pay with their own
lives if even one were to be found missing. Some of the relatives still had
valuables concealed in their clothing or on their bodies, and they offered
them to the *kapos* in return for the lives of their children. Even those who
had absolutely nothing with which to redeem their sons somehow
managed to secure small valuables from other prisoners who wished to
help. All that day of Rosh Hashanah the Jews clustered outside the doors
of the cellblock bargaining with the *kapos*. Succumbing to greed, the
kapos agreed to release some of the prisoners. But, they warned, for each
prisoner released they would have to seize some other Jewish boy who
had escaped the *selektion* or had managed to reach the bar, so that the
count would be full when the block's inmates were taken to the
crematoria.

Although they knew that their sons' lives would be spared only at the
cost of others, fathers made whatever deals they could to save their own
children. All this bargaining went on in full view of the camp inmates.
The SS guards, Rabbi Meisels writes, generally remained at the periphery
of Auschwitz and allowed the *kapos* to maintain control of the inner
blocks. While he was observing this mad trafficking in human life, Rabbi
Meisels was approached by a Jew from Oberland who said, "Rabbi, my
only son is in that cellblock. I have enough money to ransom him. But I
know for certain that if he is released, the *kapos* will take another in his
place to be killed. So, Rabbi, I ask of you a *she'elah le'halakhah
u'lema'aseh* (a question which demands an immediate response to an actual situation). Render a judgment in accordance with the Torah. May I
save his life at the expense of another? Whatever your ruling, I will obey
it."

Rabbi Meisels replied, "My beloved child: How can I determine the
Halakhah in such a grave matter under these conditions? Even when we
possessed the Holy Temple, a capital matter such as this required determination by a Sanhedrin. Here I am in Auschwitz, without any halakhic
source books, with no other rabbis with whom to consult, and without
the necessary clarity of mind because of these dreadful circumstances."
Rabbi Meisels reasoned that if the *kapos* were first to release the ransomed boy and then capture another in his place, the Halakhah might
possibly permit the father to redeem his child. This, because the *kapos*,

who, after all, were Jews, however degraded and corrupt, might somehow relent after releasing the first child and not attempt to take another. Where it is not absolutely certain that saving the one life will cost another, the Halakhah might not forbid the ransom attempt. But the *kapos*, fearful that the SS might come at any time and hold them responsible for the full count, made certain to sieze another victim before they would release the first. So, unable to give halakhic permission to the father, and unwilling to deny it, Rabbi Meisels continued to implore the Jew from Oberland not to ask his *she'elah*.

But the distraught father refused to accept Rabbi Meisel's evasions and said, "Rabbi, you must give me a definite answer while there is still time to save my son's life." Rabbi Meisels replied, "My dear and beloved Jew, please, I beg you, desist from asking me this *she'elah*. I cannot give you any kind of answer without consulting sources, especially under such fearful and terrible circumstances." The father responded, "Rabbi, this means that you can find no *heter*—permission—for me to ransom my only son. So be it. I accept this judgment in love." The rabbi continued to implore the man not to rely upon him. "Beloved Jew, I did not say that you could not ransom your child. I cannot rule either yes or no. Do what you wish as though you had never asked me." After much entreaty, the father finally said, "Rabbi, I have done what the Torah has obligated me to do. I have asked a *she'elah* of a *rav*. There is no other *rav* here. And if you cannot tell me that I may ransom my child, it is a sign that in your own mind, you are not certain that the Halakhah permits it. For if you were certain that it is permitted, you would unquestionably have told me so. So for me your evasion is tantamount to a *pesak din*—a clear decision—that I am forbidden to do so by the Halakhah. So my only son will lose his life according to the Torah and the Halakhah. I accept God's decree with love and with joy. I will do nothing to ransom him at the cost of another innocent life, for so the Torah has commanded!"[6]

In spite of the rabbi's importuning, the father persisted in his decision. All that day of Rosh Hashanah, Rabbi Meisels writes, the Jew from Oberland went about murmuring joyfully that he had the merit of giving his only son's life in obedience to the will of the Creator and His Torah. He prayed that his act might be as acceptable in the sight of the Almighty as Abraham's binding of Isaac, of which we are reminded in the Rosh Hashanah Torah reading and prayers.

Throughout this tragic interchange of question and answer, neither Rabbi Meisels nor the father raised the one question which to those outside the world of the Halakhah would seem to be the most urgent and demanding: "Shall not the Judge of all the earth do justly?"[7] Indeed, in almost all the halakhic literature of the Holocaust there is hardly any attempt at questioning, let alone vindicating, the justice of the Almighty. To some extent this avoidance of theodicy may be explained by the apothegm attributed to the great spiritual leader of East European Jewry, Rabbi Israel Meir Hacohen, the *Hafetz Hayyim* (d. 1933): "For the believer there are no questions; and for the unbeliever there are no answers." But the more essential reason was that personal and national tragedies had long since prompted the raising of all the possible questions. They are strewn throughout the Bible, the Talmud, the Midrash, and the post-Talmudic literature. The answers, however unconvincing or unsatisfying or even contradictory they might be, were well known to anyone at all familiar with Jewish tradition. The Halakhah maintained that the only tenable response of the believing Jew to the chastisements of God—deserved or not—was that of Moses himself, who, after describing God's outpouring of wrath upon His people, declared, "The secret things belong unto the Lord our God, but the things that are revealed belong unto us and to our children forever, *that we may do all the words of this law*" (Deut. 29:28). The one course of action which remained mandatory under even the most calamitous circumstances was the fulfillment of the *mitzvot*.

This basic principle was applicable no less to the Holocaust than it was to every personal and national tragedy that preceded it. It was clearly enunciated in the second century in the response of the Sages to the apostasy of Elisha ben Abuyah. Observing that the consequences of the fulfillment of the commandments of *shiluah ha-kan* (not taking fledglings in the presence of the mother bird) (Deut. 22:6) and *kibbud av* (parental honor) (Exod. 20:12) were not, as the Torah promised, "well-being and length of days," but, at least on one occasion, violent and untimely death, Elisha concluded *let din ve'let dayyan* ("there is no justice and no Judge"), and abandoned the Halakhah. Rabbi Jacob, however, declared that the "well-being" and "long life" promised by the Torah to those who observed its commandments were not necessarily to be enjoyed in this world, but in the next.[8] As Rabbi Yannai summed it up, "It is not in our power to explain either the prosperity of the wicked or the afflictions of the righteous" (*Avot* 4:19). Whether one met with sorrow and suffering or happiness and rejoicing, he was still obligated to praise and bless God (*Berakhot* 48b).

But a Jew did not need to be a Talmudic or Rabbinic scholar to know that the Halakhah provided for and was operative in death and pain as it was in life and joy. The beloved and well-known texts of the *siddur* (prayerbook), the *tehilim* (Psalms), the *ḥumash* (Pentateuch), the *seliḥot*, (penitential prayers) and the *kinot* (elegiac prayers for Tisha b'Av) had familiarized him with the lot which had befallen pious Jews in the past with no consequent impairment of their piety. It may be said that in a very real sense this daily, albeit vicarious, experience of suffering prepared the observant Jew for the agonies of the Holocaust. Conversely, the "culture shock" of the alienated and emancipated Jew of the Western world was infinitely greater when he was confronted with the actual experience of the Holocaust, or even with a mere historical account of its events. The Jew who lived by the Halakhah, reciting the 137th Psalm each weekday before saying grace, was aware that the ancient Babylonians had dashed Jewish infants to death upon the rocks. In the daily *taḥanun* (petitionary) prayers he proclaimed, "Our soul is shrunken by reason of the sword and capitivity and pestilence and plague and every trouble and sorrow. . .O God, sunken is our glory among the nations, and they hold us in abomination, as of utter defilement."[9] On fast days, in the *avinu malkenu*, he recalled the Roman persecutions or the medieval massacres of the First Crusade, or the Chmielnicki decimation of East European Jewry in 1648, or the more recent Czarist pogroms or Petlura riots—"Our Father our King, have compassion upon us and upon our children and our infants; do it for the sake of them that were slaughtered for Thy holy name; do it for the sake of them that were slaughtered for Thy unity; do it for the sake of them that went through fire and water for the sanctification of Thy name; avenge before our eyes the blood of Thy servants that hath been shed; do it for Thy sake if not for ours. . ."[10]

On Mondays and Thursdays, after the reading of the Torah, he joined in the prayer, "May it be the will of our Father who is in heaven to have mercy upon us and upon our remnant, and to keep destruction and the plague from us and from all His people, the house of Israel. . .As for our brethren, the whole house of Israel, such as are given over to trouble or captivity, whether they be on the sea or on land, may the All-Present have mercy upon them and bring them forth from trouble to deliverance, from darkness to light and from subjection to redemption, now, speedily, and very soon, and let us say, Amen."[11]

On most Sabbaths of the year he recited the *av haraḥamim*, composed after the First Crusade in 1096, when the Jewish communities of the Rhineland were annihilated: "May the Father of Mercies who dwelleth on high, in his mighty compassion remember those loving, upright, and blameless ones, the holy congregations who laid down their lives for the sanctification of the Divine Name, who were lovely and pleasant in their lives; and in their death were not separated. . .May God remember them for good with the other righteous of the world and render retribution for the blood of his servants which hath been shed. . ."[12]

In the *seliḥot* prior to and on Rosh Hashanah and Yom Kippur, he chanted the harrowing accounts of many Jewish martyrdoms. Even if he were barely literate, he was familiar with the account of the Ten Martyred Scholars of the Hadrianic persecutions (135 C.E.) and the question placed by the poet of the *maḥzor* in the mouths of the *Seraphim* when they saw the rabbis tortured and murdered: "Is this, then, the reward for the Torah?" The response of the Almighty, as the *maḥzor* has it, was also known to him: "It is a decree from before Me. . .accept it, all of you who love the Law!"[13]

The *kinot* recited on Tisha b'Av, the Book of Lamentations, the *tokhaḥah* in Deuteronomy (28:15-68), all provided graphic descriptions of the starvation, torture, death, exile, madness, and degradation which had been, or might be, the lot of the Jewish people. Halakhic Judaism had not obliterated the memory of these tragedies. On the contrary it had reinforced them so that at least on a subliminal level, and generally on a conscious level as well, Jews who observed the Torah and its commandments were aware that the Halakhah had enabled their predecessors to survive, and even to surmount, the enemies and afflictions of earlier times. Thus, in the ghettos of Kovno, Warsaw, and Lodz, in the concentration camps of Auschwitz, Bergen-Belsen, and Mauthausen, they were able to face life with dignity, death with serenity—and sometimes even ecstasy.

To be sure, there must have been thousands of observant Jews who did ask Abraham's question, "Shall not the Judge of all the earth do justly?" and who found the conventional answers wanting. They could find no sin heinous enough to warrant the punishment they were receiving, and no promised bliss in the hereafter adequate to outweigh the hellish tortures they were suffering in this world. They abandoned and rejected the Halakhah at the same time that they denied God. But there were thousands more to whom the *mitzvot* were as important, perhaps more important, during the Holocaust as they were in normal times. For them the Rabbinic observation, "Since the day the Temple was destroyed, the Holy One, blessed be He, is only to be found in the 'four cubits' of Halakhah" (*Berakhot* 8a), became almost literally true. Their one sure link with the Divine was the performance of His commandments. The one universe in which they could be certain He was to be found was the universe of Halakhah. It is these men and women, who lived in the Holocaust and Halakhah kingdoms at the same time, with whom this volume is concerned.

The Origins of Holocaust Responsa

A brief examination of the methodology of the Nazis in attempting to achieve the "final solution" of the "Jewish problem" is necessary to an understanding of the halakhic response to the Holocaust.[14] The first stage of an anti-Jewish activity was from the accession of Hitler to power on January 30, 1933, until the outbreak of World War II in 1939. During this period the aim of the Nazi policy was to make Germany and German-controlled areas free of Jews. Using "legal" means to eliminate Jews from the German state and society, the Nazis sought to make life unbearable for Jews and to force them to emigrate. Jews were eliminated from citizenship, public office, the professions, and the intellectual and artistic life of Germany. The Nuremberg Laws (September 1935) were but the forerunners of a series of "legal" measures designed to achieve Hitler's purpose. These "legal" steps were accompanied by acts of degradation and violence, deportation and destruction, culminating in the demolishing of German synagogues on *Kristallnacht*, November 9, 1938. In the short period of six and one-half years, the German Jewish Community, numbering 500,000 in 1933, was uprooted and reduced to a group of some 220,000 outlaws.

Until the latter part of this period, the primary effect of the Nazi persecutions on Jewish religious observance concerned the slaughtering of kosher meat—*shehitah*. On the pretext of a concern for cruelty to animals, the Germans outlawed *shehitah* unless the animal had previously been stunned by an electric shock. The pre-stunning of the animal raised grave questions since it could very easily cause lesions which would render the animal *terefah*—unfit for kosher use—even if it were slaughtered in kosher fashion after the stunning. After a time the Nazis also banned the importing of kosher meat from other countries. In any event, by virtue of their difficult financial straits, German Jews were unable to purchase such meat. By 1934, confronted with a situation in which not only individual Jews but also Jewish communal institutions, orphan homes, hospitals, and homes for the aged, which had previously adhered to strict standards of *kashrut*, would be compelled to use *terefah* meat if they did not comply with the regulations concerning *shehitah*, Rabbi Jehiel Jacob Weinberg, head of the department of Talmud and Codes at the *Bet Midrash Le'Rabbanim* in Berlin, and an acknowledged halakhic authority, prepared an exhaustive treatise on the subject. In it he found some warrant for permitting *shehitah* of electrically stunned animals—particularly under the difficult conditions which obtained in Germany, and especially for those who were ill, aged, or infirm. A number of other German rabbis agreed with him. However, the leading scholars of Poland and Lithuania, to whom he traveled personally, and with whom he corresponded, could not countenance this drastic change in the method of *shehitah*. They were concerned not only about the grave halakhic difficulties which it raised, but also with the impression which might be conveyed to Jews and their enemies that the Germans had been successful in causing Jews to abandon their religious practices. They felt, too, that permitting such questionable *shehitah* in Germany would set a precedent for the adoption of such practices in other countries by those who were concerned with cruelty to animals.[15]

Still another *she'elah* was directed to Rabbi Weinberg during this early period, when Jews were forbidden to appear, or were fearful of being present, in places of public assembly, such as concert and lecture halls. Was it permissible to conduct lectures and concerts in the synagogue, or would such programs be considered as violating its sanctity? Rabbi Weinberg concluded that lectures were permitted, as were concerts of sacred music. However, discussion periods after lectures (because of the likelihood of unseemly or irreligious controversy) and secular concerts were forbidden.[16]

With each succeeding year, the *teshuvot* of the period begin to take on a more foreboding and ominous note. Rabbi Menahem Mendel Kirschboim, who was the rabbi of the *Kehilah ha-Kelalit* in Frankfurt-am-

Main, was perhaps one of the first to be confronted with the harsh realities of the German plans for the Jews. In 1934 he too had traveled to Eastern Europe to discuss the problems of *shehitah* with the rabbis of that area. He was one of the authorities who sought to find some solution to the problem. In 1938, after the *Kristallnacht* episode, thousands of Jews were imprisoned in concentration camps. Many of them were killed, and their bodies were cremated by the Germans. In that still "civilized" period, the Nazis sent the ashes back to the victim's family for burial. A number of halakhic questions arose concerning the observing of mourning practices and the disposition of the ashes. Rabbi Kirshboim, on January 4, 1939, issued a four-page decision covering all these matters. Since it was forbidden to print Hebrew works in Germany, he sent it to his brother in Cracow, who arranged for its publication. His *teshuvah* concluded that the *shivah* mourning period was to begin upon notification of death from the authorities. The chest in which the ashes reposed was to be borne to the cemetery in the same manner as the coffin usually was. If possible, the ashes were to be buried in a coffin. In any event, a *tallit* and *takhrikhin* were to be wrapped around them as a confident indication of the belief in immortality and resurrection.[17]

Undoubtedly a great many more *she'elot u'teshuvot* relating to conditions during this early period have been lost. Rabbi Weinberg points out that he was compelled to leave hundreds of his *teshuvot* behind when he was expelled from Berlin by the Gestapo in 1939.[18] These were destroyed, as were those of the other rabbinic leaders of Germany. There are, however, a number of responsa from the satellite countries of Hungary and Slovakia dating from 1941 and 1942, when the conditions of the Jewish community there were roughly comparable to those of the last pre-1939 years in Germany.[19] Two *teshuvot* from this period are cited in *Mekadeshei ha-Shem*, vol. 1, pp. 150-151. These *she'elot* reveal the difficult, but not yet desperate, situation of Hungarian Jews. The first, dated Tamuz 5701 (July 1941), is from Rabbi Yitzhak Weiss of Werbau, who was asked, "Since Tisha b'Av falls this year on Saturday night, and since there is a decree from the *goyim* that Jews are not allowed on the streets after 8:00 P.M., how will we recite the *ma'ariv* evening service and the Book of Lamentations?" Was it permissible to advance the time of *ma'ariv* until just after *pelag ha-minha* (about one and one-quarter hours before sunset), at which time the Jews would still be allowed to be outside? According to Talmudic practice this is permissible in time of emergency. Or should we follow the *Magen Avraham* in *Oraḥ Ḥayyim* 292, who rules, according to the *Maharshal* and the *Bah*, that even though the Talmud permits it, one should not do so, since reciting the *ma'ariv* service before the Sabbath is over at nightfall would cause wonderment and perplexity among the public? While the *Shakh* (*Yoreh Deah* 247) says that one may render such a decision, despite the "wonderment" it may cause, if the reason for the decision is made known, others do not agree.

Further, because of the principle "we do not hasten the approach of trouble" (*Megillah* 5a), it may not be proper to recite *ma'ariv* early, thereby ushering in the Tisha b'Av fast before it should really begin. After considering all these issues, Rabbi Weiss ruled that it would be improper to recite *ma'ariv* early because of the reservations about this practice expressed the *Magen Avraham*. To begin the fast and to recite the Book of Lamentations publicly after *pelag ha-minḥah* would con- travene the principle of "we do not hasten." Therefore, he proposed that the Jews of his community recite *ma'ariv* at home privately after the conclusion of the Sabbath at nightfall. They should also read the Book of Lamentations privately at that time. However, in order to fulfill the requirement of a public reading of Lamentations, it should be read at the synagogue on Tisha b'Av morning, although it is not customarily read then. This procedure would satisfy the requirements of the *Levush* (*Oraḥ Ḥayyim* 559), who insists on a public reading of Lamentations, as well as the *Ḥayyei Adam* (402), who accepts a private reading as valid.

The second *she'elah* is dated the eve of *shabbat ha-gadol*, 5702 (March 28, 1942). It was directed to Rabbi Weiss by Rabbi Yitzhak Friedman of Tirnau. He writes that because of the decree prohibiting Jews from being outside after 6:00 P.M., a difficulty had arisen for women whose ritual immersion in the *mikveh* fell due on a Friday night. This immersion ordinarily must be performed after nightfall after the counting of seven "clean days," but because of the curfew regulations they were unable to go to the *mikveh* on both Friday night and Saturday night. While in case of emergency the Halakhah permits ritual immersion during the day after the seven-day period, they would not be able to go until Sunday morning. However, this undue delay in the opportunity of fulfilling the commandment of "be fruitful and multiply," and the denial of the opportunity for marital relations, goes counter to the letter and spirit of the Torah concerning marriage. Since the *Ḥokhmat Adam*, 118:5, rules that in emergency situations it is permissible to visit the *mikveh* on the seventh day during the daylight hours (in this case on Friday), provided the husband is unaware of this, and provided marital relations are not had until after nightfall, Rabbi Friedman asks whether we may allow this procedure and permit ritual immersion on Friday during the day for the women affected. After considerable searchings of heart, and of the sources, Rabbi Weiss reluctantly indicated that such permission might be granted on an individual, rather than a general, basis, and records that he had heard that such a decision had also been rendered in one of the large cities of Hungary.

Another *she'elah* apparently from this period, although it is undated, appears in the collection of responsa *Yerushat Pelatah*, pp. 8 ff. In the face of a government decree requiring Jewish-owned shops to be opened on *shabbat*, Rabbi Pinḥas Tzimetboim of Grossvarden was asked if it was permissible for the shops to remain open, since the penalty for not doing so was the total shuttering of the stores by the government. Such action would be disastrous, resulting in a total loss of livelihood for the many Jews affected. After exploring the possibilities of keeping the shops open on the *shabbat* by having a non-Jew handle all transactions, Rabbi Tzimetboim writes,

> And even if one can find a *heter*, permission, to open the shops on *shabbat* during this time of persecution by having a non-Jew handle all buying and selling, it is necessary to make an important *takanah* that each person so doing give his solemn word (*t'kiat kaf*), staking his share in the world to come in the presence of a *rav* or a *bet din*, that he will not personally sell on the *shabbat* and that he will renounce any profit from these Sabbath transactions. Even so, it may be advisable for no official ruling to be issued, but for each person to determine his own course of action and not be able to point to an official *heter* from a *bet din*. It is necessary to take counsel with the "great ones of the generation" on this matter and for a general ruling for the entire country to be decided—whether it is *le'issur* or *le'heter*, so that some rabbis do not rule one way and others another.

While the problems raised in these *she'elot* of the early Nazi period are by no means inconsequential, they cannot compare in poignancy and tragedy with those which arose during the second period of the Nazi campaign against the Jews, which began with the invasion of Poland in September of 1939. During this period, from September 1939 until April 1942, a systematic process of physical destruction was launched in

Greater Germany and the Polish areas annexed to Germany. Jews were deprived of elementary human rights, including freedom of movement; robbed of their properties and businesses; dismissed from the professions; crowded in restricted quarters under outrageous conditions; forced to wear the yellow badge; compelled to work at forced labor without remuneration, and subjected to starvation and savage brutality. Synagogues were burned, Torah scrolls desecrated, and rabbis taunted and tormented. This, then, was the Nazi-created ghetto.

The ghetto was both an instrument of physical and psychological warfare against the Jew and a control device designed to facilitate his ultimate destruction. The isolation of the Jewish population behind barbed wire and high walls did succeed in reducing their number through starvation, debilitating forced labor, disease, and overcrowding. The concentration of the Jews in the ghetto also made it a superb waystation for the assembly and transfer of Jews to labor and extermination camps.

Yet while it would be fatuous to minimize the severe psychological trauma which ghettoization must have had upon the Jewish population, it did not at all fulfill the Nazi expectation that it would crush the Jewish spirit. Despite the appalling circumstances of Ghetto life, Jews managed to maintain a remarkable level of human dignity and sanity—even sanctity, *kiddush ha-ḥayyim*.[20] They organized employment and established welfare institutions. There were public soup kitchens for children, the aged, and the needy. Clinics and hospitals were maintained. In many cases a network of elementary, secondary, and even higher schools functioned—most of them illegal. Public prayer and religious studies did not cease despite their strict prohibition, and underground *yeshivot* were set up. Scholars, poets, writers, and artists continued their work; and historians compiled documentation to supply evidence of Jewish suffering and heroism for future generations.

It is from this ghetto milieu that most of the responsa in this volume are drawn. The largest number come from the ghetto of Kovno (Kaunas), Lithuania. During the period of Nazi occupation—from June 24, 1941 until August 1, 1944—Rabbi Ephraim Oshry, one of the few halakhic authorities of Kovno who remained alive, was asked many *she'elot* by the Jews of that city, long noted for its scholarship and piety. He committed his responsa to writing on whatever scraps of paper he could find, and buried them in the ground, confident that someday redemption would come. He was in a unique position to determine the requirements of the Halakhah, not only because of his scholarship, but also because he was appointed for a time by the Nazis as one of the custodians of the warehouse of Jewish books which they had set up in Kovno. Rabbi Oshry thus had access to a least some of the major works of Rabbinic literature necessary in formulating his *teshuvot*. He indicates in his three-volume publication of these responsa that, except for an occasional passage or citation, they appear precisely as he prepared them during the Nazi occupation.[21] Other *teshuvot* from the ghettos are not as complete as those of Rabbi Oshry. In some instances they are a simple yes or no ruling; in others they are a "*teshuvah* of the deed," where the halakhic response to a particular situation is evident not from a literary fragment, but from an eyewitness account of what was actually done. It would also appear that the halakhic decisions of some rabbis either were not rendered in written form or, if they were, did not survive the war.[22]

With the German invasion of the Soviet Union in June of 1941, the process of the physical destruction of the Jews was accelerated. While ghettos were set up in large Jewish population centers, such as Kovno and Vilna, at the same time the immediate liquidation of vast numbers of Jews was begun. In the Soviet areas the shooting and occasional gassing of Jews by the *Einsatzgruppen* (special-action groups) reached gigantic proportions. There were two waves of intensive extermination; the first from June through October, 1941. The second, after stabilization of the Russian front, began in January of 1942.

In Poland, mass murder centers had begun operation in November of 1941. Perhaps the most infamous of these was Auschwitz. Opened in May of 1941, the extermination operation began there in March of 1942. Auschwitz II (Birkenau), with its extensive gas installations and crematoria, was opened on November 26, 1941 and continued in operation until the end of 1944. Like many other camps, Auschwitz was a multi-purpose installation. It was used for the execution of non-Jewish Poles, the physical destruction of sick and debilitated inmates—particularly Jews—shipped from various other camps, and also for medical experiments. However, it was primarily the site of the destruction of the countless Jews transported there, gassed either immediately upon arrival or after a period of debilitating work in the widespread military-industrial installations in or near the camp.

It is from the Jews working at forced labor in Auschwitz or similar camps that most of the "*teshuvot* of the deed" in this volume are drawn.

While many of those who were at the gates of the gas chamber and crematorium demonstrated a remarkable fidelity to the Halakhah until the very last moment, their *she'elot* were essentially reducible to one—how to die as a Jew. However, for those who worked under conditions of semi-starvation and degradation in the camps, the question of how to live as a Jew had many halakhic aspects. Their responses to this question while not formal responsa, have much to say about the Holocaust and Halakhah.

Notes

1. *Encyclopaedia Judaica*, s.v. "Holocaust." See also *Entziklopedia Shel Galuyot* (Jerusalem, 1966), vol. 4, pt. 1, in which N. M. Gelber, the editor of the section on Lvov, writes, "I have seen this time and again in the hundreds of memorial volumes which ignore the truth, that the great majority of Jews in the destroyed communities were believing Jews."

2. For an excellent and succinct summary of the relationship of the responsa to the sources of Jewish law, the general reader is referred to David Feldman, *Birth Control in Jewish Law*, pp. 3–18 [See Kellner, pp. 21–37]. Solomon Freehof's *The Responsa Literature* (Philadelphia, 1959), pp. 21–45, may also be of interest.

3. *Einsatzgruppen* were special-action units entrusted with the mobile killing operations of Jews. See Raul Hilberg, *The Destruction of the European Jews*, pp. 183 ff.

4. Zvi Hirsch Meisels, *Mekadeshei ha-Shem*, vol. 1, p. 8.

5. A *kapo* was a prisoner in charge of a group of inmates in the concentration camps. According to some the word derives from the Italian *capo*, "boss." Others derive it from *Kameradschaftpolizei*. *Kapos* were appointed by the SS to carry out its orders and insure absolute control over the prisoners. They were initially appointed from the ranks of German criminal prisoners. Jews were appointed *kapos* only in camps where the prisoners were primarily Jewish. The majority of them were cruel and repressive and imitated the conduct of the SS. A few did help their fellow prisoners.

6. Rabbi Meisels reveals the halakhic considerations which did not permit him to render a clear-cut decision under the circumstances prevailing at Auschwitz to be as follows: In the *Shulhan Arukh, Hoshen Mishpat* 388:2, the *Rama* rules that if a man sees impending danger to himself, he may save himself even if by so doing he endangers his neighbor. However, the *Sema* quotes the *Nimukei Yosef* as holding that this applies only when the danger is potential and not actual. However, once he is in the actual situation of damage or danger, he may not save himself by diverting the threat to his neighbor. In his commentary to *Hoshen Mishpat* 163:11, the *Shakh* cites a *teshuvah* of the *Maharival* to the effect that if a man has been seized and is being held for ransom, and it is known that if he is rescued another will be seized in his place, it is forbidden for others to attempt to rescue him. However, the prisoner himself may certainly attempt to extricate himself from the impending or certain danger of harm from those who have seized him. This is the opinion of

the *Yad Avraham, Yoreh Deah* 157. Now Rabbi Meisels's concern was whether or not a father's relationship to his son is so close that he is considered "the same person." If so, then he would be permitted to rescue his son even though another would be seized in his place. For a man may rescue himself even though another will suffer. However, if a father is considered "another person," he has no right to save the son at the expense of a third party. There is no clear opinion as to which is the correct halakhic evaluation of this situation. This same source material was cited by Rabbi Oshry in a somewhat different context.

It is interesting to note that Shlomo Rozman, an eyewitness to the episode involving Rabbi Meisels and this *she'elah*, gives a more detailed account in *Zikhron Kedoshim*, pp. 380 ff. Rozman's version, however, differs in one essential particular. As he recalls it, after Rabbi Meisels's unsuccessful attempt to persuade the father to follow the dictates of his own conscience, "the father insisted; he had the golden coin with which he could quickly ransom his only son, but he wanted to know whether he could do this according to the Halakhah. Both shed bitter tears, and the rabbi rendered the *pesak din* [quoting the Talmud, *Sanhedrin* 74a], 'Who can say that your blood is redder? How do you know that your son's blood is redder than that of the other child [who would be taken in his stead]?' " Whether, in fact, Rabbi Meisels meant this reference as a *pesak din*, as Rozman assumes, or was simply musing aloud about the various halakhic considerations involved in the tragic situation, did not, of course, affect the outcome. In either event, whether Rabbi Meisels specifically ruled that the son could not be ransomed, or whether the father assumed from his silence that this would be what the Halakhah required, he felt he had no other course but to obey that Halakhah willingly.

7. Gen. 18:26.

8. *Kiddushin* 39b; *Hullin* 142a.

9. Joseph H. Hertz, ed., *The Authorized Daily Prayer Book* (New York, 1948), p. 179.

10. Ibid., p. 162.

11. Ibid., p. 195.

12. Ibid., p. 511.

13. H. Adler, ed., *Service of the Synagogue: Day of Atonement* (New York), p. 180.

14. This description of the stages in the Nazi program for the "final solution" is based on Hilberg, op. cit.: *Encyclopaedia Judaica*, s.v. "Holocaust"; and *The Holocaust and the Resistance* (Jerusalem: Yad Vashem, 1972).

15. Jehiel Weinberg, *Seridei Esh*, vol. 1, pp. 4-8.

16. Ibid., vol. 2, p. 22.

17. Menahem Kirschboim, *Tziyyun le-Menahem*, p. 361. In 1939, just before the outbreak of World War II, Rabbi Kirschboim fled to Brussels. On *shabbat shuvah* of 1942 (September 19), during the Nazi occupation of Belgium, he was arrested by the Gestapo. Since it was the Sabbath, he had not been carrying his identification pass. He was sent to Auschwitz, where he perished.

18. *Seridei Esh*, vol. 1, p. 2.

19. For a description of the situation in Hungary, see Hilberg, pp. 509 ff., and Eugene Levai, *Black Book of Hungarian Jewry* (Zurich, 1948).

20. "Santification of life"—this term was coined by Rabbi Yitzhak Nissenbaum in the Warsaw ghetto. "This is the hour of *kiddush ha-hayyim*. . .the enemy demands the physical Jew, and it is incumbent upon every Jew to defend it: to guard his own life." Also related to this concept was "confronting death with an inner peace, nobility, upright stance, without lament and cringing to the enemy." Cf. Peter Schindler, "Responses of Hassidic Leaders and Hassidim during the Holocaust," p. 138.

21. Students of the Halakhah who may have reservations or questions concerning the reasoning or conclusions in the cited responsa should, of course, consult the full text of the *teshuvah* in question. The study of each step in the argument should, in most cases, resolve their difficulties. It must be remembered that all these rulings were rendered *be'sha'at ha- dehak*, in emergency situations, where a great deal of flexibility is possible in selecting the earlier and later authorities whose views lead to a halakhic decision which best meets the emergency conditions. The emotional and physical pressures which existed at the time these responsa were formulated should also be borne in mind.

22. Shimon Huberband, in *Kiddush Hashem*, p. 94, reports that while there were few *she'elot* concerning the dietary laws in the Warsaw ghetto (because of the virtual absence of kosher meat), there were a great many relating to other problems engendered by the Nazi persecutions. Most of those he lists are quite similar to the ones encountered by Rabbi Oshry in the ghetto of Kovno. Among them are questions concerning the observance of mourning and the recitation of *kaddish* for victims of the Nazis; the manner of conducting a *seder* without the Four Cups of Wine or *matzot*; permission to eat on Yom Kippur for those who were weak or sick; the permissibility of eating *terefah* meat for those who were ill or weak; the permissibility of using leavened bread which had not been legally sold before Passover, after the Passover was over. Unfortunately, these *she'elot u'teshuvot* were not committed to writing or were destroyed in the ghetto uprising.

28

Jewish Resistance

"Like Sheep to the Slaughter"

ALEXANDER DONAT

Truth and Interpretation

To Dr. Isaac Schipper, the Polish-Jewish historian who was my closest neighbor in the potato-peeling brigade at the Maidanek concentration camp, I owe an insight which has haunted me ever since my stay there.

"There is no such thing as historical truth," he would say with his sad smile when we dreamed about how after the war the survivors of the camps would tell the world *the whole truth*. "There is just interpretation," he said. "It depends on who writes the history of our time. Should *they* write the story of this war, our destruction will be presented as one of the most glorious exploits in world history. But if *we* write the story we will have the thankless task of proving to a disbelieving world that we really are Abel, the murdered brother."

Not even twenty years have passed since Schipper spoke these words, and reality has already proved darker than his forebodings. Our tragedy has not yet had time to become history, its witnesses and survivors still live, their memories remain vivid; yet a malicious myth about our experience keeps rising before our eyes. The myth is both open and covert; its sources are at best ignorance and misinformation—at worst, vested interest. After the initial shock, the truth proved too horrible to live with. Then, so much the worse for the truth; it must be doctored, and of doctors there is no lack: the Germans, the Poles, the Vatican, the capitals of the world, and, worst, the Jews themselves.

Reprinted by permission of the author from *Out of the Whirlwind*, Albert H. Friedlander (Ed.). Copyright © 1968 by Union of American Hebrew Congregations.

We are now far from the time when Karl Jaspers could blame every German for "crimes committed in his presence or with his knowledge. If I fail to do whatever I can to prevent them, I too am guilty. If I was present at the murder of others without risking my life to prevent it, I feel guilty."[1] According to Raul Hilberg,[2] about two million Germans were connected with the Nazi genocide organization. Other millions profiteered from the loot. Today, it seems that all the crimes were committed by a handful of Nazi criminals; the German people were not present, they "didn't know." Not only were the Germans "ignorant of the crimes," but the measly flicker of German resistance—late in the day (1944) and actually an ultranationalist response to the possibility of Hitler's losing—has now been inflated by some historians into a "soundless rebellion" in which almost the whole German nation ("soundlessly") took part.[3] Everything becomes simple. The small Nazis carried out the orders of the bigger ones, and the bigger ones the orders of the Führer himself. Since Hitler is dead, the guilt and responsibility are heaped on a small group of Nazi villains—most of them now conveniently dead—so that the German conscience is left free and clear.

Konrad Adenauer is perhaps an enlightened representative of the German conscience—or perhaps he is simply smarter. One thing is sure: he made the better deal with his "Reparations" and "Restitutions" to the victims and to Israel, than the claimants. He did just enough to disarm the victims morally and to buy Germany's respectability in the eyes of the world. At the same time his countrymen—the murderers, their spouses, their families—are comfortably immersed in the prosperity of the *Wirschaftswunder*, pump-primed by U. S. dollars. Such a spectacle could only come about as the result of the shameful American-Soviet race for the favors of their yesterday's enemy. The political wisdom of this race is, for my purpose, irrelevant; the moral aspects are my concern; the depraved spectacle of the *Faust-Volk* periodically selling its soul to the devil, turning into a nation of barbarians, and then being promoted to the role of defender of civilization.

As for Poland, it now seems there is hardly a man in that country who somehow hadn't "participated" in rescuing Jews from the Nazi murderers. This legend, carefully fomented by the official propaganda, is so well-rooted that the young Polish generation, Jews as well as Gentiles, believe in it entirely.

Each of the political parties participating in the revolt of the Warsaw Ghetto and the Jewish resistance has tried its best to appropriate the biggest slice of posthumous glory: the Zionists, the Bund, the Communists. The Communists tend to grossly overstate their part in the Ghetto resistance and in the aid they rendered to the Ghetto.[4] The Polish non-Communist underground, the Home Army (Armia Krajowa), states through one of its leaders, Andrzej Pomian, that "we Poles are not burdened by the sin of indifference to the Jews' sufferings. In order to alleviate their fate, the leadership of our Underground did everything within the limits of our then very modest means."[5]

But the historical facts are not exactly thus. The late Dr. Isaac Schwarzbart, deputy in the Polish National Council in London during the war, told me more than once, with tears in his eyes, how it really looked—and inside Poland it was even worse. I cite from my yet unpublished memoirs:

> In vain did we implore help from our Polish brothers, with whom we had shared good and bad fortune alike for seven centuries. They were utterly unmoved in our hour of need. They did not even express ordinary human compassion at the spectacle of our ordeal—let alone some manifestation of Christian charity. They did not even let political good sense guide them—after all, objectively, we *were allies* in a struggle against a common enemy. While we bled and died, their attitude was at best indifference and all too often it was "friendly neutrality" toward the Germans. ("Let the Germans do this dirty job for us.") And there were far too many cases of willing, active, enthusiastic Polish assistance to the Nazi murderers.
>
> There was a handful of noble Poles, of course, but nobody listened to them. Their voices never carried above the continual screams of hatred. Heroically, they managed to save individuals, but they could not bring about the slightest mitigation of Nazi ferocity.

Two forces only were in a position to influence the Polish masses: the London-led underground, and the pulpit. Neither used its influence to change the climate of indifference toward the martyred Jews.

The question of the clergy and its role in our tragedy is a very delicate one, but of extreme importance. "A Christian who witnesses inactively a crime becomes its accomplice." In our crucial moment in two nominally Christian nations there were to be found only a handful of true Christians. Of course, it is common knowledge that some Catholic priests both at the very top and the bottom of the hierarchy, assumed a courageous attitude in a true Christian spirit.[6] But the over-all picture, it must in candor be said, is most depressing. The Vatican's archives are locked, and the true story of the Church's role in our holocaust has not been revealed to the world. The Vatican and Treblinka, the Vatican and Auschwitz—when will the Vatican archives be opened? When will we obtain the fully documented answer: did the Vatican play the part of Pilate, or did it side with the crucified martyrs?

Only the great capitals of the world might have stopped the eradication of the Jews: by a simple threat of retaliation. What was done? They followed the letter of the gospel: they were silent. From paper protests, of course, they never shirked. But practically they did nothing to relieve the plight of six million innocent Jews. There is reason to believe that the Nazis would have retreated before a strong worldwide reaction to their atrocities, and that they took world passivity as a green light to go ahead with their genocide. The reasons and excuses for this passivity can all be reduced to two: genuine indifference, and fear lest the Western powers be suspected of waging a "Jewish war." A too-resourceful defense of the Jews just "didn't pay," politically and diplomatically.[7] The sympathies of world Jewry were taken for granted (what alternative did they have?), and there was no need, as in World War I, to win them over with a Balfour declaration.

And the Jews, last and most painful of all. What did the free Jews in America and Europe do when the abyss of biological destruction opened in front of one-third of their people, the crux and the reservoir of their national existence? Did they stone the parliaments, ministries and embassies? Did they besiege the Congress, and the White House? Did they dynamite the diplomatic outposts of the Nazis? Shmul Zygelboim ("Artur"), representative of the Bund in the Polish National Council in London, committed suicide when his efforts to stir world opinion against the Nazi murders proved futile, in the hope that his sacrifice would arouse the world; but how many Shmul Zygelboims were there, and how many *were* aroused by his act among the millions of Jews spared by the conflagration? Certainly they talked a great deal, and even wept and passed resolutions. But, what did they really *do*?

Thus the litmus test "What did you do *then*?" is amazingly efficient. There are too many participants and onlookers who don't care to remember the details of the spectacle, let alone to be reminded of it.

By a sad irony, all the escapist, revisionistic, and distorting versions of the martyrdom, some arising from guilty consciences, others from shame and still others from "the anti-Semitism of guilt," were helped by some voices coming from Israel. These voices, by no means general, were conceived in a desperate negation of the *galuth*, in a determined dissociation from the tragic yesterday of the ghetto. Helpless hatred of the murderers turned into shame and hatred toward the victims—"Why did they let themselves be murdered?" They forget that Israel owes to the *sherit hapleta*, the survivors, at least what they owe her, that Israel is the bone and flesh of the Jewish people all over the world and that it cannot sever the umbilical cord with two thousand years of Jewish history. They seem to forget that the new Jew-as-warrior was cast in the crucible of a profound moral revolution that the People of the Book went through in the flames of the Warsaw Ghetto revolt. In hating the murderers of their people, in painfully reflecting upon the world gone forever, they were the first to coin the self-flagellating indictment-lamentation: "The European Jewry left the historical stage without dignity," declared Itzhak Greenbaum, one of the leaders of Polish Jewry in the twenties and early thirties, who emigrated to Palestine before World War II.[8]

There came also to light a purely pragmatic attitude of "nation-building realism." Out of the blood of the ghettos and gas chambers came the realization of the 2000-year-old dream, the State of Israel—and now practically the sole beneficiary of the billion-dollar reparations, and one of the few friends of West Germany! "Let's be realistic." The murdered millions cannot be restored to life anyway, and sound geopolitical realism suggests that "our social scriptures teach that sons cannot be held responsible for their fathers' sins." So let bygones be bygones! Let's bury the past. . .And to those of us who cannot so swiftly change our hearts a bitter reproach is thrown: "We *read* memoirs, you still *live* them!"

The Victims on the Defendants' Bench

And then—it was but one more step—the defendants' bench was marked by a new addition: the victims. From all sides obliging pseudoscientists, historians and psychoanalysts started amassing "learned evidence" that the victims were actually co-guilty. These experts said that not only did the Jews not defend themselves but that by their attitude, due to a centuries-long tradition of passivity and servility, "they went like sheep to the slaughter. . ." and "collaborated in their own destruction." (Trevor-Roper.)

In this campaign desecrating the memory of our martyrs, the lead belongs to a professor of history at the University of Vermont, Dr. Raul Hilberg. In his 800-page work, *The Destruction of the European Jews,* he concludes with the following verdict: "The reaction pattern of the Jews is characterized by almost complete lack of resistance." "Anticipatory compliance" with the murderers' orders was the only weapon in the Jewish arsenal. Conditioned by 2000 years of submission and passivity they displayed an exceptional capacity for self-delusion. "The Jewish victims, caught in the straitjacket of their history, plunged themselves physically and psychologically into catastrophe." Thus the author condemns the Jews for their "role in their own destruction."

Even more appalling are the pseudo-scientific utterances of the Chicago psychologist Bruno Bettelheim. Because of his work in the Viennese Social Democratic party, he spent a year in 1938 in Dachau and Buchenwald. After his release he went to the USA where he became an "expert" on concentration camps and published several books, the latest of which, *The Informed Heart,*[9] analyzes the behavior of individuals and groups in concentration camps. From the safety of America, Bettelheim chose to start a war against—Anne Frank. "There is little doubt," he writes, "that the Franks could have provided themselves with a gun or two had they wished. They could have sold their lives dearly instead of walking to their deaths." "Millions of the Jews of Europe who did not or could not escape in time or go underground as many thousands did, could at least have marched as free men against the SS, rather than to first grovel, then wait to be rounded up for their own extermination, and finally walk themselves to the gas chambers."[10]

In 1962, from the comfort of Chicago, Bettelheim presumes to award patents of heroism and/or cowardice to Hitler's martyrs. In 1962, armed with a knowledge which the Jews *and everyone else* lacked in 1942, Bettelheim lectures them on how they should have behaved. The moral level of this advice is best illustrated by the story he admiringly tells of his Hungarian-Jewish relatives who, looking typically "Aryan," *joined the Hungarian SS* and so enabled themselves and some few other Jews to survive. He does not even realize the moral degradation unavoidably involved in such "heroism." Is Bettelheim naive enough to suppose that by serving the SS these Hungarian Jews didn't become participants in and accessories to the crimes of the SS? Survival at any price—is this Bettelheim's notion of heroism?

Bettelheim freely applies his experiences of the "extreme situations" in Dachau and Buchenwald in 1938 to the "extreme situations" in the Warsaw Ghetto, Maidanek and Auschwitz in 1943. *He forgets that by comparison to the later camps, the camps in 1938 were like summer resorts.* Bettelheim is fully aware that "one could easily arrive at erroneous opinions if findings made in the psychoanalytic setting were applied outside the context of that particular environment." But the temptation to do just that is too strong for him, and so he commits this gross error.

In his masterly and unfortunately too short article, "Jewish Resistance to the Nazis" (*Commentary*, November 1962), Professor Oscar Handlin disposes of these charges: "It is simply not true that the Jews did not resist; there are ample instances of their capacity for fighting back. Nor is it true that greater, or more persistent, or better organized efforts of resistance would have staved off the catastrophe."

In my already mentioned memoirs I find the following paragraphs about the Warsaw Ghetto:

> There was a stubborn, unending, continuous battle to survive. In view of the unequal forces, it was a labor of Sisyphus. Jewish resistance was the resistance of a fish caught in a net, a mouse in a trap, an animal at bay. It is pure myth that the Jews were merely "passive," that they did not resist the Nazis who had decided on their destruction. The Jews fought back against their enemies to a degree no other community anywhere in the world would have been capable of doing were it to find itself similarly beleaguered. They fought against hunger and starvation, against epidemic disease, against the deadly Nazi economic blockade. They fought against the German murderers and against the traitors within their own ranks, *and they were utterly alone in their fight.* They were forsaken by God and man, surrounded by the hatred or indifference of the Gentile population.
>
> Ours was not a romantic war. Although there was much heroism, there was little beauty; much toil and suffering, but no glamor. We fought back on every front where the enemy attacked—the biological front, the economic front, the propaganda front, the cultural front—with every weapon we possessed.
>
> In the end it was ruse, deception and cunning beyond anything the world has ever seen, which accomplished what hunger and disease could not achieve. What defeated us, ultimately, was Jewry's indestructible optimism, our eternal faith in the goodness of man—or rather, in the limits of his degradation. For generations, the Jews of Eastern Europe had looked to Berlin as to the very symbol of lawfulness, enlightenment and culture. We just could not believe that a German, even disguised as a Nazi, would so far renounce his own humanity as to murder women and children—coldly and

systematically. We paid a terrible price for our hope, which turned out to be a delusion: the delusion that the nation of Kant, Goethe, Mozart and Beethoven cannot be a nation of murderers. And when, finally, we saw how we had been deceived, and we resorted to the weapons for which we were least well prepared—historically, philosophically, psychologically—when we finally took up arms, we inscribed in the annals of history the unforgettable epic of the Warsaw Ghetto uprising.

A few basic facts, and I commend them particularly to Trevor-Roper, Hilberg, Bettelheim and all the other retrospective heroes: at the start of the big "Resettlement" action in Warsaw (July 22, 1942) a clandestine meeting of representatives of all organizations active in the Ghetto (except the Revisionists) was urgently summoned. The majority was against an immediate resistance, arguing that it would serve as an excuse for a total massacre. "Painful as it is," they argued, "it is better to sacrifice 70,000 Jews destined for deportation than to endanger the lives of half a million. Since the Nazis apply the principle of collective responsibility, it will bring disaster." The participants in the meeting did not know at the time that deportation meant death. Dr. Emanuel Ringelblum, the archivist of the Ghetto, testifies: "To normally thinking people it was difficult to accept the idea that a Government pretending to the name of European can be found on the globe which would murder millions of innocent people." Today it is easy to sneer at such pathetic delusions and wax morally superior; but what would our combative professors and psychologists have done if they had been confronted, day by day, with the agony of such choices?

The more-militant Left-Zionist youth groups disagreed with the majority and decided to act on their own. *Six* days later (July 28, 1942) the nucleus of what was later to become the Jewish Fighters' Organization was born. *In the second half of August one revolver was smuggled into the Ghetto as a gift from the Polish Workers Party.* Note this well, Messrs. Bettelheim and Hilberg, our resistance began with *one* revolver. This revolver was used by the *Shomer* Israel Kanal in his attempt on the chief of the Ghetto police, Szerynski, on August 25, 1942, the date that is considered the beginning of the armed Ghetto resistance. By the end of December 1942 (when the massacre was practically completed) the Home Army turned over to the Jewish fighters in Warsaw *ten* pistols, and then *fifty* grenades and *fifty* revolvers in February 1943. In Bialystok and Vilna the Jewish fighters received nothing.

Just consider the *quantities* involved: *one, ten, fifty*. This was the help received from the Polish underground. But to Bruno Bettelheim it seems that the Franks (and of course all the remaining million Jewish families in Europe) could "easily" get "one or two" guns—which would have amounted to 1 or 2 million guns! To say things like this is not merely to mock the victims, but to reveal a total failure to imagine what life was like under the Nazis.

Mr. Bettelheim also disapproves of "the Franks' selection [!] of a hiding place that was basically a trap without an outlet." Doesn't the man know that hundreds of thousands of Jews perished because they had *no* place to hide, with or without an outlet? That it wasn't a matter of choice—we could not advertise in the *New York Times*—but of grasping whatever we could? How relevant and realistic Bettelheim's advices are is best illustrated by my own experience: In our shelter in the Warsaw Ghetto there was *one* revolver among the forty persons present. The man with the gun was very anxious to make the Nazis pay dearly for our lives. *He was not even given the chance.* The Germans were careful enough never to approach us within shooting (let alone stabbing) distance. The SS General Stroop, responsible for the destruction of the Warsaw Ghetto, ordered his troops to set fire to *every* building in the Ghetto. Special engineer brigades poured gasoline on the ground floors and wooden staircases, then threw grenades and gas bombs into cellar bunkers. Thousands of Jews perished in flames and smoke without a physical chance to fight, even if they *had* had the weapons. For Mr. Bettelheim's comfort: Our shelter *did* have an emergency exit. When flames and smoke reached our shelter, the man with the gun ordered its evacuation. About half of the occupants preferred potassium cyanide to surrender. The others momentarily escaped, only to be captured and killed eventually, one way or another. Balance: only *two survived* (my wife and I). Not because we "did not believe in business as usual" and they did. It was just a succession of miracles. Ironically, the man with the gun did not survive.

Bettelheim says: "Anne Frank died because her parents could not get themselves to believe in Auschwitz." But the truth is, Mr. Bettelheim, that nobody could, not you nor I nor anyone else at the time. But what can one expect from a man who could bring himself to write so calloused, so ignorant a sentence as: "Most Jews in Poland who did not believe in business as usual survived the Second World War." Before such a display of bad faith and outrageous stupidity, language is helpless.

Says the Polish journalist Wanda Pelczynska in her review of Hilberg's book:

> Hilberg, educated and living in a free world, doesn't understand how people locked-up in jail, in camp, in the ghetto, people not protected by any law, exposed to enemy violence—save themselves by an illusion of hope. These people are easily told lies and by lies are brought without resistance to the execution trench. Thus the NKVD doublecrossed thousands of Polish officers [presumably not contaminated by the Jewish ethos of passivity]; they transported them to Katyn by telling them that this was a change from a worse camp to a better one. And these people, mind you, were brought up on the principle that "violence will be met with violence" and "when our hour to die will come—it will be in combat."

Says Walter Z. Laqueur (*Survey*, October 1962):

> In more than one sense the Russians were unprepared for the German onslaught in June 1941. Sholokhov, in his *The Science of Hatred*, has described the shock experienced by Soviet citizens when they realized that the behavior of the Germans in the occupied territories was very far indeed from their traditional image of the civilized and orderly German; they could not believe the news about mass killings, mass robbery and brutal oppression. They had always held the Germans in special esteem. As Stalin told Emil Ludwig in a famous interview, "The Germans were a solid, reliable, sober people who could be trusted."

Witnesses Higher SS and Police Chief Erich von dem Bach Zelewsky:

> The mass of the Jewish people were taken completely by surprise. Never before has a people gone so unsuspectingly to its disaster. After the first anti-Jewish actions of the Germans, they thought now the wave was over and so they walked back to their undoing.

Hilberg himself admits that "one of the most giant hoaxes in world history was perpetrated on five million people noted for their intellect."

There is abundant evidence that Jews took at face value German assurances that it was a bona fide resettlement. Resettlements and relocations of one kind or another had been commonplace since the beginning of the war, and no one for a moment imagined that *this one* would be different. Hundreds of thousands came to Auschwitz, loaded with food and clothes and their life's savings. Thousands of young people in the Warsaw Ghetto with knapsacks and bags volunteered at the *Umschlagplatz* to "join their families previously resettled." Full credit must be given to the Nazi stage-managers that the deceiving appearances, camouflage, psychological warfare and the torture of hope were maintained to the very last moment. Any unbiased person can see the tragedy of the Jews' ignorance. But not Bettelheim and Hilberg: to them the Jews "collaborated in self-destruction."

The tragic truth is, and this is to a great extent our fault as survivors, that twenty years after it occurred, the catastrophe of European Jewry and the epic of the Warsaw Ghetto uprising is little known and even less understood. For three years the Warsaw Ghetto had been systematically bled: by savage Nazi repression and discrimination, by famine and disease, by the Gestapo, by traitors among us, by the misgovernment of the *Judenrat*. The toll of deaths was 100,000 human beings, 25 per cent of its entire population. It was stripped of its political and intellectual leaders who were abroad as a result of the 1939 exodus. The same applies also to the majority of its young men who were either in USSR or in other countries. For some reasons, the male mortality in the Ghetto was twice that of females. Thus, in 1943, the Ghetto was a famished, broken city of women and children.

And still our record stands the toughest scrutiny when compared to the French Huguenots, to the massacred Armenians, not to mention Andersonville, Eupen-Malmedy, or Soviet prisoners-of-war. And what about Czechoslovakia in 1938? And France in 1940?

Let us remember too the anything but heroic performance of the American people, including the intellectuals, in the McCarthy era. Try to imagine McCarthy in war time, endowed with total power, with limitless facilities for terror and destruction, with no legal opposition and with full control of press, radio and television. Imagine McCarthy with his cohorts determined to physically exterminate and plunder a minority segment of the nation, all "for the glory of America." I am by no means sure about the conduct under such circumstances of the majority of Americans nor of the reaction of our vociferous "heroes," had they had the misfortune to belong to that doomed minority.

Lord Moran, who spent three years as army physician in Flanders during World War I, and a year with the RAF in World War II, observes how soldiers' morale cracks under the strain of tension, shock, and monotony in the trenches, and how their resistance to fear is lowered by sickness, fatigue, loss of sleep and other hardships. "Courage is willpower, whereof no man has an unlimited stock; and when in war it is used up, he is finished."[11] Has it ever occurred to our retrospective heroes who now assault the victims of Nazism that after years in the ghetto and camps, after endless "conditioning," after the loss of their dearest ones, a point comes when it no longer matters whether one dies with a piece of hardware in his hand—the so-called "hero's death"—or dies passively in a gas chamber? Bettelheim has written about "extreme situations," but he does not know—and perhaps no one can who did not live through it—what an extreme situation really is.

I purposely leave aside the wide range of problems that border on psychology, philosophy, and ethics: where does the natural self-preservative instinct stop and fear and anxiety begin? Where is the line between controlled fear and cowardice? Is discipline cowardice or courage, collaboration or responsibility? And, on the other side of the spectrum: how long can responsibility (individual and collective) be stretched before it becomes courage, and at what point does an idea greater than fear transform courage into heroism? Heroism carried one step too far can be irresponsibility. Was the Warsaw uprising in 1944 an act of heroism or suicidal folly? Was Czechoslovakia's surrender after Munich an act of cowardice or tragic realism? And, in purely practical terms and not just for the glorious record, did Poland with her romantic adventurism fare better than Czechoslovakia with her pragmatism?

The heroism of the handful of Warsaw youths shook the imagination of our generation, blasés as we have become toward acts of daring. But that heroism at the same time concealed the much more profound and shattering sacrifice of 50,000 defenseless men, women and children, who in a magnificent gesture of unarmed resistance defeated the Nazi bestial violence. As never before in mankind's history, heroism and martyrdom flashed in the lightning of doom. It takes a Tolstoy or a Gandhi to appreciate the grandeur of the spectacle. In the climax of our history martyrdom reached its most sublime expression, and in the unprecedented revolutionary tension there appeared a heroism that was the turning point of Jewish history and created a new type of Jew. Martyrdom was the mainstream of Jewish history for millennia. In our catastrophe martyrdom and heroism became inseparable ingredients. No one can tell whether and when the two ingredients will cross again. They are both equally tragic and equally sublime.

We are blessed and burdened with the memory of both; neither can be taken from us; and neither could save us.

Hatred and Soap

There is a widespread belief that the Jewish tragedy is a result of Hitler's psychopathic hatred of the Jews, that it was conceived in the obsession of a maniac. William Shirer defines our catastrophe as "the shattering cost of [Hitler's] aberration." Handlin thinks that "Hitler. . .was determined, for reasons which were totally irrational, expensive, and contrary to the interests of the state, to liquidate the Jews."

To reduce the origins of genocide to Hitler's psychopathic hatred is both historically and politically naive. The anti-Jewish policy of the Nazis was a worked-out calculation. Hermann Rauschning (*Gesprache mit Hitler*, Zurich 1940) quotes Hitler that anti-Semitism is "die wichtigste Waffe in unserem Propaganda-Arsenal."[12] And Robert Ley, the leader of the Deutsche Arbeitsfront, stated in May 1944: "Anti-Semitism is our second secret weapon."

Irrational hatred sometimes results in murder, but a passionate murderer does not manufacture soap out of the fat of his victim. The anti-Jewish war was a coldly premeditated political action carried out with the most monstrous precision. Says Professor Golo Mann, the son of Thomas Mann: "The German nation in its overwhelming majority was not at all passionately anti-Semitic, no more so than other peoples are. . . .Maybe this makes it even more appalling. That they have murdered without belief, without hatred, without conviction, without any sense; only upon order." (*Der Anti-semitismus*, Frankfort, 1961.) Of course, the war on the Jews eventually became a gathering point for the wicked and the sadistic, a mobilization of scum and degeneration, a university of cruelty and crime. Many a murderer became a captive of the ideology, and intoxicated by hatred. Perhaps the calculation did turn out to be erroneous and, as Handlin wrote, "contrary to the interests of the [German] state," but nobody can deny that for years it was a powerful weapon. Torture of Jews not only sowed demoralization among the vanquished nations; anti-Semitism was the link uniting the scum of the world with the Nazi masterminds.

"Soapmaking," the cold-blooded machinery to exploit all the advantages of the murder—financial, economic, political, propagandistic—was by no means a by-product of the extermination of the Jews, but a basic ingredient of this action. Plundering Jewish property, exploitation of the Jewish labor force, filling all the Jewish economic and cultural positions with Germans, bribing the native mob with shreds of Jewish "wealth," and, finally, the bestial machinery of destruction and exploitation even of human fat and hair—all these stages of soapmaking were by no means accidental.

That anti-Semitism was a powerful weapon in the Nazi aggression is shown by a host of shameful instances. Even Roosevelt and Churchill did not dare to wage an open war on this front. Stalin didn't even try to resist.

Viewed in this light the Jewish resistance against the Nazis must be thoroughly reappraised. To begin with, we have to expose the fallacy which equates the Jewish resistance with the general resistance movements in Europe. The difference consists not only in the two-front situation of the Jews, so penetratingly pointed out by Handlin: Jews fought as members of the general resistance of a given nation, not as Jews but as nationals, but in addition to this they fought as a branded community pushed to a uniquely "extreme situation."[13] It is clear that from the moment the decision for their extermination was taken, their destiny was sealed and the diapason of Jewish resistance could not influence the result. European Jewry was an object and not a subject in this struggle, and as the death sentence came from the outside so too could salvation come only from the outside, through the counter-action of the Great Powers, and the Gentile population. The resistance and partisan movements of other nations had the support of their governments (whether in exile or at home), commanding centers, supplies of arms and funds, not to mention a base among the majority of the populace. The situation of the Jews was different in every respect.

Under these circumstances it would not have been surprising had the Jews really given up all resistance. It is a miracle that in spite of these appalling conditions the Jews often did fight, and heroically.

The Central Issue

Abundant factual material proves beyond a doubt that allegations of the Bettelheim-Hilberg kind are false. True, history did not make us into a trigger-happy nation, but we are by no means exceptions in this respect. We did not believe that the enlightened Germans could be transformed into a nation of soapmakers, but in 1942 neither Mr. Bettelheim nor Mr.

Hilberg knew about it. We dearly paid for this delusion about the nature of Germans, and we should not feel ashamed of it.

With each passing day the tragedy of European Jewry, the greatest crime in the annals of mankind, recedes into the storehouse of history. A new generation arises that "knew not Joseph." Less and less is it a political, financial, demographic problem. But it will never cease to be a moral problem.

And as a moral problem, paradoxical as this may sound, it is less and less a Jewish problem, and more and more a universal one. Auschwitz is modern civilization's declaration of bankruptcy. It is a disaster of humanity. It explodes as the anti-Semitism of guilty conscience: one hates the innocent victim whom one wronged. It makes the East European governments dismally surrender to Hitler's heritage, helpless to cope with the scourge of anti-Semitism. And, finally, the worst loser of all is Christianity itself, whose two thousand years turned out to be an historical mirage.

I do not believe in metaphysical historical justice. But we have daily evidence that crime has in it the seeds of forthcoming punishment, and that unpunished crime boomerangs on the criminals.

Item: When the fighting Warsaw Ghetto begged for arms from the alert and combat-ready "Aryan" Warsaw, icy silence was the answer. What moral right of protest had this very same Warsaw less than a year and a half later when it begged for help from the Red Army across the river, obtaining in answer a similarly "political" silence?

Item: What moral right of protest do the Germans have against the Berlin wall, they who invented this disgrace? Germany from wall to wall—this certainly has its irony.

Item: How can Christianity regain its face? What does it have to offer post-war man, horrified by the specter of atomic war? How can an honest man believe, after Auschwitz?

Item: What moral right of protest do we all have against atomic holocaust? In the name of what principle? If one can with impunity murder six million people, why not six hundred million? Will tomorrow's genocide be stopped by the technicality that the next victim will not be Jewish any more but German, Russian or American? Morals know neither arithmetic nor geography.

There is a sense in which nothing anyone writes or does can redeem the tragedy of our century. But the one thing that those of us who have survived can do is to keep clean the memory of the victims.

Meanwhile, a few concluding remarks may be useful. Whether the Jews resisted or were able to resist, whether they should or could have behaved other than they did—such questions reveal, as a rule, an incapacity even to imagine the extremity of our situation under Nazi totalitarianism. The shame and horror of our century have to do with the conduct of the European powers, the Gentile world. Even if not one Jew had resisted, there would be no justification either to condemn the victims or to divert attention from the crimes of the murderers. The central issue must not be forgotten; it is a moral issue, the issue of what the world has done and permitted to be done. To insist upon making the world uncomfortable with the memory of its guilt is a necessity for that moral reconstruction which may alone prevent a repetition of our holocaust.

Notes

1. Karl Jaspers, *The Question of German Guilt*, New York, 1947.
2. Raul Hilberg, *The Destruction of the European Jews*, Chicago, 1961.
3. Gunther Weisenborn, *Der lautlose Aufstand*, Hamburg, 1953.
4. B. Mark, *Walka i zaglada warszawskiego getta*, Warsaw, 1959.
5. Zygmunt Nagórski, Sr. et al, *Dialog polsko-zydowski*, New York, 1958.
6. The names of the Archbishop of Toulouse, later elevated to Cardinal Monsignor Jules Gerard Saliège; the Bishop of Montauban, Monsignor Pierre-Marie Theas; the Primate of France and Archbishop of Lyons, Cardinal Gerlier; Father Marie-Benoit (Padre Benedetti, "Father of the Jews"); Metropolitan Andreas Szeptycki, Archbishop of Lvov, the head of the Ukrainian Greek Catholic (Uniate) Church in Galicia; and many superiors of monasteries, convents and Catholic orphanages, will forever remain in the grateful hearts of the persecuted. (Cf. Philip Friedman, *Their Brothers' Keepers*, New York, 1957.)
7. Cf. G. Reitlinger, *The Final Solution of the Jewish Question*, New York, 1953. See also H. G. Adler, *Der Kampf gegen die "Endlösung der Judenfrage,"* Bonn, 1958.
8. The very same people from the ghettos and camps were to become the most devoted soldiers of the Israel underground and Liberation War.
9. Bruno Bettelheim, *The Informed Heart*, New York, 1961.

10. Amazingly soon Bettelheim found willing disciples and imitators. A particularly coarse example: In their best-selling novel *Fail-Safe*, Eugene Burdick and Harvey Wheeler, without any logical context within the narrative, treat us to the following tirade: "Anne Frank and her family acted like imbeciles. . . .If each Jew in Germany had been prepared to take one SS trooper with him before he was sent to the camps and the gas ovens, precious few Jews would have been arrested. At some point Hitler and the SS would have stopped. . . .If every Jew who was arrested had walked to the door with a pistol in his hand and started shooting at the local heroes, how long would the Nazis have kept it up? But the first Jews who shuffled quietly off to death camps or hid like mice in attics were instruments of destruction of the rest."

11. Lord Moran, *The Anatomy of Courage*, London, 1945.

12. The most important weapon in our propaganda arsenal.

13. And in this last capacity they were in most cases left to their own fate. "Where a government and a people fought Nazi encroachments," states Philip Friedman (*Their Brothers' Keepers*), "many Jews were saved from extermination. Such were the experiences in Denmark, Finland, Bulgaria, and Italy."

Bibliography

Bibliography

The bibliography presented here does not pretend to be comprehensive. It includes a selected list of recent and generally available books and articles in English on the subjects discussed in this volume. (Works of or about Jewish ethics generally are cited in the notes to the General Introduction.) Further bibliographical material may be found in Sid Z. Leiman's excellent, "Jewish Ethics 1970-1975: Retrospect and Prospect," in *Religious Studies Review* 2 (1976), 16-22. The *Encyclopaedia Judaica* (Jerusalem, 1972) contains articles (with bibliographies) on many of the subjects covered here. There are also two journals which should be mentioned in this connection: 1) *Sh'ma: A Journal of Jewish Responsibility* (bi-weekly) provides a forum for the discussion of contemporary Jewish issues. 2) *Tradition* has a department called "Survey of Recent Halakhic Periodical Literature," edited by J. David Bleich, in which many of the issues dealt with in this volume are discussed.

The abbreviations used in this bibliography are as follows:

> MJE   *Modern Jewish Ethics*, edited by Marvin Fox (Columbus, Ohio, 1975).
>
> J   *Judaism* (quarterly) published by the American Jewish Congress.
>
> T   *Tradition* (quarterly) published by the Rabbinical Council of America (Orthodox).
>
> CJ   *Conservative Judaism* (semi-annually) published by the Rabbinical Assembly and the Jewish Theological Seminary of America.
>
> R   *The Reconstructionist* (monthly) published by the Jewish Reconstructionist Foundation.

Morality and Religion

Bergman, Shmuel H., *The Quality of Faith: Essays on Judaism and Morality* (Jerusalem, 1970).

Bokser, Ben Zion, "Morality and Religion in the Theology of Maimonides," in J. L. Blau (ed.), *Essays in Jewish Life and Thought Presented in Honor of Salo Wittmayer Baron* (New York, 1969), 139-158.

Cohen, Jack, "Toward a Theology of Jewish Ethics," *J* 7 (1958), 56-63.

Ellenson, David, "Emil Fackenheim and the Revealed Morality of Judaism," *J* 25 (1976), 402-413.

Greenberg, Simon, "Ethics, Religion, and Judaism," *CJ* 26 (1972), 85-126 and *CJ* 27 (1972), 75-129.

Kadushin, Max, *Worship and Ethics: A Study in Rabbinic Judaism* (Chicago, 1964).

Kaplan, Mordecai, *Basic Values in the Jewish Religion* (New York, 1957).

Roth, Leon, "Moralization and Demoralization in Jewish Ethics," *J* 11 (1962), 291-302.

Schwarzschild, Steven S., "Moral Radicalism and 'Middlingness' in Medieval Jewish Ethics," *Studies in Medieval Culture* XI.

Silberg, Moshe, "Law and Morals in Jewish Jurisprudence," *Harvard Law Review* 75 (1961), 306-331.

Waxman, Mordecai, *Judaism: Religion and Ethics* (New York, 1958).

Morality and *Halakhah*

Cohen, Boaz, "Law and Ethics in the Light of Jewish Tradition," in his *Law and Tradition in Judaism* (New York, 1969), 182-238.

idem, "Letter and Spirit in Jewish and Roman Law," *Mordecai M. Kaplan Jubilee Volume* (New York, 1953), 109-135.

Dorff, Elliot N., "The Interaction of Jewish Law with Morality," *J* 26 (1977), 455-466.

Fauer, Jose, "Law and Justice in Rabbinic Jurisprudence," *S. K. Mirsky Memorial Volume* (New York, 1970), 13-20.

Fox, Marvin, "Law and Ethics in Modern Jewish Philosophy: The Case of Moses Mendelssohn," *Proceedings of the American Academy of Jewish Research* 43 (1976), 1-14.

Gordis, Robert, "The Ethical Dimension in the Halakha," *CJ* 26 (1972), 70-74.

Konvitz, Milton R., "Law and Morals: In the Hebrew Scriptures, Plato, and Aristotle," L. Finkelstein (ed.), *Social Reponsibility in an Age of Revolution* (New York, 1971).

Korn, Eugene B., "Ethics and Jewish Law," *J* 24 (1975), 201-214.

Lauterbach, Jacob Z., "The Ethics of the Halakha," *CCAR Yearbook* (1913), 249-287. Reprinted in his *Rabbinic Essays* (Cincinnati, 1951), 259-296.

Rabinovitch, Nachum, "Halakha and Other Systems of Ethics: Attitudes and Interactions," *MJE*, 89-102.

Ross, J.J., "Morality and the Law," *T* 10 (1968), 5-16.

Siegel, Seymour, "Ethics and the Halakha," *CJ* 25 (1971), 33-40.

Steinsaltz, Adin, "Ethics and *Halakha*," in his *Essential Talmud* (New York, 1976), 199-205.

Schwarzschild, Steven S., "The Question of Jewish Ethics Today," *Sh'ma* 7/124 (Dec. 24, 1976). This essay, which deals directly with the issue of *halakhah* and ethics, prompted considerable debate in the pages of *Sh'ma* and a large number of rejoinders to it were published in subsequent issues.

Love of Neighbor

Brenner, R.R., "The Golden Rule Controversy Reconsidered," *R* 34 (1968), 23-26.

Cohen, Hermann, *Religion of Reason Out of the Sources of Judaism* (New York, 1972), 144-164.

Fisch, Harold, "A Response to Ernst Simon," *MJE*, 57-61.

Petuchowsky, Jakob J., "The Limits of Self-Sacrifice," *MJE*, 103-120.

Polish, David, "Love and Law in Judaism," *CCAR Journal* 16 (1969) 7-20.

Simon, Ernst, "The Neighbor (*Re'a*) Whom We Shall Love," *MJE*, 29-56.

Pacifism

Finn, James (ed.), *Protest and Pacifism* (New York, 1968), contains interviews on the subject of Judaism and pacifism with Everett Gendler, Arthur Gilbert, Abraham Joshua Heschel and Steven S. Schwarzschild.

Kimmelman, Reuven, "Non-Violence in the Talmud," *J* 17 (1968), 316-334.
Kornfield, Joseph S., "War and Peace in the Jewish Tradition," *CCAR Yearbook* (1936), 198-221.
Neher, Andre, "Rabbinic Adumbrations of Non-Violence: Israel and Canaan," in R. Loewe (ed.), *Studies in Rationalism, Judaism, and Universalism* (London, 1966), 169-196.
Schwarzschild, Steven S., "The Religious Demand for Peace," *J* 15 (1966), 412-418.
Shapiro, David, "The Jewish Attitude Towards War and Peace," in Leo Jung (ed.), *Israel of Tomorrow* (New York, 1946), 215-254. Reprinted in his *Studies in Jewish Thought* (New York, 1975), 316-363.
Siegman, Henry (ed.), *Judaism and World Peace: Focus Vietnam* (New York, 1966). (Booklet published by the Synagogue Council of America containing articles by Seymour Siegel, Irving Greenberg, Arthur J. Lelyveld, and Wolfgang G. Friedmann.)
Simonson, S., "Violence from the Perspective of the Ethics of the Fathers," *T* 10 (1968), 35-41.
Szajkowski, Zosa, "The Pacifism of Judah Magnes," *CJ* 22 (1968), 36-55.

Disobedience to Authority

Bamberger, Bernard J., "Individual Rights and the Demands of the State: The Position of Classical Judaism," *CCAR Yearbook* 54 (1944), 197-211.
Broude, S.G., "Civil Disobedience in the Jewish Tradition," in D.J. Silver (ed.), *Judaism and Ethics* (New York, 1970), 231-239.
Kimmelman, Reuven, "Rabbinic Ethics of Protest," *J* 19 (1970), 38-58.
Kirschenbaum, Aaron, "A Cog in the Wheel: The Defense of 'Obedience to Superior Orders' in Jewish Law," *Israel Yearbook on Human Rights* 4 (1974), 168-193.
Landman, Leo, "Civil Disobedience: The Jewish View," *T* 10 (1969), 5-14.
Roth, S., "The Morality of Revolution: A Jewish View," *J* 20 (1971), 431-442.
Schindler, R., "Civil Disobedience: A Secular and Jewish View," *Journal of Jewish Communal Service* 50 (1974), 322-326.
Waskow, Arthur, "*Malkhut Zadon M'hera T'aker*," *J* 20 (1971), 404-415.
Zimmerman, S., "Confronting the Halakha on Military Service," *J* 20 (1971), 204-212.

Medical Ethics

On this subject generally, see Immanuel Jakobovits, *Jewish Medical Ethics* (New York, 1975); Fred Rosner, *Modern Medicine and Jewish Law* (New York, 1972); and Moshe Tendler (ed.), *Medical Ethics: A Compendium of Jewish Moral, Ethical and Religious Principles in Medical Practice*, 5th ed. (New York, 1975).

Abortion

Bleich, J. David, "Abortion in Halakhic Literature," *T* 10 (1968), 72-120.
Bokser, Ben Zion, "Problems in Bio-Medical Ethics: A Jewish Perspective," *J* 24 (1975), 134-143.
Feldman, David, *Marital Relations, Birth Control, and Abortion in Jewish Law* (New York, 1974).

idem, "Abortion and Ethics," *CJ* 29 (1975), 31-38.

idem, "When Does Human Life Begin?" *Keeping Posted* 20 (1975), 3-7.

Klein, Isaac, "Teshuva [Responsum] on Abortion," *CJ* 14 (1959).

Kushner, R., "Tay-Sachs and Abortion Legislation," *National Jewish Monthly* 88 (1974), 49-55.

Nitowsky, H., "Abortion and Ethics," *CJ* 29 (1975), 26-30.

Rosner, Fred, "Tay-Sachs Disease: To Screen or Not to Screen," *T* 15 (1976), 101-112.

Schneider, I., "Abortion and Jewish Law," *R* 40 (1974), 26-30.

Euthanasia

Barram, A.S., "Modern Trends in Violence," *R* 41 (1975), 7-18.

Bleich, J. David, "Establishing Criteria of Death," *T* 13 (1973), 90-113.

Bokser, Ben Zion, "Problems in Bio-Medical Ethics: A Jewish Perspective," *J* 24 (1975), 134-143.

Brill, M., "The Sanctity of Life," *Jewish Spectator* 39 (1974), 60-61.

Dagi, T.F., "The Paradox of Euthanasia, *J* 24 (1975), 157-167.

Federbusch, Simon, "The Problem of Euthanasia in the Jewish Tradition," *J* 1 (1952), 64-68.

Goldfarb, Daniel C., "The Definition of Death," *CJ* 30 (1976), 10-22.

Greenberg, Hayim, "The Right to Kill?" in Jack Riemer (ed.), *Jewish Reflections on Death* (New York, 1974), 107-116.

Kass, Leon, "Averting One's Eyes or Facing the Music — On Dignity in Death," *Hastings Center Studies* 2 (1974), 67-80.

Lerner, L.D., "On Death and Dying — Jewishly," *R* 40 (1974), 11-15.

Rosenfeld, Azriel, "The Jewish Attitude Towards Euthanasia," *New York State Journal of Medicine* 67 (1967), 2499-2506.

Siegel, Seymour, "Updating the Criteria of Death," *CJ* 30 (1976), 23-39.

Singer, Daniel J., "The Right to Die?" in Jack Riemer (ed.), *Jewish Reflections on Death* (New York, 1974), 117-125.

Symposium on Euthanasia (E. Horowiz, M. Forse, S. Siegel, M. Tendler, H. Cohn and J. D. Bleich), in *Sh'ma* 7/132 (April 15, 1977), 93-102.

Sexual Equality

The literature on this subject is very large. Many of the more important items, however, are collected in two anthologies, both edited by Elizabeth Koltun. They are *The Jewish Woman: An Anthology* (Waltham, Mass., 1973), a special issue of *Response* (No. 18; Summer, 1973) and *The Jewish Woman: New Perspectives* (New York, 1976). Both of these volumes include extensive bibliographies.

Sexual Relations

Brav, Stanley R., "Reform and the Jewish Sex Ethic," *CCAR Journal* (January, 1963), 10-13, 26.

Borowitz, Eugene B., *Choosing a Sex Ethic* (New York, 1969).

Epstein, Louis M., *Sex Laws and Customs in Judaism* (New York, 1968).

Feldman, David, *Marital Relations, Birth Control and Abortion in Jewish Law* (New York, 1968, 1974).

Freehof, Solomon B., "The Pregnant Bride: A Responsum," *CCAR Journal* (Winter, 1974), 24-26.

Gordis, Robert, "The Synagogue, the Family, and Sex," *Jewish Heritage* 14 (1972), 54-59.

Harris, Monford, "The Way of a Man With a Maid: Romantic or Real Love," *CJ* 14 (1960), 29-39.

idem, "Reflections on the Sexual Revolution," *CJ* 20 (1968), 1-17.

idem, "Premarital Sexual Experience: A Covenantal Critique," *J* 19 (1970), 134-144.

Lamm, Norman, "The New Morality Under Religious Auspices," *T* 10 (1968), 17-30.

Maller, A.S., "Is Marriage Obsolete?" *R* 40 (1974), 7-10.

Rackman, Emanuel, "Ethical Norms in the Jewish Law of Marriage," in his *One Man's Judaism* (New York, 1970), 225-237.

Shapiro, David S., "Be Fruitful and Multiply," *T* 13 (1973) 42-67.

Homosexuality

Feldman, David, "Homosexuality and the Halakha," *Sh'ma* 2/33 (1972), 99-102.

Spiegler, S., "Gay Reform," *Journal of Jewish Community Services* 49, 329-330.

Symposium on "Judaism and Homosexuality" (S.B. Freehof, B. Herman, S. Ragins, J. Marmor and A. Lipton) in *CCAR Journal* (Summer, 1973).

Holocaust

Schindler, Pesach, "The Holocaust and Kiddush Hashem in Hassidic Thought," *T* 13-14 (1973), 88-104.

Wiesenthal, Simon, *The Sunflower* (New York, 1976).

Glossary

Glossary

Aggadah	Extra-legal rabbinic teachings.
Agunah	lit: chained. A woman whose husband has disappeared, or whose supposed death cannot be proven, and who therefore may not remarry.
Ahavah	Love.
Aharonim	Commentators and decisors who flourished after the publication of the *Shulḥan Arukh* of Joseph Caro (1488-1575). *Aharonim* have less authority than *Rishonim*, those decisors and commentators who preceded the *Shulḥan Arukh*.
Akedah	The binding of Isaac (Genesis 22: 1-19).
Amora	Sage of the *Gemara*.
Averah	Transgression of religious law.
Derekh Eretz	Civility, manners, decency.
Din	Law, in the narrow, concrete sense (a particular law).
Dina Debar Mezra	Rabbinic law requiring a seller of land to give first option to his neighbor.
D'oraita	A law of Biblical authority.
D'rabbanan	A law of rabbinic authority.
Gemara	Text composed of commentary upon, and exposition and analysis of, the *Mishnah*. Second component (with the *Mishnah*) of the *Talmud*.
Gemilut Ḥasadim	Benevolent action.
Ger	Stranger, alien, non-Jew.
Ger tzedek	Convert to Judaism.
Get	Document of divorce.
Halakhah	Law, in both the general and specific sense (pl: *halakhot*).
Ḥazal	Acronym for "Our Sages of Blessed Memory"; Talmudic sages (*tannaim* and *amoraim*).
Ḥerem	Excommunication, ban.
Ḥesed	Lovingkindness.
Ḥillul Hashem	Profanation of God's name.
Kiddush Hashem	Sanctification of God's name; martyrdom.
Kedushah	Holiness.
Ketubah	Marriage contract.
Lifnim Meshurat Hadin	lit: Within the line of the law. Going beyond the letter of the law.
Midat Ḥasidut	Act or characteristic of special piety or saintliness.

Midrash	lit: exposition. Rabbinic Bible interpretations not found in the Talmud.
Milḥemet Mitzvah	Mandatory war.
Milḥemet Reshut	Discretionary war.
Mishkav Zakhur	Homosexuality.
Mishnah	Earliest written text based on the Oral Torah. Edited by Rabbi Judah the Prince about 200 CE.
Mishnat Ḥasidim	A teaching that saintly people ought to follow; above and beyond the call of duty.
Mishneh Torah	Influential code of Jewish law by Moses Maimonides (1135-1204).
Mitzvah	Commandment (pl: *mitzvot*).
Moredet	Rebellious wife.
Nefesh	Soul, person.
Ones	Duress.
Oral Torah	Unwritten tradition, supplementing and elucidating the *Written Torah*. Edited first into the *Mishnah* and then, with the *Gemara,* into the *Talmud.*
Piskei Halakhah	Halakhic decisions (sing: *psak halakhah; also psak din*).
Re'a	Neighbor, as in "You shall love your neighbor as yourself."
Responsa	Collections of questions addressed to halakhic authorities with their responses (hence *responsa*).
Rishonim	Commentators and decisors who flourished after the close of the *Talmud* and before the publication of the *Shulḥan Arukh* of Joseph Caro (1488-1575). Their authority is inferior to that of the sages of the *Talmud* and superior to that of the *Aḥaronim.*
Shalom	Peace.
She'elah	Question of law addressed to an halakhic authority (see *Responsa*).
Sheḥitah	Ritual slaughtering.
Shulḥan Arukh	Widely-accepted code of Jewish law by Joseph Caro (1488-1575).
Talmud	Basic text of *halakhah* composed of *Mishnah* and *Gemara.*
Tanna	Sage of the *Mishnah.*
Teshuvah	Response to an halakhic question (*she'elah*). (See *Responsa.*) In other contexts, repentance.
To'evah	Abomination.
Torah	lit: teaching; the word may refer to the Pentateuch, the entire Hebrew Bible, or all normative Jewish teachings.
Tosafot	Short, note-like medieval commentaries on the Talmud.
Tzaddik	Saint (pl: *tzaddikim*).
Tzedek	Righteousness.
Written Torah	Bible, especially the Pentateuch.

Biographical Notes

Biographical Notes

Rachel Adler is a Jewish feminist writer and teacher in Minneapolis, Minn.

Eliezer Berkovits was Professor of Jewish Philosophy at the Hebrew Theological College. Now living in Israel, he is the author of *Faith After the Holocaust, Crisis and Faith*, and many other books.

Ezra Bick teaches Talmud at Yeshivat Har Etzion in Israel.

J. David Bleich is Professor of Talmud at Yeshiva University and the author of *Providence in the Philosophy of Gersonides*, and of *Contemporary Halakhic Problems*.

Gerald Blidstein is Professor of Jewish Thought at Ben Gurion University and author of *Honor Thy Father and Mother*.

Balfour Brickner is the Director of the Department of Inter-Religious Affairs of the Union of American Hebrew Congregations, and writes on problems of contemporary Jewish interest.

Martin Buber (1878-1965), the religious existentialist philosopher, is best known for his *I and Thou*.

Alexander Donat, a survivor of the Holocaust who now lives in New York City, is the author of *Jewish Resistance* and *The Holocaust Kingdom*.

David Feldman, rabbi of the Bay Ridge Jewish Center in Brooklyn, New York, is the author of *Birth Control, Marital Relations, and Abortion in Jewish Law*.

Emil Fackenheim, Professor of Philosophy at the University of Toronto, is the author of *God's Presence in History* and other works.

Everett E. Gendler is a rabbi in Lowell, Mass. and is active in the Jewish peace movement.

Moshe Greenberg is Professor of Bible at the Hebrew University and the author of many scholarly studies.

Louis Jacobs is the rabbi of the New London Synagogue and the author of many works, including *A Jewish Theology* and *Theology in the Responsa*.

Leo Jung was Professor of Jewish Ethics at Yeshiva University. He is the founder and original editor of the *Jewish Library* and Emeritus Rabbi of the Jewish Center, New York.

Israel Kazis is a rabbi in Newton, Mass. and the editor and translator of *The Book of the Gests of Alexander of Macedon* by Immanuel ben Jacob Bonfils.

Isaac Klein, formerly president of the Rabbinical Assembly, is the author of *The Ten Commandments in a Changing World* and the translator of Book XII of Maimonides' Code of Law.

Milton R. Konvitz was Professor of Law at Cornell University. He is the author of many books on U.S. Consititutional law and the editor of *Judaism and Human Rights.*

Maurice Lamm is a rabbi in Los Angeles, California, and the author of *The Jewish Way in Death and Mourning.*

Norman Lamm is President of Yeshiva University and the author of *Faith and Doubt* and other works.

Sid Z. Leiman is Associate Professor of Religious Studies at Yale University and the editor of a forthcoming anthology of medieval Jewish ethics.

Aharon Lichtenstein is the head of Yeshivat Har Etzion in Israel and the author of *Henry More: The Rational Theology of the Cambridge Platonists.*

Chaim Reines taught Jewish studies for many years and is the author of several books on Biblical and rabbinic ethics.

Irving J. Rosenbaum is President of the Hebrew Theological College and author of *Holocaust and Halakhah.*

Fred Rosner is Director of the Hematology Division at Queens Hospital Center, New York. He is the author of many studies in Jewish medical ethics, and is the translator of Julius Preuss' *Biblical and Talmudic Medicine.*

Norbert Samuelson is Associate Professor of Religion at Temple University and the author of *The Problem of God's Knowledge in Gersonides.*

David Shapiro, a rabbi in Milwaukee for many years, has written extensively in the field of Jewish studies.

Seymour Siegel is Professor of Jewish philosophy at the Jewish Theological Seminary of America. He has written widely in the fields of Jewish theology and ethics.